Peschel Press ~ P.O. Box 132 ~ Hershey, PA 17033 ~ Email: Bpeschel@Gmail.com ~ www.PeschelPress.com

The Times Report of the Trial of William Palmer

BOOKS FROM PESCHEL PRESS

The Rugeley Poisoner Series
The Illustrated Life and Career of William Palmer
The Times Report of the Trial of William Palmer
The Life and Career of Dr. William Palmer of Rugeley

Career Indie Author Series
Career Indie Author by Bill Peschel and Teresa Peschel
Career Indie Author Quote Book by Bill Peschel

The 223B Casebook Series, Notes & Annotations by Bill Peschel
The Best Sherlock Holmes Parodies and Pastiches: 1888-1930
Sherlock Holmes Victorian Parodies and Pastiches: 1888-1899
Sherlock Holmes Edwardian Parodies and Pastiches I: 1900-1904
Sherlock Holmes Edwardian Parodies and Pastiches II: 1905-1909
Sherlock Holmes Great War Parodies and Pastiches I: 1910-1914
Sherlock Holmes Great War Parodies and Pastiches II: 1915-1919
Sherlock Holmes Jazz Age Parodies and Pastiches I: 1920-1924
Sherlock Holmes Jazz Age Parodies and Pastiches II: 1925-1930
The Early Punch Parodies of Sherlock Holmes
The Cases of Blue Ploermell

Annotated Editions by Bill Peschel
The Complete, Annotated Secret of Chimneys
By Agatha Christie
The Complete, Annotated Murder on the Links
By Agatha Christie
The Complete, Annotated Secret Adversary
By Agatha Christie
The Complete, Annotated Mysterious Affair at Styles
By Agatha Christie
The Complete, Annotated Whose Body?
By Dorothy L. Sayers

The Steppes of Mars Series by Odessa Moon
The Bride from Dairapaska
The White Elephant of Panschin
The Vanished Pearls of Orlov

Other Books
Suburban Stockade by Teresa Peschel
Sew Cloth Grocery Bags by Teresa Peschel
A Dictionary of Flowers and Gems by Skye Kingsbury
Hell's Casino by Bill Peschel
Writers Gone Wild by Bill Peschel
The Casebook of Twain and Holmes by Bill Peschel

Learn more about the "history behind the mystery" by signing up for the newsletter at www.PeschelPress.com.

THE TIMES REPORT OF THE TRIAL OF WILLIAM PALMER

THE TALBOT ARMS, RUGELEY, THE SCENE OF COOK'S DEATH

From the short-hand notes taken in the
Central Criminal Court From Day to Day

Notes and Essays by Bill Peschel

PESCHEL PRESS ~ HERSHEY, PA.

THE TIMES REPORT OF THE TRIAL OF WILLIAM PALMER. Book format, modified transcript, modified artwork, footnotes and essays copyright 2015 by Bill Peschel. All rights reserved. Printed in the United States of America.

No part of the footnotes or essays may be used or reproduced in any manner without written permission except in cases of brief quotations embodied in critical articles or reviews. For information, email peschel@peschelpress.com or write to P.O. Box 132, Hershey, PA 17033.

Cover design by Bill Peschel. Art from *The Most Extraordinary Trial of William Palmer for the Rugeley Poisonings*. Artist unknown.

www.peschelpress.com

ISBN-13: 978-1-950347-22-3

Second printing: March 2021

SUMMARY OF THE TWELVE DAYS' PROCEEDINGS.

FIRST DAY.—May 14, 1856.
[Wednesday] The Attorney-General's Opening Address for the Prosecution. — Evidence for the Prosecution commences, Ishmael Fisher (wine merchant) being the first witness examined. — The following witnesses were also examined this day:— Thomas Jones (law stationer) — George Read (sporting-house keeper) — William Scaife Gibson (surgeon of Shrewsbury) and Elizabeth Mills (chambermaid at the Talbot Arms) 16

SECOND DAY.—May 15.
[Thursday] The Court opened this day with a continuation of Elizabeth Mills's evidence;— the evidence of the following witnesses was also taken: Mr. James Gardner (solicitor at Rugeley) — Mrs. Ann Brooks (a lady who attends races) — Lavinia Barnes (waitress at the Talbot Arms) — Ann Rowley (Palmer's charwoman) — Charles Horley (gardener to Palmer) — Sarah Bond (housekeeper at the Talbot) — William Henry Jones (surgeon at Lutterworth) — Dr. Henry Savage (physician) and Charles Newton (assistant to Mr. Salt, chemist), who supplied Palmer with strychnine 62

THIRD DAY.—May 16.
[Friday] The proceedings opened this day with the examination of Charles Joseph Roberts, apprentice to Mr. Hawkins, druggist at Rugeley, and who sold Palmer six grains of strychnine. — Depositions of Dr. Bamford read. — Mr. William Stevens, stepfather of the deceased Cook, gives his evidence, which is followed by that of Mary Keeling (who laid out Cook's body) — John Thomas Harland (physician at Stafford) — Charles James Devonshire (undergraduate of the University of London, and late assistant to Dr. Monckton) — Dr. Henry Monckton (physician at Rugeley) — Mr. John Boycott (clerk to Messrs. Lander and Gardner, attorneys at Rugeley) — James Myatt (postboy at the Talbot) — Samuel Cheshire (late post-master at Rugeley) — Captain John Haines Hatton (chief constable of Stafford) — Ellis Crisp (inspector of police at Rugeley) — Daniel Scully Burgen (inspector of police in Staffordshire) — Juliet Elizabeth Hawkes (boarding-house-keeper, Strand) — George Herring — Frederick Slack (porter at Mrs. Hawkes's) 90

FOURTH DAY.—May 17.
[Saturday] The business of this day opened with the examination of George Bates ("a gentleman of good property, and possessing a capital

cellar of wine") — Thomas Blizard Curling (member of the College of Surgeons) — Dr. Robert Bentley Todd (physician at King's College Hospital) — Sir Benjamin Brodie (senior surgeon to St. George's Hospital) — Dr. Henry Daniel (retired surgeon to the Bristol Hospital) — Mr. Samuel Solly (surgeon of St. Thomas's Hospital) — Mr. Henry Lee (surgeon to King's College and the Lock Hospitals) — Dr. Henry Corbett (physician of Glasgow) — Dr. Ebenezer Watson (surgeon at Glasgow Infirmary) — Dr. James Patterson (also of the Glasgow Infirmary) — Mary Kelly (a patient of the Glasgow Infirmary) — Caroline Hickson (nurse and lady's maid in the family of Mr. Sarjantson Smyth) — Mr. Francis Taylor (surgeon at Romsey) — Charles Broxholme (chemist at Romsey) — Jane Witham (attendant to a lady who died with similar symptoms to those experienced by the deceased, Cook) — Mr. George Morley (surgeon at Leeds) — Mr. Edward D. Moore (surgeon) 121

FIFTH DAY.—May 19.
[Monday] The Trial was continued this day with the examination of Dr. Alfred Swaine Taylor. Fellow of the College of Physicians; and which nearly occupied the attention of the Court the whole of the day. When Dr. Taylor's evidence was concluded, Dr. George Owen Rees, Professor William Thomas Brande, and Professor Robert Christison, were examined, and thus the day closed 151

SIXTH DAY.—May 20.
[Tuesday] The Prosecution was opened this day with Dr. John Jackson's evidence. — Daniel Scully Bergen (chief superintendent of police at Stafford) — Henry Augustus Deane (of the firm of Chubb Deane and Chubb, Gray's Inn) — John Espin (solicitor) — William Bamford (surgeon at Rugeley) — Thomas Pratt (solicitor of London) — John Armshaw (attorney at Rugeley) — John Wallbank (butcher at Rugeley) — John Spillbury (Staffordshire farmer) — Mr. Thomas Smerdon Strawbridge (of the bank)— Herbert Wright (solicitor of Birmingham) 176

SEVENTH DAY.—May 21.
[Wednesday] The Case for the Prosecution was closed this day with the examination of Charles Weatherby (secretary to the Jockey Club) — and Mr. Johnson Rogerson Butler (a well-known sporting character) — Serjeant Shee occupied the remainder of the day (eight hours) in his address for the Defence 194

EIGHTH DAY.—May 22.
[Thursday] Thomas Nunneley (Professor of Surgery at the Leeds

School of Medicine) was the first evidence submitted for the Defence. — He was followed by Mr. William Herapath (professor of Chymistry and Toxicology) — Mr. Julian Edward Disbrowe Rogers (professor of Chymistry at St. George's School of Medicine) — Dr. Henry Letheby (Medical Officer of Health to the City of London) — and Mr. Robert Edward Gay (member of the Royal College of Surgeons) whose testimony closed the proceedings of the day.. 248

NINTH DAY.—May 23.
[Friday] Evidence for the Defence was opened by the examination of Mr. John Brown Ross (house-surgeon to the London Hospital); followed by Mr. Ryners Mantell (also House-surgeon to the London Hospital) — Dr. Francis Wrightson (pupil of Liebig's) — Professor Richard Partridge (Professor of Anatomy in King's College) — Mr. John Gay (Surgeon to the Royal Free Hospital) — Dr. William Macdonald (licentiate of the Royal College of Surgeons of Edinburgh) — Dr. John Nathan Bainbridge (medical officer to St. Martin's Workhouse) — Mr. Edward Austin Steddy (Member of the Royal College of Surgeons, and of Chatham) — Dr. George Robinson (physician to the Newcastle-on-Tyne Dispensary) — Dr. Benjamin Wall Richardson (London physician) — Catherine Watson (of Garnkirk), whose evidence closed the proceedings of the day 273

TENTH DAY.—May 24.
[Saturday] Oliver Pemberton (lecturer on anatomy, Queen's College) was the first person examined this day — Henry Matthews (inspector of police at the Euston-square railway station) — Joseph Foster (farmer and grazier at Sibbertoft) — George Myatt (saddler at Rugeley) — John Serjeant (attendant at races) — Jeremiah Smith (attorney at Rugeley) whose examination closed the evidence for the Defence. — The Attorney General's reply wound up the day 294

ELEVENTH DAY.—May 26.
[Monday] The Lord Chief Justice commenced this day with his summing up the case to the Jury, and commented on the whole of the Evidence for the Prosecution, when the Court adjourned................ 351

TWELFTH AND LAST DAY.—May 27.
[Tuesday] The Lord Chief Justice resumed his summing up, which he closed at eighteen minutes after two. — The case was left in the hands of the Jury, who, after retiring for one hour and seventeen minutes, return with their verdict. 372

APPENDIX.
The Execution of William Palmer 392
Glossary of Medical Terms, Doctors and Hospitals 405
Profiles of the Justices and Counsel 413
Bibliography 423
Index to Witnesses, Medical Evidence and Counsel..........................424

How This Book Was Edited

The text was taken from Google Books, which scanned a printed copy using optical-character recognition and converted it into text. The quality was scattershot, as anyone who has bought a printed copy of the PDF file will see. So the manuscript was read four times, twice on the computer screen and twice in the printed version by myself and a copy editor. Problem areas were identified and corrected after comparison to the PDF.

That was the easy part. We had to decide how faithful this edition should be to the first edition. Should we recreate the book or should it be improved, and if so, how far? Should we ignore factual errors, footnote them or silently correct them? Should the illustrations be kept in their original locations, even when they're clearly out of place? How far should we go to make the book useful to modern readers without losing the flavor of how the language was used at the time?

To find an answer, we had to decide between preserving the past, mistakes and all, and providing an edition that would provide a better reading experience. At first the choices were made piecemeal, as they arose, but as the decisions piled up, it became clear that we wanted to sell a definitive, edited version. Understanding the case, particularly the medical evidence, will be hard enough without throwing more obstacles in the reader's way. We decided to make minor corrections to the text silently, while footnoting testimony that needed correction or clarification.

After that, the editing process fell into place. We did not standardize the spelling of "chymist" and "chemist" since both appear in the manuscript — reflecting a transition in the language — but we used the British spelling of "cheque" even though "check" was used as well, favoring clarity here (for the same reason, we changed Gray's-inn to Gray's Inn and defense to defence). Words that were capitalized that wouldn't be today were retained, but we removed the spaces before semi-colons and question and exclamation marks. Spaces were inserted around long dashes. Long blocks of text were broken into paragraphs as a concession to the reader's eyes.

A similar question arose with the use of the pound sign, which was represented in both the old and new fashions (10*l.* and £10). For clarity's sake, it was decided to retain the pound sign in all uses.

Then there were questions of fact. Palmer's hired man was spelled Bate here, Bates elsewhere. I used Bates. The chemist's apprentice Blocksome had his correct name — Broxholme — restored as it appeared in the Old Bailey transcript. Witnesses whose names were accidentally omitted from the index were added, and partial names of those testifying were changed to their full names after consulting the Old Bailey and Notable British Trials transcripts.

The illustrations were cleaned up as best they could be. Those spread over two pages presented impossible challenges since so much of the art was lost in the gutter. Many woodcuts were moved to more appropriate locations. Witness portraits were matched to their testimony. The *Times* jammed in as many pictures as it could, whether they were appropriate or not. Some reflected scenes that were not mentioned at the trial at all, such as the Shoulder of Mutton Inn, the town hall, and the Palmer family vault. But they were in the Peschel Press edition of "The Illustrated Life and Career of William Palmer," so they were moved there.

Added material was included in footnotes, such as coroner's reports and newspaper accounts. If it was easier on the reader to include material in the text, we did it between square brackets [like this].

The book's fourth edition contained an account of Palmer's imprisonment and execution, and the list of jurors. They were added. The profiles of the judges and counsel were taken from the Notable British Trials edition. Also added to the end was the list of books for sale from the publisher because they conveyed a flavor of what was read at the time.

Converting a pound in 1856 to today that would have any meaning is difficult. There's inflation and deflation to consider. Some products, such as computers, modern drugs and digital watches, didn't exist in 1856. Lower energy prices and international trade have dramatically changed the value of goods such as clothing and out-of-season produce. The factors that go into setting wages have changed as well. Today's business owners must take into account taxes, pensions, insurance, and other costs that were not considered in Palmer's time. There were also marked differences in wages paid to skilled workers, semi-skilled workers, and laborers. The Measuring Worth website (www.measuringworth.com) offers several methods of determining the true value of a pound. They show that the relative value of an 1856 pound ranges from £82 (how much that pound would buy today) to £2,060 (the economic power of that pound when compared to the gross domestic product). Since we want to know how valuable that pound would be to us, we'll use the historic standard of living measurement, in which a pound then would be worth £82 or $134, rounded off, as of Sept. 3, 2014 (when £1 is worth $1.64).

Before I go, I'd like to make a personal request. If you like this book, tell your friends. Mention it on your social network or the website where you bought this book. If you like, email me at bpeschel@gmail.com or write to Bill Peschel, P.O. Box 132, Hershey,

PA 17033-0132. Tell me I'm not alone in thinking annotations and extras helped you enjoy the book.

Word of mouth spurs sales, helps me support my family and encourages me to publish more annotations.

Bill Peschel
Hershey, Pa.
Feb. 1, 2015

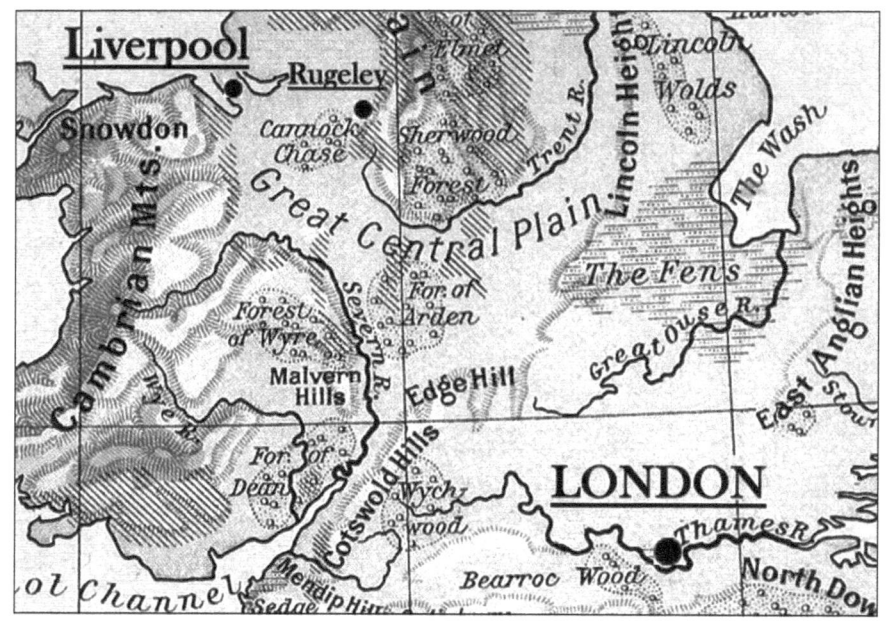

LONDON, LIVERPOOL, AND RUGELEY

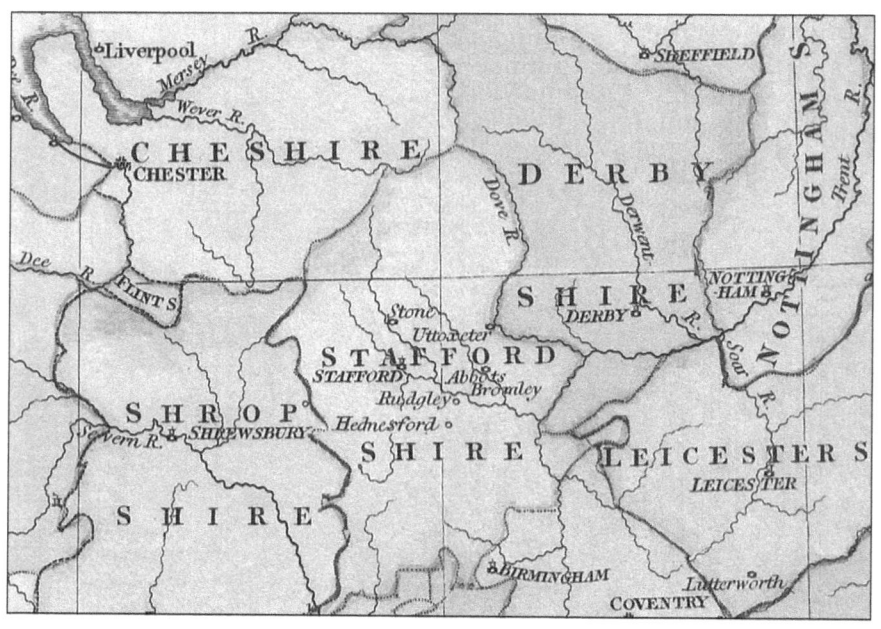

DR. PALMER'S WORLD

TRIAL OF WILLIAM PALMER FOR POISONING JOHN PARSONS COOK, AT RUGELEY.

CENTRAL CRIMINAL COURT.

The Trial of William Palmer at the Central Criminal Court

JUSTICE CRESSWELL, LORD CHIEF JUSTICE CAMPBELL, BARON ALDERSON

FIRST DAY.—MAY 14, 1856.

The long-deferred trial of William Palmer, which, owing to the necessity of passing a special act of Parliament[1] to enable it to take place in this court, had been delayed for a period of several months since the finding of a true bill[2] by the Grand

---

[1] The act allowed a trial for a crime committed anywhere to be tried at London's Central Criminal Court, also called the Old Bailey. This was the unexpected consequence of a move, beginning in the 1830s, to remove all taxes and duties imposed on newspapers. Reducing the cost of production allowed newspapers to lower their prices to within the reach of lower- and middle-class readers. To attract these readers, this led to newspapers focusing on human-interest stories, particularly crime and scandal. Circulation boomed from 39 million newspapers sold in 1836 to 122 million by 1854.

The Palmer case was the first to suffer from this new kind of saturation coverage. Much of the news came from the inquests, but there was also a hefty dose of reporting based on rumor, opinion, and innuendo. The storm of publicity was so unfavorable to Palmer that it inspired Parliament to act.

[2] Also known as an indictment. A grand jury would receive the accusation written on a piece of paper called a bill. After listening to the testimony from witnesses, they would decide if there is enough evidence to warrant a trial. If so, the foreman would write "a true bill" on the back of the sheet and send it to the judge.

Jury of Staffordshire, commenced to-day at the Old Bailey;[3] and, notwithstanding the interval which has elapsed since this extraordinary case was first brought under the notice of the public, the intense interest and excitement which it then occasioned seemed in no degree to have abated. Indeed, if the applications for admission to the court which were made so soon as the trial was appointed, and the eager endeavours of large crowds to gain an entrance to-day, may be regarded as a criterion of the public anxiety upon the progress and issue of the trial, the interest would seem to have augmented rather than diminished.

At a very early hour every entrance to the court was besieged by persons of respectable appearance, who were favoured with cards giving them a right of entrance. Without such cards no admittance could on any pretence be obtained, and even the fortunate holders of them found that they had many difficulties to overcome, and many stern janitors to encounter, before an entrance to the much-coveted precincts could be obtained. On the whole, however, the arrangements of the Under-Sheriffs Stone and Ross were excellent, and, although there may be individual cases of complaint, as there always will be when delicate and important functions have to be performed with firmness, it is but justice to testify to the general completeness and propriety of the regulations which the Sheriffs had laid down.

Among the distinguished persons who were present at the opening of the Court were the Earl of Derby, Earl Grey,[4] the Marquis of Anglesea,[5] Lord Lucan, Lord Denbigh, Prince Edward of Saxe Weimar, Lord W. Lennox, Lord G.G. Lennox, and Lord H. Lennox. The Lord Advocate of Scotland sat by the side of the Attorney-General during the trial.

At five minutes to ten o'clock the learned Judges, Lord Chief Justice Campbell, Mr. Baron Alderson, and Mr. Justice Cresswell,

---

[3] The Central Criminal Court building in London, named for the street outside it. Its location next to Newgate Prison made it easy to move prisoners back and forth safely. The courtroom where Palmer was tried has since been torn down and rebuilt.
[4] The 3rd earl, Henry George Grey (1802-1894), had been Secretary of War (1835-1839) and Secretary of State for War and the Colonies (1846-1852). He was the son of the earl whose name inspired Earl Grey tea, notable for being flavored with oil from the bergamot orange tree.
[5] According to George Fletcher's biography, the Palmer family's fortune was founded with the unknowing assistance of the marquis' father. Palmer's father, Joseph, a sawyer by trade, had an agreement to cut down trees on the estate for a share of the proceeds. Palmer cut down more trees than agreed and shared the profits with the marquis' steward who turned a blind eye to the theft.

THE TIMES REPORT

CLOCKWISE FROM LOWER LEFT: THE ATTORNEY-GENERAL, MR. HUDDLESTONE, MR. BODKIN, MR. WELSBY, MR. JAMES

accompanied by the Lord Mayor, and Aldermen Sir G. Carroll, Humphrey, Sir R.W. Carden, Finnis, Sir F.G. Moon, and Sidney, Mr. Sheriff Kennedy, Mr. Sheriff Rose, Mr. Under-Sheriff Stone, and Mr. Under-Sheriff Rose, took their seats on the bench.

The prisoner, William Palmer, was immediately placed in the dock; and to the indictment which charged him with the wilful murder of John Parsons Cook, who died at Rugeley upon the 21st of November last, he pleaded, in a clear, low, but perfectly audible and distinct tone, "Not Guilty." The prisoner is described in the Calendar as "William Palmer, 31, surgeon, of superior degree of instruction." In appearance Palmer is much older, and, although there are no marks of care about his face, there are the set expression and rounded frame which belong to the man of forty or forty-five. His countenance is clear and open, the forehead high, the complexion ruddy, and the general impression which one would form from his appearance would be rather favourable than otherwise, although his features are of a common and somewhat mean cast. There is certainly nothing to

COUNSEL FOR THE PRISONER, CLOCKWISE FROM LEFT:
MR. SERJEANT SHEE, MR. GRAY, MR. KENEALY, MR. GROVE

indicate to the ordinary observer the presence either of ferocity or cunning, and one would expect to find in him more of the boon companion than the subtle adversary. His manner was remarkably calm and collected throughout the whole of the day. It was altogether devoid of bravado, but was respectful and attentive, and was calculated to create a favourable impression. He frequently conversed with Mr. Smith, his professional adviser, and remained standing until the close of the speech for the prosecution, when at his request his counsel asked that he might be permitted to sit — an application which was at once acceded to by Lord Campbell.

The counsel engaged in the case were:— The Attorney-General, Mr. E. James, Q.C.,[6] Mr. Bodkin, Mr. Welsby, and Mr. Huddlestone, for the Crown; and Mr. Serjeant Shee, Mr. Grove, Q.C., Mr. Gray, and

---

[6] Queen's Counsel, a status granted by the queen — so during a king's reign they're known as K.C.s — in which lawyers, among other privileges, are permitted to wear silk gowns indicating they're senior members of the profession. This award is known as "taking silk."

Mr. Kenealy, for the prisoner.

A most respectable jury having been empanelled, and all the witnesses, with the exception of the medical men, having been ordered out of court,

THE ATTORNEY-GENERAL
proceeded, amid breathless silence, to open the case on the part of the prosecution. He said — Gentlemen of the jury, the duty you are called upon to discharge is the most solemn which a man can by possibility have to perform — it is to sit in judgment and to decide an issue on which depends the life of a fellow human being who stands charged with the highest crime for which a man can be arraigned before a worldly tribunal. I am sure that I need not ask your most anxious and earnest attention to such a case; but there is one thing I feel it incumbent on me to urge upon you. The peculiar circumstances of this case have given it a profound and painful interest throughout the whole country. There is scarcely a man, perhaps, who has not come to some conclusion on the issue which you are now to decide. All the details have been seized on with eager avidity, and there is, perhaps, no one who is not more or less acquainted with those details.

Standing here as a minister of justice, with no interest and no desire save that justice shall be done impartially, I feel it incumbent on me to warn you not to allow any preconceived opinion to operate on your judgment this day. Your duty — your bounden duty — is to try this case according to the evidence which shall be brought before you, and according to that alone. You must discard from your minds anything that you may have read or heard, or any opinion that you may have formed. If the evidence shall satisfy you of the prisoner's guilt, you will discharge your duty to society, to your consciences, and to the oaths which you have taken, by fearlessly pronouncing your verdict accordingly; but if the evidence fail to produce a reasonable conviction of guilt in your minds, God forbid that the scale of justice should be inclined against the prisoner by anything of prejudice or preconceived opinion.

My duty, gentlemen, will be a simple one. It will be to lay before you the facts on which the prosecution is based, and in doing so I must ask for your most patient attention. They are of a somewhat complicated character, and they range over a considerable period of time, so that it will be necessary, not merely to look to circumstances which are immediately connected with the accusation, but to go back to matters of an antecedent date. I may safely say, however, that, in my conscience, I believe there is not a fact to which I'm about to ask your patient attention which has not an immediate and most important bearing on this case.

The prisoner at the bar, William Palmer, was by profession a medical practitioner, and he carried on that profession in the town of Rugeley, in Staffordshire, for several years. In later years, however, he became addicted to turf pursuits, which gradually drew off his attention and weaned him from his profession. Within the last two or three years he made over his business to a person named Thirlby, formerly his assistant, who now carries it on. In the course of his pursuits connected with the turn, Palmer became intimate with the man whose death forms the subject of this inquiry — Mr. John Parsons Cook.

Now, Mr. Cook was a young man of decent family, who originally had been intended for the profession of the law. He was articled to a solicitor;[7] but after a time, inheriting some property, to the extent, I think, of some £12,000 or £15,000,[8] he abandoned the laborious profession of the law, and betook himself also to the turf. He kept racehorses, and betted considerably; and in the course of his operations he became much connected and familiarly intimate with the prisoner William Palmer.

It is for the murder of that Mr. John Parsons Cook that the prisoner stands indicted to-day,[9] the charge against him being that he took away that man's life by poison. It will be necessary to show you the circumstances in which the prisoner Palmer was then placed, and the position in which he stood relatively to the deceased Cook. It will be impossible thoroughly to understand this case in all its bearings without those circumstances being laid before you, and it will be necessary, therefore, that I should go into them particularly.

The case which, on the part of the prosecution, I have to urge against Palmer is this — that, being in desperate circumstances, with ruin, disgrace, and punishment staring him in the face, which could only be averted by means of money, he took advantage of his intimacy with Cook, when Cook had become the winner of a considerable sum, to destroy him, in order to obtain possession of his money. Out of the

---

[7] A trainee who was bound by an agreement called the "articles of clerkship" to undergo training with a firm or individual for a fixed period of time.

[8] Using the conversion ratio discussed in the Preface (£1 in 1856 = £82 or $134 in 2015), this is the equivalent of £984,000 or $1,230,000. This was at a time when Palmer was paying workers at his training facility 12 to 14 shillings a week.

[9] The word "today" was originally two words that over time was melded into one. People speaking Old English, an early form of the English language from roughly 650 to 1150, would say "to daege" for "on (the) day." Sometime during the 16th century, the word came to be written with the hyphen and would stay that way until the early 20th century. The same process happened with "tomorrow," which you will see written as "to-morrow" (in Old English they'd say "to morgenne" for "on (the) morrow").

circumstances of Palmer at that time arose, as we say, the motive which induced him to commit this crime. If I show you upon evidence which can leave no reasonable doubt in your minds that he committed that crime, motives become a matter of secondary importance. Nevertheless, in inquiries of this kind, it is natural and right to look to see what may have been the motives by which a man has been induced to commit the crime charged against him; and if we find strong motives, the more readily shall we be led to believe in the probability of the crime having been committed; but if we find an absence of motive the probability is the other way. In this case, the motive will be matter for serious consideration; and inasmuch as the circumstances out of which we say that the motive arose come first in order of time, I will deal with them before I come to that which is the more immediate subject matter of our inquiry.

It seems to me that it would be most convenient that I should follow the chronological order of events, and I will therefore pursue that course. It appears that as early as the year 1853 Palmer had got into difficulties, and that he began to raise money upon bills.[10] In 1854 his circumstances became worse, and he was at that time indebted to different persons in a large sum of money. He then had recourse to an expedient which it is important that I should bring before you; but, as it will become necessary for me to detail to you transactions involving fraud, and, what is worse, forgery, I wish to make a few observations to you before I detail those transactions.

Although I am anxious, where I feel it to be absolutely necessary for the elucidation of the truth, that those circumstances should be brought before you, I wish that they should not have more than their fair and legitimate weight. You must not allow them to prejudice your minds against the prisoner with reference to that which is the real matter of inquiry. I cannot avoid bringing them forward; but I would anxiously caution you and pray you not to allow any prejudice by reason of those transactions to operate against the prisoner; for, though a man may be guilty of fraud and forgery, it does not follow, therefore, that he is guilty of murder.

---

[10] Borrowing money in Victorian England was fraught with peril. Unregulated moneylenders charged between 60 and 100 percent interest on their bills, making it nearly impossible for borrowers to pay them off. As we see in the Palmer case, the need to raise fresh money meant unending rounds of visiting lenders, pledging whatever security was at hand — sometimes several times over — until the person's finances collapse. Defaulters risked reputation-damaging exposure and jail time. Younger members of wealthy families were especially vulnerable. They were inexperienced to the point of gullibility about contracts. Sometimes, they would sign them without reading them, with the expectation that they would be bailed out by their family.

Among the bills on which Palmer raised money in 1853 was one for £2,000, which he had discounted by a person named Padwick. That bill bore the acceptance of Sarah Palmer, the mother of the prisoner. She was, and is, a woman of considerable property, and her acceptance being believed to be genuine, was a security upon which money could be readily raised. The prisoner forged that acceptance, and that was, if not the first, at all events one of the earliest transactions of that nature by means of which for a long period of time money was obtained by him upon bills, with his mother's acceptance forged by him. This shows how, when things came to a climax and he found himself involved in a position of great peril and emergency, he had recourse to a desperate expedient to avoid the consequences which seemed inevitably to press upon him.

He owed in 1854 a very large sum of money. On the 29th of September in that year his wife died. He had effected an insurance upon her life for £13,000, and the proceeds of that insurance were realised, and by means of them he discharged some of his most pressing liabilities. In dealing with a portion of these liabilities he employed a gentleman named Pratt, a solicitor in London, who was in the habit of discounting bills. Mr. Pratt received from him £8,000, and Mr. Wright, a solicitor of Birmingham, received £5,000; and with those two sums £13,000 of debt was disposed of; but that still left Palmer with considerable liabilities, and among other things, the bill of £2,000, which was discounted by Padwick, remained unpaid.

In the course of the same year he effected an insurance on his brother's life, and upon the strength of that policy Palmer proceeded to issue fresh bills, which were discounted by Pratt at the rate of 60 per cent., who kept the policy as collateral security. The bills which were discounted in the course of that year amounted in the whole to £12,500. I find that there were two bills discounted as early as June, 1854, which were held over from month to month. In March, 1855, two bills were discounted for £2,000 each, with the proceeds of which Palmer bought two racehorses, called Nettle and Chicken. Those bills were renewed in June, and one became due on the 28th of September, and the other on the 2nd of October, when they were again renewed. The result of the bill proceedings of the year was that in November, when the Shrewsbury races took place, there were in Pratt's hands one bill for £2,000, due the 25th of October; another for £2,000, due the 27th of October; two for the joint sum of £1,500, due on the 9th of November; one for £1,000, due on the 30th of September; one for £2,000, due on the 1st January; one for £2,000, due on the 5th January; and another for £2,000, due on the 15th January; making altogether £12,500. £1,000 of this sum, however, he had contrived to pay off, so that there was due in November, 1855, no less than

£11,500 upon bills, every one of which bore the forged acceptance of the prisoner's mother.

Under these circumstances, a pressure naturally arose — the pressure of £11,500 of liabilities, with not a shilling in the world to meet them, and the still greater pressure resulting from a consciousness that the moment when he could no longer go on and his mother was resorted to for payment, the fact of those forgeries would at once become manifest, and would bring upon him the peril of the law for the crime of forgery.

The prisoner's brother died in August, 1855. His life had been insured, and the policy for £13,000 had been assigned to the prisoner who, of course, expected that the proceeds of that insurance would pay off his liabilities; but the office in which the insurance was effected declined to pay, and consequently there was no assistance to be derived from that source.[11]

Now, in these transactions to which I have referred, the deceased John Parsons Cook had been to a certain extent concerned. It seems that in May, 1855, Palmer was pressed to pay £500 to a person named Serjeant. He had at that time in the hands of Palmer a balance upon bill transactions of £310 to his credit, and he wanted Pratt to advance the £190 necessary to make up £500. Pratt declined to do that, except upon security; upon which Palmer offered him the acceptance of Cook, representing him to be a man of substance. Accordingly the acceptance of Cook for £200 was sent up, and upon that Pratt advanced the money. When that bill for £200 became due, Palmer failed to provide for it, and Cook had to meet it himself.

In August of the same year, an occurrence took place to which I must call your particular attention. Palmer wrote to Pratt to say that he must have £1,000 by a day named. Pratt declined to advance it without security; upon which Palmer offered the security of Cook's acceptance for £500. Pratt still declined to advance the money without some more tangible security. Now Palmer represented this as a transaction in which Cook required the money, and it may be that such was the fact. I have no means of ascertaining how that was; but I will give him the credit of supposing it to be true.

---

[11] The life insurance industry grew rapidly during the first half of the 19th century. Anyone could insure anyone so long as they had a financial interest in that person staying alive, so husbands insured their wives' marriage settlement and creditors insured debtors. In "Bitter Nemesis," John Buckingham writes that the formation of burial societies, a form of group insurance families could draw on for funeral expenses, led to widespread abuses: "The epidemic of child-poisoning reached its zenith in 1846-1851 when the abuses led to the closure of the societies."

Pratt still declining to advance the money, Palmer proposed an assignment by Cook of two racehorses, one called Polestar, which won the Shrewsbury races, and another called Sirius. That assignment was afterwards executed by Cook in favour of Pratt, and Cook, therefore, was clearly entitled to the money which was raised upon that security, which realised £375 in cash, and a wine warrant[12] for £65. Palmer contrived, however, that the money and wine warrant should be sent to him and not to Cook. Mr. Pratt sent down his cheque to Palmer, in the country, on a stamp as the Act of Parliament required, and he availed himself of the opportunity now offered by law of striking out the word "bearer," and writing "order," the effect of which was to necessitate the endorsement of Cook on the back of the cheque.

It was not intended by Palmer that these proceeds should fall into Cook's hands, and accordingly he forged the name of John Parsons Cook on the back of that cheque. Cook never received the money, and you will see that within ten days from the period when he came to his end, the bill in respect to that transaction, which was at three months, would have fallen due, when it must have become apparent that Palmer received the money; and that, in order to obtain it, he had forged the endorsement of Cook.

I wish these were the only transactions in which Cook had been at all mixed up with the prisoner Palmer; but there is another to which it is necessary to refer. In September, 1855, Palmer's brother having died, and the proceeds of the insurance not having been realised, Palmer induced a person named Bates to propose his life for insurance. Palmer had succeeded in raising money upon previous policies, and I have no doubt that he persuaded Cook to assist him in that transaction, so that, by representing Bates as a man of wealth and substance, they might get a policy on his life, by which policy, deposited as a collateral security, they might obtain advances[13] of

---

[12] England was undergoing a long transition from a barter economy to one based on currency tied to the value of gold. A warrant fell somewhere in between. It was a note made out to the keeper of a bonded warehouse, who agreed to deliver wine of a certain value upon receipt.

[13] This passage raises an interesting and terrible implication. If it's possible to obtain a loan using the policy as security, what was in it for the moneylender? Why would they be willing to lend thousands of pounds today only to cash in years, possibly decades, later? Or was there hanging in the air the unspoken assumption that the policy will pay off sooner than the assurance company expected? That Cook was a party to fraud is not disputed; were his hands bloody as well? Or was he financially naïve? Fletcher's biography quotes George Herring asking Cook, the day after he was drugged in Shrewsbury, why he was returning to Rugeley with Palmer. When Cook replied "I really must go — you don't know all," was this what he was thinking of?

money. Bates had been somewhat better off in the world, but he had fallen into decay, and he had accepted employment from Palmer as a sort of hanger-on in his stables. He was a healthy young man; and, being in the company of Palmer and Cook at Rugeley, on the 5th of September, Palmer asked him to insure his life, and produced the form of proposal to the office.

Bates declined, but Palmer pressed him, and Cook interposed and said, "You had better do it; it will be for your benefit, and you'll be quite safe with Palmer." At length they succeeded in persuading him to sign the proposal for no less a sum than £25,000, Cook attesting the proposal, which Palmer filled in, Palmer being referred to as medical attendant, and his former assistant, Thirlby, as general referee. That proposal was sent up to the Solicitors and General Insurance Office, and in the ensuing month — that office not being disposed to effect the insurance — they sent up another for £10,000 to the Midland Office on that same life. That proposal also failed, and no money, therefore, could be obtained from that source. All these circumstances are important, because they show the desperate straits in which the prisoner at that time found himself.

[The learned counsel then read a series of letters from Mr. Pratt to the prisoner, all pressing upon the prisoner the importance of his meeting the numerous bills which Pratt held, bearing the acceptance of Mrs. Sarah Palmer; and these letters appeared to become more urgent when the writer found that the insurance office refused to pay the £13,000 upon the policy effected on the life of the prisoner's brother, and which Pratt held as collateral security. The letters were dated at intervals between the 10th of September and the 18th of October, 1855. He then continued.]

On the 6th of November, two writs were issued by Pratt for £4,000, one against Palmer, and the other against his mother; and Pratt wrote on the same day to say that he had sent the writs to Mr. Crabbe, but that they were not to be served until he sent further instructions, and he strongly urged Palmer to make immediate arrangements for meeting them, and also to arrange for the bills for £1,500 due on the 9th of November. Between the 10th and the 13th of November, Palmer succeeded in paying £600; but on that day Pratt again wrote to him, urging him to raise £1,000, at all events, to meet the bills due on the 9th.

That being the state of things at that time, we now come to the events connected with Shrewsbury races. Cook was the owner of a mare called Polestar, which was entered for the Shrewsbury Handicap. She had been advantageously weighted, and Cook, believing that the mare would win, betted largely upon the event. The race was ran upon the 13th of November — the very day on which that last letter was written by Pratt, which would reach Palmer on the 14th. The result of the race was that Polestar won, and that Cook was entitled, in the first place, to the stakes, which amounted to £424, minus certain deductions, which left a net sum of £381 19s. His bets had also been successful, and he won, upon the whole, a total sum of £2,050.[14] He had won also in the previous week, at Worcester, and I shall show that at Shrewsbury he had in his pocket, besides the stakes and the money which he would be entitled to receive at Tattersall's,[15] between £700 and £900. The stakes he would receive through Mr. Weatherby, a great racing agent in London, with whom he kept an account, and upon whom he would draw; and, the race being run on Tuesday, he would be entitled on the ensuing Monday to receive his bets at Tattersall's, which amounted to £1,020.

Within a week from that time Mr. Cook died, and the important inquiry which we have now to make is how he came by his death — whether by natural causes or by the hand of man? and if the latter, by whose hand?

It is important, in the first place, that I should show you what was his state of health when he went down to Shrewsbury. He was a young man, but twenty-eight when he died. He was slightly disposed to a pulmonary[16] complaint, and, although delicate in that respect, he was in all other respects a hale and hearty young man. He had been in the habit, from time to time, especially with reference to his chest, of consulting a physician in London — Dr. Savage, who saw him a fortnight before his death. For four years he had occasionally consulted Dr. Savage, being at that time a little anxious about the state of his throat, in which there happened to be one or two slight eruptions. He had been taking mercury for these eruptions, having mistaken the character of the complaint.[17] Dr. Savage at once saw that he had made a mistake, and desired him to discontinue the use of mercury, substituting for it a course of tonics. Mr. Cook's health

---

[14] The equivalent of roughly £220,000 or $350,000 today. See "How This Book Was Edited" for an explanation.
[15] An auction house that specialized in race horses and gambling, founded in 1766 by Richard Tattersall (1724-1795). The business's willingness to transact bets attracted sporting men and gamblers from all classes. It was located until 1865 near Hyde Park Corner, then on the edge of London. It still operates as an auction house in Newmarket, Suffolk.
[16] Something that is related to or affecting the lungs.
[17] The implication is that Cook was taking mercury to treat syphilis, a venereal disease that can lead to a horrible degrading death. Mercury is a highly toxic metallic element notable for being the only one that remains liquid at room temperature. It has been used as a medicine since ancient times, and in Victorian England it was an ineffectual treatment for syphilis. Palmer's defense will argue that Cook's dissipated life led to his death.

immediately began to improve; but, inasmuch as the new course of treatment might have involved serious consequences in case Dr. Savage had been mistaken in the diagnosis of the disease, he asked Cook to look in upon him from time to time, and Cook had, as recently as within a fortnight of his death, gone to call upon Dr. Savage. Dr. Savage then examined his throat and whole system carefully, and he will be prepared to tell you that at that time he had nothing on earth the matter with him, except a certain degree of thickening of the tonsils, or some of the glands of the throat, to which anyone is liable, and there was no symptom whatever of ulcerated[18] sore throat, or any thing of the sort.

Having then seen Dr. Savage, he went down to Shrewsbury races, and his horse won. After that he was somewhat excited, as a man might naturally be under the circumstances of having won a considerable sum of money, and he asked several friends to dine with him to celebrate the event. They dined together at the Raven,[19] the hotel where he was staying, and had two or three bottles of wine; but there was no excess of any sort, and no foundation for saying that Cook was the worse for liquor. Indeed, he was not addicted to excesses, but was, on the contrary, an abstemious man on all occasions. He went to bed that night, and there was nothing the matter with him. He got up the next day, and went again on the course, as usual.

That night, Wednesday, the 14th November, a remarkable incident happened, to which I beg to draw your attention. A friend of his, a Mr. Fisher, and a Mr. Herring, were at Shrewsbury races, and Fisher, who, besides being a sporting man, was an agent for receiving winnings, and who received Cook's bets at the settling day at Tattersall's, occupied the room next to that occupied by Cook. Late in the evening Fisher went into a room in which he found Palmer and Cook drinking brandy and water. Cook gave him something to drink, and said to Palmer. "You'll have some more, won't you?" Palmer replied, "Not unless you finish your glass." Cook said, "I'll soon do that;" and he finished it at a gulp, leaving only about a tea-spoonful at the bottom of the glass. He had hardly swallowed it, when he exclaimed, "Good God! there's something in it, it burns my throat." Palmer immediately took up the glass, and drinking what remained, said, "Nonsense, there's nothing in it" and then pushing the glass to Fisher and another person who had come in, said, "Cook fancies there is something in the brandy-and-water — there's nothing in it — taste it." On which one of them replied, "How can we taste it? you've drank it all."

---

[18] An opening in the skin caused by the disintegration of tissue.
[19] The Raven Hotel on Castle Street was one of Shrewsbury's principal inns for more than 200 years. The elegant three-story building was demolished in 1960.

Cook suddenly rose and left the room, and called Fisher out, saying that he was taken seriously ill. He was seized with a most violent vomiting, and became so bad that after a little while it was necessary to take him to bed. He vomited there again and again in the most violent way, and as the sickness continued after the lapse of a couple of hours, a medical man was sent for. He came and proposed an emetic[20] and other means for making the sick man eject what he had taken. After that, medicine was given him — at first some stimulant of a comforting nature, and then a pill as a purgative dose. After two or three hours he became more tranquil, and about two o'clock he fell asleep and slept till next morning. Such was the state of the man's feelings all that time that I cannot tell what passed; but he gave Fisher the money which he had about him, desiring him to take care of it, and Mr. Fisher will tell you that that money amounted to between £800 and £900 in notes.

The next morning, having passed a quiet night, as I have said, and feeling better, he went out on the course; and he saw Fisher, who gave him back his notes. That was the Thursday. He still looked very ill, and felt very ill; but the vomiting had ceased. On that day Palmer's horse, the Chicken, ran at Shrewsbury. He had backed his mare heavily, but she lost. When Palmer went to Shrewsbury he had no money, and was obliged to borrow £25 to take him there. His horse lost, and he lost bets upon the race. He and Cook then left Shrewsbury, and returned to Rugeley, Cook going to the Talbot Arms Hotel, directly opposite the prisoner's house.

There was an incident however, connected with the occurrence at Shrewsbury, which I must mention. About eleven o'clock that night, a Mrs. Brooks, who betted on commission, and had an establishment of jockeys, went to speak to the deceased upon some racing business, and in the lobby she saw Palmer holding up a tumbler to the light; and, having looked at it through the gas, he withdrew to an outer room, and presently returned with the glass in his hand, and went into the room where Cook was, and in which room he drank the brandy and water, from which I suppose you will infer that the sickness came on. I do not charge that by anything which caused that sickness Cook's death was occasioned; but I shall show you that throughout the ensuing days at Rugeley he constantly received things from the prisoner, and that during those days that sickness was continued. I shall show you that after he died antimony[21] was found in the tissues of his body, and in his

---

[20] A drug or object, such as a toothbrush, used to induce vomiting.
[21] A naturally occurring chemical element. While it is poisonous — its symptoms make it easy to mistake for arsenic — it was used in low doses to cause vomiting.

blood — antimony, administered in the form of tartar emetic,[22] which, if continued to be applied, will maintain sickness.

It was not that, however, of which this man died. The charge is, that having been prepared by antimony, he was killed by strychnine. You have, no doubt, heard of the vegetable product known as *nux vomica*.[23] In that nut, or bean, there resides a subtle and fatal poison, which is capable of being extracted from it by the skill of the operative chemist, and of which the most minute quantity is fatal to animal life. From half to a quarter of a grain will destroy life — you may imagine, therefore, how minute is the dose.[24]

In the human organization, the nervous system may be divided into two main parts — the nerves of sensation, by which a consciousness of all external sensations is conveyed to the brain; and the nerves of motion, which are, as it were, the agents between the intellectual power of man and the physical action which arises from his organization. Those are the two main branches, having their origin in the immediate vicinity of the seat of man's intellectual existence. They are entirely distinct in their allocations, and one set of nerves may be affected, while the other is left undisturbed. You may paralyse the nerves of sensation, and may leave the nerves which act upon the voluntary muscles of movement wholly unaffected; or you may reverse that state of things, and may affect the nerves and muscles of volition, leaving the nerves of sensation wholly unaffected.

Strychnine affects the nerves which act on the voluntary muscles, and it leaves wholly unaffected the nerves on which human consciousness depends; and it is important to bear this in mind — some poisons produce a total absence of consciousness, but the poison to which I refer affects the voluntary action of the muscles of the body, and leaves unimpaired the power of consciousness.

Now, the way in which strychnine acting upon the voluntary muscles is fatal to life is that it produces the most intense excitement of all those muscles. Violent convulsions take place — spasms which affect the whole body, and which end in rigidity. All the muscles

---

[22] Potassium antimony tartrate, a compound used to treat animals, in dyes, and to cause vomiting in patients (which is what an emetic does).

[23] A substance containing strychnine and brucia, derived from grinding into a powder seeds from the tree of the same name.

[24] A grain is a obsolete unit of weight based on the size of a cereal seed. Its weight varied from country to country; in England it was equal to 64.8 milligrams. Since a standard aspirin tablet of 325 milligrams is five grains, the equivalent of one-fifth of a tablet of pure strychnine is enough to kill a person.

become fixed, and the respiratory muscles[25] in which the lungs have play are fixed with an immovable rigidity. Respiration consequently is suspended, and death ensues. These symptoms are known to medical men under the term of tetanus.[26] There are other forms of tetanus which produce death, and which arise from other causes than the taking of strychnine, but there is a wide difference between the various forms of the same disease, which prevents the possibility of mistake.

[The learned counsel then explained the different symptoms which characterize traumatic tetanus and idiopathic tetanus, which latter is of comparatively rare occurrence in this country; but, as this is a matter which he hereafter dwelt upon with great detail in the medical testimony, it is unnecessary to burden our report with it at any length here. He then continued.]

I have reason to believe that an attempt will be made to confound those different classes of disease, and it will be necessary therefore for the jury to watch with great minuteness the medical evidence upon this point. It will show that both in traumatic and idiopathic tetanus the disease commences with the milder symptoms, which gradually progress towards the development and final completion of the attack. When once the disease has commenced, it continues without intermission, although, as in every other form of malady, the paroxysms will be from time to time more or less intense. In the case of tetanus from strychnine it is not so. It commences with paroxysms which may subside for a time, but are renewed again; and whereas other forms of tetanus almost always last during a certain number of hours or days, when we deal with strychnine we deal with cases not of hours but of minutes — in which we have no beginnings of the disease, and then a gradual development to the climax; but in which the paroxysms commence with all their power at the very first, and terminate, after a few short minutes of fearful agony and struggles, in the dissolution of the victim.

Palmer was a medical man, and it is clear that the effect of

---

[25] Muscles responsible for breathing. In the human body, the intercostal muscles that run between the ribs expand and shrink to help the chest cavity bring in and expel oxygen.

[26] Nowadays, it is recognized as a medical condition, characterized by the contraction of muscle fibres throughout the body, caused by a bacterium. But at the time of Palmer's trial, it was defined simply as a type of convulsion. It was divided into three groups: idiopathic, or spontaneous tetanus, a rare disease with an unknown origin; traumatic tetanus caused by external wounds, open sores or lockjaw; and tetanus caused by strychnine. The trial's medical evidence hinged on whether Cook died from traumatic tetanus or strychnine.

strychnine had not escaped his attention; for I have a book before me[27] which was found in his house after his arrest, called "Manual for Students Preparing for Examination at Apothecaries' Hall"; and on the first page, in his handwriting, I observe this remark, "Strychnine kills by causing tetanic fixing of the respiratory muscles." I don't wish to attach more importance to that circumstance than it deserves, because nothing is more natural than that, in a book of this kind belonging to a professional man, such notes should be made; but I refer to it to show that the effect of poison on human life had come within his notice.

I now revert to what took place after the arrival of these people at Rugeley. They arrived on the night of Thursday, the 15th of November, between ten and eleven o'clock, when Mr. Cook took some refreshment and went to bed. He rose next morning and went out, and dined that day with Palmer. He returned to the inn about ten o'clock that evening, perfectly well and sober, and went to bed.

The next morning, at an early hour, Palmer was with him, and from that time throughout the whole of Saturday and Sunday he was constantly in attendance on him. He ordered him coffee on Saturday morning. It was brought in by the chambermaid, Elizabeth Mills, and given to the prisoner, who had an opportunity of tampering with it before giving it to Cook. Immediately after taking it the same symptoms set in which had occurred at Shrewsbury.

Throughout the whole of that day and the next, the prisoner constantly administered various things to Cook, who continued to be tormented with that incessant and troublesome sickness. Again, toast and water was brought over from the prisoner's house, instead of being made at the inn, as it might have been, and again the sickness ensued.

It seems also that Palmer desired a woman named Reney to procure some broth for Cook from the Albion. She obtained it, and gave it to Palmer to warm, and when Palmer had done so he told her to take it to the Talbot for Mr. Cook, and to say that Mr. Smith had sent it — there being a Mr. Jeremiah Smith, an intimate friend of Cook. Cook tried to swallow a spoonful of the broth, but it

---

[27] Dr. John Stegall's 500-plus page book, which ran to multiple editions, contained extensive chapters on botany, anatomy, toxicology, chemistry (organic, animal and general), midwifery and the practice of medicine. If that wasn't enough help, Stegall even includes an offer in the back to personally tutor up to two students a term. The number of "principal diseases" reflects the state of medical science then: fevers (13), digestion (17), lungs (10), circulation (2), skin (1), and brain and nervous system (9). John Buckingham's "Bitter Nemesis: The Intimate History of Strychnine" called it "a farrago of medieval alchemy and ill-described medicine."

immediately made him sick, and he brought it off his stomach.

The broth was then taken down stairs, and after a little while the prisoner came across and asked if Mr. Cook had had his broth. He was told, "No; that he had tried to take it, but that it had made him sick, and that he could not retain it on his stomach." Palmer said that he must take it, and desired that the broth should be brought upstairs. Cook tried to take it again, but again he began to vomit and throw the whole off his stomach.

It was then taken down stairs, and a woman at the inn, thinking that it looked nice, took a couple of tablespoonfuls of it; within half an hour she also was taken severely ill. Vomiting came on, and continued almost incessantly for five or six hours. She was obliged to go to bed, and she had exactly the same symptoms which manifested themselves in Cook's person after he drank the brandy and water at Shrewsbury.

On that Saturday, about three o'clock, Dr. Bamford, a medical man at Rugeley, was called in, and Palmer told him that Cook had a bilious attack[28] — that he had dined with him on the day before, and had drunk too freely of champagne, which had disordered his stomach.

Now, I shall show to you, by the evidence of medical men, both at Shrewsbury and Rugeley, that although Palmer had on one or two occasions represented Cook as suffering under bilious diarrhœa, there was not, during the continuance of the violent vomiting which I have mentioned, a single bilious symptom of any sort whatever. Dr. Bamford visited him at half-past 3, and when he found Mr. Cook suffering from violent vomiting, and the stomach in so irritable a state that it would not retain a tablespoonful of anything, he naturally tried to see what the symptoms were which could lead him to form a notion as to the cause of that state of things. He found to his surprise that the pulse of the patient was perfectly natural — that his tongue was quite clean, his skin quite moist, and that there was not the slightest trace of fever, or, in short, of any of those symptoms which might be expected in the case of a bilious man. Having heard from Palmer that he ascribed his illness to an excess of wine on the previous day, he informed Cook of it, and Cook then said, "Well, I suppose I must have taken too much, but it's very odd, for I only took three glasses."

The representation, therefore, made by Palmer, that Cook had taken an excess of champagne, was not correct. Coffee was brought up to Cook at 4 o'clock when Palmer was there, and he vomited immediately. At 6 some barley-water[29] was taken to him when Palmer was not there,

---

[28] An ailment caused by the disruption of the digestion system or excessive secretions of bile.
[29] A drink made from boiled pearl barley with helpings of lemon, fruit juice and sugar to taste.

and the barley-water did not produce vomiting. At 8 some arrowroot[30] was given him, Palmer was present, and vomiting took place again.

These may, no doubt, be mere coincidences, but they are facts, which, of whatever interpretation they may be susceptible, are well deserving of attention, that during the whole of that Saturday Palmer was continually in and out of the house in which Cook was sojourning; that he gave him a variety of things, and that whenever he gave him anything sickness invariably ensued.

That evening Dr. Bamford called again, and finding that the sickness still continued he prepared for the patient two pills containing half a grain of calomel, half a grain of morphia, and four grains of rhubarb.[31]

On the following day, Sunday, between 7 and 8 o'clock in the morning, Dr. Bamford is again summoned to Cook's bedside, and finds the sickness still recurring, but fails to detect any symptoms of bile. He visited him repeatedly in the course of that day, and on leaving him in the evening found, that though the sickness continued, the tongue was clean, and there was not the slightest indication of bile or fever. And so Sunday ended.

On Monday, the 19th, Palmer left Rugeley for London — on what business I shall presently explain. Before starting, however, he called in the morning to see Cook, and ordered him a cup of coffee. He took it up himself, and after drinking it Cook, as usual, vomited. After that Palmer took his departure.

Presently Dr. Bamford called, and, finding Cook still suffering from sickness of the stomach, gave him some medicine. Whether from the effect of that medicine, or from whatever other cause, I know not; but it is admitted that from that time a great improvement was observed in Cook. Palmer was not present, and during the whole of the day Cook was better.

Between 12 and 1 o'clock he is visited by Dr. Bamford, who, perceiving the improvement, advised him to get up. He does so, washes, dresses, recovers his spirits, and sits up for several hours. Two of his

---

[30] A powdered starch obtained from the root of the tropical plant. Ground into a powder, it was used in biscuits, cakes, puddings, and jellies. Easily digestible and nourishing, it was boiled with flavoring or dissolved in beef tea or milk and fed to children and invalids.

[31] *Calomel*, also called mercury chloride, is a chemical compound used as a laxative, a purgative and to treat syphilis. *Morphia* is an outdated term for morphine, the main chemical found in the opium poppy plant. Morphine operates on the central nervous system to relieve pain. It is effective, but also has a high potential for addiction. It was isolated in 1804 and reached commercial markets in 1827, but it wasn't until the hypodermic needle was invented in 1857 that its use exploded. *Rhubarb*: A plant used as a laxative.

jockeys and his trainer called to see him, are admitted to his room, enter into conversation with him, and perceive that he is in a state of comparative ease and comfort, and so he continued till a late hour.

I will now interrupt for a moment the consecutive narration of what passed afterwards at Rugeley, to follow Palmer through the events in which he was concerned in London. He had written to a person named Herring to meet him at Beaufort-buildings,[32] where a boarding-house was kept by a lady named Hawks.

Herring was a man on the turf, and had been to Shrewsbury races. Immediately on seeing Palmer he inquired after Cook's health. "Oh," said Palmer, "he is all right; his medical man has given him a dose of calomel and recommended him to come out, and what I want to see you about is the settling of his accounts." Monday, it appears, was settling-day[33] at Tattersall's, and it was necessary that all accounts should be squared. Cook's usual agent for effecting that arrangement was a person named Fisher, and it seems not a little singular that Cook should have told Palmer why Fisher should not have been employed on this as on all other similar occasions. On this point, however, Palmer offered no explanation. He was himself a defaulter, and could not show at Tattersall's.

He produced a piece of paper which he said contained a list of the sums which Cook was entitled to receive, and he mentioned the names of the different persons who were indebted to Cook, and the amounts for which they were respectively liable. Herring held out his hand to take the paper, but Palmer said, "No, I will keep this document; here is another piece of paper, write down what I read to you, and what I have here I will retain, as it will be a check against you." He then dictated the names of the various persons, with the sums for which they were liable.

Herring observed that it amounted to £1,020. "Very well," said Palmer, "pay yourself £6, Shelly, £30, and if you see Bull, tell him Cook will pay him on Thursday or Friday. And now," he added, "how much do you make the balance?"

Herring replied that he made it £984. Palmer replied that the tot was right, and then went on to say, "I will give you £16, which will make it £1,000. Pay yourself the £200 that I owe you for my bill; pay Padwick £350, and Pratt £450."

So we have it here established, beyond all controversy, that Palmer did not hesitate to apply Cook's money to the payment of his own debts. With regard to the debt due to Mr. Padwick, I am assured

---

[32] Palmer rented rooms at the site off The Strand. The building was torn down to build the Savoy Theatre, which opened in 1881.

[33] The day, usually a week after the race was run, when betters and bookies meet to pay off losing bets and receive their winnings for successful wages.

that it represents moneys won by that gentlemen, partly from Cook, and partly from Palmer, but that Mr. Padwick held Palmer to be the responsible party, and looked to him for payment. The debt to Pratt was Palmer's own affair.

Such is the state of things as regards the disposition of money. Palmer desired Herring to send cheques to Pratt and Padwick at once, and without waiting to draw the money from Tattersall's.

To this Herring objected, observing that it would be most injudicious to send the cheques before he was sure of getting the money.

"Ah, well," said Palmer, "never mind — it is all right; but come what will, Pratt must be paid, for his claim is on account of a bill of sale for a mare."

Finding it impossible to overcome Herring's objection to send the cheques until he had got the money at Tattersall's, Palmer then proceeded to settle some small betting transactions between himself and that gentleman amounting to £5, or thereabouts. He pulled out a £50 note, and Herring, not having full change, gave him a cheque for £20. They then parted, Palmer directing him to send down word of his proceedings either to him (Palmer) or to Cook.

With this injunction Herring complied, and I shall prove in the course of the trial that the letters he wrote to Cook were intercepted by the postmaster at Rugeley. Not having received as much as he expected at Tattersall's, Herring was unable to pay Padwick the £350; but it is not disputed that he paid £450 to Pratt.

On the same day, Palmer went himself to the latter gentleman, and paid him other moneys, consisting of £30 in notes, and the cheque for £20 which he had received from Herring and a memorandum was drawn, and to which I shall hereafter have occasion to call attention.

So much for Palmer's proceedings in London. On the evening of that same day (Monday) he returned home. Arriving at Rugeley about 9 o'clock at night, he at once proceeded to visit Cook, at the Talbot Arms; and from that time till 10 or 11 o'clock he was continually in and out of Cook's room.

In the course of the evening he went to a man named Newton, assistant to a surgeon named Salt, and applied for three grains of strychnine, which Newton, knowing Palmer to be a medical practitioner, did not hesitate to give him. Dr. Bamford had sent on this day the same kind of pills that he had sent on Saturday and Sunday. I believe it was the doctor's habit to take the pills himself to the Talbot Arms, and intrust them to the care of the housekeeper, who carried them upstairs; but it was Palmer's practice to come in afterwards, and, evening after evening, to administer medicine to the patient.

There is no doubt that Cook took pills on Monday night. Whether he took the pills prepared for him by Dr. Bamford, and similar to those which he had taken on Saturday and Sunday, or whether Palmer substituted for Dr. Bamford's pills some of his own concoction, consisting in some measure of strychnine, I must leave for the jury to determine. Certain it is, that when he left Cook at 11 o'clock at night, the latter was still comparatively well and comfortable, and cheerful as in the morning. But he was not long to continue so.

About 12 o'clock the female servants in the lower part of the house were alarmed by violent screams proceeding from Cook's room. They rushed in and found him in great agony, shrieking dreadfully, shouting "Murder!" and calling on Christ to save his soul. He was in intense pain. The eyes were starting out of his head. He was flinging his arms wildly about him, and his whole body was convulsed. He was perfectly conscious, however, and desired that Palmer should be sent for without delay. One of the women ran to fetch him, and he attended in a few minutes. He found Cook still screaming, gasping for breath, and hardly able to speak. He ran back again to procure some medicine; and on his return Cook exclaimed, "Oh dear, doctor, I shall die!"

"No, my lad, you shall not," replied Palmer; and he then gave him some more medicine. The sick man vomited almost immediately, but there was no appearance of the pills in the utensil.

Shortly afterwards he became more calm, and called on the women to rub his limbs. They did so, and found them cold and rigid. Presently the symptoms became still more tranquil and he grew better; but the medical men will depose that the tetanus that afflicted him was that occasioned by strychnine. His frame, exhausted by the terrible agony it had endured, now fell gradually into repose; nature asserted her claim to rest, and he began to doze.

So matters remained till the morrow, Tuesday, the 20th, the day of his death. On the morning of that day, Cook was found comparatively comfortable, though still retaining a vivid impression of the horrors he had suffered the night before. He was quite collected, and conversed rationally with the chambermaid. Palmer meeting Dr. Bamford that same day, told him that he did not want to have Cook disturbed, for that he was now at his ease, though he had had a fit the night before.

This same morning, between the hours of eleven and twelve o'clock, there occurred a very remarkable incident. About that time Palmer went to the shop of a certain Mr. Hawkings, a druggist, at Rugeley. He had not dealt with him for two years before, it being his practice during that period to purchase such drugs as he required from Mr. Thirlby, a former assistant of Mr. Hawkings, who had set up

THE TIMES REPORT

THIRLBY'S SHOP, RUGELEY

in business for himself. But on this day Palmer went to Mr. Hawkings's shop, and, producing a bottle, informed the assistant [Charles Roberts] that he wanted two drachms[34] of prussic acid. While it was being prepared for him, Mr. Newton, the same man from whom he had on a former occasion obtained strychnine, came into the shop, whereupon Palmer seized him by the arm, and observing that he had something particular to say to him, hurried him into the street, where he kept talking to him in the matter of the smallest possible importance, relating to the precise period at which his employer's son meant to repair to a farm he had taken in the country. They continued to converse on this trivial topic until a gentleman named Brassington (or Grassington) came up, whereupon Mr. Newton turned aside to say a few words to him. Palmer, relieved by this accident, went back into the shop, and asked, in addition, for six

---

[34] A unit of measurement, also called a dram, equal to an eighth of an ounce.

grains of strychnine and a certain quantity of Batley's liquor of opium. He obtained them, paid for them, and went away. Presently Mr. Newton returned, and being struck with the fact of Palmer's dealing with Hawkings, asked out of passing curiosity what he had come for, and was informed.

And here I must mention a fact of some importance respecting Mr. Newton. When examined before the coroner, that gentleman only deposed to one purchase of strychnine by Palmer at Mr. Salt's surgery, and it was only as recently as yesterday that, with many expressions of contrition for not having been more explicit, he communicated to the Crown the fact that Palmer had also bought strychnine on Monday night. It is for you, gentlemen, to decide the amount of credit to be attached to this evidence; but you will bear in mind that whatever you may think of Mr. Newton's testimony, that of Mr. Roberts, on whom there is no taint of shadow of suspicion, is decisive with respect to the purchase which the prisoner made on Tuesday at the shop of Mr. Hawkings.

I now resume the story of Tuesday's proceedings with the observation that Cook was entitled to receive the stakes he had won at Shrewsbury. On that day Palmer sent for Mr. Cheshire, the postmaster at Rugeley. He owed Cheshire £7 odd, and the latter, supposing that he was about to be paid, came with a stamped receipt in his hand. Palmer produced a paper, and remarking "that Cook was too ill to write himself," told Cheshire to draw a cheque on Weatherby's in his (Palmer's) favour for £350. Cheshire thereupon filled up a piece of paper purporting to be the body of a cheque, addressed in the manner indicated to the Messers. Weatherby, and concluding with the words, "and place the same to my account." Palmer then took the document away, for the purpose, as he averred, of getting Cook's signature to it. What became of it I do not undertake to assert; but of this there is no question, that by that night's post Palmer sent up to Weathersby's a cheque which was returned dishonoured. Whether it was genuine, or like so many other papers with which Palmer had to do, forged, is a question which you will have to determine.

And now, returning to Cook, it may be observed that in the course of that morning coffee and broth were sent him by Palmer, and, as usual, vomiting ensued and continued through the whole afternoon.

And now a new person makes his appearance on the stage. You must know that on Sunday, Palmer wrote to Mr. W.H. Jones, a surgeon, of Lutterworth,[35] desiring him to come over to see Cook. Cook was a personal friend of Mr. Jones, and had occasionally been in the habit of residing at his house. It is deserving of remark that

---

[35] A market town in Leicestershire, about 40 miles southeast of Rugeley.

Palmer, in his letter to Jones, describes Cook as "suffering from a severe bilious attack, accompanied with diarrhœa," adding, "it is desirable for you to come and see him as soon as possible." Whether this communication is to be interpreted in a sense favourable to the prisoner, or whether it is to be taken as indicating a deep design to give colour to the idea that Cook died a natural death, it is at least certain that the statement that Cook had been "suffering from a bilious attack attended with diarrhœa," was utterly untrue.

Mr. Jones being himself unwell, did not come to Rugeley till Tuesday. He arrived at about three o'clock on that day, and immediately proceeded to see his sick friend. Palmer came in at the same moment, and they both examined the patient. Mr. Jones paid particular attention to the state of his tongue; remarking, "That is not the tongue of bilious fever."

About seven o'clock that same evening Dr. Bamford called, and found the patient pretty well. Subsequently the three medical men (Palmer, Bamford, and Jones) held a consultation, but before leaving the bedroom for that purpose, Cook beckoned to Palmer, and said, "Mind, I will have no more pills or medicine to-night." They then withdrew and consulted. Palmer insisted on his taking pills, but added, "Let us not tell him what they contain, as he fears the same results that have already given him such pain." It was agreed that Dr. Bamford should make up the pills, which were to be composed of the same ingredients as those that had been administered on the three preceding evenings. The doctor repaired to his surgery, and made them up accordingly. He was followed by Palmer, who asked him to write the directions how they were to be taken. Dr. Bamford, though unable to understand the necessity of his doing so, under the circumstances, complied with Palmer's request, and wrote on the box that the pills were to be taken at "bed-time."

Palmer then took them away, and gave either those pills or some others to Cook that night. It is remarkable, however, that half or three-quarters of an hour elapsed from the time he left Dr. Bamford's surgery until he brought the pills to Cook. When, at length, he came, he produced two pills, but before giving them to Cook he took especial care to call Mr. Jones's attention to the directions on the lid, observing that the writing was singularly distinct and vigorous for a man upwards of eighty. If the prisoner be guilty, it is a natural presumption that he made this observation with the view of identifying the pillbox as having come from Dr. Bamford, and so averting suspicion from himself.

This was about half-past ten at night. The pills were then offered to Cook, who strongly objected to taking them, remarking that they had made him ill the night before. Palmer insisted, and the sick man at last consented to take them. He vomited immediately after, but did not bring up the pills.

Jones then went down and took his supper, and he will tell you that up to the period when the pills were administered, Cook had been easy and cheerful, and presented no symptom of the approach of disease, much less of death. It was arranged that Jones should sleep in the same room with Cook, and he did so; but he had not been more than fifteen or twenty minutes in bed when he was aroused by a sudden exclamation, and a frightful scream from Cook, who, starting up, said, "Send for the doctor immediately; I am going to be ill, as I was last night."

The chambermaid ran across the road, and rang the bell of Palmer's house, and in a moment Palmer was at the window. He was told that Cook was again ill. In two minutes he was by the bedside of the sick man, and, strangely, volunteered the observation, "I never dressed so quickly in my life." It is for you, gentlemen, to say whether you think he had time to dress at all.

Cook was found in the same condition, and with the same symptoms as the night before, gasping for breath, screaming violently, his body convulsed with cramps and spasms, and his neck rigid. Jones raised him and rubbed his neck. When Palmer entered the room, Cook asked him for the same remedy that had relieved him the night before. "I will run back and fetch it," said Palmer, and he darted out of the room.

In the passage he met two female servants, who remarked that Cook was as "bad" as he had been last night. "He is not within fifty times as bad as he was last night; and what a game is this to be at every night!" was Palmer's reply. In a few minutes he returned with two pills, which he told Jones were ammonia,[36] though I am assured that it is a drug that requires much time in the preparation, and can with difficulty be made into pills. The sick man swallowed these pills, but brought them up again immediately.

And now ensued a terrible scene. He was suddenly seized with violent convulsions; by degrees his body began to stiffen out; then suffocation commenced. Agonised with pain, he repeatedly entreated to be raised. They tried to raise him, but it was not possible. The body had become rigid as iron, and it could not be done. He then said, "Pray turn me over." They did turn him over on the right side. He gasped for breath, but could utter no more. In a few moments all was tranquil — the tide of life was ebbing fast. Jones leant over him to listen to the action of the heart. Gradually the pulse ceased — all was over — he was dead. (Sensation.)

---

[36] A chemical compound of nitrogen and hydrogen, noted for its pungent odor. Used as an emetic and to relieve dyspeptic flatulence or heart palpitations.

I will show you that his was a death referable in its symptoms to the tetanus produced by strychnine, and not to any other possible form of tetanus.

Scarcely was the breath out of his body when Palmer begins to think of what is to be done. He engages two women to lay out the corpse, and these women, on entering the room, find him searching the pockets of a coat which, no doubt, belonged to Cook, and hunting under the pillows and bolsters. They saw some letters on the mantelshelf, which, in all probability, had been taken out of the dead man's pocket; and, what is very remarkable is, that from that day to this, nothing has been seen or heard either of the betting-book or of any of the papers connected with Cook's money affairs.

On a subsequent day (Thursday) he returned, and, on the pretence of looking for some books and a paper knife, rummaged again through the documents of the deceased. On the 25th November he sent for Cheshire, and, producing a paper purporting to bear the signature of Cook, asked him to attest it. Cheshire glanced over it. It was a document in which Cook acknowledged that certain bills, to the amount of £4,000 or thereabouts, were bills that had been negotiated for his (Cook's) benefit, and in respect of which Palmer had received no consideration.

Such was the paper to which, forty-eight hours after the death of the man whose name it bore, Palmer did not hesitate to ask Cheshire to be an attesting witness. Cheshire, though, unfortunately for himself, too much the slave of Palmer, peremptorily refused to comply with this request; whereupon Palmer carelessly observed, "It is of no consequence; I dare say the signature will not be disputed, but it occurred to me that it would look more regular if it were attested."

On Friday Mr. Stevens, Cook's father-in-law, came down to Rugeley, and, after viewing the body of his relative, to whom he had been tenderly attached, asked Palmer about his affairs. Palmer assured him that he held a paper drawn up by a lawyer, and signed by Cook, stating that, in respect of £4,000 worth of bills, he (Cook) was alone liable, and that Palmer had a claim to that amount against his estate. Mr. Stevens expressed his amazement, and replied that there would not be 4,000 shillings for the holders of the bills.

Subsequently Palmer displayed an eager officiousness in the matter of the funeral, taking upon himself to order a shell and an oak coffin, without any directions to that effect from the relatives of the deceased, who were anxious to have the arrangements in their own hands.

Mr. Stevens ordered dinner at the hotel for Bamford, Jones, and himself, and finding Palmer still hanging about him, thought it but civil to extend the invitation to him. Accordingly they all sat down together. After dinner, Mr. Stevens asked Jones to step upstairs and bring down all books and papers belonging to Cook. Jones left the room to do so, and Palmer followed him. They were absent about ten minutes, and on their return Jones observed that they were unable to find the betting-book or any of the papers belonging to the deceased.

Palmer added, "The betting-book would be of no use to you if you found it, for the bets are void by his death."

Mr. Stevens replied, "The book must be found;" and then Palmer, changing his tone, said, "Oh, I dare say it will turn up." Mr. Stevens then rang the bell, and told the housekeeper to take charge of whatever books and papers had belonged to Cook, and to be sure not to allow any one to meddle with them until he came back from London, which he would soon do, with his solicitor.

He then departed, but, returning to Rugeley after a brief interval, declared his intention to have a *post-mortem*[37] examination. Palmer volunteered to nominate the surgeons who should conduct it, but Mr. Stevens refused to employ any one whom he should recommend.

On Sunday, the 26th, Palmer called on Dr. Bamford, and asked him for a certificate attesting the cause of Cook's death. The doctor expressed his surprise, and observed — "Why, he was your patient." But Palmer importuned him, and Bamford, taking the pen, filled up the certificate, and entered the cause of death as "apoplexy."[38] Dr. Bamford is upwards of eighty, and I hope that it is to some infirmity connected with his great age that this most unjustifiable act is to be attributed. However, he shall be produced in court, and he will tell you that apoplexy has never been known to produce tetanus.

In the course of the day Palmer sent for Newton, and after they had some brandy and water, asked him how much strychnine he would use to kill a dog. Newton replied, "from half a grain to a grain." "And how much," inquired Palmer, "could be found in the tissues and intestines after death?" "None at all," was Newton's reply; but that is a point on which I will produce important evidence.

The *post-mortem* examination took place the next day, and on that occasion Palmer assured the medical men, of whom there were many present, that Cook had had epileptic fits[39] on Monday and Tuesday, and that they would find old disease in the heart and head. He added, that the poor fellow was "full of disease," and had "all kinds of complaints."

---

[37] An autopsy in which the corpse is examined to determine the cause of death.

[38] The medical term for a stroke or a fit. Nowadays, it is used to describe a stroke, an inability to feel or move a part of the body due to a loss of blood flow to the brain, or a hemorrhage in a body cavity or organ.

[39] Abnormal brain activity that can cause reactions from a momentary loss of awareness to violent, uncontrolled jerking movements. These seizures also can occur in people who do not have epilepsy.

These statements were completely disproved by the *post-mortem* examinations. At the first of them, conducted by Dr. Devonshire, the liver, lungs, and kidneys were all found healthy. It was said that there were some slight indications of congestion of the kidneys, whether due to decomposition or to what other cause was not certain; but it was admitted on all hands that they did not impair the general health of the system, or at all account for death. The stomach and intestines were examined, and they exhibited a few white spots at the large end of the stomach, but these marks were wholly insufficient to explain the cause of dissolution. Dr. Bamford contended that there was some slight congestion of the brain, but all the other medical men concurred in thinking that there was none at all.

In the ensuing month of January the body was exhumed with a view to a more accurate examination, and the body was then found to be in a perfectly normal and healthy condition. Palmer seemed rejoiced at the discovery, and turning to Dr. Bamford exclaimed, "Doctor, they won't hang us yet!" The stomach and intestines were taken out and placed in a jar, and it was observed that Palmer pushed against the medical man who was engaged in the operation, and the jar was in danger of being upset. It escaped, however, and was covered with skins, tied down, and sealed.

Presently one of the medical men turned round, and finding that the jar had disappeared, asked what had become of it. It was found at a distance, near a different door from that through which people usually passed in and out, and Palmer exclaimed, "It's all right. It was I who removed it. I thought it would be more convenient for you to have it here, that you might lay your hands readily on it as you went out."

When the jar was recovered it was found that two slits had been cut in the skins with a knife. The slits, however, were clean, so that, whatever his object may have been in making the incisions, it is certain that nothing was taken out of the jar. He goes to Dr. Bamford, and remonstrates against the removal of the jars. He says, "I do not think we ought to allow them to be taken away."

Now, if he had been an ignorant person, not familiar with the course likely to be pursued by medical men under such circumstances, there might be some excuse for this; but it is for you to ask yourselves whether Palmer, himself a medical man, knowing that the contents of the jars were to be submitted to an analysis, might not have relied with confidence on the honour and integrity of the profession to which he belonged. You must say whether his anxiety to prevent the removal of the jars was not a sign of a guilty conscience. Dr. Bamford was a most respectable physician, and his character and position were well known to Palmer.

But the case does not stop here. The jar was delivered to Mr.

Boycott, the clerk to Mr. Gardner, the solicitor. Palmer, finding that it was to be sent to London for chemical analysis was extremely anxious that it should not reach its destination. It was going to be conveyed by Mr. Boycott to the Stafford station in a fly, driven by a postboy. Palmer goes to this postboy and asks him whether it is the fact that he is going to drive Boycott to Stafford? He is answered in the affirmative. He then asks, "Are the jars there?" He is told that they are. He says, "They have no business to take them; one does not know what they may put in them. Can't you manage to upset the fly and break them? I will give you £10, and make it all right for you." The man said, "I shall do no such thing I must go and look after my fly." That man will be called before you, and he will have no interest to state anything but the truth.

I have now gone through the painful history, yet there are some points of minor importance which I ought not altogether to pass over, as nothing connected with the conduct of a man conscious that an imputation of this kind rests upon him can be immaterial.

After the *post-mortem* examination it was thought right to hold a coroner's inquest. On two or three occasions in the course of that inquiry, Palmer sent presents to the coroner. The stomach of the deceased and its contents were sent to Dr. Taylor and Dr. Rees, at Guy's Hospital,[40] who were known to be in communication with Mr. Gardner.[41] A letter was sent by Dr. Taylor to Mr. Gardner stating the result of the investigation; that letter was betrayed to Palmer by the postmaster, Cheshire, and Palmer then wrote to the coroner, telling him that Dr. Taylor and Dr. Rees had failed in finding traces of poison, and asking him to take a certain course with respect to the evidence. Why should he have done this if there had not been a feeling of uneasiness upon his mind? These matters must not be wholly overlooked, although I will not ask you to give them any undue importance.

I should have told you, in addition, that the prisoner had no money prior to Shrewsbury races, while afterwards he was flush of cash. Sums of £100 and £150 were paid by him into the bank at Rugeley, two or three persons received sums of £10 each, and he seemed, in fact, to be giving away money right and left. I think I shall be able to show that he had something like £400 in his possession. Now, Cook had £700 or £800 when he left Shrewsbury on the Thursday morning. None is found. It may be that Cook, who, whatever his faults, was a kind-hearted creature, compassionating

---

[40] A teaching hospital founded in 1721 by Thomas Guy (1644-1724), funded with the fortune he made in the South Sea Bubble, a notorious investment scandal.

[41] James Gardner was a solicitor in Rugeley working for Cookson and Co., the solicitors of Stevens, Cook's stepfather.

Palmer's condition, and, influenced by his representations, assisted him with money. That I do not know. I do not wish to strain the point too far, but one cannot imagine that Cook, who had no money but what he took with him to Shrewsbury, should have given Palmer everything and left himself destitute.

The case then stands thus:— Here is a man overwhelmed with pecuniary difficulties, obliged to resort to the desperate expedient of forging acceptances to raise money, hoping to meet them by the proceeds of the insurances he had effected upon a life. Disappointed in that expectation by the board; told by the gentleman through whom the bills had been discounted, "You must trifle with me no longer — if you cannot find money, writs will be served on you." Cook's name forged to an endorsement for £375; ruin staring him in the face: You, gentlemen, must say whether he had not sufficient inducement to commit the crime.

He seems to have had a further object. No sooner is the breath out of the dead man's body than he says to Jones, "I had a claim of £3,000 or £4,000 against him on account of bills." Besides, he believed that Cook had more property than it turns out he really had. The valuable mare, Polestar, belonged to him when the assignment had been paid off, and Palmer would have been glad to obtain possession of her. The fact, too, that Cook was mired up in the insurance of Bates may lead one to surmise that he was in possession of secrets relating to the desperate expedients to which this man has resorted to obtain money. I will leave you to say whether this combination of motives may not have led to the crime with which he is charged. This you will only have to consider, supposing the case to be balanced between probabilities; but if you believe the evidence that will be given as to what took place on the Monday and the Tuesday — if you believe the paroxysms of the Monday, the mortal agony of the Tuesday — I shall show that things were administered, on both those days, by the hand of Palmer, by a degree of evidence almost amounting to certainty.

The body was submitted to a careful analysis, and I am bound to say that no trace of strychnine was found. But I am told that, although the presence of strychnine may be detected by certain tests, and although indications of its presence lead irresistibly to the conclusion that it has been administered, the converse of that proposition does not hold. Sometimes it is found, at other times it is not. It depends upon circumstances.

A most minute dose will destroy life, from half to three-quarters of a grain will lay the strongest man prostrate. But in order to produce that fatal effect it must be absorbed into the system, and the absorption takes place in a greater or less period according to the manner in which the poison is presented to the surfaces with which it comes in contact. If it is in a fluid form it is rapidly taken up and soon produces the effect; if not, it requires to be absorbed, and the effects are a longer time in showing themselves. But in either case there is a difficulty in discovering its presence. If it acts only on the nervous system through the circulation, an almost infinitesimal dose will be present. And, as it is a vegetable poison, the tests which alone can be employed are infinitely more delicate and difficult than those which are applied to other poisons. It is unlike a mineral poison, which can soon be detected and reproduced. If the dose has been a large one death ensues before the whole has been absorbed, and a portion is left in the intestines; but if a minimum dose has been administered, a different consequence follows, and the whole is absorbed.

Practical experience bears out the theory that I am enunciating. Experiments have been tried which show that where the same amount of poison has been administered to animals of the same species death will ensue in the same number of minutes, accompanied by precisely the same kinds of symptoms; while in the analysis afterwards made, the presence of poison will be detected in one case and not in another. It has been repeated over and over again that the scientific men employed in this case had come to the conclusion that the presence of strychnine cannot be detected by any tests known to science. They have been grievously misunderstood. They never made any such assertion. What they have asserted is this — the detection of its presence, where its administration is a matter of certainty, is a matter of the greatest uncertainty. It would, indeed, be a fatal thing to sanction the notion that strychnine administered for the purpose of taking away life cannot afterwards be detected! Lamentable enough is the uncertainty of detection! Happily, Providence, which has placed this fatal agent at the disposition of man, has marked its effects with characteristic symptoms distinguishable from those of all other agents by the eye of science.

It will be for you to say whether the testimony that will be laid before you with regard to those symptoms does not lead your mind to the conclusion that the deceased came to his death by poison administered to him by the prisoner. There is a circumstance which throws great light upon this part of the case. Some days before his death the man was constantly vomiting. The analysis made of his body failed to produce evidence of the presence of strychnine, but did not fail to produce evidence of the presence of antimony.

Now, antimony was not administered by the medical men, and unless taken in a considerable quantity it produces no effect and is perfectly soluble. It is an irritant, which produces exactly the symptoms which were produced in this case. The man was sick for a week, and antimony was found in his body afterwards.

For what purpose can it have been administered? It may be that the original intention was to destroy him by means of antimony — it may be that the only object was to bring about the appearance of disease so as to account for death. One is lost in speculation. But the question is whether you have any doubt that strychnine was administered on the Monday, and still more on the Tuesday when death ensued? And if you are satisfied with the evidence that will be adduced[42] on that point, you must then determine whether it was not administered by the prisoner's hand.

I shall produce testimony before you in proof of the statements I have made, which I am afraid must occupy some considerable portion of your time; but in such an inquiry time cannot be wasted, and I am sure you will give it your most patient attention. I have the satisfaction of knowing that the prisoner will be defended by one of the most eloquent and able men who ever adorned the bar of this country or any other forum, and that everything will be done for him that can be done. If in the end all should fail in satisfying you of his guilt, in God's name let not the innocent suffer! If, on the other hand, the facts that will be presented to you should lead you to the conclusion that he is guilty, the best interests of society demand his conviction.

The opening address of the Attorney-General occupied upwards of four hours in its delivery. At its conclusion (at a quarter past two o'clock) the jury retired for a short time for refreshment, and upon their return the following witnesses were called in support of the prosecution:—

EVIDENCE FOR THE PROSECUTION.

ISHMAEL FISHER, examined by Mr. *E. James*.

I am a wine merchant at 4, Victoria-street, City,[43] I am in the habit of attending races and betting. I knew John Parsons Cook. I had known him for about two years before his death. I was at Shrewsbury races in November, 1855. I remember the Shrewsbury Handicap. It was won by the mare called Polestar, the property of Cook. It took place on Tuesday, November 13th. I saw Cook upon the course. He looked

---

[42] To cite as evidence. From the Latin *adducere* for "lead towards."
[43] A street in the Westminster district of central London, running from Victoria Station to Westminster Cathedral. "The City" refers to the roughly square-mile district within London that has been inhabited since Roman times. Because many financial and trading companies are located there, it's common for workers to say they work "in the City" instead of "in London." The City of London is one of two districts within the metropolis to hold city status. The other is the adjacent City of Westminster.

as well as he had looked at any time since I had known him.

I was stopping at the Raven Hotel, at Shrewsbury. I know Palmer (the prisoner) very well. I have known him rather more than two years. Cook and Palmer were stopping at the same hotel, and occupied a room separated from mine only by a wooden partition. It was a sitting room, and they occupied it jointly.

On the Wednesday night, between 11 and 12 o'clock, I went into the sitting-room. I found there Cook, Palmer, and Mr. Myatt, a saddler at Rugeley, a friend of Palmer's. They had grog[44] before them. I was asked to sit down by Cook, and I sat down. Cook asked Palmer to have some more brandy and water. Palmer said, "I will not have any more till you have drunk yours." Cook said, "Then I will drink mine." He took up his glass and drank the grog off immediately. He said within a minute afterwards, "There is something in it; it burns my throat dreadfully." Palmer then got up, took the glass, sipped up what was left in it, and said, "There is nothing in it." There was not more than a teaspoonful in the glass when he emptied it.

In the mean time Mr. Read had come in. Palmer handed the glass to Read and to me, and asked if we thought there was anything in it. We both said the glass was so empty that we could not recognise anything. I said I thought there was rather a strong scent upon it, but I could not say it arose from anything but brandy.

Lord CAMPBELL — Did you put your lips to it?

Witness — I did not. It was completely drained. Within ten minutes I retired. Cook had left the room, and then came back and called me from it. We went to my own sitting-room. He there told me he was very ill and very sick, and asked me to take his money.

Mr. *E. James* — Did he state what he was suffering from?

Mr. *Serjeant Shee* objected to this question.

Lord CAMPBELL — Surely his statement of the effect produced on him by what he had just swallowed is admissible.

Witness — He said he was very sick, and he thought "that d———d Palmer" had dosed him. He handed me over some money, between £700 and £800, in bank notes, to take care of. He did not sleep in the same room with Palmer. He was seized with vomiting after he had given me the money, and left the room. He afterwards came back to my room, and again complained of what he had been suffering. He asked me to go to his bedroom. I went with him. Mr. Jones, (a law stationer[45]) went with

---

[44] A drink consisting of rum and water, traditionally the noontime tipple of sailors aboard Royal Navy vessels, where it is mixed with lime to prevent outbreaks of scurvy. Other witnesses testified that they were drinking brandy and water.

[45] A dealer in paper and supplies used by lawyers. Also, a person who makes official copies of legal documents.

me. He then vomited again violently, and was so ill that I sent for a doctor, Mr. Gibson, who came about half-past twelve or a quarter to one. I remained with Cook till two o'clock. I sent for Mr. Gibson a second time, and he sent some medicine, which Cook took. After seeing the doctor and taking the medicine, he became more composed. Mr. Jones and I gave him the medicine.

Next morning, about 10 o'clock, I saw Palmer. I found him in my sitting-room when I came down stairs. He said, "Cook has been stating that I gave him something in his brandy. I never play such tricks with people. But I can tell you what he was. He was d———d drunk." I should say Cook was certainly not drunk.

Lord CAMPBELL — Was he affected by liquor?

Witness — Not at all approaching drunkenness, my Lord. Cook came into my bedroom before I was up, the same morning. He was much better, but still looked ill. I gave him back his money.

About three o'clock on that day (Thursday) I saw Cook on the racecourse. He looked very ill. I had always settled Cook's bets for him, when he did not settle them himself. I saw his betting book in his hand. It was dark in colour, and about half the size of this. (The witness here produced a small black pocketbook.)

On the 17th of November (Saturday), by Cook's request, I paid Pratt £200. His account, in the ordinary course, would have been settled at Tattersall's on Monday, the 19th. I advanced the £200 to pay Pratt. I knew that Cook had won at Shrewsbury, and I should have been entitled to deduct that £200 from his winnings if I had settled his account at Tattersall's. I did not settle that account, and I have not been paid my advance.

Cross-examined by Mr. *Serjeant Shee*. I had known Cook about two years, and Palmer longer. They were a good deal connected in racing transactions.

Do you know that they were partners? — I don't remember settling any transactions in which they were jointly interested, and I don't know that they owned horses jointly. They appeared very intimate and were much together, generally staying at the same hotels. I was not at the Worcester meeting. I don't know whether Palmer won at Shrewsbury as well as Cook. The races began on the Tuesday, about 2 o'clock. Polestar ran about an hour afterwards, but I cannot tell the exact time. I saw Cook on the course after the race, and he appeared much elated. Polestar won easily.

In the evening when I went into the sitting-room there was a candle on the table. A glass was ordered for me when I sat down. I don't remember drinking anything, but I cannot swear that I did not. I am a good judge of brandy by the smell. I said there was nothing particular in the smell, but the glass was so completely drained that there was very little to smell. I counted the money Cook gave me. I had been at the Unicorn that evening quite an hour before. I dined at the Raven about six o'clock. I did not see Cook after the race on the Wednesday till I saw him at the Unicorn, between 9 and 10 o'clock in the evening. I merely looked into the room. I saw Saunders, the trainer, Cook, Palmer, and a lady. I can't say whether they were drinking.

Did it happen that a good many people were ill on that Wednesday at Shrewsbury — I mean people connected with the races? No. — I do not know that there were. On the Wednesday it was damp underfoot, but I forget whether it rained. I saw Cook several times on the course. On the Thursday the weather was cold and damp. I don't know that Cook and Palmer breakfasted together on the Thursday morning.

On the 17th of November I received a letter from Cook. [The letter was read. It was dated, "Rugeley, Nov. the 16th," and in it Cook said it was of very great importance to Palmer and to himself that £500 should be paid to Pratt on the next day, that £300 should be sent, and he would be greatly obliged if Fisher would pay the other £200 immediately on receipt of the letter, promising to give it him back on the following Monday at Tattersall's. He added that he was much better.]

Re-examined by the *Attorney General*. I never intended to say that Cook and Palmer were partners.

Did you notice any change of feeling on the part of Cook towards Palmer? He never had any great respect for Palmer, but I did notice a change in him. It was a handicap race that Polestar won. Palmer had a horse called Chicken, which ran on the Thursday and lost. He had betted upon the race. Cook was not more elated at winning than people usually are. I am not sure that I drank any brandy and water while I was staying at the Raven.

THOMAS JONES, examined by Mr. *Welsby*.

I am a law stationer in Carey-street, London. I was at Shrewsbury races last November, and I lodged at the Raven. I arrived there on a Monday night. I supped with Cook, Herring, Fisher, and Gravatt. Cook appeared well. I saw him on the Tuesday and Wednesday, and he then also seemed quite well. Fisher and I went to the Raven between eleven and twelve o'clock on Wednesday night. Read was there, and he invited Cook into my room. Palmer was also there.

After the party broke up, Fisher came and told me something about Cook, in consequence of which I went with him to Cook's bedroom. He complained of something burning at his throat and of vomiting. Some medicine was brought — pills and a draught. Cook refused to take the pills. I then went to the doctor's and got some liquid medicine, and gave him a small quantity in a wine glass. He was in bed. About a quarter of an hour afterwards he took the pills also, and I left him. Between six and seven o'clock next morning I saw him again. He said he felt easier and better. He looked pale.

This witness was not cross-examined.

GEORGE READ, examined by Mr. *Bodkin*.

I live in Victoria-street, near Farringdon-market. I keep a house frequented by sporting characters. I am acquainted with Palmer. I saw him at Shrewsbury races on Tuesday, as well as Cook. He appeared to be in his usual health. I saw him also the next day, and he was apparently in the same health. I stayed at the Raven.

On the Wednesday night I went between eleven and twelve into the room in which were Palmer and Cook. There was more than one gentleman in the room. I had some brandy and water there. I saw that Cook was in pain almost immediately after I entered. He said to us there is something in the brandy and water. Palmer handed me the glass after it had been emptied. I said, "What is the use of examining a glass which is empty?" I believe Cook left the room. I did not see him again. I saw him on the following morning at eleven o'clock. He was in his sitting-room. He said in my hearing that he was very ill.

Cross-examined. On Tuesday he was as well as usual. He never looked a strong man, but one having delicate health. He was not in the habit of complaining of ill-health.

By the Court — I had some of the brandy and water, and it did not make me ill.

Re-examined by the *Attorney-General.* My brandy was taken from another decanter, which was sent for when I went in. Cook appeared to be a delicate man, but I never knew anything to be the matter with him. He frequented races everywhere. I never knew him prevented by illness from going to races.

WILLIAM SCAIFE GIBSON, examined by Mr. *Huddleston*.

I am assistant to Mr. Heathcote, surgeon, of the town of Shrewsbury. On the 14th day of November last, I was sent for, and went to the Railway Hotel, Shrewsbury, between twelve and one o'clock at night. I saw Mr. Cook there. He was in his bedroom, but not in bed. He complained of pain in his stomach, and heat in his throat. He also said he thought he had been poisoned. I felt his pulse and looked at his tongue, which was perfectly clean. He appeared much distended[46] about the abdomen. I recommended an emetic. He said that he could make himself sick with warm water. I sent the waitress for some. She brought about a pint. I recommended him to use a feather. He said he could do it with the handle of a toothbrush. He drank all the warm water. Having used the toothbrush he was sick. I examined the vomit; it was perfectly clear. I then told him I would send him some medicine. I sent him two pills and a draught. The pills were a compound rhubarb pill and a three-grain calomel pill. They were ordered to be taken immediately, and the draught, which was sennica — a compound of senna, magnesia, and aromatic spirit — was to be taken twenty minutes afterwards. It was what is called a black draught.[47] Half an hour afterwards I gave to Jones, for Cook, an anodyne draught.[48] I did not see Cook afterwards.

Cross-examined by Mr. *Serjeant Shee*. Did you form any opinion as to what was the matter with Cook? — I treated it as a case of poisoning.

Did you observe anything in the vomit which led you to believe he had been poisoned? — Nothing at all.

Did he appear to have been drinking? — He appeared to be a little excited, but he was quite sensible what he was doing and saying.

By "excited" do you mean to say he was tipsy? — No; but his brain had been stimulated with brandy and water. The idea of having taken poison would have some effect upon it.

In your judgment, was what you had prescribed a good thing, supposing Cook had taken poison? — According to the symptoms, I should say it was.

Would it not have been better to get the poison up at once, if possible? — He threw up the warm water.

Lord CAMPBELL — Did that cleanse the stomach? Yes.

Cross-examination continued. — Yet you thought calomel necessary? — Yes; on account of the distended state of the bowels.

Did you see anything like bile in the basin? — There was some on the edge of the basin, but it must have been thrown up before he took the warm water.

Re-examined by the *Attorney-General*. The piece of bile was about the size of a pea? — The water thrown up was perfectly clean. Cook's tongue was quite clean.

Is that usual in the case of a bilious attack? — If the stomach had been wrong any length of time the tongue would have been discoloured.

---

[46] A swelling caused by pressure from inside the organ.
[47] A mixture used as a purgative to encourage the bowels to empty. *Senna:* A flowering plant used as a laxative.
[48] A drug such as laudanum (tincture of liquid opium) used to relieve pain.

ELIZABETH MILLS, CHAMBERMAID AT THE TALBOT ARMS.

ELIZABETH MILLS, examined by Mr. *James*.

In November last I was chambermaid at the Talbot Arms, Rugeley. I had been so about two years. I knew the prisoner Palmer, who was in the habit of coming to the Talbot Arms. I also knew Cook, the deceased. On Thursday, the 15th of November, he came to the Talbot Arms. He came between 9 and 10 o'clock at night. The prisoner was with him. They came in a fly.[49] Cook went to bed at half-past 10 o'clock. When Cook arrived he said he had been poorly, and was poorly then. I don't remember seeing Palmer after he got out of the fly.

About 12 o'clock on the following day I took Cook some hot water, and he went out about 1 o'clock. He then appeared poorly. He said he felt no worse, but was not well. He returned about 10 o'clock in the evening.

---

[49] A light carriage drawn by a horse, used to ferry passengers or goods.

In about half-an-hour he went to bed. I asked him if he felt any worse than when he went out in the morning. He said he did not. He said that he had been dining with Palmer. He was perfectly sober. He asked me for an extra piece of candle to read by. I saw no more of him that night.

On Saturday morning, about 8 o'clock, I saw Palmer at the Talbot Arms. I do not know whether Cook had sent for him. Palmer ordered from me a cup of coffee for Cook. I gave it to Cook in the bedroom. I believe Palmer was then in the room. I left the coffee in Cook's hands, but did not see him drink it. Afterwards I went up stairs, and found the coffee in the chamber utensil. That might be an hour, or it might be a couple of hours after I had taken up the coffee. The utensil was on the table by the side of the bed. I do not remember that I spoke to Palmer, nor he to me, about this. I did not see any toast and water in the bed room; but a jug, not belonging to the inn. It was about 10 o'clock in the evening it was sent down for some fresh toast and water.[50] The waitress, Lavinia Barnes, brought it down. I am sure the jug which was brought down from Cook's room did not belong to the Talbot Arms. I saw Palmer go in and out of Cook's room, perhaps four or five times, on that Saturday.

I heard Palmer tell Cook that he would send him over some broth. I saw some broth in the kitchen, which some person had brought there ready made. After Barnes had taken some broth up, ten minute or a quarter of an hour after the broth came over, I met Palmer going upstairs towards Cook's room. He asked if Mr. Cook had had his broth? I told him I was not aware that any had come for him. While I was speaking, Lavinia Barnes came out of the commercial-room,[51] and said she had taken the broth up to Cook when it came, but that he refused to take it, saying it would not stay on his stomach. Palmer said that I must go and fetch the broth; he (Cook) must have it. I fetched the broth and took it into Cook's room.

---

[50] The Notable British Trials transcript records this paragraph this way: "On Saturday morning about eight, Palmer, who lived opposite to the Talbot Arms, came over. He ordered a cup of coffee for Mr. Cook, which I believe I gave to Mr. Cook in his bedroom. Mr. Palmer was in the room at the time. I did not see Cook drink it, but about half an hour afterwards I returned into the room and found that the coffee had been vomited. On that occasion I observed a jug in the room which did not belong to the Talbot Arms. It was sent down to me by Lavinia Barnes to make some more toast and water."

Toast-and-water was a drink for invalids, prepared by pouring boiling water over a nicely browned, if possible stale, heel from a loaf. The mixture was allowed to cool, then strained. "Mrs. Beeton's Book of Household Management" (1861) stressed that it should be served cold, as "if drunk in a tepid or lukewarm state, it is an exceedingly disagreeable beverage."

[51] A room at a hotel reserved for use by traveling salesmen for dining and relaxing.

Palmer was there. I cannot say whether it was to him or Cook that I gave the broth, but I left it there. I am sure that this was some of the broth which had been sent in.

Some time afterwards (about an hour or two), I went up to Cook's room again, and found that the broth had been vomited.

About six o'clock in the evening, some barley-water was made for Cook. I took it up to him. I cannot say whether Palmer was with him. I cannot say whether or not that barley-water stayed upon Cook's stomach. At eight o'clock in the evening some arrowroot was made in the kitchen. I took it up to Cook. I cannot say whether Palmer was there, nor can I remember whether the arrowroot remained on Cook's stomach.

On Saturday, about three o'clock in the afternoon, I saw Mr. Bamford, the surgeon. On Sunday morning I went to Mr. Cook's room, about seven or eight o'clock. Mr. Smith, called "Jerry Smith," slept in Mr. Cook's room during Saturday night. He is a friend of the prisoner Palmer. I asked Cook if he was any worse? He said he felt pretty comfortable, and had slept well since twelve o'clock. On Sunday more broth, a large breakfast-cup full, was brought over for Cook. That was between twelve and one o'clock. I believe Charles Horley brought it. I took some of that broth up to Cook's room in the same cup in which it was brought. It was hot. I tasted it. I drank about two table spoonfuls. In about half-an-hour or an hour I was sick. I vomited violently during the whole afternoon till about 5 o'clock. I was obliged to go to bed. I vomited a great many times. During the morning I had felt perfectly well, and had not taken anything that could disagree with me. It was before dinner that I took the broth. I went down to work again about a quarter before 6 o'clock.

On the Sunday evening I saw Mr. Cook; he did not appear to be any worse. He seemed to be in good spirits. The illness seemed to be confined to vomitings after taking food. On Sunday night I saw Cook last about 10 o'clock.

On Monday morning I saw him between 7 and 8 o'clock, when I took up to him a cup of coffee. I did not remain to see him drink it. He did not vomit it. Palmer was coming down stairs, as though from Cook's room, about 7 o'clock. To my knowledge Palmer was not there on Monday. Cook got up about 1 o'clock, and appeared to be a great deal better. He shaved, washed and dressed himself as if he was going out. Ashmall the jockey, and his brother and Saunders the trainer, came to see him. As soon as he got up I gave him some arrowroot, which remained on his stomach. He sat up until about 4 o'clock, when he returned to bed. Between 9 and 10 o'clock at night I saw Palmer; he was sitting down in Cook's room. I saw Cook about half-past ten o'clock, and not again until about a quarter before 12 o'clock.

On the Monday night, about 8 o'clock, a pill-box wrapped in

white paper was brought from Mr. Bamford's. It was given to me by Miss Bond, the housekeeper, to take up to Cook's room. I took it up and placed the box on the dressing-table. That was before Palmer came. When I saw Palmer he was sitting by the fire in Cook's room. I went to bed between 10 and 11 o'clock.

About eight or ten minutes before 12 o'clock the waitress, Lavinia Barnes, called me up. While I was dressing I twice heard screams from Cook's room. My room is above, but not immediately over Cook's. I went down to Cook's room. As soon as I entered the room I saw him sitting up in bed. He desired me to fetch Palmer directly. I told him Palmer was sent for, and walked to his bedside. I found the pillow upon the floor. There was one mould candle[52] burning in the room. I picked up the pillow, and asked Cook if he would lay his head down. He was sitting up, beating the bedclothes with both his hands and arms, which were stretched out. When I asked him to lay his head down, he said, "I can't lie down; I shall be suffocated if I lie down. Oh, fetch Mr. Palmer!" The last words he said very loud, I did not observe his legs, but there was a sort of jumping or jerking about his head and neck, and his body. Sometimes he would throw back his head upon the pillow, and then raise it up again. He had much difficulty in breathing. The balls of his eyes projected very much. He screamed again three or four times while I was in the room. He was moving and knocking about all the time. Twice he called aloud, "Murder!" He asked me to rub one hand. I found it stiff. It was the left hand.

By the COURT — It was stretched out. It did not move. The hand was about half shut. All the upper part seemed to be stiff.

Examination resumed — I did not rub it long. As soon as he thought I had rubbed it sufficiently he thanked me, and I left off. Palmer was there while I was rubbing the hand. While I was rubbing it the arm and also the body seemed to twitch. Cook was perfectly conscious. When Palmer came in he recognized him. He was throwing himself about the bed, and said to Palmer, "Oh, doctor, I shall die." Palmer replied, "Oh, my lad, you won't!" Palmer just looked at Cook, and then left the room, asking me to stay by the bedside.

In about two or three minutes he returned. He brought with him some pills. He gave Cook a draught in a wineglass, but I cannot say whether he brought that with him. He first gave the pills, and then the draught. Cook said the pills stuck in his throat, and he could not swallow them. Palmer desired me to give him a teaspoonful of toast and water, and I did so. His body was still jerking and jumping. When I put the spoon to his mouth he snapped at it and got it fast between his

---

[52] A candle made by pouring wax or tallow into a mould containing a wick.

teeth, and seemed to bite it very hard. In snapping at the spoon he threw forward his head and neck. He swallowed the toast and water, and with it the pills. Palmer then handed him a draught in a wineglass, which was about three parts full. It was a dark, thick, heavy-looking liquid. Cook drank this. He snapped at the glass as he had done at the spoon. He seemed as though he could not exactly control himself. He swallowed the draught, but vomited it immediately into the chamber utensil. I supported his forehead. The vomit smelt like opium. Palmer said he hoped either that the pills had stayed on his stomach or had not returned. He searched for the pills in the vomit with a quill. He said, "I can't find the pills," and he then desired me to take the utensil away, and pour the contents out carefully to see if I could find the pills. I did so, and brought back the utensil, and told him I could not see the pills at all. Cook afterwards seemed to be more easy. That was about half an hour or more after I had first gone into the room. During the whole of that time he appeared to be quite conscious.

When Cook was lying more quiet he desired Palmer to come and feel how his heart beat, or something of that sort. Palmer went to the bedside, and pressed his hand, I cannot say whether to the heart or to the side of the face, but he said it was all right.

I left Cook about 3 o'clock in the morning. He was not asleep, but appeared to be dozing. Palmer was sitting in the easy chair, and I believe he was asleep. I went into the next room and laid down. About 6 o'clock I saw Cook again. I asked if Palmer had gone, and Cook said he left at a quarter before 5 o'clock. I asked if he felt any worse, and he said, no, he had been no worse since I left him. I said, "You were asleep when I left." He replied, "No. I heard you go." He asked me if I had ever seen any one suffer such agony as he did last night? I said, no, I never had. He said he should think I should not like to see any one like it again. I said, "What do you think was the cause of all that agony?" He said, "The pills which Palmer gave me at half-past 10." I do not think anything more was said. I asked him if he would take anything and he said, "No."

I do not remember seeing Palmer on that day (Tuesday) until he was sent for. On that morning Cook seemed quite composed and quiet, but his eyes looked wild. There was no motion about the body. About twelve o'clock at noon he rang his bell, and desired me to send the "boots"[53] over to Palmer to ask if he might have a cup of coffee. Boots returned and said he might, and Palmer would be over immediately. I took the coffee up to Cook a little after twelve o'clock. Palmer was then in Cook's room. I gave the coffee to Palmer. He tasted it to see whether it was too strong, and I left the room.

---

[53] A common nickname for a servant responsible for cleaning boots and running odd jobs at a hotel. Used both as a noun and a proper name, as "send the boots on an errand" or "send Boots on an errand."

Mr. Jones arrived by the three o'clock train from Lutterworth. I saw him in Cook's room. About four o'clock I took Cook another cup of coffee. I cannot say whether Palmer was there. Afterwards I saw Palmer. He opened the bed-room door and gave me the chamber utensil, saying that Cook had vomited the coffee. There was coffee in the utensil.

I saw Cook several times before I went to bed. He appeared to be in very good spirits, and talked about getting up next morning. He said he would have the barber sent for to shave him. I believe I gave him some arrowroot. I did not see him later than half-past ten.

Palmer was with him when I last saw him. I gave Palmer some toast and water for Cook at the door. Palmer then said to Cook, "Can this good girl do anything more for you to-night?" Cook said, "No: I shall want nothing more till morning." He spoke in a composed and cheerful manner. I remained in the kitchen all night, to see how Cook went on, and did not go to sleep.

About ten minutes before twelve o'clock the bell of Cook's room was rung violently. Jones was sleeping in a second bed in the same room. On hearing the bell I went up to Cook's room. Cook was sitting up. I think Jones was supporting him, with his arms round his shoulders. Cook said, "Oh, Mary, fetch Mr. Palmer directly." I went to Palmer's, and rang the surgery bell. As soon as I had rung I stepped off the steps to look at Palmer's bed-room window, where I expected him to appear, and he was there. He did not lift up the sash, but opened a small casement and spoke to me. I could not see whether he was dressed, but I heard and knew his voice. I asked him to come over to Mr. Cook directly, as he was much the same as he had been the night before. I don't remember what he replied. I went back to the hotel, and in two or three minutes Palmer came. I was then in the bed-room. Jones was there supporting Cook. Palmer said he had never dressed so quickly in his life.

The question which elicited this answer was, "Did Palmer make any remark about his dress?" After the answer had been given,

Mr. SERJEANT SHEE objected to the form in which the question had been put.

Lord CAMPBELL — It seems to me that the examination is conducted with perfect fairness. No leading question, nor any one which could be considered doubtful, has been put to the witness.

Examination continued — I left the room, but remained on the landing. After I had been waiting there a short time (about a minute or two) Palmer came out. I said, "He is much the same as last night." Palmer said, "Oh, he is not so ill by a fiftieth part." He then went down stairs as though going to his own house. He was absent but a very short time, and then returned to Cook's room. I also went in. I believe Cook said, "Turn me over on my right side." I was then outside, but the door was open. I do not think that I was in the room at the time he died. I went in just before, but came out again. Jones was there at the time, and had his right arm under Cook's head. Palmer was then feeling Cook's pulse, and said to Jones, "His pulse is gone." Jones pressed the side of his face to Cook's heart, lifted up his hands, but did not speak. Palmer asked me to fetch Mr. Bamford, and I went for him. Cook's death occurred about three-quarters of an hour after I had been called up.

Mr. Bamford came over. I did not return to Cook's room. When Mr. Bamford came down stairs he said, "He is dead: he was dead when I arrived." After Mr. Bamford had gone I went up to the landing, and sat upon the stairs. I had sat there about ten minutes when Jones came out of the room, and said, "Mr. Palmer wants you," or "Will you go into the room?" I went into the room where Cook was lying dead. Palmer was there. I said to him, "It is not possible that Mr. Cook is dead?" He said, "Oh yes, he is dead." He asked me who I thought would come and lay him out. I mentioned two women whom I thought Palmer knew. He said, "Those are just the women." I said, "Shall I fetch them?" and he said, "Yes."

I had seen a betting-book in Cook's room. It was a dark book, with gold bands round the edges. It was not a very large book, rather more long than square, and had a clasp at one end. I saw Cook have this book when he stopped at Talbot Arms, as he went to the Liverpool[54] races some months before. There was a case at the one side containing a pencil. I saw the book in Cook's room on Monday night, I took it off the dressing-table and gave it to him in bed. He asked me to give him the book, pen, and ink, and some paper. I gave him all. That was between seven and eight o'clock. He took a postage stamp[55] from a pocket at one end of the book. I replaced the book on the frame of the looking-glass on the dressing-table. Palmer was in the room after that time. To my knowledge I never saw the book afterwards. I afterwards searched the room for it, but could not find it.

When I went into the room after Cook's death, the clothes he had worn were lying on a chair. I saw Palmer searching the pockets of the coat. That was about ten minutes after the death. When I went into the room Palmer had in his hand, searching the pockets, the coat which I had seen Cook wear. Palmer also searched under the pillow and bolster. I saw two or three letters lying upon the chimney-piece. I never saw them again, but I was not much in the room afterwards. I

---

[54] A port about 75 miles northwest of Rugeley. It is noted as a center for ship-building and related industries.

[55] In 1840, Great Britain became the first nation to introduce postage stamps when it introduced the "penny black" bearing an engraving of a young Queen Victoria. Stamps had to be cut apart before use, and it wasn't until 1854 that perforating the sheets became common.

had not seen the letters before Cook's death.

The examination in chief of this witness being concluded, the Court adjourned, at twenty minutes past six o'clock, till next morning, when it met at ten o'clock.

THE MAYPOLE, RUGELEY

SECOND DAY.—May 15, 1856.

Among the distinguished persons present were the Earl of Derby, Earl Grey, Lord W. Lennox, Lord G.G. Lennox, Lord H. Lennox, &c.

The learned Judges, Lord Chief Justice Campbell, Baron Alderson, and Mr. Justice Cresswell, accompanied by the Recorder, the Sheriffs, the Under-Sheriffs, and several members of the Court of Aldermen, took their seats on the bench at ten o'clock.

The prisoner was then placed at the bar. The expression of his countenance was sadder and more subdued than on the preceding day. He maintained his usual tranquillity of demeanour, seldom changing his position, and gazing steadfastly at the witnesses.

The same counsel were again in attendance:— The Attorney-General, Mr. E. James, Q.C., Mr. Bodkin, Mr. Welsby, and Mr. Huddleston, for the Crown; and Mr. Serjeant Shee, Mr. Grove, Q.C., Mr. Gray, and Mr. Kenealy, for the prisoner.

The Jury, who had been all night at the London Coffee House,[1] were conducted into court by the officer who had them in charge.

Elizabeth Mills, who was under examination the previous evening, was again placed in the witness-box. She deposed as follows:—

I had been engaged at the Talbot Arms for about three years previous to Cook's death. Cook first came to that inn in the month of May, 1855, and was off and on for some months. I never heard him complain of any illness during that time except of an affection in his throat. I heard him complain of a sore throat two or three months before his death. He said it resulted from cold. He took a gargle for it. I believe he had it from Mr. Thirlby. I did not observe any sores about his mouth. I never heard him complain of a difficulty in swallowing. I have seen him with a "loaded" tongue[2] occasionally, but I never heard him complain of a sore tongue, nor have I heard of caustic[3] being applied to his tongue. It was a month, if not more, before his death, that I heard him say he had a sore throat. I never knew him to take medicine before his last illness. He had a slight cough through cold,

---

[1] A tavern in Ludgate Hill near the Old Bailey where jurors in murder trials were lodged overnight if they couldn't reach a verdict. It opened in 1731 as "a punch-house, Dorchester Beer, and Welsh Ale Warehouse." The tavern closed in 1867 and was replaced by the "Ye Olde London" pub.

[2] Thick with mucus.

[3] A substance that dissolves organic tissue by chemical action. For example, a stick with lunar caustic (silver nitrate) would be brushed on the tongue to heal ulcers.

The High Street, Rugeley, showing Palmer's House, right, and the Talbot Arms Hotel, left.

but never to my knowledge a violent one. He had not been ailing just before he went to Shrewsbury. On his return from Shrewsbury he complained of being poorly.

I left my situation at Christmas, and went to my home in the Potteries.[4] Since then I have been in another situation, which I left in February. I have seen Mr. Stevens, Mr. Cook's father-in-law, since I have been in London. I cannot say how many times I have seen him, but it is not more than six or seven times. Sometimes we conversed together in a private room. He only came to see whether I liked the place or whether I liked London. We used to converse together about Mr. Cook's death; I have talked to him about Mr. Cook's death at Rugeley. I cannot remember anything else that we talked about except the death. He has never given me a farthing of money or promised to get me a place.

I saw Mr. Stevens last Tuesday at Dolly's Hotel,[5] where I had been in service. Lavinia Barnes was with us. She was the waitress at the Talbot Arms when Mr. Cook died. Two other persons were present, Mr. Hatton, the chief officer of Rugeley, and Mr. Gardner, an attorney at the same place. Mr. Cook's death may have been mentioned at this meeting. Other things were talked of which I do not wish to mention.

Mr. SERJEANT SHEE — But you must mention them.

Witness — I cannot remember what they were. I do not know whether we talked about the trial. They did not ask me what I could prove. My deposition was not read over to me; and Mr. Stevens did not talk to me about the symptoms that were exhibited by Mr. Cook before his death. I had seen Mr. Hatton a few times before. I once saw him at Dolly's. He merely dined there. I cannot remember whether he spoke to me about Cook's death. He might have done so. I cannot remember whether he did or not. I know he asked me how I did. (A

---

[4] The area now called Stoke-on-Trent in Staffordshire, about 22 miles north of Rugeley. The name comes from the pottery industry which was centered in North Staffordshire beginning in the early 17th century.

[5] The Old Bailey transcript adds "Paternoster-row" to her testimony, which places the hotel within sight of St. Paul's Cathedral. "Gilbert's Visitor's Guide to London" (1851) further narrows it down by listing a Dolly's Hotel and Chop-House in Queen's Head Passage, east of what is now Paternoster Square. The place was a tavern in Queen Anne's reign (1702-1707) and was known for attracting wits and eccentrics. A measure of the hotel's quality can be found in a 1874 story from the Suez Mail, which mentions a celebratory dinner held at the hotel by the passengers of the British ship Duke of Edinburgh after they arrived in London from New Zealand: "As may be judged from the character of the house, the dinner was excellent in every respect, and after full justice had been done to the good things provided, a silver tea and coffee service was presented to the captain of the ship."

laugh.) I saw Mr. Gardner once at Dolly's, and once in the street, and I swear these were the only occasions I ever saw him. I never went with him to a solicitor's office.

At present I am living with my mother at Rugeley. Before that I had been living among my friends. I know a man named Dutton. He is a friend of mine; I have been staying at his house. His mother lives in the same house. He is a labouring man. I used to sleep with Dutton's mother. I swear that I slept with his mother. I have also been staying with a cousin of mine in the Potteries. I left Dolly's of my own accord, because I did not like the place; I can read, and I read the newspapers.

I have heard of the case of a person named Dove,[6] who was supposed to have murdered his wife at Leeds. I merely heard that it was another strychnine case, but the symptoms of strychnine were not mentioned.

I will swear that I mentioned "twitching" to the coroner. If I did not use the exact word, I said something to the same effect. I will swear that I have used the word "twitching" before I came to London. The words "twitching" and "jerking" were not first suggested to me.[7]

I did not say anything about the broth having made me sick before the coroner, because it did not occur to me. I did tell the coroner that I tasted the broth, and that I did not observe anything particular about

---

[6] The Dove case reflected a recent development in the relationship between newspapers and its readers, where information spread through society faster than before. Palmer's defense contended that Mills' testimony, particularly her description of strychnine symptoms, was influenced by newspaper articles about the Dove case. Two months before the Palmer trial, Harriet Dove died in Leeds. Her husband, William, a drunkard who suffered from delusions, had fed her small doses of strychnine for two weeks before her death. He had read about Palmer's arrest and the debate about whether strychnine could be detected and decided to try the drug on his wife. The jury found him guilty, but their recommendation for mercy on the basis of insanity was rejected, and he was hanged. The Dove case was also discussed in the testimony of Jane Witham and George Morley.

[7] The Old Bailey transcript expands her testimony on this point, suggesting that Shee was implying that Mills' testimony was coached:

"I will swear that — I first used the expression "twitching" to the Coroner, or if I did not mention "twitching," I mentioned words to the same effect — I cannot swear that I used that word to the Coroner, I used it before I came to London, but I do not know to whom — I will swear I used it before I came to London — I believe I used it in mother's house — I swear I did, and I described to her the symptoms that the young man died under — I will swear I used the word "twitching" to mother — she is not here — I cannot remember when I first used the word "jerking" to anybody — it has never been used to me by anybody — I have never been asked by anybody whether there was not jerking or twitching, not that I can remember."

it. I was examined several times, and I was questioned particularly upon the subject of the broth, and I said on one occasion that I thought the broth was very good. I did not at the time think it was the broth that had caused the sickness. I was so ill that I was obliged to go to bed; but I could not at all account for it. I only took two tablespoonfuls, and the sickness came on in about half an hour.

I never knew of Mr. Cook taking coffee in bed before those occasions. If I have said that Mr. Palmer ordered coffee for Cook, I have no doubt that it is correct. I cannot remember so well to-day as I did yesterday. I cannot remember whether I told the coroner that I had not seen Mr. Palmer when I gave the deceased the coffee.

I don't remember whether I said anything before the coroner about seeing a box of pills in the deceased's bedroom on the Monday night, and that Palmer was in the room at the time. Perhaps I was not asked the question. I did nothing but answer questions that were put to me. I am sure that Palmer was in the room on that night. I remember that he brought a jar of jelly, and I opened it. I swear that the deceased told me that the pills Palmer had given him had made him ill. I did not say this before the coroner. I was asked some questions by Dr. Collier with regard to what I had stated to the coroner, and I said that my evidence had been altered, as some things had occurred to me since, and I had made another statement to a gentleman. I gave this additional statement to a gentleman at Dolly's. I don't know who the gentleman was. I did not ask him, and he did not tell me. He did not ask me many questions. He put a few to me and wrote down my answers. He mentioned Mr. Stevens' name. Mr. Stevens was there.

Serjeant Shee — Why did you not tell me that? — Because you did not ask me. (A laugh.)

Cross-examination continued: I did not tell the coroner that Mr. Cook was beating the bedclothes on the Monday night. I did say that he sometimes threw his head back, and then would raise himself up again, and I believe I also said that he could hardly speak for shortness of breath. I did not say that he called "Murder!" twice, and I do not remember saying that he "twitched" while I was rubbing his hands. I did not say anything about toast and water being given to Mr. Cook, by order of Palmer, in a spoon; or that he snapped at the spoon, and bit it so hard that it was difficult to get it out of his mouth.

The LORD CHIEF JUSTICE here interposed, and intimated his opinion that it would be a fairer course to read the witness' depositions.

The other Judges concurred.

The *Attorney-General* said, he should have interposed, but it was his intention to adduce evidence to show the manner in which the case was conducted by the coroner, and that he was expostulated with upon omitting to put proper questions, and also omitting to take down the answers that were given.

Cross-Examination continued. — I should have answered all those questions if they had been put to me. I was not purposely recalled to state the symptoms of the deceased in the presence of Dr. Taylor. When the prisoner came to the Talbot on the Tuesday night, he had a plaid dressing-gown on, but I cannot say whether he had a cap or not. I did not observe that the prisoner appeared at all confused at the time he was examining the clothes and the bed of the deceased.

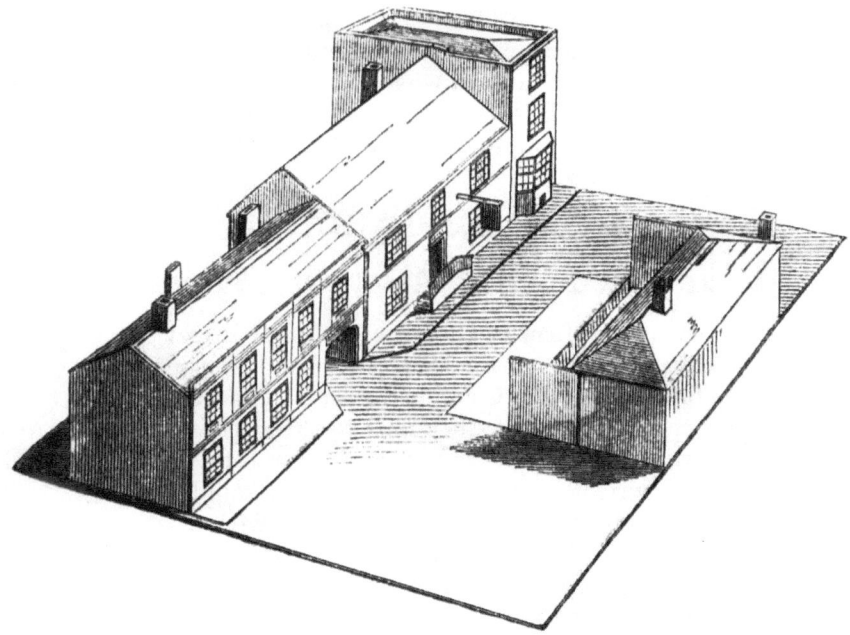

THE MODEL EXHIBITED IN COURT
OF THE TALBOT ARMS AND PALMER'S HOUSE

A model of the prisoner's house and of the hotel was here produced. The deposition of the witness was put in and read, for the purpose of showing that the statements made by her in her examination on Wednesday were omitted when she was examined by the coroner.

Re-examined by Mr. E. *James*. I was examined on a great many different days by the coroner. I was not asked to describe all the symptoms I saw. The coroner himself put the questions to me, and his clerk took down the answers. I merely answered the questions, and I was not told to describe all I saw.

The coroner asked me if the broth had any effect upon me, and I said, "Not that I was aware of." I don't know what brought the sickness to my mind afterwards, but I think that some one else in the house brought the fact to my memory. I certainly did vomit after I took the broth, and was obliged to go to bed.

I am quite sure the deceased told me that it was the pills Palmer had given him that had made him ill. When Mr. Collier came to me he said that he was for the Crown, and he then asked me questions about the inquest and the death of Mr. Cook. I answered all the questions he put to me, and he took them down in writing, and carried the statement away with him. Two other persons waited outside the house.

I am engaged to be married to one of the Duttons.

Mr. *Serjeant Shee* — Did not Dr. Collier tell you that he was neither for the Crown nor for the defence, but for the truth?

Witness — No; what he said was that he was for the Crown; but what he desired above all things was to know the truth, and that he asked me to tell him without fear, favour or affection.

Mr. JAMES GARDNER,
examined by the *Attorney-General*.

I am a member of the firm of Gardner & Co., of Rugeley. I acted in this matter for the firm of Cookson and Co., the solicitors of Mr. Stevens, the father-in-law of Cook. I attended the inquest on the body of Cook, and occasionally put questions to the witnesses. Mr. Ward, an attorney, was the coroner. He put questions to the witnesses, and his clerk took down the answers. The inquest lasted five days, and several times upon each day I expostulated with the coroner on account of his omitting to put questions.

Mr. *Serjeant Shee* submitted that what was said by the coroner was no evidence against the prisoner.

The *Attorney-General* — It is not intended as evidence against the prisoner, but to rebut the effect of evidence that you have put in. I will ask — had you occasion to expostulate with the coroner as to the omission of his clerk to take down the answers of witnesses?

Mr. *Serjeant Shee* — I object to the question being put in that form.

The *Attorney-General* — Did you observe that the clerk omitted to take down the answers of Elizabeth Mills?

Witness — Not in reference to that particular case.

Mr. Baron ALDERSON — Her account of the matter is that the questions were not put.

The *Attorney-General* — Did Dr. Taylor object that questions were not put which ought to have been put?

Interior of the Town Hall, Rugeley, during the Inquest on the Body of John Parsons Cook.
Ward, Coroner. Dr. Rees. Thirlby. Smith, Solicitor. Sup. Hatton. Dr. Taylor.

Witness — I do not recollect it.

Lord CAMPBELL — It is not suggested, as I understand, that the coroner refused to correct any mistakes that were made.

The *Attorney-General* — I am prepared to show that there was such misconduct on the part of the coroner as led to expostulation.

Mr. *Serjeant Shee* — Don't state that unless you are going to prove it.

The *Attorney-General* — It is suggested that a witness has given evidence here which she did not give before the coroner; my object is to show, first, that questions were not put to her which might and ought to have been put; secondly, that her answers to other questions were not taken down.

Lord CAMPBELL held that the evidence was not admissible.

Cross-examined by *Serjeant Shee*. The jury put a great many questions.

Re-examined by the *Attorney-General*. The jury made very strong observations as to the necessity of putting questions.

The *Attorney-General* — Did they assign any reason for interfering when they put questions?

Mr. *Serjeant Shee* objected to this question, on the ground that it did not arise out of his cross-examination.

Lord CAMPBELL — My learned brethren think that evidence upon this point is not admissible.

Mr. Justice CRESSWELL said, the depositions which had been put in did not show that any questions had been put by the jurymen. If they had contained such questions they would have shown the motive of the jury in putting them. But the Court was left totally in the dark as to whether questions had been put by the coroner or any other person. For any thing that appeared to the contrary, the witnesses might have made a voluntary statement without any questions at all being put to them. No foundation was laid therefore for the Attorney-General's question.

Mr. Baron ALDERSON concurred.

Mrs. ANN BROOKS,
examined by the *Attorney-General*.

I live at Manchester. I am in the habit of attending races. I was at Shrewsbury races in November, 1855. I saw Palmer there. On the 14th (Wednesday), about eight o'clock in the evening, I met him in the street, and asked him whether he thought his horse Chicken would win? He desired me if I heard anything further about a horse belonging to Lord Derby,[8] which was also to run, to call and tell him on the following day.

I went to the Raven to see him at half-past ten o'clock on the Thursday evening.[9] Some friends waited for me in the road. I went upstairs and asked a servant to tell Palmer that I wished to speak to him. The servant said he was there.

At the top of the stairs there are two passages, one facing the other, to the left. I turned to the left. I saw Palmer standing by a small table in the passage. He had a tumbler-glass in his hand, in which there appeared to be a small quantity of water. I did not see him put anything into it. There was a light between him and me, and he held it up to the light. He said to me, "I will be with you presently." He saw me the moment I got to the top of the stairs. He stood at the table a minute or two longer with the glass in his hand, holding it up to the light once or twice, and now and then shaking it. I made an observation about the fineness of the weather. The door of a sitting-room, which I supposed was unoccupied, was partially open, and he went into it, taking the glass with him. In two or three minutes he came out again with the glass. What was in the glass was still the colour of water. He then carried it into his own sitting-room, the door of which was shut.

He afterwards came out and brought me a glass with brandy-and-water in it. It might have been the same glass. I had some of the brandy-and-water. It produced no unpleasant consequences. We had some conversation about the races. In the course of it he said he should back his own horse, Chicken. I was present at the race, when Chicken ran and lost.

Cross-examined by Mr. *Serjeant Shee*. I am married. Brooks is the name of my husband. He never goes with me to races. I live with him. I don't attend many races in the course of a year. My husband has a high appointment, and does not sanction my going to races.

---

[8] Edward Smith-Stanley, the 14th Earl of Derby (1799-1869) was three times prime minister, never for very long, and the longest-serving leader of the Conservative Party. His second son, as Governor General of Canada, donated a cup to the nation's top-ranking ice hockey club, which subsequently was named for him: the Stanley Cup.

[9] The Old Bailey transcript gives more background on Brooks' meetings with Palmer: "I had occasion to go and speak to him; that was on the 14th, Wednesday — I met him in the street on the first occasion, that was about 8 o'clock in the evening — I asked him if he thought his horse would win on the following day — that horse was called Chicken, and was to run on the Thursday — Mr. Palmer said, if I heard anything further, I was to call in at the Raven Hotel that evening, and tell him — the information was in reference to another horse called Lord Alfred, which was to run in the race — he merely said, 'Be sure you call if you hear anything' — I went to see him that evening at the Raven, it was about half past 10 o'clock when I went . . ."

MRS. ANN BROOKS, A LADY WHO ATTENDS RACES

A great number of racing men were ill at Shrewsbury on the Wednesday. There was a wonder as to what had caused their illness, and something was said about the water being poisoned. People were affected by sickness and purging. I knew some persons who were so affected.

The passage in which I saw Palmer holding the glass led to a good many rooms. I think it was lighted by gas. I supposed that he was mixing some cooling drink.

Re-examined by the *Attorney-General*. I was not examined before the coroner. The brandy-and-water which Palmer gave me was cold. I had been on friendly terms with him, I had known him a number of years as a racing man.

LAVINIA BARNES, examined by Mr. *E. James*.

In November, 1855, I was a waitress at the Talbot Arms. I knew

Palmer and Cook. Cook called thereon the 12th (Monday) as he was going to the races. He did not complain of illness. I saw him when he returned on the 15th.

On the Friday he came between nine and ten o'clock in the evening, after dining with Palmer. He spoke to me. He was sober.

On the Saturday I saw him twice. Some broth was sent over and taken up to him by me. He could not take it; he was too sick. I carried it down and put it into the kitchen. I afterwards saw Palmer, and told him Cook was too sick to take it. Palmer said he must have it. Elizabeth Mills afterwards took it up again. She was taken ill with violent vomiting on the Sunday, between twelve and one o'clock. She went to bed, and did not come down stairs till four or five o'clock. I saw some broth on that day in the kitchen. It was in a "sick-cup," with two handles, not belonging to the house. I did not see it brought. The cup went back to Palmer's.

On the Monday morning, between seven and eight o'clock, I saw Palmer. He told Mills he was going to London. I also saw Cook during the day. Saunders came to see him, and I took him up some brandy-and-water. I slept that night in the next room to Cook's. Palmer came between eight and nine o'clock in the evening, and went upstairs, but I did not see whether he went into Cook's room.

About twelve o'clock I was in the kitchen, when Cook's bell rang violently. I went upstairs. Cook was very ill, and asked me to send for Palmer. He screamed out "Murder!" He exclaimed that he was in violent pain — that he was suffocating. His eyes were wild-looking, standing a great way out of his head. He was beating the bed with his arms. He cried out, "Christ, have mercy on my soul!" I never saw a person in such a state.

Having called up Mills, I left to send "Boots" for Palmer. Palmer came, and I again went into the room. Cook was then more composed. He said, "Oh, doctor, I shall die." Palmer replied, "Don't be alarmed, my lad." I saw Cook drink a darkish mixture out of a glass. I don't know who gave it to him. I both saw and heard him snap at the glass. He brought up the draught. I left him between twelve and one o'clock, when he was much more composed.

On the Tuesday he seemed a little better. At night, a little before twelve o'clock, the bell rang again. I was in the kitchen. Mills went up stairs. I followed her, and heard Cook screaming, but did not go into the room. I stood outside the door, and saw Palmer come. He had been fetched. I said as he passed me, "Mr. Cook is ill again." He said, "Oh, is he?" and went into the room. He was dressed in his usual manner, and wore a black coat and a cap. I remained on the landing when Palmer came out. As he went down stairs, Mills asked him how Cook was? He said to her and to me, "He is not so bad by fifty parts as he was last night." I heard Cook ask to be turned over before I went in, while Palmer was there. I went in after Palmer had left, but I came out before Cook died.

After he died on the Tuesday I went into the room, and found Palmer with a coat in his hand. He was clearing out the pockets of the coat, and looking under the bolster. I said, "Oh! Mr. Cook can't be dead!" Palmer said, "He is. I knew he would be," and then left the room.

I saw him on the Thursday following. He came into the body of the hall, and asked for the key to Mr. Cook's bedroom, in which the body was lying. The key was in the bar. He said he wanted some books and papers and a paperknife,[10] for they were to go back to the stationer's, or else he would have to pay for them. I went with him into the room. He then requested me to go to Miss Bond for some books. I went down stairs and fetched the books. When I returned he was still in the room looking for the paperknife on the top of the chest of drawers among books, papers, and clothes. He said, "I can't find the knife anywhere." Miss Bond, the housekeeper, afterwards came up, and I left.

On the Friday, between three and four o'clock, I saw Mr. Jones with Palmer. Jones said he thought Palmer knew where the betting-book was. Palmer asked me to go and look for it, and said it was sure to be found, but it was not worth anything to any one but Cook. Mills and I went up to look for it, but we could not find it. We searched everywhere, in the bed and all round the room, but not in the drawers. We went down and told Palmer and Jones that we could not find it. Palmer said, "Oh, it will be found somewhere. I'll go with you and look myself." He did not go with us, but left the house. I did not see him come out of the room on the Thursday. There was no reason for our not looking in the drawers. Some people were in the room at the time nailing the coffin.

Cross-examined by Mr. *Serjeant Shee*. Cook had some coffee on the Saturday between 12 and 1. I did not pay any particular attention to the time when Palmer went up on the Monday. I am not sure it was before half-past nine, but I am sure it was before 10.

I didn't remember whether Cook touched the glass from which he drank the mixture. I think some one else was holding it.

---

[10] A knife-like object used to open letters or books whose pages were sold uncut. Originally, books were sold without covers, and the customer had to take them to his binder. The binder would attach a cover and then slit the pages, or the customer would do it himself. Even when books were being issued with covers, printers left the pages uncut until machinery was designed to take over that task.

There was some of Cook's linen[11] in several of the drawers. There was a portmanteau[12] containing other things besides those in the drawers. There were dress clothes, an overcoat, and morning clothes.

The door was locked on the night of the death. The women were sent for to lay out the corpse before it was light. The undertakers went on the following morning, and the door was locked after they left. They came again on the Thursday night, had the key, and went up by themselves. The body was put into the coffin the day Stevens was there. The women were in the room with the three undertakers when I looked for the book.

Re-examined by the *Attorney-General.* The chambermaid and I were in and out of the room while the women were laying out the body, but they were sometimes left alone. I saw nothing of the book at that time. I had seen it before in Cook's hand, but I don't remember seeing it in the room.

ANN ROWLEY, examined by Mr. *Welsby.*

I live at Rugeley, and have frequently been employed as charwoman by Palmer. On the Saturday before Cook died Palmer sent me to Mr. Robinson's, at the Albion Inn,[13] for a little broth for Cook. I fetched the broth, took it to Palmer's house, and put it to the fire in the back kitchen to warm. After doing so, I went about my work in other parts of the house. When the broth was hot, Palmer brought it to me in the kitchen, and poured it into a cup. He told me to take it to the Talbot Arms for Cook, to ask if he would take a little bread or toast with it, and to say that Smith had sent it.

By Lord CAMPBELL — He did not say why I was to say that.

Examination resumed. — There is a Mr. Jeremiah Smith at Rugeley. He is called "Jerry Smith." He is a friend of Palmer's. I took the broth to the Talbot Arms, and gave it to Lavinia Barnes.

Cross-examined by Mr. *Serjeant Shee.* Mr. Smith was in the habit of putting up at the Albion. He was friendly with Cook. Cook was to have dined with Smith that day, but was not able to go. Mrs. Robinson, the landlady of the Albion, made the broth, but I do not know by whose orders.

By Lord CAMPBELL — The broth was at the fire in Palmer's kitchen, about five minutes.

---

[11] The underclothes worn next to the skin, such as shirts, drawers and stockings. These were usually made of linen or cotton and could be easily laundered.

[12] A large traveling bag that opened into two equal parts. The word is also used to define a word created from two or more distinct words. For example, combining "brother" and "romance" creates the portmanteau word "bromance"

[13] The Albion is still in business at 17 Albion St. in Rugeley.

CHARLES HORLEY, examined by Mr. *Bodkin*.

I am a gardener living at Rugeley, and was occasionally employed by the prisoner in his garden. On the Sunday before Cook died, Palmer asked me to take some broth to Cook. That was at Palmer's house, where I was in the habit of going. It was between 12 and 1 o'clock. He gave me the broth in a small cup, with a cover over it, and told me to take it to the Talbot Arms for Cook. I did so. I cannot say whether or not the broth was hot. I gave it to one of the servant girls at the Talbot Arms, but which I cannot say.

The witness was not cross-examined.

SARAH BOND, examined by Mr. *Huddleston*.

In November last I was housekeeper at the Talbot Arms. I knew Cook. He stayed at the Talbot Arms. I remember his going to Shrewsbury races on the 12th of November. He returned on the Thursday. I heard him say that he was very poorly. I did not see him on the Friday or Saturday.

On Sunday I saw him about 8 o'clock in the evening. He was in bed. He said that he had been very poorly, but was better. Very soon afterwards I saw Palmer. I asked him what he thought of Cook, and he replied that he was better. On Saturday night Smith had slept in the room with Cook. On the Sunday evening I asked Palmer if Cook would not want somebody with him that night, and Palmer replied that he was so much better that it would not be necessary that any one should be with him. I asked if Daniel Jenkins, the boots, should sleep in the room? Palmer said that Cook was so much better he had much rather he did not.

On the Monday morning, a little before 7 o'clock, I saw Palmer again. He came into the kitchen to me. I asked him how Cook was. He said he was better, and requested me to make him a cup of coffee. He did not say anything about its strength. He remained in the kitchen, and I made the coffee and gave it to him. He told me that he was going to London, and that he had written for Mr. Jones to come to see Cook. On the Monday night, hearing from the waitress that Cook was ill, I went up to his room between 11 and 12 o'clock. When I went into the room Cook was alone. He was sitting up in bed, resting on his elbow. He seemed disappointed, and said that he did not want to see me, but Palmer. I went out on to the landing, and soon afterwards Palmer came. Palmer went into the room. I could not see what was done in the room. Palmer came out, went away for a few minutes, and then returned. After he came back I heard that Cook had vomited. Cook said he thought he should die. Palmer cheered him up, and said that he would do all he could to prevent it. When Palmer came out of the room again, I asked him if Cook had any relatives, and he said that he had only a step-father.

I saw Cook again between 3 and 4 o'clock on Tuesday. That was when Mr. Jones came. A little after 6 o'clock I took some jelly up to Cook. He seemed very anxious for it, and said that he thought he should die. I thought he seemed better. I did not see him again alive.

Between 8 and 9 o'clock on Wednesday morning, I locked the door of the room in which Cook's body lay. About 9 o'clock I gave the key to Mr. Tolly, the barber, when he came to shave the corpse.

On Thursday I gave it to Lavinia Barnes. After that I went up to the room and met Palmer coming out of it. After I came out the door was locked, and I had the key.

On Friday, when Mr. Stevens came, I gave the key to the undertaker.

Cross-examined by Mr. *Grove*. The passengers by the express train from London arrived at Rugeley about 10 o'clock in the evening. They come by fly from Stafford.[14]

WILLIAM HENRY JONES,
examined by the *Attorney-General*.

I am a surgeon, living at Lutterworth. I have been in practice fifteen years. I was acquainted with Cook, who from time to time resided at my house. I had been on terms of intimacy with him nearly five years. He was 28 years of age when he died, and unmarried. He was originally educated for the law, but of late years had devoted himself to agriculture and the turf. The last year or two he had no farm. He kept racehorses, and betted. I had known Palmer about 12 months. Lately Cook considered my house at Lutterworth as his home. I have attended him professionally. His health was generally good, but he was not very robust. He was a man of active habits. He both hunted and played cricket.

In November last he invited me to go to Shrewsbury to see his horse run, and I went. I spent Tuesday, the 13th, with him there. That was the day on which Polestar ran and won. I dined with Cook and other friends

---

[14] The Old Bailey transcript explains further what this cross-examination was about:

Q. What time did you see Mr. Palmer on the Monday evening?

A. A little before 12 o'clock — I had not seen him before in the course of the evening — the last train that stops at Rugeley is between 7 and 8 o'clock — that is not the express, the express does not stop at Rugeley — it is necessary for passengers coming from the express to have a fly, or some conveyance, from Stafford — I cannot tell at what time they would arrive in the ordinary course, I should say about 10 o'clock.

at the Raven Hotel, where he was staying. The horse having won, there was a little extra champagne drunk. We dined between 6 and 7 o'clock, and the party broke up between 8 and 9. Cook afterwards accompanied me round the town. We went to Mr. Fraill's, who is Clerk of the Course. I saw Cook produce his betting-book to Whitehouse, the jockey. He calculated his winnings on Polestar. There were figures in the book. Cook made a statement as to his winnings.

Mr. *Serjeant Shee* objected to this statement being given in evidence, and the Attorney-General therefore did not ask any questions as to its purport.

Examination resumed. — I left the Raven Hotel at 10 o'clock. Cook was then at the door. He was not at all the worse for liquor. He was in his usual health. On the following Monday I received a letter from Palmer.

This letter, which was put in and read, was as follows:—

"MY DEAR SIR,— Mr. Cook was taken ill at Shrewsbury, and obliged to call in a medical man. Since then he has been confined to his bed here with a very severe bilious attack, combined with diarrhœa. I think it desirable for you to come to see him as soon as possible.

"November 18, 1855.

"WILLIAM PALMER."

Examination resumed. — On that day (Monday) I was very unwell. On the next day I went to Rugeley. I arrived at the Talbot Arms about half past 3 o'clock in the afternoon, and immediately went up to Cook's room. He said that he was very comfortable, but he had been very ill at Shrewsbury. He did not detail the symptoms, but said he was obliged to call in a medical man. Palmer came in. I examined Cook in Palmer's presence. He had a natural pulse. I looked at his tongue, which was clean. I said it was hardly the tongue of a bilious diarrhœa attack. Palmer replied — "You should have seen it before." I did not then prescribe for Cook.

In the course of the afternoon I visited him several times. He changed for the better. His spirits and pulse both improved. I gave him, at his request, some toast and water, and he vomited. There was no diarrhœa. The toast and water was in the room.

Mr. Bamford came in the evening about 7 o'clock. Palmer had told me that Mr. Bamford had been called in. Mr. Bamford expressed his opinion that Cook was going on very satisfactorily. We were talking about what he was to have, and Cook objected to the pills of the previous night. Palmer was there all the time. Cook said the pills made him ill. I do not remember to whom he addressed this observation. We three (Palmer, Bamford, and myself) went out upon the landing. Palmer proposed that Mr. Bamford should make up some morphine pills as before, at the same time requesting me not to mention to Cook what they contained, as he objected to the morphine so much. Mr. Bamford agreed to this, and he went away.

I went back to Cook's room, and Palmer went with me. During the evening I was several times in Cook's room. He seemed very comfortable all the evening. There was no more vomiting nor any diarrhœa, but there was a natural motion of the bowels. I observed no bilious symptoms about Cook.

By Lord CAMPBELL — Did he appear to have recently suffered from a bilious attack? — No.

Examination resumed. — Palmer and I went to his house about 8 o'clock. I remained there about half an hour, and then returned to Cook. I next saw Palmer in Cook's room at nearly 11 o'clock. He had brought with him a box of pills. He opened the paper, on which the direction was written, in my presence. That paper was round the box. He called my attention to the paper, saying, "What an excellent handwriting for an old man!" I did not read the direction, but looked at the writing, which was very good.

Palmer proposed to Cook that he should take the pills. Cook protested very much against it, because they had made him so ill on the previous night. Palmer repeated the request several times, and at last Cook complied with it, and took the pills. The moment he took them he vomited into the utensil. Palmer and myself (at Palmer's request) searched in it for the pills, to see whether they were returned. We found nothing but toast-and-water. I do not know when Cook had drunk the toast-and-water, but it was standing by the bedside all the evening. The vomiting could not have been caused by the contents of the pills, nor by the act of swallowing. After vomiting, Cook laid down and appeared quiet.

Before Palmer came Cook had got up and sat in a chair. His spirits were very good; he was laughing and joking, talking of what he should do with himself during the winter. After he had taken the pills I went down stairs to my supper, and returned to his room at nearly 12 o'clock. His room was double-bedded, and it had been arranged that I should sleep in it that night. I talked to Cook for a few minutes, and then went to bed. When I last talked to him he was rather sleepy, but quite as well as he had been during the evening. There was nothing about him to excite any apprehensions.

I had been in bed about 10 minutes, and had not gone to sleep, when he suddenly started up in bed, and called out, "Doctor, get up, I am going to be ill! Ring the bell and send for Palmer." I rang the bell. The chambermaid came, and Cook called out to her, "Fetch Mr. Palmer." He asked me to give him something; I declined, and said, "Palmer will be here directly." Cook was then sitting up in bed. The room was rather dark, and I did not observe anything particular in his countenance. He asked me to rub the back of his neck. I did so. I supported him with my arm. There was a stiffness about the muscles of his neck.

Palmer came very soon, two or three minutes at the utmost after the chambermaid went for him. He said, "I never dressed so quickly in my life." I did not observe how he was dressed. He gave Cook two pills, which he told me were ammonia pills.[15] Cook swallowed them. Directly he did so he uttered loud screams, threw himself back in the bed, and was dreadfully convulsed. That could not have been the result of the action of the pills last taken. Cook said, "Raise me up! I shall be suffocated." That was at the commencement of the convulsions, which lasted five or ten minutes. The convulsions affected every muscle of the body, and were accompanied by stiffening of the limbs. I endeavoured to raise Cook with the assistance of Palmer, but found it quite impossible, owing to the rigidity of the limbs.

When Cook found we could not raise him up he asked me to turn him over. He was then quite sensible. I turned him on to his side. I listened to the action of his heart. I found that it gradually weakened, and asked Palmer to fetch some spirits of ammonia, to be used as a stimulant. Palmer went to his house and fetched the bottle. He was away a very short time.

When he returned the pulsations of the heart were gradually ceasing, and life was almost extinct. Cook died very quietly a very short time afterwards. From the time he called to me to that of his death there elapsed about ten minutes or a quarter of an hour.[16]

He died of tetanus, which is a spasmodic affection of the muscles of the whole body. It causes death by stopping the action of the heart. The sense of suffocation is caused by the contraction of the respiratory muscles.

The room was so dark that I could not observe what was the outward appearance of Cook's body after death. When he threw himself back in bed he clinched his hands, and they remained clinched after death. When I was rubbing his neck his head and neck were unnaturally bent back by the spasmodic action of the muscles. After death his body was so twisted or bowed that if I had placed it upon the back it would have rested upon the head and the feet.

By Lord CAMPBELL — When did you first observe that twisting or bowing? — When Cook threw himself back in bed.

---

[15] Pills containing ammonia and carbon dioxide, used as a stimulant to treat problems such as chronic bronchitis, dyspepsia, and heart palpitations.
[16] According to George Fletcher's biography, in the immediate silence after Cook's death, Palmer shocked Jones and the maids by saying "The poor devil has gone."

Examination resumed. — The jaw was effected by the spasmodic action. Palmer remained half an hour or an hour after Cook's death. I suggested that we should have some women to lay Cook out. I left the room to speak to the housekeeper about this. Seeing two maids on the landing I sent them into the room where Palmer was with Cook's body. I went down stairs and spoke to the housekeeper, and then returned to the bedroom.

When I went back Palmer had Cook's coat in his hand. He said to me, "You, as his nearest friend, had better take possession of his effects." I took Cook's watch and his purse, containing five sovereigns and five shillings, which was all I could find. I saw no betting-book nor any papers or letters belonging to Cook. I found no banknotes.

Before Palmer left did he say anything to you on the subject of affairs between himself and Cook? — He did. Soon after Cook's death he said, "It is a bad thing for me that Mr. Cook is dead, as I am responsible for £3,000 or £4,000, and I hope Mr. Cook's friends will not let me lose it. If they do not assist me all my horses will be seized." He said nothing about securities or papers.

I was present when Mr. Stevens, Cook's stepfather, came. Palmer said that if Mr. Stevens did not bury Cook he should. I do not recollect that there was any question about burying him. Mr. Stevens, Palmer, Mr. Bamford, and myself dined together. After dinner, Mr. Stevens, in Palmer's presence, asked me to go and look for Cook's betting-book. I went to look for it, and Palmer followed me. The night that Cook died the betting-book was mentioned.

What was said about it? — Palmer said that it would be of use to no one.

What led to this? — My taking possession of the effects.

Did you make any observation about the book? — I cannot recollect.

Did you find it? — No.

Did you make any remark? — No particular remark.

Did Palmer know what you were looking for? — Yes.

How? — I said, "Where is the betting-book?" Upon that he said, "It is of no use to any one."

You are sure he said that? — Yes. When I went to look for the book, at Mr. Stevens's request Palmer followed me. I looked for the book for two or three minutes, but did not find it. I told the maidservants that I could not find it. Palmer returned with me to the dining-room, and I told Mr. Stevens that I could not find the book.

By Lord CAMPBELL — When Palmer, Mr. Bamford, and myself held the consultation on the landing on the Tuesday night, nothing was said about the spasms of the night before.

Cross-examined by Mr. *Serjeant Shee*.

I am a regular medical practitioner, and have for 15 years practised medicine as a means of gaining a living. I am a licentiate of the Apothecaries' Company,[17] and have endeavoured, both as a young man and since, to qualify myself for my profession.

When I saw Cook his throat was slightly ulcerated, but he could swallow very well, although with a little pain. I know that he had applied caustic to his tongue, but he had ceased to do so for two months. He did not after that continue to complain of pain in his throat or tongue. I saw him frequently during the races, and never heard him express any apprehension about spots which appeared upon his body, although he did express apprehensions of secondary symptoms resulting from syphilis.[18] I am not aware that at the time he died he was suffering from the venereal disease, but I know that he had it about a twelvemonth ago.

He had been reduced in circumstances some time before he died, but he was redeeming them. I do not know that he was frequently in want of small sums of money. I believe that he owned a mare in conjunction with Palmer named Pyrrhine, which was under the care of Saunders, the trainer.

The race which Polestar won was a matter of very great importance to the deceased. He was much excited at the race, and more particularly so after it. Deceased was a very temperate man and did not exceed in wine on the evening of the race.

The next I heard of him was through the letter from Palmer. Palmer knew perfectly well who I was, and that I was in practice as a surgeon at Lutterworth. When I saw deceased he objected to taking morphia pills, because they had made him ill the night before. He did not say that Dr. Savage had forbidden him to take the morphia, but he said that he had been directed not to take mercury or opium. The effect of morphia would be to soothe and to cause slight constipation. When I saw him and he roused up a little, he said "Palmer, give me the remedy you gave me last night." I rubbed the deceased's neck for

---

[17] A society, founded in 1617, that until 1999 was responsible for licensing doctors in England. It wasn't until soon after Palmer's time, however, that doctors had to meet any general set of standards to practice medicine.

[18] A sexually transmitted disease caused by a spiral-shaped bacterium. It initially appears as ulcers on the skin, particularly in the groin, then forms large, painful abscesses and sores all over the body. The disease would fall dormant, sometimes for years, before returning with more painful and wide-spreading symptoms until the victim became insane, disfigured, and then died. Syphilis was treated with mercury, which was ineffective and caused severe mouth ulcers, teeth loss, and, at high levels, death. The first effective treatment against syphilis didn't appear until 1943 with the introduction of penicillin.

about five minutes. He died very quietly.

I had seen cases of tetanus before. I think I mentioned tetanus at the inquest. I am sure, if you refer to my depositions, you will find that I mentioned tetanus and convulsions both. (The depositions were referred to, and there was no mention of tetanus in them.) Witness continued, however, "I am sure that I mentioned tetanus."

The *Attorney-General* — I must set this right. I have here the original deposition, and I find that the matter stands thus: — "There were strong symptoms of" — then there is the word "compression" struck out; and then there is the word "tetanus" also struck out — it is evident that the clerk did not know the meaning of what he was writing — and then the words "violent convulsions" are added; so that the sentence stands, "There were strong symptoms of violent convulsions."

By Mr. *Serjeant Shee* — I also said before the Coroner that I could not tell the cause of death, and that I imagined at the time that it was from over-excitement.

The LORD CHIEF JUSTICE said, that the learned counsel must not read detached portions of the depositions — the whole must be read. (The depositions were accordingly read by the Clerk of the Arraigns.)

Cross-examination continued. — I do not recollect that I ever said that deceased died of epilepsy. Dr. Bamford said he died in an apoplectic fit, and I said that I thought he did not. I said that, it was more like an epileptic than an apoplectic fit. I do not know Mr. Pratt, but I took a letter from him to Cook. Cook did not open it, but said, "I know the contents of it — let it be till to-morrow morning." I have seen Palmer's racing establishment at Rugeley. I saw a number of mares in foal, and others in the paddock, and some very valuable horses. The stables were good, and the establishment appeared to be a large and expensive one.[19]

Re-examined by the *Attorney-General*. I am not a good judge of the value of racing horses, but I understand other horses very well. I have only seen one case of tetanus, and that case resulted from a wound. The patient in that case lasted three days before death ensued. I am satisfied that the death of Mr. Cook did not arise from epilepsy. In epilepsy consciousness is lost, but there is no rigidity or convulsive spasm of the muscles. The symptoms are quite different. I am equally certain that death was not the result of apoplexy.

---

[19] Palmer's establishment consisted of 17 race horses plus stablemen to care for them. Boarding them at Hednesford alone cost him £1,600 a year, plus the cost for food, training, transportation, jockey fees, and his own travels and bets. Small wonder he ran up huge debts to Pratt, Padwick and Wright.

PALMER'S STABLES FOR BROOD MARES AT RUGELEY

LAVINIA BARNES,
re-examined by Mr. *Serjeant Shee*

On Monday morning Mr. Cook said to me that he had been very ill on Sunday night, just before 12 o'clock, and that he had rung the bell for some one to come to him; but he thought that they had all gone to bed.

ELIZABETH MILLS, recalled by the *Attorney-General*, and examined on the same point.

I remember on Monday morning asking Mr. Cook how he was, and he said that he had been disturbed in the night, adding, "I was just mad for two minutes." I said, "Why did you not ring the bell?" and he replied, "I thought you would be all fast asleep, and would not hear me. The illness passed away, and I managed to get over it without." He also said that he thought he had been disturbed by the noise of a quarrel in the street.

Dr. HENRY SAVAGE,
examined by the *Attorney-General*.

I knew John Parsons Cook. He had been in the habit of consulting me professionally during the last four years. He was a man not of robust constitution; but his general health was good.

He came to me in May, 1855, but I saw him about November of the year before, and early in the spring of 1855. In the spring of 1855 the old affair — indigestion — was one cause of his visiting me, and he had some spots upon his body, about which he was uneasy. He had also two shallow ulcers on his tongue, which corresponded with two bad teeth. He said that he had been under a mild mercurial course, and he imagined that those spots were syphilitic; I thought they were not, and I recommended the discontinuance of mercury. I gave him quinine as a tonic, and an aperient[20] composed of cream of tartar, magnesia, and sulphur. I never at any time gave him antimony. Under the treatment which I prescribed the sores gradually disappeared, and they were quite well by the end of May.

I saw him, however, frequently in June, as he still felt some little anxiety about the accuracy of my opinion. If any little spot made its appearance he came to me, and I also was anxious on the subject, as my opinion differed from that of another medical man in London.

Every time he came to me I examined him carefully. There were no indications of a syphilitic character about the sores, and there was no ulceration of the throat, but one of the tonsils was slightly enlarged and tender.

I saw him last alive, and carefully examined him, either on the 3rd or 5th of November. There was, in my judgment, no venereal taint about him at the time.

Cross-examined by Mr. *Serjeant Shee*. I do not think that the deceased was fond of taking mercury before I advised him against it; but he was timid on the subject of his throat, and was apt to take the advice of any one. No; I don't think that he would take quack medicines. I don't think he was so foolish as that.

CHARLES NEWTON,
examined by Mr. *James*, Q.C.

I am assistant to Mr. Salt, a surgeon at Rugeley. I know the prisoner, William Palmer. I remember Monday, the 19th of November I saw Palmer that evening at Mr. Salt's surgery, about 9 o'clock. I was alone when he came there. He asked me for three grains of strychnine, and I weighed it accurately and gave it to him, enclosed in a piece of paper. He said nothing further but "Good night," and took it away with him. I knew

---

[20] Any medicine used to relieve constipation.

him to be a medical man and gave it him — made no charge for it. The whole transaction did not occupy more than two or three minutes.[21]

I again saw Palmer on the following day, between 11 and 12 o'clock. He was then at the shop of Mr. Hawkins, a druggist.[22] He asked me how I was, and put his hand upon my shoulder and said he wished to speak with me. Accordingly I went out into the street with him, and he then asked me when Mr. Edwin Salt was going to his farm. The farm in question was at a place about 14 miles distant from Rugeley. Palmer had nothing whatever to do with that farm; but Mr. Salt's going there was a rumour of the town.[23]

While we were talking a Mr. Brassington came up and spoke to me, and during our conversation Palmer went into Hawkins's shop again. Palmer came out of the shop a second time, while I was still talking to Brassington. I am not sure whether Palmer spoke to me at that time; but he went past me in the direction of his own house, which is about 200 yards from Hawkins'.

I then went into Hawkins' shop, where I saw Roberts, Mr. Hawkins' apprentice, and I had some conversation with him about Palmer.[24] I knew a man named Thirlby, who had been an assistant and a partner of Palmer. Palmer usually dealt with Thirlby for his drugs — in fact, Thirlby dispensed Palmer's medicine.

On Sunday, the 25th of November, about 7 o'clock in the evening, I was sent for and went to Palmer's house. I found Palmer, when I got there, in his kitchen. He was sitting by the fire reading. He asked me how I was, and to have some brandy-and-water. No one else was present. He asked me what was the dose of strychnine to give to kill a dog? I told him a grain. He asked me what would be the appearance of the stomach after death? I told him that there would be no inflammation, and that I did not think it could be found. Upon that he snapped his finger and thumb in a quiet way, and exclaimed, as if communing with himself, "That's all right." (Sensation.) He made some other remarks of a commonplace character, which I do not recollect. I was with him altogether about five minutes.

---

[21] Mr. Salt was a surgeon, not a chemist, and was not allowed to sell drugs. Because of the backdoor nature of this transaction, Newton was not officially obliged to register the sale in the poison book. According to Fletcher, Newton was a "dissipated companion of Palmer's" and therefore willing to do him a favor.

[22] Fletcher mentions that Newton came in to pick up a particular brand of calomel pills a patient wanted that Mr. Salt did not have in stock.

[23] It was commonly known that Mr. Salt had recently bought the farm, so the speculation was about when he would move there.

[24] According to Roberts' testimony at the inquest, Newton said, "Whatever is the matter with Palmer this morning?" Roberts replied, "Matter! Why, he has bought enough poison for the whole parish."

On the following day — Monday, the 26th of November — I heard that a *post-mortem* examination was to take place. I went to Dr. Bamford's house, intending to accompany him to the examination, and I found Palmer there in the study. That was about 10 o'clock in the day. Palmer asked me what I wanted. I told him that I had come to attend the *post-mortem*. He asked whether I thought Mr. Salt was going; and I replied that he was engaged and could not go. I took the necessary instruments with me, and went down to the Talbot Arms. Dr. Harland, and Mr. Frere, a surgeon, practising at Rugeley, were both there. They went away, however, for a short time, and left Palmer and me together in the entrance to the hall at the Talbot Arms. He spoke to me. He said, "It will be a dirty job; I will go and have some brandy." I went with him to his house, which was just opposite. He gave me two wine-glasses of neat brandy, and he took the same quantity himself. He said — "You'll find this fellow suffering from a diseased throat — he has had syphilis, and has taken a great deal of mercury." I afterwards went over with Palmer to the *post-mortem*, and found the other doctors there.

During the *post-mortem* Palmer stood near to Dr. Bamford, against the fire. I was examined before the coroner, and did not state before that functionary that I had given Palmer three grains of strychnine on the night of the 19th of November. The first person that I told of it was Cheshire, the post-master.

Mr. *Serjeant Shee* objected to anything that this witness had said to Cheshire being admitted as evidence against the prisoner.

The Court ruled in favour of the objection.

Cross-examined by Mr. *Grove*, Q.C. It might have been a week, or two or three days after I gave Palmer the strychnine, that I first mentioned the occurrence to any one. I think I may undertake to say that it was not a fortnight afterwards. Subsequently to the inquest I was examined for the purpose of giving evidence on the part of the Crown. I cannot say how long after the inquest that was. When I was first examined on behalf of the Crown I did not mention the three grains of strychnine, but I did mention the conversation about the poisoning of the dog. That was not the first time that I had mentioned that conversation; for I had mentioned it before to Mr. Salt; but I cannot tell how long before. I was examined twice for the purpose of the prosecution by the Crown. I did not mention Cook's suffering from sore throat at the inquest, but I did mention the conversation which took place at Hawkins's shop. At that time I knew it had been alleged that Palmer had purchased strychnine at Hawkins's, and I presumed that my evidence was required with reference to that point. I first stated on Tuesday last, for the purposes of this prosecution, the fact of my having given Palmer three grains of strychnine. I cannot say whether in that examination I said that Palmer said, "You will find this 'poor' fellow suffering from a diseased throat." I don't know whether I said "poor fellow" or "rich fellow."

Do you not know that there is a difference in the expression "fellow", and "poor fellow?" — I know there is a difference between rich and poor. It is impossible to recollect all that I said upon every occasion.

Re-examined by the *Attorney-General*. I did not mention the circumstance of my having given the strychnine to Palmer, because Mr. Salt, my employer, and Palmer were not friends, and I thought it would displease Mr. Salt if he knew that I had let Palmer have anything. I first mentioned it to Boycott, the clerk of Mr. Gardner, the solicitor, at the Rugeley station, where I and a number of other witnesses were assembled for the purpose of coming to London. As soon as I arrived in London, Boycott took me to Mr. Gardner's. I communicated to him what I had to say; and I was then taken to the solicitor of the Treasury, and I made the same statement to him.

Mr. *Serjeant Shee* — Have you not given another reason for not mentioning the occurrence about the three grains of strychnine before — that reason being that you were afraid you could be indicted for perjury? — No, I did not give that as a reason, but I stated to a gentleman that a young man at Wolverhampton had been threatened to be indicted for perjury by George Palmer,[25] because he had said at the inquest upon Walter Palmer, that he had sold the prisoner prussic acid, and he had not entered it in the book and could not prove it. I stated at the same time that George Palmer said he could be transported for it. I did not enter the gift of the three grains of strychnine from Mr. Salt's surgery in a book. The inquest upon Walter Palmer did not take place till five or six weeks after the inquest upon Mr. Cook.[26]

The Court then adjourned at 25 minutes past 6 o'clock until 10 o'clock next day, the jury being conducted, as on the previous evening, to the London Coffee House in charge of the officers of the Court.

---

[25] George Palmer was William Palmer's older brother and a solicitor. Walter Palmer was a timber merchant who lost his employment and his wife to alcohol. William insured Walter's life for £13,000, then hired a man to take care of Walter and make sure he was provided with enough gin to drink himself to death. The story of Walter's fatal decline is described in "The Illustrated Life and Career of William Palmer" (Peschel Press, 2015).

[26] Newton's recollections grew with each retelling. First, he saw Palmer buy strychnine at Hawkins. Three months later, he disclosed the conversation about poisoning a dog. Three months after that, he revealed that he, too, had provided Palmer with strychnine. To a suspicious mind, it's as if his desire to keep himself in the center of the trial encouraged these revelations. While we'll never know Newton's true motives, there's no doubt that, in George Fletcher's words, he was "a most doubtful, unsatisfactory character . . . a real shuffler."

THE JURORS' SLEEPING APARTMENT AT THE LONDON COFFEE HOUSE.

THIRD DAY.—May 16, 1856.

The Court was quite as full at the commencement of the proceedings this morning, as it had been upon either of the preceding days. The Earl of Derby, Earl Grey, and other noble lords were again present.

The jury took their seats shortly before ten o'clock. The learned Judges, Lord Chief Justice Campbell, Mr. Baron Alderson, and Mr. Justice Cresswell, soon afterwards entered the Court, accompanied by the Recorder and Sheriffs, and the prisoner was then placed at the bar. He appeared rather more anxious than on the two previous days, but was still calm and collected, and paid the greatest attention to the evidence.

Counsel for the Crown: The Attorney-General, Mr. E. James, Q.C., Mr. Bodkin, Mr. Welsby, and Mr. Huddleston; for the prisoner: Mr. Serjeant Shee, Mr. Grove, Q.C, Mr. Gray, and Mr. Kenealy.

CHARLES JOSEPH ROBERTS,
examined by Mr. *E. James*.

In November last, I was apprentice to Mr. Hawkins, a druggist, at Rugeley. I know Palmer. On Tuesday, November the 20th, between eleven and twelve in the day, he came into Mr. Hawkins's shop. He first asked for two drachms of prussic acid, for which he had brought a bottle. I was putting it up when Newton, the assistant of Salt, came in. Palmer told him he wanted to speak to him, and they went out of the shop together.

I then saw Brassington, the cooper, take Newton away from Palmer, and enter into conversation with him. Palmer then came back into the shop, and asked me for six grains of strychnine and two drachms of Batley's solution of opium, (commonly called "Batley's sedative"). I had put up the prussic acid, which was lying upon the counter. He stood at the counter when he ordered the things, and while I was preparing them behind the counter, he stood at the shop door, with his back to me, looking into the street. I was about five minutes preparing them. He stood at the door till they were ready, when I delivered them to him — the prussic acid in the bottle he had brought, the strychnine in a paper, and the opium in a bottle. He paid me for them, and took them away. No one else was in the shop from the time when Palmer and Newton went out, till I delivered the things to him.

When Palmer had left, Newton came in, and we had some conversation. I had at that time been six years in Mr. Hawkins's employment. Palmer had not bought any drugs at the shop for about two years. I know Thirlby, Palmer's assistant. He had started a shop about two years before.

By Lord CAMPBELL — Thirlby was carrying on business as a druggist at the time.

Cross-examined by Mr. *Serjeant Shee*. I did not make entries of any of these things in the books.

Re-examined. When articles are paid for across the counter I am not in the habit of making entries of them in the books.

The *Attorney-General* stated that Dr. Bamford was seriously ill, and unable to attend, but his depositions would be read.

MR. WM. STEVENS, COOK'S STEPFATHER

THE TIMES REPORT

Mr. WILLIAM STEVENS,
examined by the *Attorney-General.*

I have been a merchant in the City, but am now out of business. Was stepfather to the deceased Mr. Cook. I married his father's widow 15 (or 18) years ago, and I have known him intimately ever since. I was made executor to his grandfather's will. I was always on friendly terms with him, and constantly had the care of him. He had property worth altogether about £12,000. He was articled to a solicitor at Worthing, in Sussex,[1] but he did not follow the profession. He had been connected with the turf about three or four years — perhaps not so much. I did everything in my power to withdraw him from that pursuit.

Lord CAMPBELL — But you still remained on friendly terms?

Witness — On affectionate terms. The last time I saw him alive was at the station at Euston-square,[2] about two on the afternoon of the 5th of November. I think he told me he was going to Rugeley, but I am not quite sure; he looked better than I had seen him for a very long time. I was so gratified that I said, "My boy, you look very well now; you don't look anything of an invalid." He said he was quite well, and struck himself on the chest. I think he added he should be quite right if he was happy.

In point of appearance he was not a robust man. His complexion was pale. During the previous winter he had had a sore throat for some months. I first heard of his death on the evening of Wednesday, Nov. 21. Mr. Jones, of Lutterworth, called at my house and informed me of it.

The next day I went down to Lutterworth with Mr. Jones for the purpose of searching for the will and papers. The day after I went to Rugeley. I arrived between twelve and one. I asked to see the body when I got to the inn. I met Palmer in the passage. I had seen him once before, and Mr. Jones introduced me to him. He followed us upstairs to see the body, and removed the sheet from it to rather below the waist. I was much struck with its appearance. I first noticed the tightness of the muscles across the face. There did not appear to me to be any emaciation or disease. We all went down stairs to one of the sitting rooms.

In a short time I said to Palmer, "I hear from Mr. Jones that you know something of my son's affairs. Can you tell me anything about them?" He replied, "Yes; there are £4,000 worth of bills out of his, and I am sorry to say my name is to them; but I have got a paper drawn up by a lawyer and signed by him to show that I never had any

---

[1] A county on the southeastern coast of England, due south of London.
[2] Euston railway station in central London provides passenger service to northwest Britain, including parts of Scotland and Wales.

money from them." I expressed great surprise at this, and said, "I fear there won't be 4,000 shillings to pay you."

"But," I asked, "had he no horses, no property?" Palmer replied, "Yes, he has some horses, but they are mortgaged." I said, "Has he no sporting bets, nor anything of that sort?" He mentioned one debt of £300. I would rather not state the name of the person who owed it. It is a relation of his, not a sporting gentleman. (The witness wrote down the name, and handed it to the counsel on both sides and the Judges.)

Lord CAMPBELL — The name is immaterial.

COOK'S GRAVE

Examination continued. — Palmer said he did not know of any other debt. I said I thought his sporting creditors would have to take his sporting effects, as I should have nothing to do with them. I added, "Well, whether he has left anything or not, poor fellow, he must be buried." Palmer immediately said, "Oh! I will bury him myself, if that is all." I said, "I certainly cannot think of your doing that; I shall do it." Cook's brother-in-law, who had come to meet me, was then present and also expressed a great wish to be allowed to bury him. I said, "No; as his executor, I shall take care of that. I cannot have the funeral immediately, because I intend to bury him in London, in his mother's grave.[3] I shall be sorry to inconvenience the

---

[3] For reasons unknown, Cook was buried in St. Augustine's churchyard in Rugeley. Fletcher adds that a public subscription was raised to pay for his burial.

people here at the inn, but I will get it done as soon as possible." Palmer said, "Oh! that is of no consequence, but the body ought to be fastened up at once." He repeated that observation — "So long as the body is fastened up, it is of no consequence."

While I was talking to Cook's brother-in-law, Palmer and Jones left the room. They returned in about half an hour. I then asked Palmer for the name of some respectable undertaker at Rugeley, that I might at once order a coffin and give directions. He said, "I have been and done that. I have ordered a shell and strong oak coffin." I expressed my surprise. I said, "I did not give you any authority to do so, but I must see the undertaker to let him have my instructions." I think he told me the name of the undertaker. I ordered dinner for myself, my son-in-law, and Jones, and I asked Palmer to come in. We all dined together at the inn at about three. I was going back to London that afternoon.

After dinner, Palmer being still present, I desired Mr. Jones to be so good as to go upstairs and get me Cook's betting-book, or pocket-book, or books or papers that might be there. I had seen him with a betting-book — a small one with clasps. Mr. Jones then left the room, and Palmer followed him. They were away ten minutes.

Mr. Jones said, on their return, "I am very sorry to say I cannot find any betting book or papers." I exclaimed, "No betting-book, Mr. Jones?" Turning towards Palmer, I said, "How is this?" Palmer said, "Oh, it is no manner of use if you find it." I said, "No use, Sir! I am the best judge of that." He again said, "It is of no manner of use." I said, "I am told it is of use. I understand my son won a great deal of money at Shrewsbury, and I ought to know something about it." He replied, "It is of no use, I assure you. When a man dies his bets are done with. Besides, Cook received the greater part of his money on the course at Shrewsbury." I said, "Very well, the book ought to be found, and must be found." Palmer then said, in a quieter tone, "It will be found, no doubt." I again said, "Sir, it shall be found."

I then went to the door, and, calling to the housekeeper, I desired that everything in the bedroom should be locked up, and nothing touched until I returned or sent some one. Before leaving I went upstairs to take a last look at the body. Some servants were in the room, turning over the bed clothes, and also the undertaker. I had given him instructions before dinner to place the body in the coffin. He was standing by the side of the shell. The body was in it, uncovered. I knelt down by the side of the shell, and, taking the right hand of the corpse, I found it clinched. I looked across the body, and saw that the left hand was clinched in the same manner.

I returned to town, and communicated next morning with my solicitor, who gave me a letter to Mr. Gardner, of Rugeley. I returned to Rugeley, where I arrived at eight o'clock next evening (Saturday). I started from Euston-square at two o'clock, and on the platform I met Palmer. He said he had received a telegraphic message summoning him to London after I had left Rugeley. I asked him where Cook's horses were kept. He told me at Eddisford, near Rugeley, and said he would drive me out there if I wished.

When I got to Wolverton, where the train stops, I saw him again in the refreshment-room. I said, "Mr. Palmer this is a very melancholy thing, the death of my poor son happening so suddenly; I think, for the sake of his brother and sister, who are somewhat delicate, it might be desirable for his medical friends to know what his complaints were." Cook had a sister and a half-brother. Palmer replied, "That can be done very well." The bell then rang, and we went to our seats.

He travelled in a different carriage till we reached Rugby where I saw him again in the refreshment room. I said, "Mr. Palmer, as I live at a distance, I think I ought to ask a solicitor at Rugeley to look after my interest." He said, "Oh, yes you might do that. Do you know any solicitor?" I said, "No." I then got some refreshment, and went back to my carriage; I found Palmer sitting there. I had no conversation with him before I reached Rugeley, but continued talking to a lady and gentleman, with whom I had been conversing since I left town.

After we arrived at Rugeley, Palmer said, "Do you know any solicitor here?" I said, "No, I don't; I am a perfect stranger." He said, "I know them all intimately, and I can introduce you[4] to one. When I get home I must have a cup of coffee, and I will then come over and take you all about." I thanked him, as I had done once or twice before, and said I wouldn't trouble him. He repeated his offer. Altering my tone and manner, I said, "Mr. Palmer, if I should call in a solicitor to give me advice, I suppose you will have no objection to answer any question he may put to you?" I altered my tone purposely; I looked steadily at him, but, although the moon was shining, I could not see his features distinctly. He said, with a spasmodic convulsion of the throat, which was perfectly apparent, "Oh, no, certainly not."

At Wolverton I had purposely mentioned my desire that there should be a *post-mortem* examination, and I ought to say that he was quite calm when I mentioned it. After I asked him that question, there was a pause for three or four minutes. He then again proposed to come over to me after he had had his coffee, and I again begged he would not trouble himself.

I went to Mr. Gardner, and then came back to the inn. Palmer came to me and began to talk about the bills. He said, "It is a very unpleasant

---

[4] Palmer probably would have introduced Stevens to Jeremiah Smith, his longtime solicitor. Smith will provide dramatic testimony on the tenth day of the trial.

affair for me." I said, "I think it right to tell you that since I saw you I have had rather a different account of Mr. Cook's affairs." He said, "Oh, indeed! I hope at any rate, they will be settled pleasantly." I said, "His affairs can only be settled in a Court of Chancery." He asked me what friends Mr. Cook visited in the neighbourhood of London, I said, "Several."

The next day (Sunday) I saw him again between five and six in the evening. He said, "You were talking of going to Eddisford. If I were you I would not take a solicitor with me there." I said, "Why not? I shall use my own judgment."

Later in the evening he came again to my room, holding a piece of paper as if he wished to give it me. I went on with my writing and said, "Pray, who is Mr. Smith?" He repeated "Mr. Smith" two or three times, and I said, "I mean a Mr. Smith who sat up with my son one night." He said, "He is a solicitor in the town." I asked if he was in practice. He replied, "Yes." I said, "I ask you the question because, as the betting-book is lost, I should wish to know who has been with the young man." After a pause I said, "Did you attend my son in a medical capacity?" He said, "Oh dear no." I said, "I ask you, because I am determined to have his body examined; and if you had attended him professionally I suppose the gentleman I shall call in would think it proper that you should be present." He asked who was to perform the examination. I said, "I cannot say; I shall not know myself until to-morrow. I think it right to tell you of it; but whether you are present at it or not is a matter of indifference to me."

On the Friday, when Palmer gave orders for the shell, did you perceive any sign of decomposition in the body, or anything which would render its immediate enclosure necessary? — On the contrary, the body did not look to me like a dead body. I was surprised at its appearance.

Cross-examined by Mr. *Serjeant Shee*. The last time Cook stayed at my house was in January or February last year, for about a month. He then had a sore throat. I do not remember that it was continually sore. He had not the least difficulty in swallowing. I did not notice any ulcers about his face. In the spring he complained of being an invalid, and said his medical friends told him that if he was not better in the winter he ought to go to a warm climate. No communication was made to me about insuring his life.

I was dissatisfied about the loss of the betting-book. I desired that everything belonging to the deceased might be locked up. When I returned to Rugeley with Palmer I went to seek for Mr. Gardner. I saw him on the following (Sunday) morning. I have once been in communication with the police officer Field. That was a fortnight or three weeks after my son's death. Field called upon me. I never applied to him.

By Mr. BARON ALDERSON — I never called upon Mr. Bamford, but he dined with me at the Talbot Arms.

MARY KEELING, examined by Mr. *Welsby*.

I am a widow, living at Rugeley. On the morning of Wednesday, the 21st of November last, I was sent for to lay out Cook's body. My sister-in-law went with me. That was about 1 o'clock in the morning.

The body was still warm, but the hands and arms were cold. The body was lying on the back. The arms were crossed before the chest. The head lay a little turned on one side. The body was very stiff indeed. I have laid out many corpses. I never saw one so stiff before. We had difficulty in straightening the arms. We could not keep them straight down to the body. I passed a piece of tape under the back, and tied it round the wrists to fasten the arms down. The right foot turned on one side, outwards. We were obliged to tie both the feet together. The eyes were open. We were a considerable time before we could close them, because the eyelids were very stiff. The hands were closed, and were very stiff.

Palmer was upstairs with us. He lighted me while I took two rings off Cook's fingers. That was off one hand. The fingers were very stiff, and I had difficulty in getting off the rings. I got them off, and when I had done so the hand closed again. I did not see anything of a betting-book, nor any small book like a pocket-book.

Re-examined by the *Attorney-General*. I cannot say how many bodies I have laid out, but I have laid out a great many of all ages. I never knew of the arms being tied before this instance. It is usual to lay the arms by the sides within a few minutes after death.

I was called up at half-past twelve. It was half-past one when I went up stairs to the room where Cook lay. Sometimes the feet of corpses get twisted out; it is then that they are tied. That occurs within about half-an-hour after death. I have never known the eyelid so stiff as in this case. I have put penny pieces on the eyes.[5] In those cases the lids were stiff, but not so stiff as in this instance.

---

[5] The tradition of placing coins on the eyes of the dead has been traced back to ancient Greece, where the coins were intended to pay Charon for ferrying the soul across the River Styx. They were probably placed on the eyes for cosmetic reasons. After death, the liquid inside the eyeballs evaporates, making them sink into the skull and create an unsettling sight. In some places, it was important to keep the eyes closed as the body is moved out of the house, so that its ghost could not find its way back and take away another member of the household.

John Thomas Harland, Physician

JOHN THOMAS HARLAND,
examined by Mr. *Bodkin*.

I am a physician residing at Stafford. On the 26th of November last I went from Stafford to Rugeley to be present at a *post-mortem* examination.

I arrived at Rugeley at ten o'clock in the morning. I called at the house of Mr. Bamford, surgeon. As I went there Palmer joined me in the street. He came from the back of his own house. I had frequently seen him and had spoken to him before. He said, "I am glad that you have come to make a *post-mortem* examination. Some one might have been sent whom I did not know."[6] I said, "What is this case? I hear there is a suspicion of poisoning." He said, "Oh, no; I think not. He

---

[6] Palmer had known Harland for years, raising the suspicion that he knew how to manipulate him.

had an epileptic fit on Monday and Tuesday last, and you will find old disease in the heart and in the head."

We then went together to Mr. Bamford's. I had brought no instruments with me, having only been requested to be present at the examination. Palmer said that he had instruments, and offered to fetch them and lend them to me. He (Palmer) said there was a very queer old man who seemed to suspect him of something, but he did not know what he meant or what he wanted. He also said, "He seems to suspect that I have got the betting-book. Cook had no betting-book that would be of use to anyone."

Mr. Bamford and I then went to the house of Mr. Frere, who is a surgeon at Rugeley. Palmer did not go with us. Thence we went to the Talbot Arms, where the *post-mortem* examination was proceeded with.[7] Mr. Devonshire operated, and Mr. Newton assisted him. There were in the room Mr. Bamford, Palmer, myself, and several other persons. I stood near Mr. Devonshire. The body was very stiff.

By Lord CAMPBELL — It was much stiffer than bodies usually are five or six days after death.

Examination resumed. — The muscles were very highly developed. By that I mean that they were strongly contracted and thrown out. I examined the hands. They were stiff and were firmly closed. The abdominal viscera[8] were first examined.

[At the suggestion of Lord CAMPBELL, the witness read a report[9]

---

[7] At the time there were no official procedures for conducting a post-mortem and preserving forensic evidence. If conducted today, it would be considered slipshod, maybe even a farce. Stevens had asked Harland to conduct it, but the doctor chose instead to observe and take notes. The cutting was done by both Devonshire, an unqualified medical assistant, and Newton, a clerk who dispensed drugs. Dr. Salt was present, but he had no experience in pathology and had never conducted a post-mortem. No record was kept of who was in the room. There was no official report signed by the attending physicians, just Harland's report sent to Stevens, and a doctor with personal ties to the deceased (and who might have been suspected of doing the deed) was allowed to participate! Only one glass jar was provided to hold all the organs, and instead of preserving the stomach contents separately, the stomach was cut open and its contents mixed with fecal matter from the intestines. Under these circumstances, it was a miracle that Dr. Taylor found anything at all!

[8] The organs in the abdominal cavity below the diaphragm, including the stomach, liver, intestines, spleen, and pancreas.

[9] From the Old Bailey transcript:

"Post-mortem examination of John Parsons Cook, Esq., Rugeley, Nov. 26th, 1855. — The body is moderately muscular; the back and most depending parts of the body are discoloured from blood having gravitated there. Pupils of the eyes neither contracted nor dilated. No serum in the peritoneal cavity; the peritoneum slightly injected; no adhesions — stomach as now exposed is rather distended, and the course of some of its vessels is which he prepared on the day on which this *post-mortem* examination took place, November 26, 1855, and transmitted to Mr. Stevens, the stepfather of the deceased. This report described the state of the various internal organs as being perfectly healthy and natural. The material statements were all repeated in the subsequent examination of the witness. After reading the report, the witness continued:—]

The abdominal viscera were in a perfectly healthy state. They were taken out of the body. We examined the liver. It was healthy. The lungs were healthy, but contained a good deal of blood. Not more than would be accounted for by gravitation[10] after death. We examined the head. The brain was quite healthy. There was no extravasation[11] of blood, and no serum.[12] There was nothing which, in my judgment, could cause pressure. The heart was contracted, and contained no blood. That was the result not of disease, but of spasmodic action. At the larger end of the stomach there were numerous small yellowish-white spots, about the size of mustard

---

seen beneath the peritoneal coat. The stomach, on being removed, contained some ounces of a brown fluid — the large curvature resting on the spleen was of dark colour. The internal mucous membrane of the stomach was without ulceration or excoriation. On the inferior surface of the cardiac extremity were minute yellowish-white specks, of the size of mustard seeds. The small intestines contained some bilious fluid in the duodenum; they were altogether small and contracted, but presented no other remarkable appearance. The large intestines contained some fluid feculent matter. The spleen and pancreas seemed to be healthy. The right kidney was rather large, soft, and its whole texture full of blood; there were no granulations, nor coagulable lymph. The left kidney was of less size, but its appearance was the same as the right, in less degree. Between the base of the tongue and epiglottis were numerous enlarged follicles like warts. The œsophagus and epiglottis were natural. The larynx was stained with dark blood, which had penetrated through all its tissues. The lungs contained much fluid blood in their posterior parts, which would be accounted for by gravitation. The lungs everywhere contained air. The pleura were healthy, the heart was of natural size, and in every part healthy. In the aorta, immediately behind the valves, were some yellow-greyish-white patches like soft cartilage. The heart presented no remarkable appearance. The skull was of natural thickness. The dura mater had its arteries injected with blood. There was no excess of serum, nor adhesions. The pia mater and arachnoid, as well as the brain, appeared altogether healthy; all the blood was fluid and uncoagulated. Signed, J. T. HARLAND, M.D."

[10] The effect of gravity on an object.

[11] A forcing of fluid, such as blood, from the body or an organ.

[12] No blood was forced out of the veins and into the brain tissue. The serum is the thin watery part of the blood. After death, the heavier red blood cells separate from the serum and settle at the lowest points of the body. This process is called lividity.

seeds. They would not at all account for death. I doubt whether they would have any effect upon the health. I think they were mucous follicles. The kidneys were full of blood, which had gravitated there. They had no appearance of disease. The blood was in a fluid state. That is not usual. It is found so in some cases of sudden death, which are of rare occurrence. The lower part of the spinal cord was not very closely examined. We examined the upper part of that cord. It presented a perfectly natural appearance.

On a subsequent day, I think the 25th of January, it was thought right to exhume the body, that the spinal cord might be more carefully examined. I was present at that examination. The lower part of the spinal cord was then minutely examined. A report was made of that examination.

This report was put in, and was read by the witness.[13] It

---

[13] From the Old Bailey transcript, subdivided by the editor into paragraphs:

"Report of an examination of the spinal cord of the exhumed body of John Parsons Cook, Esq., on Friday, Jan. 25th, 1856. We, the undersigned, were shown the corpse which, to the certain knowledge of one of us, namely, Mr. Bamford, was that of the late John Parsons Cook, Esq., who died at Rugeley, Staffordshire, Nov. 20th, 1855, and were requested by the officers of the Crown to institute an examination into the condition of the spinal cord.

"The body was enclosed in both a shell and a coffin, and was found lying on its back. The cranium, thorax, and abdomen had been opened at a previous examination, and decomposition had proceeded rapidly in these parts in consequence of the admission of air. There was much rigidity of some of the muscles of the body, considerable force being required to flex the legs or to alter the position of the different limbs. The thumbs and fingers were partially but firmly flexed; the toes as firmly extended, and the inner edge of each foot drawn up by the tibiales antici et postici, as in talipes," (Old Bailey transcriber's note: that is a species of club foot,) "the postici slightly predominating, so as to point the toes downwards. The muscles of the neck and trunk were relaxed.

"We observed much lividity of the integuments of the dorsal surface of the body, putrefaction having softened and discoloured them. A longitudinal incision having been made along the course of, and down to, the spines of the vertebra, from occiput to sacrum, the muscles were reflected on either side from off the vertebral laminæ, these muscles presenting no other evidence of putrefaction than some softening but slight sero-sanguineous infiltration. Sawing through the laminá, we removed the spinet of the vertebras, and so opened the spinal canal in its whole length. These portions of the posterior wall of the canal were successively and minutely examined, but no roughness, spicula, or other irregularity could be discovered. The medulla spinalis now lay beneath our view, enclosed in its fibrous sheath, and surrounded on all sides by loose areolar tissue and fat, traversed in all directions by veins. This areolar tissue had not the colour ordinarily possessed by it in the recent state, but was of a livid hue, or of deep prune juice colour. This was, doubtless, owing to its being saturated, as a sponge would be, with the sanguineo-serous fluid which occupied the canal to a considerable extent, having gravitated to this dependent part of the body subsequent to its death.

"The chest having been raised on a large block, so as to give a proper curve to the dorsal portion of the spine, this fluid had mainly gravitated to the lumbar region; but the areolar tissue, lining the walls of the vertebral canal, was throughout its whole length infiltrated, saturated, and stained with this bloody serum. We now divided the dura mater, or medullary sheath, longitudinally, in its whole length, reflecting it off the cord on either side, a very small quantity of sanguinolent serum had gravitated within the sheath to the lumbar region, where it was lying staining the canal equina. The arachnoid was glistening and perfectly transparent. The medulla oblongata had been separated from the medulla spinalis on a level with the atlas, and the medulla spinalis, as it lay in situ, presented a most healthy appearance, smooth, glistening, and of a greyish-white colour; presenting, in fact, no departure from its usual normal character and condition. The post roots of the spinal nerves were regular in their origin and course, and when traced to their points of emergence from the canal exhibit no abnormal appearance whatsoever; they had a somewhat darker grey colour than had the cord itself.

"The cord was next raised from its sheath, and its nerves being one by one divided, it was removed from the canal, its anterior surface and the anterior roots of the spinal nerves being now scrutinized, they appeared in every way as healthy and free from disease as did the posterior. Stains or discolorations of the cords or nerves were readily removed by the effusion of water. There was no appearance of fulness of the veins of the spinal cord, or its members; the upper part of the cord, being more exposed by the previous opening of the skull, was softened by decomposition, but, upon examination, neither it nor any other part of the spinal cord showed any signs of disease. The proper envelope of the cord contained the nervous matter in a pulpy state, being softened by decomposition.

"After the removal of the cord, its fibrous sheath and osseous canal were carefully examined by the eye and finger, cast along its whole length, and this proved the absence of all unnatural appearance or condition, roughness, irregularity, fracture, dislocation, exostosis, or spicula of bone, except at a point opposite the third and fourth cervical vertebrá where both the eye and the finger detected a slightly granular roughness of the arachnoid surface of the dura mater. Upon closer examination this slight roughness was found to depend upon the presence beneath the arachnoid of some twenty or thirty minute irregularly shaped granules, of some hard material barely raising the surface in a perceptible degree, they were found scattered over a space of less than an inch square. No more could be found elsewhere, each granule was gritty and hard under the point of the scalpel, and under the microscope had an appearance rather of calcareous than of osseous matter. The dura mater of the brain was next carefully examined, but nothing abnormal was found; no spiculae nor granules such as described above were detected. We believe that these granules could have no connection whatsoever with the death of deceased.

"Deduction: The only conclusion, therefore, at which we could arrive after this examination was a negative one. That there was nothing in the condition of described minutely the appearance and condition of the spinal cord and its envelopes, and concluded with this statement:— "There is nothing in the condition of the spinal cord or its envelopes to account for death; nothing but the most normal and healthy state, allowance being made for the lapse of time since the death of the deceased."

Examination resumed. — I am still of the opinion that there was nothing in the appearance of the spine to account for the death of the deceased, and nothing of an unusual kind which might not be referred to changes after death. When the stomach and intestines were removed from the body on the occasion of the first examination, they were separately emptied into a jar, and were afterwards placed in it. Mr. Devonshire and Mr. Newton removed them from the body. They were the only two who operated.

At that time the prisoner was standing on the right of Mr. Newton. While Mr. Devonshire was opening the stomach, a push was given by Palmer, which sent Mr. Newton against Mr. Devonshire, and shook some of the contents of the stomach into the body. I thought a joke was passing among them, and said, "Don't do that."

By Lord CAMPBELL — Might not Palmer have been impelled by some one outside him? — There was no one who could have impelled him.

What did you observe Palmer do? — I saw Mr. Newton and Mr. Devonshire pushed together, and Palmer was over them. He was smiling at the time.

Examination continued. — After this interruption the opening of the stomach was pursued. The stomach contained about three ounces of a brownish fluid. There was nothing particular in that. Palmer was looking on, and said, "They won't hang us yet." He said that to Mr. Bamford in a loud whisper. That remark was made upon his own observation of the stomach.

The stomach, after being emptied, was put into the jar. The intestines were then examined, but nothing particular was found in them. They were contracted and very small. The viscera, with their contents, as taken from the body, were placed in the jar, which was then covered over with two bladders,[14] which were tied and sealed. I

---

the spinal cord or its envelopes to account for death; nothing but the most normal and healthy state, allowance being made for the lapse of time since the death of deceased. J. T. Harland, M.D., William Bamford, apothecary, D. Henry Monckton, M.D."

[14] Animal bladders, usually pigs, were used to seal specimen jars. To do it correctly required skill and careful attention to detail. According to "The Medico-Chiurgical Review & Journal of Practical Medicine" (Vol. 25, 1836), the bladder had to be soaked in water for a week to ten days then carefully dried. The specimen jar needed to be filled to the brim with spirits and the rim wiped dry. The bladder was laid on top, inner side down, then tied off

tied and sealed them.

After I had done so, I placed the jar upon the table by the body. Palmer was then moving about the room. In a few moments I missed the jar from where I had placed it. During that time my attention had been withdrawn by the examination. On missing the jar I called out, "Where's the jar?" and Palmer from the other end of the room, said, "It is here; I thought it would be more convenient for you to take away." There was a door at the end of the room where he was. He was within a yard or two of that door, and about 24 feet from the table on which the body was lying. [Before making this last statement the witness referred to a plan of the room which was put in by the Attorney-General.]

The door near which Palmer was standing was not the one by which he had entered the room. I called to Palmer, "Will you bring it here?" I went from the table and met Palmer half-way, coming with the jar. The jar had since I last saw it been cut through both bladders The cut was hardly an inch long. It had been done with a sharp instrument. I examined the cut. The edges were quite clean. No part of the contents of the jar could have passed through it. Finding this cut, I said, "Here is a cut; who has done this?" Palmer and Mr. Devonshire and Mr. Newton all said that they had not done it, and nothing more was said about it.

When I was about to remove the jar from the room the prisoner asked me what I was going to do with it. I said I should take it to Mr. Frere's. He said, "I had rather you would take it to Stafford than take it there." I made no answer that I remember.

I took it to Mr. Frere's house. After doing so I returned to the Talbot Arms. I left the jar in Mr. Frere's hall, tied and sealed. Immediately upon finding the slit in the cover I cut the strings and altered the bladders, so that the slits were not over the top of the jar. I resealed them.

After going to Mr. Frere's I went to the Talbot Arms. I went into the yard to order my carriage, and while I was waiting for it the prisoner came across to me. He asked me what I had done with the jar. I told him that I had left it at Mr. Frere's. He inquired what would be done with it, and I said that it would go either to Birmingham or London that night for examination. I do not recollect that he made any reply.

When I re-covered the jar, I tied each cover separately, and sealed it with my own seal. During the first *post-mortem* examination there were several Rugeley persons present, but I believe no one on

---

with twine. The extra material was trimmed away and the bladder pressed onto the rim. When it dried, it created a seal that kept air out and the contents from decaying.

behalf of the prisoner.[15] At the second examination there was some one there on behalf of Palmer.

Cross-examined by Mr. *Serjeant Shee*. In the course of the *post-mortem* examination Palmer said, "They won't hang us yet." I am not sure whether that observation was addressed to Dr. Bamford, or whether he prefaced it by the word "Doctor." I think that he first said it to Dr. Bamford in a loud whisper, and afterwards repeated it to several persons.

I had said to him that I had heard that there was a suspicion of poisoning.

I made notes in pencil at the time of the *post-mortem* and I wrote a more formal report from those notes as soon as I got home. The original pencil notes are destroyed. I sent the fair copy to Mr. Stevens, Cook's father-in-law, the same evening. They were not produced before the coroner.

At the base of the tongue of the deceased I observed some enlarged mucous follicles; they were not pustules containing matter, but enlarged mucous follicles of long standing. There were a good many of them, but I do not suppose that they would occasion much inconvenience. They might cause some degree of pain, but I think that it would be slight. I do not believe that they were enlarged glands.

I should not say that deceased's lungs were diseased, although they were not in their normal state. The lungs were full of blood and the heart empty. I had no lens at the *post-mortem*, but I made an examination which was satisfactory to me, without one.

The brain was carefully taken out; the membranes and external parts were first examined, and thin slices of about a quarter of an inch in thickness were taken off and subjected to separate examination. I think that by that means we should have discovered disease if any had existed; and if there had been any indication of disease I should have examined it more carefully.

I examined the spinal cord as far down as possible, and if there had been any appearance of disease I should have opened the canal. There was no appearance of disease however. We opened down to the first vertebra. If we had found a softening of the spinal cord I do not think that it would have been sufficient to have caused Mr. Cook's death; certainly not. A softening of the spinal cord would not produce tetanus — it might produce paralysis. I do not think, as a medical man investigating the cause of death, that it was necessary carefully to examine the spinal cord. I do not know who suggested that there should be an examination of the spinal cord two months after death. There were

---

[15] Palmer was in attendance along with his solicitor and friend Jeremiah Smith, who will later commit perjury at the trial, and the postmaster Sam Cheshire, who ended up doing time for opening letters on his behalf.

some appearances of decomposition when we examined the spinal cord, but I do not think that there was sufficient to interfere with our examination.

I examined the body to ascertain if there was any trace of venereal disease. I did find certain indications of that description, and the marks of an old excoriation, which were cicatriced over.[16]

Re-examined by the *Attorney-General*. There were no indications of wounds or sores such as could by possibility produce tetanus. There was no disease of the lungs to account for death. The heart was healthy, and its emptiness I attribute to spasmodic action. The heart being empty, of course death ensued. The convulsive spasmodic action of the muscles of the body, which was deposed to yesterday by Mr. Jones, would, in my judgment, occasion the emptiness of the heart.

There was nothing whatever in the brain to indicate the presence of any disease of any sort; but if there had been, I never heard or read of any disease of the brain ever producing tetanus.

There was no relaxation of the spinal cord which would account for the symptoms accompanying Mr. Cook's death as they have been described. In fact, there was no relaxation of the spinal cord at all, and there is no disease of the spinal cord with which I am acquainted which would produce tetanus.

Mr. CHARLES JAMES DEVONSHIRE, examined by Mr. *Huddleston*.

[EDITOR'S NOTE: Devonshire was undergraduate of the University of London and late assistant to Dr. Monckton.]

I made the first *post-mortem* examination on the body of Mr. Cook in November last. The body was pale and stiff; the hands were clinched, and the mouth was contorted.

I opened the body. The liver was very healthy. The heart also seemed healthy, but it was perfectly empty. The lungs contained a considerable quantity of dark fluid blood. The blood was perfectly fluid. The brain was healthy throughout. I examined the medulla oblongata[17] and about a quarter or half an inch of the spinal cord. It was perfectly sound. I took out the stomach and opened it with a pair of scissors. I put the contents in a jar, which was taken to Mr. Frere's, the surgeon. I obtained the jar from Mr. Frere's on Monday in the same state as it was before, and I gave it Mr. Boycott, clerk to Mr.

---

[16] *Excoriation:* An abrading or wearing off of the skin. *Cicatriced:* Healed over.
[17] The part of the spinal cord that extends into the skull.

Gardner the attorney.[18]

I examined the body again on the 29th, and took out the liver, kidneys, spleen, and some blood. I put them in a stone jar, which I covered with washleather[19] and brown paper, and sealed up. I delivered that jar also to Boycott. Palmer said at the examination that we should find syphilis upon the deceased. I therefore examined the parts carefully and found no indications of the sort. I also took out the throat. The papilla[20] were slightly enlarged, but they were natural, and one of the tonsils was shrunk.

Cross-examined by Mr. *Grove*, Q.C. Tetanic convulsions are considered to proceed from derangement of the spine and from complaints that affect the spine. These derangements are not always capable of being detected by examination. In examining the body of a person supposed to have died from tetanus the spinal cord would be the first organ looked to. About half an inch of the spinal cord, exterior to the aperture of the cranium,[21] was examined on the first occasion. I was not present when the granules were discovered on the second examination.

The learned counsel was proceeding to cross-examine this witness upon some minute points of a scientific nature, when

Baron ALDERSON, interposing, said — When you have all the medical men in London here, you had better not examine an Undergraduate of the University of London upon such points, I should think.

Dr. HENRY MONCKTON,
examined by the *Attorney-General*.

I am a physician in practice, and reside at Rugeley. On the 28th of January I made a *post-mortem* examination of the spinal cord and marrow of the deceased, J.P. Cook. I found the muscles of the trunk in a state of laxity, which I should attribute to the decay of the body which had set in; but that laxity would not be at all inconsistent, in my opinion, with a great rigidity of those muscles at the time of death. The muscles of the arms and legs were in a state of rigidity, but they were

---

[18] In the Old Bailey transcript, Devonshire also said: "As I was opening the stomach there was a pressure, or push from behind, and I went a little forward, but I did not pay any attention to it — I was carried a little forward by it. (Q. What was the effect of that; did anything happen to the contents of the stomach?) A. I cannot say if any escaped — I punctured the anterior surface of the stomach, and some of the contents fell out, about a spoonful went into the jar."

[19] A piece of pliable leather made from a chamois, sheepskin or lambskin.

[20] A small protuberance from an organ. One example would be the taste buds on the tongue.

[21] The part of the skull that encloses the brain.

not more rigid than usual in dead bodies. The muscles of the arms had partially flexed the fingers of the hand. The feet were turned inwards to a much greater extent than usual. I carefully examined the spinal cord. The body was then in such a condition as to enable me to make a satisfactory examination of it; and if prior to death there had been any disease of a normal character on the spinal cord and marrow, I should have had no difficulty in detecting it. There was no disease. I discovered certain granules upon it. It is difficult to account for their origin, but they are frequently found in persons of advanced age. I never knew them to occasion sudden death. I agree entirely in the evidence which has been given by Dr. Harland.

This witness was not cross-examined.

Mr. JOHN BOYCOTT, examined by Mr. *Welsby*.

I am clerk to Messrs. Landor, Gardner, and Landor, attorneys at Rugeley. On the 26th of last November I received a jar from Mr. Devonshire, covered with leather and brown paper, and sealed up. I took it to London, and delivered it on the next day to Dr. Taylor at Guy's Hospital. On a subsequent day I received another jar, similarly secured, from Mr. Devonshire, and I also brought that to London and delivered it to Dr. Taylor. I was not present at the inquest on Cook's body, and did not fetch Newton to be examined there. On Tuesday last, when at the Rugeley station, previous to my departure for London, Newton came and made a communication to me. He knew that Mr. Gardner was not there; and when we reached London I took him to Mr. Gardner, and I heard him make the same communication to Mr. Gardner which he had made before to me.

This witness was not cross-examined.

JAMES MYATT, examined by Mr. *James*.

In November last I was postboy at the Talbot Arms at Rugeley. I know Palmer, the prisoner, and I remember Monday, the 26th of November last I was ordered on that night, a little after five o'clock, to take Mr. Stevens to the Stafford station in a fly.

Before I started I went home to get my tea, and on returning from my tea to the Talbot Arms I met the prisoner. He asked me if I was going to drive Mr. Stevens to Stafford. I told him I was.

What did he say to you then? — He asked me if I would upset them.

JAMES MYATT, POSTBOY AT THE TALBOT ARMS

"Them?" Had anything been said about a jar? — He said he supposed I was going to take the jar.

What did you say then? — I said I believed I was.

What did he say after that? — He said "Do you think you could upset them?"

What answer did you make? — I told him "No."

Did he say anything more? — He said, "If you could there's a £10 note for you." (Sensation.)

What did you say to that? — I told him I could not. I then said, "I must go, the horses are in the fly ready for us to start." I do not recollect that he said anything more about the jar. I said, that if I didn't go somebody else would go. He told me not to be in a hurry, for if anybody else went he would pay me. I saw him again next morning, when I was going to breakfast. He asked me then who went with the fly. I told him Mr. Stevens and, I believed, one of Mr. Gardner's clerks.

Cross-examined by Mr. *Serjeant Shee*. Were not the words that Palmer used — "I wouldn't mind giving £10 to break Stevens's neck?" I don't recollect the words "break his neck."

Well, "upset him." Did he say, "I wouldn't mind giving £10 to upset him?" — Yes; I believe those were the words. I do not know that Palmer appeared to have been drinking. I don't recollect that he had. I can't say that he used any epithet, applied to Stevens — he said it was a humbugging concern altogether — or something of that. I don't recollect that he said Stevens was a troublesome fellow, and very inquisitive. I don't remember anything more than I have said. I do not know whether there was more than one jar.

SAMUEL CHESHIRE, LATE POSTMASTER AT RUGELEY

SAMUEL CHESHIRE, examined by Mr. *James*.

He is an extremely respectable looking man, above the middle age, and was dressed in black. He deposed as follows: — I was for upwards of eight years postmaster at Rugeley. I come now from Newgate, where I am under sentence for having "read" a letter. [The question was "opened" a letter.] I "confessed" to having done so. [The question was "Did you plead guilty to that charge?"] I knew the prisoner William Palmer very well — we were schoolfellows together, and I have been three or four times in my life at races with him. I never made a bet but once in my life; but I was very intimate with Palmer.

THE POST-OFFICE, RUGELEY

I accompanied him to Shrewsbury races in November, 1855. I returned to Rugeley on Tuesday, the 13th, the same day on which Polestar won the handicap.

On Saturday, the 17th, I went to see Mr. Cook, who was in bed at the Talbot Arms Hotel at Rugeley. I lived at the post-office, which was 300 or 400 yards from Palmer's house.

On Tuesday evening, the 20th, I received a message from Palmer, asking me to go over to him, and to take a receipt stamp with me. In consequence of that message I went to Palmer's house, and I took a receipt stamp, as requested. When I reached Palmer's I found him in his sitting-room. He said that he wanted me to write out a cheque, and he produced a copy from which he said I was to write. I copied the document which he produced. He said that it related to money which Mr. Cook owed him; and he asked me to write it because, he said, Cook was too ill to do it, and Weatherby would know his (Palmer's) handwriting. He said that when I had written it he would take it over to Mr. Cook to sign. I then wrote as he requested me, and I left the paper with Palmer.

Mr. Weatherly was here called in order to trace this document. In answer to Mr. James, he said,— I am secretary to the Jockey Club,[22] and my establishment is in Birmingham. I keep a sort of banking account, and receive stakes for gentlemen who own racers and bet. I knew the deceased John Parsons Cook, who had an account of that nature with me. I knew Palmer slightly; he had no such account with me. On the 21st of November I received a cheque or order upon our house for £350. It came by post. I sent it back two days afterwards — on Friday, the 23rd. I sent it back by post to Palmer, the prisoner, at Rugeley.

Boycott was recalled, and proved that he had served notices upon the prisoner and upon Mr. Smith, his attorney, to produce the "cheque or order" referred to; and that it had not been produced in pursuance of those notices.

Prisoner's counsel did not now produce it.[23]

Examination of SAMUEL CHESHIRE continued.—

As far as I can remember, what I wrote was, "Pay to Mr. William Palmer the sum of £350, and place it to my account." I do not remember whether I put any date to it. I left it with Palmer, and went away. That was on Tuesday.

On the Thursday or Friday following Palmer sent again for me. I do not remember what day it was, but it was after I had heard of the death of Mr. Cook at the Talbot Arms. I went to Palmer in the evening between six and seven o'clock, in consequence of his having sent for me.

When I arrived I found him in the kitchen, and he immediately went out, and shortly after returned with a quarto sheet[24] of paper in his hand. He gave me a pen, and asked me to sign something. I asked what it was, and he replied, "You know that Cook and I have had dealings together; and this is a document which he gave me some days ago, and I want you to witness it." I said, "What is it about?" He

---

[22] An aristocratic gentleman's club, founded officially in 1750 around the members' interest in horseracing. In 1803, it published its rules for racing. By 1807, it was deciding cases brought to it and publishing the results. It also began sponsoring major races such as the 2,000 Guineas in competition with the Oakes and Derby. By the 1850s, the club was recognized by many local meetings as the ultimate authority on the conduct of races.

[23] According to another transcript, Shee "only shook his head, a painful silence reigning in Court."

[24] A sheet of paper 10 inches by 8 inches, suitable for sending letters.

said, "Some business that I have joined him in, and which was all for Mr. Cook's benefit; and this is the document stating so."

I just cast my eye over the paper. It was quarto post paper of a yellow description. I looked at the writing, and I believed that it was Mr. Palmer's. When he asked me to sign it, I told him that I could not, as I might perhaps be called upon to give evidence on the matter at some future day. I told him that I had not seen Mr. Cook sign it, and I also said that I thought the Post-office authorities would not approve my mixing myself up in a matter which might occasion my absence from my duties to give evidence. In fact, I did not give any exact reasons for refusing to sign it.

Palmer said it did not matter, as he dared say they would not object to Mr. Cook's signature. I left the paper with Palmer, and went away. I believe that there was a stamp upon it. I did not read it all, but I cast my eye down it. [Notices had also been served upon the prisoner and his attorney to produce this document, but it had not been produced.]

Witness continued. — I remember the effect of it — it was that certain bills — the dates and amounts of which were quoted, although I cannot recollect them now — were all for Mr. Cook's benefit and not for Mr. Palmer's. Those were not the exact words, but that was the purport of them. I know that the amounts were large, although I do not remember them all. I remember, however, that one was for £1,000, and another for £500. There was a signature to that document. It was either "J.P." or "J.P. Cook." I don't think the word "Parsons" was written; but either "J.P." or "J.P. Cook."

Palmer was in the habit of calling at the Post-office for letters addressed to his mother, who resided at Rugeley. I cannot remember that during the months of October and November, 1855, I gave him any letters addressed to his mother; nor can I say whether in those months I have given him letters addressed to Mr. Cook; but Cook has taken Palmer's letters and Palmer has taken Cook's letters.

I remember the inquest upon Cook. I saw Palmer frequently while that inquest was going on. He came down to me on the Sunday evening previous to the 5th of December — the date to which the inquest was adjourned — and asked me if I saw or heard of anything fresh to let him know. I guessed what he wanted, and thought that he wanted to tempt me to open a letter. I therefore told him that I could not open a letter. He said that he did not want me to do anything to injure myself. I believe that was all that passed upon that occasion.

The letter, for reading which I am now under sentence of punishment, was from Dr. Alfred Taylor, of London, to Mr. Gardner, the solicitor, of Rugeley. I read part of the letter, and told Palmer as much as I remembered of it. This took place on the morning of the 5th of December. I told Palmer that the letter mentioned that no traces of strychnine were to be found. I can't call to mind what else I told him. He said he knew there would be no traces of poison, for he was perfectly innocent. The letter I hold in my hand, signed "W.P.," and addressed to "W.W. Ward, Esq., Coroner," I believe to be in the prisoner's handwriting.

CAPTAIN JOHN HAINES HATTON, examined by Mr. *James*.

I am chief constable of Stafford. The letter now produced I obtained from the coroner.

The Clerk of Arraigns read the letter in question. It bore no date, and was to the following effect:—[25]

"MY DEAR SIR. — I am sorry to tell you that I am still confined to my bed. I don't think it was mentioned at the inquest yesterday that Cook was taken ill on Sunday and Monday night, in the same way as he was on the Tuesday, when he died. The chambermaid at the Crown Hotel (Masters's) can prove this. I also believe that a man by the name of Fisher is coming down to prove he received some money at Shrewsbury. Now, here he could only pay Smith £10 out of £41 he owed him. Had you not better call Smith to prove this? And, again, whatever Professor Taylor may say to-morrow, he wrote from London last Tuesday night to Gardner to say, 'We (and Dr. Rees) have this day finished our analysis, and find no traces of either strychnia, prussic acid, or opium.' What can beat this from a man like Taylor, if he says what he has already said, and Dr. Harland's evidence? Mind you, I know and saw it in black and white what Taylor said to Gardner; but this is strictly private and confidential, but it is true. As regards his betting-book, I know nothing of it, and it is of no good to any one. I hope the verdict to-morrow will be that he died of natural causes, and thus end it. — Ever

MR. HATTON, CHIEF OF STAFFORDSHIRE CONSTABULARY

---

[25] Accompanying this letter was a £10 note.

yours, W.P."

CHESHIRE cross-examined
by Mr. *Serjeant Shee*.

I knew Cook very well. I did not know his handwriting. I have seen it, but am not sufficiently familiar with it to be able to identify it. I have seen him write. When I refused to sign the document which Palmer presented to me for signature he observed, "Oh, it is no matter. I dare say they will not call in question Mr. Cook's signature."

What Palmer asked me was, "Whether I had seen or heard anything?" I said that I had seen something, but that it would be wrong for me to tell him what. He then inquired what I had seen. I think the phrase he used, in speaking of his own innocence, was that he was "as innocent as a baby."

I remember having been told by Palmer, the Saturday before Cook died, that the latter was very ill. On that day I saw Cook. He was ill and in bed. I saw Palmer about midday of Wednesday, the second day of the Shrewsbury races. I saw him at Rugeley on that day.

To Mr. *James* — The duration of the journey from Stafford to Shrewsbury is upwards of an hour.

ELLIS CRISP, examined by Mr. *James*.

I am inspector of police at Rugeley. On the 17th December I assisted in searching the prisoner's house. There was a sale of his furniture, &c, on the 5th January. The book now produced I found in his house, and took it away. It was being sold, and I took it away. (A laugh.)

Cross-examined by Mr. *Serjeant Shee*. It was brought out at the sale with a lot of other books. There were several medical books in the house. There was no attempt to conceal the volume I seized.

The Clerk of Arraigns read from the book referred to this sentence, proved by the witness Boycott to be in Palmer's writing:—
"Strychnia kills by causing tetanic fixing of the respiratory muscles."

DANIEL SCULLY BURGEN,
examined by Mr. *James*.

This manuscript book I found in the prisoner's house on the 16th or 17th of December. I am an inspector of police in Staffordshire.

The *Attorney-General* read an extract from the book in question.

It related to strychnine, and alluded to the mode of its operation.[26]

Lord CAMPBELL — That may be merely a passage extracted from an article on "strychnine" in some encyclopædia.

The *Attorney-General* — No doubt it may. I put it in for what it is worth.

JULIET ELIZABETH HAWKES,
examined by Mr. *Huddleston*.

I keep a boarding-house at 7, Beaufort-buildings, Strand. I know Palmer. He was at my house on the 1st of December last. He asked my porter to buy some game and fish for him. I purchased some fowls for him on the 1st of December. They consisted of a turkey and a brace of pheasants. The porter purchased the fish. I packed these things up in a hamper. I had no conversation with Palmer about these things. I bought them by Palmer's order, conveyed through the porter. I sent them somewhere. I directed them, myself, and gave them to the porter, who carried them to the railway station. I have never been paid for them. Palmer came to my house on the evening of that day, but I did not see him. The direction on the hamper was "W.W. Ward, Esq., Stoke-upon-Trent, Staffordshire."

GEORGE HERRING,
examined by Mr. *Welsby*.

I live near New Cross,[27] and am independent. I knew Cook, and met him at Shrewsbury races last November. I put up at the Raven. He appeared in his usual health. I saw him between 6 and 7 on Wednesday, the second day of the races. I had a private room, with Mr. Fisher, Mr. Reed, and Mr. T. Jones. It was next to the room occupied by Cook and Palmer.

On Thursday (the day following) I saw Cook. I do not know that at that time he had any money with him, but I saw him with Bank of England and provincial bank-notes[28] on Wednesday. He unfolded

---

[26] From the Notable British Trials transcript:
"Nux vomica; seeds of strychnine, like an orange; a certain quantity of seed contains thirty-four grains of strychnia; one grain will give a bitter taste to 80 lbs. of water; one grain of strychnia is equal to six grains of bruchia (brucin); it kills by producing tetanic contractions in the respiratory muscles."

[27] A ward in the inner-city borough of Lewisham, in South East London, south of the Thames.

[28] Privately owned banks in Great Britain and Ireland were allowed to issue

them on his knee in twos and threes. There was a considerable number of notes. He showed me at Shrewsbury his betting-book. It contained entries of bets made on the Shrewsbury races.

On Monday, the 19th of November, I received a letter from Palmer. I have it here —

The Clerk of Arraigns read the letter:—

"DEAR SIR,— I shall feel much obliged if you will give me a call at 7, Beaufort-buildings, Strand, on Monday, about half-past 2.

"I am, dear Sir, very truly yours,

"W. PALMER."

Examination continued — I received this letter on Monday, and called at Beaufort-buildings that same day at half-past 2 exactly. I found Palmer there. He asked me what I would take? I declined to take anything. I then asked him how Mr. Cook was? He said, "He's all right; his physician gave him a dose of calomel, and advised him not to come out, it being a damp day." I don't know which term he used, "damp" or "wet."

He then went on to say, in the same sentence, "What I want to see you about is settling his account." While he was speaking he took out half a sheet of note paper from his pocket, and it was open when he had finished the sentence. He held it up and said, "This is it." I rose to take it. He said, "You had better take its contents down; this will be a check against you." At the same time he pointed to some paper lying on the table. I wrote on that paper from his dictation. I have here the paper which I so wrote. [The witness read the document in question, which contained instructions as to certain payments he should make out of moneys to be received by him at Tattersall's on account of the Shrewsbury races.]29

Palmer then said that I had better write out a cheque for Pratt and Padwick — for the former £450, and for the latter £350, and send them at once. I told him I had only one form of cheque in my pocket. He said I could easily fill up a draft on half a sheet of paper. I refused to comply with his request, as I had not as yet received the money. He replied that it would be all right, for that Cook would not deceive me. He wished me particularly so to pay Mr. Pratt the £450. His words, as nearly as I can remember them were, "You must pay Pratt, as it is for

---

their own banknotes. The Bank Charter Act in 1844 gave that power to the Bank of England, but allowed existing banks to continue issuing notes. Mergers and closures gradually reduced their numbers until 1921, when the practice was halted in England. Today, three banks in Scotland and four in Northern Ireland are still permitted to issue banknotes.

29 It should be noted that the only way that Palmer would have known the details of Cook's winnings is if he had access to the betting-book.

a bill of sale on the mare." I don't know whether he said "a bill of sale," or a "joint bill of sale."

He told me he was going to see both Pratt and Padwick, to tell them that I would send on the money. Previous to his saying this, I told him that if he would give me the address of Pratt and Padwick, I would call on them, after I had got the money from Tattersall's, and give it to them.

He then asked me what was between us? There were only a few pounds between us, and, after we had had some conversation on the point, he took out of his pocket a £50 Bank of England note. He required £29 out of the note, and I was not able to give it; but he said that if I gave him a cheque it would answer as well. I gave him a cheque for £20 and nine sovereigns.

When I was going away I do not remember that he said anything about my paying the money to Pratt and Padwick. He said on parting, "When you have settled this account, write down word to either me or Cook." I turned round and said, "I shall certainly write to Mr. Cook." I said so because I thought that I was settling Mr. Cook's account. He said, "It don't much matter which you write to." I said, "If I address 'Mr. Cook, Rugeley, Stafford,' it will be correct, will it not?" He said, "Yes."

After leaving Beaufort-buildings, I went to Tattersall's. I then received all the money I expected, except £110 from Mr. Morris, who paid me £90, instead of £200. I sent from Tattersall's a cheque for £450 to Mr. Pratt. I posted a letter to Cook from Tattersall's, and directed it to Rugeley.

On Tuesday the 20th, next day, I received a telegraphic message. I have not got it here. I gave it to Captain Hatton at the coroner's inquest at Rugeley. In consequence of receiving that message, I wrote again to Cook that day. I addressed my letter as before, but I believe the letter was not posted till the Wednesday.

I have three bills of exchange with me. I know Palmer's handwriting, but never saw him write. I cannot prove his writing; but I knew Cook's writing, and I believe the drawing of two and the accepting of the three bills to be in his writing. I got them from Fisher, and gave him cash for them. [The witness Boycott was recalled and identified the signatures on the bills as those of Palmer and Cook.]

Examination continued. — The bills are each for £200. One of them was payable in a month, and when it fell due on October 18, Cook paid the £100 on account. He paid me the remaining £100 at Shrewsbury, but I cannot tell with certainty on what day. I did not pay the £350 to Mr. Padwick. I hold another bill for £500. [Thomas Strawbridge, manager of the bank at Rugeley, identified the drawing and endorsing as in the handwriting of Palmer. The acceptance, purporting to be in the writing of Mrs. Sarah Palmer, he did not believe to have been written by her.]

Examination continued. — I am sure that the endorsement on the £500 bill is in Cook's writing. I got the bill from Mr. Fisher. I paid £200 on account of it to Palmer, and £275 to Mr. Fisher. The balance was discount. It was not paid at maturity. I have taken proceedings against Palmer to recover the amount.

Cross-examined by Mr. *Grove*. Several people were ill at Shrewsbury on the second day of the races. They suffered from a kind of diarrhœa. I was one of those so affected. I had my meals at the Raven, where I put up, as also had my companions. They were not ill, but a gentleman who dined with us one day at the inn was. Palmer did not dine with me any day at the Raven. I saw Cook several times on the racecourse. The ground was wet. I remonstrated with him on Thursday for standing on it. That was after he had been taken ill on Wednesday. I was with Palmer for about an hour at Beaufort-buildings.

FREDERICK SLACK,
examined by Mr. *Huddleston*.

I am the porter at Mrs. Hawkes's boarding-house at Beaufort-buildings. On the 1st of December I saw Palmer there, and he gave me the direction to put on a hamper containing game. It was "W.W. Ward, Esq., Stoke-upon-Trent, Staffordshire." He told me to buy a turkey, a brace of pheasants, a codfish, and a barrel of oysters; and to buy them wherever I pleased. He said he did not wish the gentleman for whom they were intended to know from whom they came. I saw him write the direction in the coffee-room. I got the hamper and put all the things in it. I sewed it up and took it to the railway. Mrs. Hawkes bought the fowls, and I the other articles.

It being now within five minutes of 6 o'clock, the Court intimated its intention not to proceed further with the case that evening.

Lord CAMPBELL suggested that some facility of breathing fresh air should be afforded to the jury before the sitting of the Court on the following morning. Were it not that he made it a practice to take a walk early in the morning in Kensington-gardens,[30] he should himself find it impossible to endure the fatigue of so arduous a trial. An omnibus, or a couple of them, ought to be engaged for the accommodation of the jury, that they, too, might enjoy similar recreation.

---

[30] A 270-acre park adjacent to the west side of Hyde Park. It is one of eight Royal Parks that were originally privately owned by the Crown and converted for public use.

Mr. Baron ALDERSON — Why should they not take a walk in the Temple-gardens?[31] There could be no more tranquil spot. (A laugh.)

The Sheriffs intimated that they would attend to the recommendations of the learned Judges.

The Court then adjourned at 6 o'clock until 10 next day, the jury being conducted, as on the previous evening, to the London Coffee House in charge of the Sheriffs' officers.

THE JURORS TAKING EXERCISE IN THE GARDEN OF THE MIDDLE TEMPLE.

---

[31] An area in central London near the Inner and Middle Temples, where barristers lived and trained in their profession. Each Inns of Court had its own buildings and garden. Of the many inns, only four are left today: Inner Temple, Middle Temple, Lincoln's Inn and Gray's Inn.

FOURTH DAY.—May 17, 1856.

The adjourned trial of William Palmer for the murder of John Parsons Cook was resumed this morning. The court was densely crowded, and there was no abatement of the interest which has from the commencement been excited by these proceedings. Among the distinguished persons present were Earl Grey, and Mr. Dallas, the American Minister.

The jury, who, in accordance with the suggestions made by the learned judges on the previous day, had during the morning been conducted to the Middle Temple-gardens by the officer who had them in charge, and allowed to walk there for some time, entered the court about ten o'clock, and almost immediately afterwards the learned judges — Lord Chief Justice Campbell, Mr. Baron Alderson, and Mr. Justice Cresswell, accompanied by the Recorder, the Common Serjeant, the Sheriffs, and Under-Sheriffs, and several members of the Court of Aldermen, took their seats upon the bench. The prisoner was then placed at the bar. There was no change in the expression of his countenance, and during the day he maintained his usual tranquillity of demeanour.

The same counsel were again in attendance: The Attorney-General, Mr. E. James, Q.C., Mr. Bodkin, Mr. Welsby, and Mr. Huddleston for the Crown; Mr. Serjeant Shee, Mr. Grove, Q.C., Mr. Gray, and Mr. Kenealy for the prisoner.

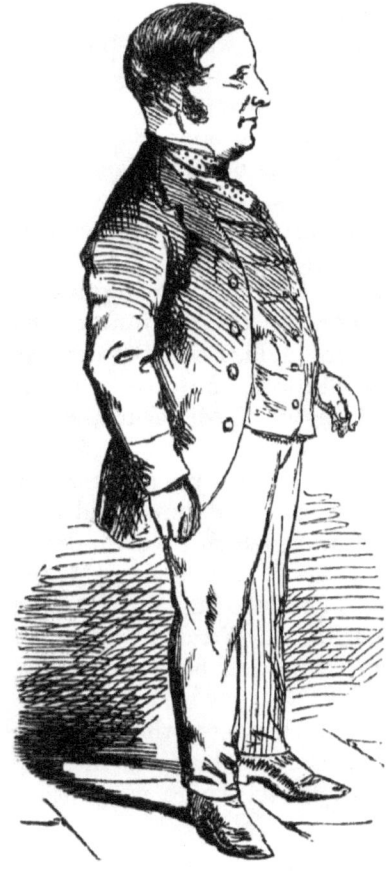

GEORGE BATES, ESQ., "A Gentleman of good Property, and possessing a Capital Cellar of Wine."

GEORGE BATES,

examined by Mr. *James*.

I was brought up a farmer, but am now out of business. I have known Palmer eight or nine years. In September, October, and November last I looked after his stud, and saw that the boys who had the care of the horses did their duty. I had no fixed salary, but used to receive money occasionally; some weeks I received two sovereigns, and some only one. I lodged in Rugeley. The rent I paid was 6s. 6d. per week. I am a single man. I knew the deceased Cook. I have no doubt that I saw him at Palmer's house in September. I cannot fix the date. I dined with him at Palmer's.

By Lord CAMPBELL — I sat at table with them.

Examination continued. — After dinner something was said of an insurance of my life. Either Cook or Palmer, which I cannot say, commenced the conversation.

Mr. *Serjeant Shee* objected to the reception of any evidence with regard to the proposal of the insurance of the witness's life.

The *Attorney-General* said that his object was to show the position of Cook's affairs at this time.

Lord CAMPBELL, after consultation with the other Judges, said — I doubted whether this would be relevant and proper evidence to receive upon this trial, and upon consultation the other Judges agree with me that it is too remote.

The examination of the witness with regard to the insurance was therefore not pursued.[1]

Witness — I remember the death of Cook, and the inquest. I know Mr. William Webb Ward, the coroner. On the morning of the 6th of December, while the inquest was being held, I saw Palmer. He gave me this letter, and told me to go to Stafford and give it to Mr. Ward. [The letter referred to was that addressed to Mr. Ward, which was on the previous day put in and read.]

That was between 9 and 10 o'clock. He also gave me a letter to a man named France, a dealer in game at Stafford. Palmer said that there would be a package of game from France, which I was to direct and send to Mr. Ward. I got a basket of game from France upon the order which that prisoner had given me. I directed it, "Webb Ward, coroner (or solicitor) Stafford," and sent it to Mr. Ward. I directed it myself. I gave a man 3d. to take the game, but I delivered the note to Mr. Ward myself.

I found him at the Dolphin Inn, Stafford. He was in the smoking-room. I told him I wanted to speak to him. He called me out into the yard or passage, and there I gave him the note. There were other

---

[1] Palmer, with the help of Cook and Jeremiah Smith, attempted to insure Bates' life. Their attempt to pass Bates off as a gentleman "with good property and possessing a fine cellar of wine" exploded when Inspector Field was sent by the insurance company. He found Bates hoeing turnips in a field. The interview showed that Bates expected to receive £1,000 and wondered if the amount would give him the right to vote!

WILLIAM WEBB WARD, ESQ., CORONER FOR STAFFORDSHIRE

people in the smoking-room. I had had no directions from the prisoner as to how I was to deliver the note. When I returned to Rugeley that night I saw the prisoner. I told him that I had delivered the letters which I took to Stafford, and had sent a boy with the game.

I remember Thursday, the 13th of December. On that day I was sent for to the prisoner's house early in the morning. About midday I went to Palmer's house. I found him in bed. He said that he wanted me to go to Stafford to take Webb Ward a letter, and to take care that no one saw me give it to him. On the Saturday, previously I had taken Palmer some money. On the Thursday Palmer told me to go to Ben and tell him he wanted a £5 note. I understood Ben to be Mr. Thirlby, his assistant. Palmer added, "Tell him that I have no small change." I believe he asked me to look in a drawer under the dressing glass, and said, "Tell me the amount of that bill." I looked in the drawer, and found there a £50 Bank of England bill. I left the bill there. This was before he gave me the letter for Ward.

After seeing the bill I went to Thirlby's for the £5. I got from Thirlby a £5 note of a local bank, and took it to Palmer. I then went downstairs, leaving Palmer in bed, with the writing materials on the bottom of it. I remained downstairs, in the yard or kitchen, about half an hour. When I went upstairs Palmer again asked me the amount of the bill which was in the drawer. I just looked at it, and thought it was the same bill I had left there. He then gave me the letter, which was sealed, and I took it to Stafford. I followed Mr. Ward through the room of the railway station, and gave it to him in the road. Mr. Ward did not open or read the letter, but crumpled it up in his hand, and put it in his pocket. I believe I told him from whom I had brought it. Having delivered the letter, I returned to Rugeley. I saw the prisoner, and told him that I had given Ward the letter. He said nothing.

Cross-examined by Mr. *Serjeant Shee*. Palmer had four brood mares, and four yearlings, and a three-year-old. I can't tell their value. I heard that one of these horses sold for 800 guineas. I can't say whether the mares were in foal in November, but I suppose some were. Palmer's stables were at the back of his house, and the paddocks, which were near them, covered about twenty acres of ground, and were fenced with a hawthorn hedge. I remember a mare called the Duchess of Kent being there. We supposed she slipped her foal, but we could not find it. I am not aware that Goldfinder's dam slipped her foal. I once saw the turf cut up with horses' feet, and attributed it to the mares galloping about. I never saw any dogs "run" them. I have seen a gun at the paddocks. I cannot say whether it belonged to Palmer. I never examined it.

I do not know Inspector Field by sight. I have seen a person whom I was told was Field. He came to me at the latter end of September, or beginning of October or November. I cannot say whether he saw Palmer. He was a stranger to me. I do not know that he put up anywhere. (A laugh.) I did not see him more than once. I do not know Field. On Thursday, December 13, I saw Gillott, who is a sheriff's officer, in Palmer's yard.

Re-examined by the *Attorney-General*. It was after the hay harvest that I saw the turf in the paddock cut up.[2] I should say that it was in the latter end of September. I cannot say how long it was before Cook's death.

THOMAS BLIZARD CURLING,
examined by the *Attorney–General*.

---

[2] In the Old Bailey transcript, Bates was answering the question "Had any complaint been made about dogs going about the paddock?" It was an attempt by the attorney general to counter a possible defense that Palmer had bought the strychnine to poison dogs that were harassing the mares.

I am a member of the College of Surgeons, and Surgeon to the London Hospital. I have particularly turned my attention to the subject of tetanus, and have published a work upon that subject. Tetanus means a spasmodic affection of the voluntary muscles. Of true tetanus there are only two descriptions — idiopathic and traumatic. There are other diseases in which we see contractions of the muscles, but we should not call them tetanus.

Idiopathic tetanus is apparently self-generated; traumatic proceeds from a wound or sore. Idiopathic tetanus arises from exposure to damp or cold, or from the irritation of worms in the alimentary canal. It is not a disease of frequent occurrence.

I have never seen a case of idiopathic tetanus, although I have been surgeon to the London Hospital for twenty-two years. Cases of traumatic tetanus are much more frequent. Speaking quite within compass, I have seen 50 such cases. I believe 100 would be nearer the mark.

The disease first manifests itself by stiffness about the jaws and back of the neck. Rigidity of the muscles of the abdomen afterwards sets in. A dragging pain at the pit of the stomach is an almost constant attendant. In many instances the muscles of the back are extensively affected. These symptoms, though continuous, are liable to aggravations into paroxysms.

As the disease goes on, these paroxysms become more frequent and more severe. When they occur the body is drawn backwards; in some instances, though less frequently, it is bent forward. A difficulty in swallowing is a very common symptom, and also a difficulty of breathing during the paroxysms.

The disease may, if fatal, end in two ways. The patient may die somewhat suddenly from suffocation, owing to the closure of the opening of the windpipe; or he may be worn out by the severe and painful spasms, the muscles may relax, and the patient gradually sink and die. The disease is generally fatal.

The locking of the jaw is an almost constant symptom attending traumatic tetanus — I may say a constant symptom. It is not always strongly marked, but generally so. It is an early symptom. Another symptom is a peculiar expression of the countenance.

Lord CAMPBELL — I believe this is not peculiar to traumatic tetanus, but my observation is taken from such cases.

Examination resumed. — There is a contraction of the eyelids, a raising of the angles of the mouth, and contraction of the brow. In traumatic tetanus the lower extremities are sometimes affected, and sometimes, but somewhat rarely, the upper ones. When the muscles of the extremities are affected, the time at which that occurs varies. If there is no wound in the arms or legs the extremities are generally not affected until late in the progress of the disease.

I never knew or read of traumatic tetanus being produced by a sore throat or by a chancre. In my opinion a syphilitic sore would not produce tetanus. I know of no instance in which a syphilitic sore has led to tetanus. I think it a very unlikely cause.

The time in which traumatic tetanus causes death varies, from 24 hours to three or four days, or longer. The shortest period that ever came to my knowledge was eight to ten hours. The disease, when once commenced, is continuous.

Did you ever know of a case in which a man was attacked one day, had 24 hours' respite, and was then attacked the next day? — Never. I should say that such a case could not occur.

You have heard the account given by Mr. Jones of the death of the deceased, — were the symptoms there consistent with any forms of traumatic tetanus that has ever come under your observation? — No.

What distinguishes it from such cases? — The sudden onset of the disease. In all cases which have come under my notice the disease was preceded by the milder symptoms of tetanus, gradually proceeding to the complete development.

Were the symptoms described by the woman Mills as being presented on the Monday night those of tetanus? — No; not of the tetanus of disease.

Assuming tetanus to be synonymous with convulsive or spasmodic action of the muscles, was there in that sense tetanus on the Monday night? — No doubt there was spasmodic action of the muscles.

There was not, in your opinion, either idiopathic or traumatic tetanus? — No.

Why are you of that opinion? — The sudden onset of the spasms and their rapid subsidence are consistent with neither of the two forms of tetanus.

Is there not what is called hysteric tetanus? — Yes. It is rather hysteria combined with spasms, but it is sometimes called hysteric tetanus. I have known no instance of its proving fatal, or of it occurring to a man. Some poisons will produce tetanus. *Nux vomica*, acting through its poisons strychnia and brucia,[3] poisons of a cognate character, produces that effect. I never saw a case of either human or animal life destroyed by strychnine.

Cross-examined by Mr. *Serjeant Shee*. Irritation of the spinal

---

[3] An alkaloid derived from the bark of the nux vomica tree whose seeds yield strychnia, used to create strychnine. Brucia is a weaker poison than strychnine, but produces the same symptoms.

cord or of the nerves proceeding to it might produce tetanus.

Do you agree with the opinion of Dr. Watson,[4] in his "Lectures on the Principles and Practice of Physic," that in four cases out of five the disease begins with lockjaw?[5] — I do.

Do you agree with Dr. Watson that all the symptoms of tetanic convulsions may arise from causes so slight as these:— the sticking of a fishbone in the fauces, the air caused by a musket shot, the stroke of a whip lash under the eye, leaving the skin unbroken, the cutting of a corn, the biting of the finger by a favourite sparrow, the blow of a stick on the neck, the insertion of a seton, the extraction of a tooth, the injection of a hydrocele, and the operation of cutting?[6] — Excepting the percussion of the air from a musket ball, I think all these causes may produce the symptoms referred to.

Do you remember reading of a case which occurred at Edinburgh, in which a negro servant lacerated his thumb by the fracture of a china dish, and was instantly, while the guests were at dinner, seized with tetanus?

The *Attorney-General*, interposing before the witness replied — I have taken some pains to ascertain what that case is, and where it is got from.

Cross-examination continued. — Could traumatic tetanus occur within so short a time as a quarter of an hour after the reception of an injury? — I know of no well authenticated instance of the kind.

Did you inquire into this case which is mentioned in your own treatise, "A negro having scratched his thumb with a piece of broken china was seized with tetanus, and in a quarter of an hour after this he was dead?" — I referred to authority as far as I could, but I did not find any reference to it except in cyclopædias. When I wrote that book I was a young man 22 years of age. I have maturer judgment and greater experience now.

You say that no case of idiopathic tetanus has come under your notice? — None.

I dare say you will tell us that such cases are not so likely to

---

[4] Sir Thomas Watson (1792-1882), a physician who was the first to describe the water hammer pulse found in aortic regurgitation. In 1859, he was appointed physician extraordinary to the queen, and was created a baronet in 1866.

[5] A condition in which the mouth is clamped shut by the jaw muscle. While it can be caused by tetanus, it can also be brought on by infections, traumatic injuries, the side effect of drugs such as antidepressants, and even tonsillitis.

[6] *Fauces:* The narrow passage that is part of the pharynx between the soft palate and the base of the tongue; *seton:* A skein of cotton inserted below the skin with the end left protruding to promote drainage and healing; *hydrocele:* An accumulation of fluids around a testicle.

come to the hospital as those of a wound ending in traumatic tetanus, they would be more likely in the first instance to come under the notice of a physician than that of a surgeon? — Certainly.

By Lord CAMPBELL — I have read of cases of idiopathic tetanus in this country.

Mr. *Serjeant Shee* — We shall be able to show that there have been such cases.

Cross-examination continued. — Do you not know that very lately there was in the London Hospital a case in which tetanus came on so rapidly and so unaccountably that it was referred to strychnine, and it was thought necessary to examine the stomach of the patient? — I know that such an opinion was entertained before the history of the case was investigated. I have heard that no strychnine was found. In that case old syphilitic sores were discovered.

By Lord CAMPBELL — I did not see the patient, who was under the care of the house-surgeons, who are now in court.

Cross-examination continued. — Might not the irritation of a syphilitic sore, by wet, cold, drink, mercury, and mental excitement lead to tetanic symptoms? — I do not think that that is very likely. The irritation which is likely to produce tetanus is the sore being exposed to friction, to which syphilitic sores in the throat are not exposed. I should class tetanus arising from the irritation of a sore as "traumatic." Cases very rarely occur which it is difficult to class as either "traumatic" or "idiopathic." I should class tetanus arising from irritation of the intestines as "idiopathic." The character of the spasms of epilepsy is not tetanic.

Not of the spasms; but are not the contractions of epilepsy sometimes continuous, so that the body may be twisted into various forms, and remain rigidly in them? — Not continuously.

For five or ten minutes together? — I think not.

Does it not frequently happen that general convulsions, no cause or trace of which in the form of disease or lesion is to be found in the body after death, occur in the most violent and spastic way so as to exhibit appearances of tetanic convulsions? — No instance of the kind has come under my observation.

Do you agree with this opinion of Dr. Copland,[7] expressed in his *Dictionary of Practical Medicine*, under the head "General Convulsions." "The abnormal contraction of the muscles is in some cases of the most violent and spastic nature, and frequently of some continuance, the relaxations being of brief duration, or scarcely

---

[7] James Copland (1791-1870) was a Scottish physician and Fellow of the Royal Society. He wrote a number of medical books, including the three-volume "Dictionary of Practical Medicine," which promoted circumcision and suggested that socialism caused insanity.

observable, and in others nearly or altogether approaching to tetanic? — I would rather speak from my own observation. I have not observed anything of the kind.

Does it not happen that a patient dies of convulsions, spastic in the sense of their being tumultuous and alternating, and chronic in the sense of exhibiting continuous rigidity, yet after death no disease is found? — It does not often happen to adults.

Does it sometimes? — I do not know, nor have I read of such a case. I have no hesitation in saying that people may die from tetanus and other diseases without the appearance of morbid symptoms after death.

Are not convulsions, not, strictly speaking, tetanic, constantly preserved by retching, distention of the stomach, flatulence of the stomach and bowels, and other dyspeptic symptoms? — Such cases do not come under my observation as a hospital surgeon. I think it is very probable that general convulsions are accompanied by yelling. I don't know that they frequently terminate fatally, and that the proximate cause of death is spasm of the respiratory muscles, inducing asphyxia.

Re-examined by the *Attorney-General*. These convulsions are easily distinguished from tetanus, because in them there is an entire loss of consciousness.

Is it one of the characteristic features of tetanus that the consciousness is not affected? — It is.

Dr. ROBERT BENTLEY TODD,
examined by the *Attorney-General*.

I am physician at King's College Hospital,[8] and have held that office about 20 years. I have also lectured on physiology and anatomy on tetanus and the diseases of the nervous system, and have published my lectures. I agree with the last witness in his distinction between idiopathic and traumatic tetanus. I have seen two cases of what appeared to me to be idiopathic tetanus, but such cases are rare in this country.

By Lord CAMPBELL — I define idiopathic tetanus to be that form of the disease which is produced without any external wound, apparently from internal causes — from constitutional causes.

Examination resumed. — In my opinion the term tetanus ought not to be applied to disease produced by poisons, but I should call the symptoms tetanic in order to distinguish the character of the

---

[8] A teaching hospital in the London borough of Lambeth that opened in 1840.

DR. TODD, PHYSICIAN OF KING'S COLLEGE HOSPITAL

convulsions. I have observed cases of traumatic tetanus. Except that, in all such cases, there is some lesion the symptoms are precisely the same as those of idiopathic tetanus. The disease begins with stiffness about the jaw. The symptoms gradually develop themselves and extend to the muscles of the trunk.

When the disease has begun is there any intermission? — There are remissions, but they are not complete; only diminutions of the severity of the symptoms, not a total subsidence. The patient does not express himself as completely well, quite comfortable. I speak from my own experience.

What is the usual period that elapses between the commencement and the termination of the disease? — The cases may be divided into two classes. Acute cases will terminate in three or four days, chronic cases will go on as long as from 19 to 22 or 23 days, and perhaps longer. I do not think that I have known a case in which death occurred within four days. Cases are reported in which it occurred in a shorter period.

In tetanus the extremities are affected, but not so much as the trunk. Their affection is a late symptom. The locking of the jaw is an early one. Sometimes the convulsions of epilepsy assume somewhat of a tetanic character, but they are essentially distinct from tetanus. In epilepsy the patient always loses consciousness. Apoplexy never produces tetanic convulsions.

Perhaps I may be allowed to say that when there is effusion of blood upon the brain, and a portion of the brain is involved, the muscles may be thrown into short tetanic convulsions. In such case the consciousness would be destroyed.

Having heard described the symptoms attending the death of the deceased, and the *post-mortem* examination, I am of the opinion that in this case there was neither apoplexy nor epilepsy.

The *Attorney-General* said that, as Dr. Bamford was so unwell that it was doubtful whether he would be able to appear as a witness, he proposed to put in his deposition, in order to found upon it a question to the witness now under examination.

Dr. Todd and Dr. Tweedie deposed that they had seen Dr. Bamford on the previous day, and that he was then suffering from a severe attack of English cholera. He was too unwell to be able to attend and give evidence.

The Court ruled that the depositions taken before the coroner might be read; and they were read accordingly by the Clerk of the Arraigns. They were to the following effect:—

"I attended the late Mr. Cook at the request of Mr. William Palmer. I first saw him about 3 o'clock on Saturday, the 17th of November, when he was suffering from violent vomiting, the stomach being in that irritable state that it would not contain a teaspoonful of milk. There was perfect moisture of the skin, and he was quite sensible. I prescribed medicine for him, and Mr. Palmer went up to my house and waited until I had made it up, and then took it away. I prescribed a saline medicine, to be taken in an effervescing state.[9]

Between 7 and 8 o'clock in the evening Mr. Palmer again requested me to visit Mr. Cook. The sickness still continued, everything being ejected which he took into his stomach. I gave him two small pills as a slight opiate. Mr. Palmer took the pills from my house. I did not accompany him, nor do I know what became of the pills.

On the following morning (Sunday) Mr. Palmer again called, and asked me to accompany him. Mr. Cook's sickness still continued. I

---

[9] *Saline medicine:* Dr. Bamford prescribed a salt-water solution used to rehydrate cholera patients. *Effervescing state:* A bubbling or foaming mixture. From the Latin *ex-* plus *fervescere* for "to begin to boil."

remained about 10 minutes. Everything he took that morning was ejected from his stomach. Everything he threw up was as clear as water, except some coffee which he had taken.

Mr. Palmer had administered some pills before I saw Mr. Cook on Saturday, which had purged him several times. Between 6 and 7 o'clock in the evening I again visited the deceased, accompanied by Mr. Palmer. The sickness still continued.

I went on Monday morning, between 8 and 9 o'clock, and changed his medicine. I sent him a draught which relieved him from the sickness, and gave him ease.

I did not see him again until Tuesday night, when Mr. Palmer called for me. I examined Mr. Cook in the presence of Mr. Jones and Mr. Palmer, and I observed a change in him. He was irritable and troubled in his mind. His pulse was firm, but tremulous, and between 80 and 90. He threw himself down on the bed and turned his face away. He said he would have no more pills nor take any more medicine.

After they had left the room Mr. Palmer asked me to make two more pills similar to those on the previous night, which I did, and he then asked me to write the directions on a slip of paper; and I gave the pills to Mr. Palmer. The effervescing mixture contained 20 grains of carbonate of potash, two drachms of compound tincture of cardamine, and two drachms of simple syrup, together with 15 grains of tartaric acid for each powder.[10] I never gave Mr. Cook a grain of antimony. I did not see the preparations after they were taken away by Mr. Palmer.

Mr. Cook did not say he had taken the pills which he had prepared, but he expressed a wish on the Sunday and Monday nights to have the pills. His skin was moist, and there was not the least fever about him. When I saw the deceased on Monday he did not say that he had been ill on the Sunday night, but Mr. Palmer told me that he had been ill.

I considered death to have been the result of congestion of the brain when the *post-mortem* examination was made, and I do not see any reason to alter that opinion.

I have attended other patients for Mr. Palmer. I attended Mrs. Palmer some days before her decease; also two children, and a

---

[10] *Carbonate of potash:* Potassium carbonate, a chemical compound used to create the bubbling in effervescence mixtures. It was used to increase urine flow and have a soothing effect on the stomach. *Tincture of cardamine:* Also called bittercress, the flowering plant was used to treat stomach and heart ailments. *Simple syrup:* Refined sugar dissolved into water. *Tartaric acid:* A type of acid found in fruits used in the creation of effervescent draughts.

gentleman from London,[11] who was on a visit at Mr. Palmer's house, and who did not live many hours after I was called in. The whole of those patients died.

Mr. Palmer first made an application to me for a certificate of Mr. Cook's death on the following Sunday morning, when I objected, saying, "He is your patient." I cannot remember his reply; but he wished me to fill up the certificate, and I did so. We had no conversation at that time as to the cause of death — nothing more than the opinion I have expressed. Mr. Palmer said he was of the same opinion as myself with respect to the death of the deceased.

I never knew apoplexy to produce rigidity of the limbs. Drowsiness is a prelude to apoplexy. I attributed the sickness on the first two days to a disordered stomach. Mr. Cook never sent for me himself.

The examination of Dr. Todd by the Attorney-General was then proceeded with as follows:— Having heard the deposition of Dr. Bamford read, I do not believe that the deceased died from apoplexy or from epilepsy. I never knew tetanus to arise either from syphilitic states or from sore throat. There are poisons which will produce tetanic convulsions. The principal of those poisons are *nux vomica* and those which contain as their active ingredients strychnine and brucia. I have never seen human life destroyed by strychnine, but I have seen animals destroyed by it frequently. The poison is usually given in a largish dose in those cases, so as to put an end to the sufferings and destroy life as soon as possible. I should not like to give a human subject a quarter of a grain. I think that it is not unlikely that half a grain might destroy life; and I believe that a grain certainly would. I think that half a grain would kill a cat.

The symptoms which would ensue upon the administration of strychnine when given in solution — and I believe that poisons of that nature act more rapidly in a state of solution than in any other form — would develop themselves in ten minutes after it was taken, if the dose were a large one; if not so large, they might be half an hour or an hour before they appeared. Those symptoms would be tetanic convulsions of the muscles, more especially those of the spine and neck; the head and back would be bent back, and the trunk would be bowed in a marked manner; the extremities also would be stiffened and jerked out. The stiffness, once set in, would never entirely disappear; but fresh paroxysms would set in, and the jerking rigidity would re-appear; and death would probably ensue in a quarter of an hour or so.

---

[11] Palmer owed London gambler Leonard Bladen £600 when he invited him to stay at his house while he gathered the money. Bladen died there on May 13, 1850, suddenly and unexpectedly.

The difference between tetanus produced by strychnine and other tetanus is very marked. In the former case the duration of the symptoms is very short, and instead of being continuous in their development, they will subside if the dose has not been strong enough to produce death, and will be renewed in fresh paroxysms; whereas in other descriptions of tetanus the symptoms commence in a mild form, and become stronger and more violent as the disease progresses. The difficulty experienced in breathing is common alike to tetanus properly so called and to tetanic convulsions occasioned by strychnine, arising from the pressure upon the respiratory muscles. I think it is remarkable that the deceased was able to swallow, and that there was no fixing of the jaw, which would have been the case with tetanus proper, resulting either from a wound or from disease.

From all the evidence I have heard, I think that the symptoms which presented themselves in the case of Mr. Cook arose from tetanus produced by strychnine.

Cross-examined by Mr. *Grove*, Q.C. There are cases sloping into each other, as it were, of every grade and degree, from mild convulsions to violent tetanic spasms. I have published some lectures upon diseases of the brain, and I adhere to the opinion there expressed, that the state of a person suffering from tetanus is identical with that which strychnine is capable of producing.

In a pathological point of view, an examination of the spinal cord shortly after death, in investigating supposed deaths from strychnine, is important. The signs of decomposition, however, could be easily distinguished from the evidences of disease which existed previously to death; but it would be difficult to distinguish in such a case whether mere softening resulted from decomposition or from pre-existing disease.

There is nothing in the *post-mortem* examination which leads me to think that the deceased died from tetanus proper. I think that granules upon the spinal cord, such as I have heard described, would not be likely to cause tetanus. I have not heard of cases treated by Mr. Travers.

In animals to which strychnine has been administered I cannot say that I have observed what you call an intolerance of touch; but by touching them the spasms are apt to be excited. That sensibility to touch continues as long as the operation of the poison continues. I have examined the interior of animals that have been killed by strychnine; but I have not observed in such cases that the right side of the heart was usually full of blood. It is some years since I made such an examination; but I am able, nevertheless, to speak positively as to the state of the heart. It was usually empty on both sides. I do not agree with Dr. Taylor, or other authorities, in the opinion that in cases of tetanus animals died asphyxiated. If they did, we should invariably have the right side of the heart full of blood, which is not the case. I think that the term asphyxiated, or suffocated, is often very loosely used.

I know from my reading that morphia sometimes produces convulsions; but I believe that they would be of an epileptic character. I think that the symptoms from morphia would be longer deferred in making their appearance than from strychnine; but I cannot speak positively on the point. Morphia, like strychnine, is a vegetable poison. I have not observed in animals the jaw fixed after the administration of strychnine.

Re-examined by the *Attorney-General*. Whatever may be the true theory as to the emptiness of the heart after strychnine, I should say that the heart is more ordinarily empty than filled after tetanus. I think that the heart would be more contracted after strychnine than in ordinary tetanus. I do not believe that a medical practitioner would have any difficulty in distinguishing between ordinary convulsions and tetanic convulsions.

I have heard the evidence of the gentlemen who made the *post-mortem* examination, and I apprehend that there was nothing to prevent the discovery of disease in the spinal cord, had any existed previously to death.

Sir BENJAMIN BRODIE, examined by Mr. *James*, Q.C.

I have been for many years Senior Surgeon to St. George's Hospital,[12] and have had considerable experience as a surgeon. In the course of my practice I have had under my care many cases of death from tetanus. Death from idiopathic tetanus is, according to my experience, very rare in this country. The ordinary tetanus in this country is traumatic tetanus.

I have heard the symptoms which accompanied the death of Mr. Cook, and I am of the opinion that so far as there was a general contraction of the muscles they resembled those of traumatic tetanus; but as to the course those symptoms took they were entirely different.

I have attended to the detailed description of the attack suffered by Mr. Cook on the Monday night, its ceasing on Tuesday, and its renewal on the Tuesday night. The symptoms of traumatic tetanus

---

[12] One of the country's largest teaching hospitals, founded at Hyde Park Corner in 1733. During the 1970s, a new school was built at Tooting in Wandsworth, South-West London.

always begin, so far as I have seen, very gradually, the stiffness of the lower jaw being, I believe, invariably, the symptom first complained of — at least, so it has been in my experience. The contraction of the muscles of the back is always a later symptom — generally much later. The muscles of the extremities are affected in a much less degree than those of the neck and trunk, except in some cases where the injury has been in a limb, and an early symptom has been spasmodic contraction of the muscles of that limb. I do not myself recollect a case of ordinary tetanus in which occurred that contraction in the muscles of the hand, which I understand was stated to have taken place in this instance.

Again, ordinary tetanus rarely runs its course in less than two or three days, and often is protracted to a much longer period. I knew one case only in which the disease was said to have terminated in so short a time as twelve hours; but probably in that case the early symptoms had been overlooked. Again, I never knew the symptoms of ordinary tetanus to last for a few minutes, then subside, and then come on again after twenty-four hours. I think that these are the principal points of difference which I perceived between the symptoms of ordinary tetanus and those which I have heard described in this case.

I have not witnessed tetanic convulsions from strychnine on animal life. I do not believe that death in the case of Mr. Cook arose from what we ordinarily call tetanus — either idiopathic or traumatic. I never knew tetanus to result from sore throat or from a chancre, or from any other form of syphilitic disease. The symptoms were not the result either of apoplexy or of epilepsy. Perhaps I had better say at once that I never saw a case in which the symptoms that I have heard described here arose from any disease. (Sensation.) When I say that, of course, I refer not to particular symptoms, but to the general course which the symptoms took.

Cross-examined by Mr. *Serjeant Shee*. I believe I remember one case in the physician's ward of St. George's Hospital which was shown to me as a case of idiopathic tetanus, but I doubted whether it was tetanus at all. It was a slight case, and I do not remember the particulars.

Considering how rare cases of tetanus are, do you think that the description given by a chambermaid and by a provincial medical man, who had never seen but one case, is sufficient to enable you to form an opinion as to the nature of the case? — I must say I thought that the description was very clearly given.

Supposing that they differed in their description, which would you rely upon — the medical man or the chambermaid?

Baron ALDERSON — That is hardly a question to put to a medical witness, although it may be very proper observation for you to make.

Cross-examination continued. — I never knew syphilitic poison to produce tetanic convulsions, except in cases where there was disease of the bones of the head.

(Sir Benjamin Brodie gave his evidence with great clearness — slowly, audibly, and distinctly — matters in which other medical witnesses would do well to emulate so distinguished an example.)

Dr. HENRY DANIEL,
examined by the *Attorney-General.*

I was for many years surgeon to the Bristol Hospital, but have been out of practice for some time. In the course of a long practice I should think that I have seen at least thirty cases of tetanus. Two of those were certainly cases of idiopathic tetanus; one of them terminated fatally, the other did not. I quite agree with the other medical witnesses that idiopathic tetanus is a very rare occurrence in this country. The only difference in the symptoms between idiopathic and traumatic tetanus that I perceived was, that the former were more modified — not so severe — in their character. I was not able to trace these two cases of idiopathic tetanus to any particular cause.

I have heard the description given of the symptoms which accompanied the attack upon Mr. Cook before his death, and it appears to me that the circumstances of that attack are assuredly distinguishable from those which came under my experience in dealing with cases of tetanus.

The evidence of Sir B. Brodie quite expresses my opinion with respect to the difference of the symptoms between ordinary tetanus and tetanic convulsions produced by strychnine. Tetanus begins with uneasiness in the lower jaw, followed by spasms of the muscles of the trunk, and most frequently extending to the muscles of the limbs. Lockjaw is almost invariably a symptom of those cases of tetanus — of traumatic tetanus especially. I do not recollect that clinching of the hands is a usual symptom of ordinary tetanus, nor do I remember any twisting of the foot.

I do not believe that any of the cases which came under my experience endured for a shorter time than from thirty to forty hours. I never knew a case of syphilitic sores producing tetanus. The symptoms as they have been described certainly cannot be referable to apoplexy or epilepsy. I never heard of such a thing. In all the cases of tetanus which came under my observation, consciousness has been retained to the last, throughout the whole disease. The symptoms have never set in their full power from the commencement, but have invariably commenced in a milder form and have then gone on increasing, being continuous in their character and without intermission.

In my judgment the symptoms in the case of Mr. Cook could not be referred either to idiopathic or traumatic tetanus.

Cross-examined by Mr. *Grove*, Q.C. I have not read Dr. Curling's or Dr. Copland's books on the subject of tetanus; nor have I of late studied much the reported cases. I am not aware that excitement or irritation from vomiting has ever been given as the cause of tetanus.

The main symptoms of tetanus are, in my opinion, always very similar, although the inferior symptoms may vary simply. I cannot undertake to say that the convulsions of tetanus arise from the spine. I do not like the term "asphyxia," but I think that death from tetanic convulsions may probably arise from suffocation. It is many years since I saw a *post-mortem* upon a case of tetanus. I cannot say whether in the case of death from suffocation the heart would be full of blood or the reverse. An examination of the spinal cord or marrow never, so far as I know, afforded evidence of the cause to which the tetanus was to be attributed.

Mr. SAMUEL SOLLY, examined by Mr. *Welsby*.

I have been connected with St. Thomas's Hospital[13] as lecturer and surgeon for 28 years, and during that time I have seen many cases of tetanus. I have had six or seven under my own care, and I may have seen ten or fifteen more. Of those cases it was doubtful in one whether the disease was idiopathic or traumatic — the wound was so slight and the symptoms so obscure that it was difficult to decide which it was. The others were all decidedly traumatic cases. The shortest period that I recollect during which the disease lasted before it terminated in death was thirty hours. The disease was always progressive in its character.

I have heard the description given by the witnesses of Mr. Cook's attacks, and they differ essentially from those cases which I have seen. In my experience of tetanus there has always been a marked expression of countenance as the first symptom. It is a sort of grin, and is so peculiar that having once seen it you can never mistake it. In the symptoms that I have heard detailed with regard to Mr. Cook there were violent convulsions on Monday night, and on the Tuesday the individual was entirely free from any discomfort about the face or jaw; whereas in the cases under my notice the disease was always

---

[13] Probably London's oldest hospital, in existence since 1215, when it was named for St. Thomas Becket. It was founded in Southwark, but moved across the Thames to Lambeth across the river from Parliament in 1871.

continuous, and the fixedness of the jaw was the last symptom to disappear.

In my judgment the symptoms detailed in Mr. Cook's case are referable neither to apoplexy, epilepsy, nor to any disease that I have ever witnessed.

Cross-examined by Mr. *Serjeant Shee*. The sort of grin which I have described is known as *risus sardonicus*.[14] It is not common to all convulsions. Epilepsy is a disease of a convulsive character.

I heard the account given by Mr. Jones of the last few minutes of Mr. Cook's death — that he uttered a piercing shriek, and died after five or six minutes quietly. That last shriek and the paroxysm which accompanied it bear in some respects a resemblance to epilepsy. All convulsions which may be designated as of an epileptic character are not attended with an utter want of consciousness. Death from tetanus accompanied with convulsions seldom leaves any trace behind it; but death from convulsions arising from epilepsy does leave its trace in the shape of a slight effusion of blood on the brain, and congestion of the vessels.

Re-examined by the *Attorney-General*. The convulsions of epilepsy are accompanied by a variety of symptoms. When a patient dies of epilepsy he dies perfectly unconscious and comatose. I never saw any case of convulsive disease at all like this. There are cases of convulsive disease which are similar to tetanus in their onset, but not in their progress. For example, laceration of the brain, a sudden injury to the spinal cord, and the irritation from teething in infants will produce convulsions resulting in death; but there would be wanting the marked expression of the face which I have described, and which I have never missed in cases of tetanus.

Mr. HENRY LEE, examined by Mr. *Bodkin*.

I am Surgeon to King's College, and to the Lock Hospital.[15] The Lock Hospital is exclusively devoted to cases of a syphilitic character, and at present I see probably as many as 3,000 of those in the course of a year. I have never known an instance of that disease terminating in tetanus.

---

[14] A facial expression caused by a spasm of the muscles creating a distorted grin. From the Latin for "sardonic smile."
[15] The world's first clinic to treat venereal diseases, founded in 1747 near Hyde Park Corner. The term "lock hospital" was a common one. As early as medieval times, they were used to confine leprosy patients. The word "lock" could come from the Anglo-Saxon *loc*, for enclosure, referring to the conditions the lepers were kept, or its alternative meaning as a tuft of cotton or wool, a reference to how the patients' lesions were wrapped.

By the Court — I have never seen or read of a case either of primary or secondary symptoms resulting in tetanus.

This witness was not cross-examined.

Dr. HENRY CORBETT,
examined by Mr. *James*, Q.C.

In September, 1845, I was Medical Clerk at the Glasgow Infirmary,[16] and I remember a patient, named Agnes Sennett, alias Agnes French, who died there on the 27th of September, 1845. It was stated that she had taken strychnine pills, which had been prepared for another patient in the ward, and the symptoms which accompanied her death were those of strychnine. The pills were for a paralytic patient.

I saw her when she was under the influence of the poison, and I had seen her the day before that perfectly well. She had been admitted for a skin disease of the head. When I saw her after she had taken the poison she was in bed. The symptoms were these:— There was a strong retraction of the mouth, the face was much suffused and red; the pupils of the eyes were dilated; the head was bent back; the spine was curved; the muscles were rigid and hard like a board; the arms were stretched out; the hands were clinched; there were severe paroxysms recurring every few seconds. She died in about an hour and a quarter after taking the pills. When I was called first the paroxysms did not last so long; but they increased in severity. According to the prescription there should have been a quarter of a grain of strychnine to each pill, and this woman had taken three. The paralytic patient was to have taken a pill each night, or one each night and morning, I forget which.

Cross-examined by Mr. *Serjeant Shee*. The retraction of the mouth was continuous, but it was worse at times. I do not think that I observed it after death. The hands were not clinched after death — they were semi-bent. She died an hour and a quarter after taking the medicine. The symptoms appeared about 20 minutes after. I tried to make her vomit, but failed. She only vomited partially after I had given her an emetic.

Re-examined by the *Attorney-General*. There was spasmodic action and grinding of the teeth. She could open her mouth and swallow. There was no lockjaw or ordinary tetanus.

---

[16] The Glasgow Royal Infirmary, a large teaching hospital founded in 1794. It was here, in the same year as the Palmer trial, that British surgeon Joseph Lister (1827-1912) began experimenting with carbolic acid to reduce the number of deaths from sepsis. His discoveries inspired American chemist to develop an antiseptic that he named "Listerine."

By Mr. *Serjeant Shee* — I do not recollect that touching her sent her into paroxysms.

Dr. EBENEZER WATSON,
examined by the *Attorney-General*.

I am a surgeon at the Glasgow Infirmary. I remember the case of Agnes Sennett. I was called in about a quarter of an hour after she was taken ill. She was in violent convulsions, and her arms were stretched out and rigid. The muscles of the body were also rigid; they were kept quiet by rigidity. She did not breathe, the muscles being kept still by tetanic rigidity. That paroxysm subsided, and fresh paroxysms came on after a short interval. She died in about half an hour. She seemed perfectly conscious. I don't recollect the state of her hands. Her body was opened. The heart was found distended and stiff. The cavities of the heart were empty. My father published an account of the case.

Cross-examined by Mr. *Grove*. The spinal cord was quite healthy.

Dr. JAMES PATTERSON,
examined by Mr. *Welsby*.

In 1845 I was engaged in the laboratory of the Infirmary at Glasgow. I dispensed the prescriptions. I made up a prescription for a paralytic patient named M'Intyre. It consisted of pills which contained strychnine. There were four pills and one grain of strychnine in the four.

Mr. Baron ALDERSON — Was any noise made about their being taken by a wrong person? — Yes.

MARY KELLY, examined by Mr. *Bodkin*.

In September, 1845, I was a patient in the Glasgow Infirmary; a paralytic patient was in the same ward, and I attended to her. There was also a patient named French or Sennett who was suffering from a sore head. She died.

I was turning a wheel near the paralytic patient on the afternoon of the day Sennett died, for the purpose of applying something to her skin. There were some pills which she was to take near her. The paralytic woman took one and swallowed it according to the orders that had been given, and she handed the box to the girl with the sore head. The girl swallowed two of the pills, and then went and sat by the ward fire. She was taken ill in about three quarters of an hour. She fell back on the floor, and I went for the nurse. We took her to bed and sent for the doctor. We were obliged to cut her clothes off, because she never moved. She was like a poker. I was by her side when she died. She never spoke after she fell down.

Cross-examined by Mr. *Serjeant Shee*. It was three-quarters of an hour from the time she took the pills till she was taken to the bed.

CAROLINE HICKSON,
examined by Mr. *E. James*.

In October, 1848, I was nurse and lady's-maid in the family of Mr. Sarjantson Smyth. The family were then residing about two miles from Romsey.[17] On the 30th of October Mrs. Smyth was unwell. We dealt with Mr. Jones, a druggist in Romsey. A prescription had been sent to him to be made up for Mrs. Smyth.

The medicine was brought back about six in the afternoon. It was a mixture in a bottle. My mistress took about half a wineglass of it the following morning at five or ten minutes past seven. I left the room when I had given it her. Five or ten minutes afterwards I was alarmed by the ringing of her bell. I went into her room, and found her out of bed leaning upon a chair, in her nightdress. I thought she had fainted. She appeared to suffer from what I thought were spasms. I ran and sent the coachman for Mr. Taylor, the surgeon, and returned to her. Some of the other servants were there assisting her. She was lying on the floor. She screamed loudly, and her teeth were clinched. She asked to have her arms and legs held straight. I took hold of her arms and legs, which were very much drawn up. She still screamed, and was in great agony. She requested that water should be thrown over her, and I threw some. Her feet were turned inwards. I put a bottle of hot water to her feet, but that did not relax them. Shortly before she died, she said she felt easier. The last words she uttered were — "Turn me over." We did turn her over on the floor. She died a very few minutes after she had spoken those words. She died very quietly. She was quite conscious, and knew me during the whole time. About an hour and a-quarter elapsed from the time I gave her the medicine till she died.[18]

---

[17] A small market town in the county of Hampshire, in the south of England.
[18] Mrs. [Sarjantson] Smyth had seen her doctor to treat weakness after suffering a miscarriage. He prescribed a painkiller consisting of nine grains of salicine (willow bark) and orange peel. But instead of salicine, the pharmacist, Mr. Jones, took down the bottle next to it containing strychnine

Cross-examined by Mr. *Grove*. She could not sit up from the time I went up to her till she died. It was when she was in a paroxysm that I endeavoured to straighten her limbs. The effect of cold water was to throw her into a paroxysm. It was a continually recurring attack, lasting about an hour or an hour and a-quarter. Her teeth were clinched during the whole time.

Re-examined by the *Attorney-General*. The fit came on five or ten minutes after I gave her the medicine. She was stiff all the time till within a few minutes after death. She was conscious all the while.

Mr. FRANCIS TAYLOR,
examined by Mr. *Welsby*.

I am a surgeon and apothecary at Romsey. I attended Mrs. Sarjantson Smyth in 1848. I was summoned to her house one morning soon after 8, and when I arrived I found her dead. The body was on the floor, near the bed. The hands were very much bent. The feet were contracted and turned inwards. The soles of the feet were hollowed up and the toes contracted, apparently from recent spasmodic action. The inner edge of each foot was turned up. There was a remarkable rigidity about the limbs.

By Lord CAMPBELL — The body was warm.

Examination continued. — The eyelids were almost adherent to the eyeballs. The druggist who made up the prescription was named Jones. I made a *post-mortem* examination three days after the death. The contraction of the feet continued, but it had gone off somewhat from the rest of the body. I found no trace of disease in the body. The heart was contracted and perfectly empty, as were all the large arteries leading from it.

I analyzed the medicine she had taken with another medical man. It contained a large quantity of strychnine. It originally contained nine grains, and she had taken one-third — three grains. I made a very casual examination of the stomach and bowels, as we had plenty of proof that poison had been taken without making use of the tests.

Cross-examined by Mr. *Serjeant Shee*. In cases of death from ordinary causes the body is much distorted. It does not generally, I should think, remain in the same position after death.

---

hydrochloride. His wife told a newspaper that he "did not feel so much the consequences to himself as the thought of having sent such a beautiful creature to another world, and such a good customer." But he must have felt worse than he let on. After being arraigned for manslaughter, he committed suicide.

If the body is not laid out immediately, is it not stiffened by the *rigor mortis*?[19] — Probably it is. The ankles were tied by a bandage to keep them together. I commenced to open the body at the thorax[20] and abdomen. The head was also opened.

CHARLES BROXHOLME, examined by Mr. *Huddleston*.

I was apprentice to Mr. Jones, the chemist, at Romsey, in 1848. My master made a mistake in preparing a prescription for Mrs. [Sarjantson] Smyth. The mistake was the substitution of strychnine for salacite (bark of willow). He destroyed himself afterwards.

JANE WITHAM, examined by Mr. *E. James*.

In March last I was in attendance upon a lady who died. [The learned counsel told the witness she had better not mention the lady's name.[21]] She took some medicine. After she took it she became ill. She complained first of her back. Her head was thrown back, her body stretched out, and I observed twitchings. Her eyes were drawn aside and staring. I put my hand upon her limbs, which did not at all relax.

She first complained of being ill in that way on Monday, the 25th of February, and died on Saturday, the 1st of March. She had attacks on the Monday, on the Wednesday, on the Thursday, on the Friday (a very slight one), and at a quarter-past eight on the Saturday morning. She died about twenty minutes to eleven that night. Between the attacks she was composed.

---

[19] The stiffening of the muscles that begins about three hours after death and can last up to three days.
[20] A part of the chest that is protected by the ribcage. From the Latin word for "breastplate."
[21] In Leeds, William Dove was tried on July 16th in the poisoning of his wife, Harriet. The case first surfaced in the testimony of Elizabeth Mills, in which the defense insinuated that she changed her testimony after reading newspaper articles about the trial.

The widowed Mrs. Witham played another role in the Dove case that did not appear in her testimony. According to an account of William Dove's trial in the Association Medical Journal, Mr. Dove told a neighbor earlier that year that his wife would soon die and that if she did, "he should make her [Mrs. Witham] an offer." His passion for the widow could not even wait until the inquest was over. "When all this is settled," he is quoted as telling her, "I hope you will let me come and talk to you." The article added helpfully, "Mrs. Witham hoped he would not, as people would talk about it." In the end, he did not get his chance to propose; he was convicted and hanged.

She principally complained of prickings in the legs and twitchings in the muscles and in the hands, which she said she could compare to nothing else than a galvanic shock. She wished her husband to rub her legs and arms. She was dead when Dr. Morley came.

Cross-examined by Mr. *Serjeant Shee*. On the Saturday night she could not bear to have her legs touched when the spasms were strong upon her. Her limbs were rigidly extended when she asked to be rubbed. That was in the intervals between the spasms. Touching her then brought on the spasms. Her body was stiff immediately after death, but I did not stay long in the house. On the Saturday she was sensible from half-an-hour to an hour, from a quarter past eight till after nine. I suppose she was insensible the remainder of the time. She did not speak.

Re-examined by Mr. *E. James*. On the Saturday before she died, the symptoms were the same as on the other days — not more violent.

Mr. GEORGE MORLEY, examined by Mr. *Welsby*.

I am a surgeon. I attended on the lady to whom the last witness has alluded for about two months before her death. On the Monday before she died she was in bed apparently comfortable, when I observed (as I stood by her side) several slight convulsive twitchings of her arms. I supposed they arose from hysteria, and ordered medicine in consequence.

The same symptoms were repeated on the following Wednesday or Thursday. I saw her on Saturday, the day she died. She was apparently better, and quite composed in the middle of the day. She complained of an attack she had had in the night. She spoke of pain and spasms in the back and neck, and of shocks. I and another medical man were sent for hastily on the Saturday night. We were met by the announcement that the lady was dead.

On the Monday I accompanied another medical gentleman to the *post-mortem* examination. We found no disease in any part of the body which would account for death. There was no emaciation, wound, or sore. There was a peculiar expression of anxiety about the countenance. The hands were bent and the fingers curved. The feet were strongly arched. We carefully examined the stomach and its contents to see if we could find poison. We applied several tests — nitric acid, chloride of sulphuric acid, bi-chloride of potash in a liquid and also in a solid state. They are the best tests to detect the presence

THE TIMES REPORT

MR. GEORGE MORLEY, SURGEON AT LEEDS

of strychnine. In each case we found appearances characteristic of strychnine. We administered the strychnine taken from the stomach to animals by inoculation. We gave it to a few mice, a few rabbits, and a guinea pig, having first separated it by chemical analysis. We observed in each of the animals more or less of the effects produced by strychnine — namely, general uneasiness, difficult breathing, convulsions of a tetanic kind, muscular rigidity, arching backwards of the head and neck, violent stretching out of the legs. These symptoms appeared in some of the animals in four or five minutes, in others in less than an hour. The guinea pig suffered but slightly at first and was left, and found dead the next day. The symptoms were strongly marked in the rabbits. After death there was an interval of flaccidity, after which rigidity commenced, more than if it had been occasioned by the usual *rigor mortis*. I afterwards made numerous experiments on animals with exactly similar results, the poison being administered in a fluid form.

Cross-examined by Mr. *Grove*. I did not see the patient during a severe attack. I have observed in animals that spasms are brought on by touch. That is a very marked symptom. The spasm is like a galvanic shock.

The patient was not at all insensible during the time I saw her, and she was able to swallow, but I did not see her during a severe attack.

After death we found the lungs very much congested. There was a small quantity of bloody serum in the pericardium.[22] The muscles of the whole body were dark and soft. There was a decided quantity of effusion in the brain. There was also a quantity of serum tinged with blood in the membranes of the spinal cord. The membranes of the spinal marrow were congested to a considerable extent. We opened the head first, and there was a good deal of blood flowing out. Part of the blood may have flowed from the heart. That might partially empty the heart, and would make it uncertain whether the heart was full or empty at the time of death.

I have often examined the hearts of animals poisoned by strychnine. The right side of the heart is generally full. In some cases I think that the symptoms did not appear for an hour after the administration of the poison. I have made the experiments in conjunction with Mr. Nunneley. We have made experiments upon frogs, but they are different in many respects from warm-blooded animals.

I have in almost all cases found the strychnine where it was known to have been administered. In one case it was doubtful. We were sure the strychnine had been administered in that case, but we doubted whether it had reached the stomach. There were appearances which might lead one to infer the presence of strychnine, but they were not satisfactory. I have detected strychnine in the stomach nearly two months after death, when decomposition has proceeded to a considerable extent.

Re-examined by the *Attorney-General*. From half a grain to a grain has been administered to cats, rabbits, and dogs. From one to two grains is quite sufficient to kill a dog.

How does the strychnine act? Is it taken up by the absorbents and carried into the system? — I think it acts upon the nerves, but a part may be taken into the blood and act through the blood. We generally examined the stomach of the animals when the poison had been administered internally. Sometimes we examined the skin. The

---

[22] A double-walled sac that contains the heart and the roots of the great blood vessels.

poison found in the stomach would be in excess of that absorbed into the system.

Are you then of the opinion that, a portion of the poison being taken into the system and a portion being left in the stomach, the portion taken into the system would produce tetanic symptoms and death?

Mr. *Serjeant Shee* objected to a question which suggested a theory.

The *Attorney-General* — What would be the operation of that portion of the poison which is taken into the system? — It would destroy life.

Mr. Baron ALDERSON — And yet leave an excess in the stomach? — That is my opinion.

The *Attorney-General* — Would the excess remaining in the stomach produce no effect? — I am not sure that strychnine could lie in the stomach without acting prejudicially.

Suppose that a minimum quantity is administered, which being absorbed into the system, destroys life, should you expect to find any in the stomach? — I should expect sometimes to fail in discovering it.

If death resulted from a series of minimum doses spread over several days, would the appearance of the body be different from that of one whose death had been caused by one dose? — I should connect the appearance of the body with the final struggle of the last day.

Would you expect a different set of phenomena in cases where death had taken place after a brief struggle, and in cases where the struggle had been protracted? — Certainly. At the *post-mortem* examination of which I have spoken, we found fluid blood in the veins.

Mr. *Serjeant Shee* — Is it your theory that in the action of poisoning, the poison becomes absorbed and ceases to exist as poison? — I have thought much upon that question, and have not formed a decided opinion, but I am inclined to think that it is so. A part may be absorbed and a part remain in the stomach unchanged.

Mr. *Serjeant Shee* — What chemical reason can you give for your opinion that strychnine, after having effected the operation of poisoning, ceases to be strychnine in the blood? — My opinion rests upon the general principle that, in acting upon living bodies, organic substances — such as food and medicine — are generally changed in their composition.

Mr. *Serjeant Shee* — What are the component parts of strychnine?

Mr. Baron ALDERSON — You will find that in any eyclopædia, brother Shee.

Mr. *Serjeant Shee* — Have you any reason to believe that strychnine can be decomposed by any sort of putrefying or fermenting process? Witness — I doubt whether it can.

Mr. EDWARD D. MOORE,
examined by Mr. *Huddleston*.

About fifteen years ago I was in practice as a surgeon, and I attended, with Dr. Chambers, a gentleman named Clutterbuck, who was suffering from paralysis. We had been giving him small doses of strychnine[23] when he went to Brighton. On his return he told us that he had been taking larger doses of strychnine, and we, in consequence, gave him a stronger dose. I made up three draughts, containing a quarter of a grain each. He took one in my presence. I remained with him a little time, and left him as he said he felt quite comfortable.

About three-quarters of an hour afterwards I was summoned to him, I found him stiffened in every limb, and the head drawn back. He was desirous that we should move and turn him and rub him. We tried to give him ammonia in a spoon, and he snapped at the spoon. He was suffering, I should say, more than three hours. Sedatives were given him. He survived the attack. He was conscious all the time.

Cross-examined by Mr. *Serjeant Shee*. The spasms ceased in about three hours, but the rigidity of the muscles remained till the next day. His hands and feet at first were drawn back, and he was much easier when we clinched them forwards. His paralysis was better after the attack.

Re-examined by the *Attorney-General*. Strychnine stimulates the nerves which act upon the voluntary muscles, and, therefore, acts beneficially in cases of paralysis.

The *Attorney-General* intimated that the next witness to be called was Dr. Taylor, and, as it was a quarter after 5, the trial was adjourned until Monday at 10 o'clock.

Lord CAMPBELL, before the jury left the box, exhorted them not to form any opinion upon the case until they had heard both sides. They should even abstain from conversing about it among themselves.

Mr. *Serjeant Shee* said that medical witnesses would be called for the defence.

His LORDSHIP also expressed a hope that, if the jury were taken out upon the following day (Sunday), they would not be allowed to go to any place of public resort, and mentioned an instance in which a jury, under similar circumstances, had been conducted to Epping Forest.[24]

---

[23] In addition to its use as a poison, strychnine was used as a stimulating tonic — its chemical makeup is similar to caffeine — and to treat paralysis.

[24] A former royal forest between northeast Greater London and Essex. The over 6,000 acres of forests, grasslands, bogs, rivers and ponds was limited to the use of the monarch for hunting. A dispute in the 19th century between landowners and commoners who had grazing and cutting rights ended with

The jury were then conveyed to the London Coffee House.

The Jurors' Sleeping Apartment at the London Coffee House

the Epping Forest Act 1878 when it was placed under the control of the City of London Corporation.

FIFTH DAY.—May 19, 1856.

The court was again crowded long before the commencement of the proceedings this morning. The Earl of Denbigh and Lord Lyttelton were among the gentlemen who occupied seats upon the bench.

The jury came into court shortly before ten o'clock, and were soon followed by Lord Campbell and Mr. Justice Cresswell, accompanied by the Recorder, the Sheriffs and Under-sheriffs, &c. Mr. Baron Alderson did not take his seat until about two o'clock.

The prisoner was immediately placed at the bar. There was no alteration perceptible in his countenance or demeanour, and he took notes of several parts of Dr. Taylor's evidence.

The Attorney-General, Mr. E. James, Q.C., Mr. Welsby, Mr. Bodkin, and Mr. Huddleston appeared for the Crown; Mr. Serjeant Shee, Mr. Grove, Q.C., Mr. Gray, and Mr. Kenealy for the prisoner.

DRS. TAYLOR AND REES PERFORMING THEIR ANALYSIS

Dr. ALFRED SWAINE TAYLOR,
examined by the *Attorney-General.*

I am a Fellow of the College of Physicians, lecturer on medical jurisprudence at Guy's Hospital, and the author of the well-known

Treatise on Poisons and on medical jurisprudence. I have made the poison called strychnia the subject of my attention. It is the produce of the *nux vomica*, which also contains brucia, a poison of an analogous character. Brucia is variously estimated at from one-sixth to one-twelfth the strength of strychnia. Most varieties of impure strychnia that are sold contain more or less brucia. Unless, therefore, you are certain as to the purity of the article, you may be misled as to its strength.

I have performed a variety of experiments with strychnia on animal life. I have never witnessed its action on a human subject. I have tried its effects upon animal life — upon rabbits — in ten or twelve instances. The symptoms are, on the whole, very uniform. The quantity I have given has varied from half a grain to two grains. Half a grain is sufficient to destroy a rabbit. I have given it both in a solid and a liquid state. When given in a fluid state, it produces its effects in a very few minutes; when in a solid state, as a sort of pill or bolus, in about six to eleven minutes. The time varies according to the strength of the dose, and also to the strength of the animal.

In what way does it operate, in your opinion? — It is first absorbed into the blood, then circulated through the body, and especially acts on the spinal cord, from which proceed the nerves acting on the voluntary muscles.

Supposing the poison has been absorbed, what time would you give for the circulating process? — The circulation of the blood through the whole system is considered to take place about once in four minutes. The circulation in animals is quicker. The absorption of the poison by rabbits is therefore quicker. The time would also depend on the state of the stomach, whether it contained much food or not, whether the poison came into immediate contact with the inner surface of the stomach.

In your opinion, does this poison act immediately on the nervous system, or must it first be absorbed? — It must first be absorbed.

The symptoms, you say, are uniform. Will you describe them? — The animal for about five or six minutes does not appear to suffer, but moves about gently; when the poison begins to act it suddenly falls on its side, there is a trembling, a quivering motion, of the whole of the muscles of the body, arising from the poison producing violent and involuntary contractions. There is then a sudden paroxysm or fit, the fore legs and the hind legs are stretched out, the head and the tail are drawn back in the form of a bow, the jaws are spasmodically closed, the eyes are prominent; after a short time there is a slight remission of the symptoms, and the animal appears to lie quiet, but the slightest noise or touch reproduces another convulsive paroxysm; sometimes there is a scream, or a sort of a shriek, as if the animal suffered from pain; the heart beats violently during the fit, and after a succession of these fits the animal dies quietly. Sometimes, however, the animal dies during a spasm, and I only know that death has occurred from holding my hand over the heart.

The appearances after death differ. In some instances, the rigidity continues. In one case the muscles were so strongly contracted for a week afterwards that it was possible to hold the body by its hind legs stretched out horizontally. In an animal killed the other day the body was flaccid at the time of death, but became rigid about five minutes afterwards. I have opened the bodies of animals thus destroyed.

Could you detect any injury in the stomach? — No. I have found in some cases congestion of the membranes of the spinal cord to a greater extent than would be accounted for by the gravitation of the blood. In other cases I have found no departure from the ordinary state of the spinal cord and the brain. I ascribe congestion to the succession of fits before death. In a majority of instances, three out of five, I found no change in the abnormal condition of the spine. In all cases the heart has been congested, especially the right side.

I saw a case of ordinary tetanus in the human subject years ago, but I have not had much experience of such cases. I saw one case last Thursday week at St. Bartholomew's Hospital. The patient recovered.

You have heard the descriptions given by the witnesses of the symptoms and appearances which accompanied Cook's attacks? — I have.

Were those symptoms and appearances the same as those you have observed in the animals to which you administered strychnine? — They were. Death has taken place in the animals more rapidly when the poison has been administered in a fluid than in a solid form. They have died at various periods after the administration of the poison.

The experiments I have performed lately have been entirely in reference to solid strychnine. In the first case the symptoms began in 7 minutes, and the animal died (including those 7) in 13 minutes. In the second case the symptoms appeared in 9 minutes, and the animal died in 17. In the third case the symptoms appeared in 10 minutes, and the animal died in 18. In the fourth case the symptoms appeared in 5 minutes, and death took place in 22. In the fifth case the symptoms appeared in 12 minutes, and death occurred in 23. If the poison were taken by the human subject in pills it would take a longer time to act, because the structure of the pill must be broken up in order to bring the poison in contact with the mucous membrane of the stomach. I have administered it to rabbits in pills.

Would poison given in pills take a longer period to operate on a human subject than on a rabbit? — I do not think we can draw any inference from a comparison of the rapidity of death in a human subject and in a rabbit. The circulation and absorption are different in the two cases. There is also a difference between one human subject and another. The strength of the dose, too, would make a difference, as a large dose would produce a more rapid effect than a small one.

I have experimented upon the intestines of animals, in order to reproduce the strychnia. The process consists in putting the stomach and its contents in alcohol, with a small quantity of acid, which dissolves the strychnia, and produces sulphate of strychnia in the stomach. The liquid is then filtered, gently evaporated, and an alkali added — carbonate of potash, which, mixed with a small quantity of sulphuric acid, precipitates[1] the strychnia. Tests are applied to the strychnia, or supposed strychnia, when extracted.

Strychnia has a peculiarly strong bitter taste. It is not soluble in water, but it is in acids and in alcohol.

The colouring tests are applied to the dry residue after evaporation. Change of colour is produced by a mixture of sulphuric and bi-chromate of potash. It produces a blue colour, changing to violet and purple, and passing to red; but colouring tests are very fallacious, with this exception — when we have strychnine separated in its crystallized state we can recognise the crystals by their form and their chemical properties, and above all, by the production of tetanic symptoms and death, when administered through a wound in the skin of animals.

Are there other vegetable substances from which, if these colouring tests were applied, similar colours would be obtained? — There are a variety of mixtures which produce similar colours. One of them has also a bitter taste like strychnia. Vegetable poisons are more difficult of detection by chemical process than mineral poisons; the tests are far more fallacious.

I have endeavoured to discover the presence of strychnine in animals I have poisoned in four cases, assisted by Dr. Rees. I have applied the process which I first described. I have then applied the tests of colouring and of taste.

Were you able to satisfy yourself of the presence of strychnia? — In one case I discovered some by the colour test. In a second case there was a bitter taste, but no other indication of strychnia. In the other two cases there were no indications at all of strychnia. In the case where it was discovered by a colour test two grains had been administered; and in the second case, where there was a bitter taste,

---

[1] Separated from the solution.

one grain. In one of the cases where we failed to detect it one grain, and in the other half a grain, had been given.

How do you account for the absence of any indication of strychnia in cases where you know it was administered? — It is absorbed into the blood, and is no longer in the stomach. It is in a great part changed in the blood.

How do you account for its presence when administered in large doses? — There is a retention of some in excess of what is required for the destruction of life.

Supposing a minimum dose, which will destroy life, had been given, could you find any? — No. It is taken up by absorption, and is no longer discoverable in the stomach.[2] The smallest quantity by which I have destroyed the life of an animal is half a grain. There is no process with which I am acquainted by which it can be discovered in the tissues. As far as I know, a small quantity cannot be discovered.

Suppose half a grain to be absorbed into the blood, what proportion does it bear to the total quantity of blood circulated in the system? — Assuming the system to contain the lowest quantity of blood, 25lbs., it would be 1·50th of a grain to a pound of blood. A physician once died from a dose of half a grain in 20 minutes. I believe it undergoes some partial change in the blood, which increases the difficulty of discovering it.

I never heard of its being separated from the tissues in a crystallised state. The crystals are peculiar in form, but there are other organic crystallized substances like them, so that a chemist will not rely on the form only.

After the *post-mortem* examination of Cook a portion of the stomach was sent to me. It was delivered to me by Mr. Boycott in a brown stone jar, covered with bladder, tied, and sealed. The jar contained the stomach and the intestines. I have experimented upon them with a view to ascertain if there was any poison present.

What poisons did you seek for in the first instance? — Various; prussic acid, oxalic acid, morphia, strychnia, veratria, tobacco poison, hemlock, arsenic, antimony, mercury, and other mineral poisons.

Did you find any of them? — We only found small traces of antimony.[3]

---

[2] Taylor is incorrect. A poison can be absorbed by the body and excreted unchanged through the kidneys. It could also be discovered through a catalytic reaction, which had been known since 1817. Dr. Nunneley would take Dr. Taylor to task over this in a letter to the British Medical Journal, and add that he didn't think a doctor like Palmer, whose medical training came from "strolling the wards" for a few months, would be competent enough to adjust the dose precisely to kill without leaving evidence behind.

[3] Taylor also found no traces of mercury or opium that would have come from

Were the parts upon which you had to operate in your search for strychnia in a favorable condition? — The most unfavourable that could possibly be, the stomach had been completely cut from end to end, all the contents were gone, and the fine mucous surface, on which any poison, if present, would have been found, was lying in contact with the outside of the intestines — all thrown together. The inside of the stomach was lying in the mass of intestinal feculent matter.

That was the fault or misfortune of the person who dissected? — I presume it was; but it seemed to have been shaken about in every possible way in the journey to London. The contents of the intestines were there, but not the contents of the stomach, in which and on the mucous membrane I should have expected to find poison.

By my own request other portions of the body were sent up to me,— namely, the spleen, the two kidneys, and a small bottle of blood. They were delivered to me by Mr. Boycott. We had no idea whence the blood had been taken. We analyzed all. We searched in the liver and one of the kidneys for mineral poison. Each part of the liver, one kidney, and the spleen all yielded antimony. The quantity was less in proportion in the spleen than in the other parts.

It was reproduced, or brought out, by boiling the animal substance in a mixture of hydrochloric acid and water. Gall and copper water were also introduced, and the antimony was found deposited on the copper. We applied various tests to it — those of Professor Brandt, of Dr. Rees, and others. I detected some antimony in the blood.

It is impossible to say with precision how recently it had been administered; but I should say within some days. The longest period at which antimony can be found in the blood after death is eight days; the earliest period at which it has been found after death, within my own knowledge, is 18 hours. A boy died within 18 hours after taking it; and it was found in the liver.

Antimony is usually given in the form of tartar emetic; it acts as an irritant, and produces vomiting. If given in repeated doses a portion would find its way into the blood and the system beyond what was ejected. If it continued to be given after it had produced certain symptoms it would destroy life. It may, however, be given with impunity.[4]

Bamford's pills that Cook should have been taking for three nights.
[4] A confusing sentence. According to the Old Bailey transcript, Taylor said, "If given in continued doses of that description, it would destroy life, if it produced certain symptoms — it may be given in frequent doses with impunity, and it may be given so as to produce symptoms which will infallibly destroy life, if continued."

I heard the account given by the female servants of the frequent vomiting of Mr. Cook, both at Rugeley and at Shrewsbury, and also the evidence of Mr. Gibson and Mr. Jones as to the predominant symptoms in his case. Vomitings produced by antimony would cause those symptoms. If given in small quantities sufficient to cause vomiting it would not affect the colour of the liquid in which it was mixed, whether brandy, wine, broth, or water. It is impossible to form an exact judgment as to the time when the antimony was administered, but it must have been within two or three weeks at the outside before death. There was no evidence that any had been given within some hours of death. It might leave a sensation in the throat — a choking sensation — if a large quantity was taken at once.

I found no trace of mercury during the analysis. If a few grains had been taken recently before death I should have expected to find some trace. If a man had taken mercury for a syphilitic affection, within two or three weeks I should have expected to find it. It is very slow in passing out of the body. As small a quantity as three or four grains might leave some trace. I recollect a case in which three grains of calomel were given three or four hours before death, and traces of mercury were found. Half a grain three or four days before death, if favourably given, and not vomited, would, I should expect, leave a trace. One grain would certainly do so. I heard the evidence as to the death of Mrs. [Sarjantson] Smyth, Agnes French, and the other lady mentioned, and also as to the attack of Clutterbuck.

From your own experience in reference to strychnine do you coincide in opinion with the other witnesses, that the deaths in those cases were caused by strychnine? — Yes.

Did the symptoms in Cook's case appear to be of a similar character to the symptoms in those cases? — They did.

As a professor of medical science, do you know any cause in the range of human disease except strychnine, to which the symptoms in Cook's case can be referred? — I do not.

Cross-examined by Mr. *Serjeant Shee*. I mean by the word "trace" a very small quantity, which can hardly be estimated by weight. I do not apply it in the sense of an imponderable quantity. In chemical language it is frequently used in that sense. An infinitesimal quantity would be called a "trace." The quantity of antimony that we discovered in all parts of the body would make up about half a grain. We did not ascertain that there was that quantity, but I will undertake to say that we extracted as much as half a grain. That quantity would not be sufficient to cause death. Only arsenic or antimony could have been deposited, under the circumstances, on the copper, and no sublimate of arsenic was obtained. [The witness, in reply to a further question, detailed the elaborate test which he had applied to the deposit, in order to ascertain that it consisted of antimony.]

Would a mistake in any one of the processes you have described, or a defect in any of the materials you used, defeat the object of the test? — It would, but all the materials I used were pure. Such an accident could not have happened without my having some intimation of it in the course of the process.

I should think antimony would operate more quickly upon animals than upon men. I am acquainted with the works of Orfila. He stood in the highest rank of analytical chemists.[5]

Did not Orfila find antimony in a dog four months after injection? — Yes; but the animal had taken about forty-five grains.

Mr. *Serjeant Shee* called the attention of the witness to a passage in Orfila's work in reference to that case, to the effect that the antimony was found accumulating in the bones, the liver contained a great deal, and the tissues a very little.

Witness — Yes; when antimony has been long in the body it passes into the bones; but I think you will find that these are not Orfila's experiments. Orfila is quoting the experiments of another person.

But is not that the case with nearly all the experiments referred to in your own book? — No; I cannot say that.

Mr. *Serjeant Shee* again referred to a case in *Orfila* in which 45 grains were given to a dog, and three and a-half months after death a quantity was found in the fat, and some in the liver, bones, and tissues.

Witness — That shows that antimony gets into the bones and flesh, but I never knew a case in which 45 grains had been given, and I have given no opinion upon such a case.

A pretty good dose is required to poison a person, I suppose? — That depends on the mode in which it is given. A dog has been poisoned with six grains. The dog died in the case you mentioned. When antimony is administered as it was in that case the liver becomes fatty and gristled. Cook's liver presented no appearance of the sort. I should infer that the antimony we found in Cook's body was given much more recently than in the experiments you have described. We cannot say positively how long it takes to get out of the body, but I have known three grains cleared out in 24 hours.

I was first applied to in this case on Thursday, the 27th of November, by Mr. Stevens, who was introduced to me by Mr. Warrington, professor of chymistry. Either then or subsequently he mentioned Mr. Gardner. I had not known Mr. Gardner before. I had never before been concerned in cases of this kind at Rugeley.

Mr. *Serjeant Shee* read the letter written by Dr. Taylor to Mr. Gardner:—

---

[5] Mathieu Orfila (1787-1853) was a French chemist credited with founding the science of toxicology.

"CHEMICAL LABORATORY, GUY'S HOSPITAL, DEC. 4, 1855.

"Re J. P. Cook, Esq., deceased.

"DEAR SIR,— Dr. Rees and I have completed the analysis to-day. We have sketched a report, which will be ready to-morrow or next day.

"As I am going to Durham Assizes on the part of the Crown, in the case of Reg. v. Wooler,[6] the report will be in the hands of Dr. Rees, No. 26, Albemarle-street. It will be most desirable that Mr. Stevens should call on Dr. Rees, read the report with him, and put such questions as may occur.

"In reply to your letter received here this morning, I beg to say that we wish a statement of all the medicines prescribed for deceased (until his death) to be drawn up and sent to Dr. Rees.

"We do not find strychnine, prussic acid, or any trace of opium. From the contents having been drained away, it is now impossible to say whether any strychnine had or had not been given just before death, but it is quite possible for tartar emetic to destroy life if given in repeated doses; and, so far as we can at present form an opinion, in the absence of any natural cause of death, the deceased may have died from the effects of antimony in this or some other form.

"We are, dear Sir, yours faithfully,

"ALFRED S. TAYLOR.

"G. OWEN REES."

Was that your opinion at the time? — It was. We could infer nothing else.

Have you not said that the quantity of antimony you found was not sufficient to account for death? — Certainly. If a man takes antimony he first vomits, and then a part of the antimony goes out of the body; some may escape from the bowels. A great deal passes at once into the blood by absorption, and is carried out by the urine.

Can you say upon your oath that from the traces in Cook's body you were justified in stating your opinion that death was caused by antimony?

---

[6] Joseph Wooler, a retired merchant, was accused of murdering his wife with arsenic. Taylor described the case in "A Manual of Medical Jurisprudence" because the three doctors treating the woman suspected but could not confirm arsenic poisoning, in part because they were treating her with prussic acid, henbane and strychnine, which mimic the symptoms of arsenic poisoning. Before they could seek another opinion, the woman had died. Taylor found arsenic everywhere in the body, but the husband was acquitted. At the trial, the judge criticized the doctors for not airing their suspicions, but other doctors, including Taylor and Christison (whose testimony will come), pointed out that doing so would have exposed the medical men to heavy damages for slander if they were wrong.

— Yes, perfectly and distinctly. That which is found in a dead body is not the slightest criterion as to what the man took when he was alive.

When you gave your opinion that Cook died from the effects of antimony had you any reason to think that an undue quantity had been administered? — I could not tell. People may die from large or small quantities; the quantity found in the body was no criterion as to how much he had taken.

May not the injudicious use of a quack medicine containing antimony, the injudicious use of James's powders,[7] account for the antimony you found in the body? — Yes; the injudicious use of any antimonial medicine would account for it.

Or even their judicious use? — It might.

With that knowledge, upon being consulted with regard to Cook, you gave it as your opinion that he died from the poison of antimony? — You pervert my meaning entirely. I said that antimony in the form of tartar emetic might occasion vomiting and other symptoms of irritation, and that in large doses it would cause death, preceded by convulsions. (The witness was proceeding to read his report upon the case, but was stopped by the Court.)

I was told that the deceased was in good health seven or eight days before his death, and that he had been taken very sick and ill, and had died in convulsions. No further particulars being given us, we were left to suppose that he had not died a natural death. There was no natural cause to account for death, and finding antimony existing throughout the body we thought it might have been caused by antimony. An analysis cannot be made effectually without information.

You think it necessary before you can rely upon an analysis to have received a long statement of the symptoms before death? — A short statement will do.

You allow your judgment to be influenced by the statement of a person who knows nothing of his own knowledge? — I do not allow my judgment to be influenced in any way; I judge by the result.

Do you mean to say that what Mr. Stevens told you did not assist you in arriving at the conclusion you state in writing? — I stated it as a possible case — not as a certainty. If we had found a very large quantity of tartar emetic in the stomach we should have come to the conclusion that the man had died from it. As we found only a small quantity, we said he might have died from it.

I attended the coroner's inquest on the body of Mr. Cook. I think I first attended on the 14th of December. Some of the evidence was

---

[7] A drug containing phosphate of lime and oxide of antimony created by Dr. Robert James (1705-1776), who claimed it cured fever, gout and rheumatism. James also known for his three-volume "Medical Dictionary" which contained a dedication from longtime friend Samuel Johnson.

read over to me. I think that Dr. Harland was the first witness I heard examined. I heard Mr. Bamford examined, and also Lavinia Barnes. I cannot say as to Newton. I heard Jones.

I had experimented some years ago on five of the rabbits I have mentioned; that is about twenty-three years ago. That is the only knowledge of my own that I had of the effect of strychnia upon animal life. I have a great objection to the sacrifice of life. No toxicologist will sacrifice the lives of a hundred rabbits to establish facts which he knows to be already well established. I experimented upon the last rabbits since the inquest.

Do not you think that is a very slight experiment? — You must add to that experiment the study of poisons and cases.

Do not you think that a rabbit is a very unfair animal to select?—No.

Would not a dog be much better? — Dogs are very dangerous to handle.(A laugh.)

Do you mean to give that answer? — Dogs and cats bear a greater analogy to man because they vomit, while rabbits do not, but rabbits are much more manageable.

Mr. *Serjeant Shee* — I will take your answer that you are afraid of dogs.

Witness — After the experiments I have tried with dogs and cats I have no inclination to go on.

Do you admit that as to the action of the respiratory organs they would be better than rabbits? — I do not.

As to the effect of the poison would they not? — I think a rabbit is quite as good as any animal. The poison is retained, and its operation is shown.

At the inquest I saw Mr. Gardner. I suggested questions to the coroner. Some of them he put to the witnesses, and others they answered upon my suggestion of them. Ten days before the inquest Mr. Gardner informed me, in his letter, that strychnia, Batley's solution, and prussic acid had been purchased on the Tuesday; that was why I used the expressions to which you have referred. We did not allow that information to have any influence upon our report.

At the request of Mr. Serjeant Shee the deposition of this witness taken at the coroner's inquest was read by the clerk of arraigns.[8]

---

[8] In "On Poisoning by Strychnia," Taylor quotes from his deposition's conclusion. The material within square brackets are his, the paragraphing mine:

"Therefore the result is, we find antimony in the body, but cannot account for the cause of death. The heart might have been emptied [as the result of] by spasm [either from disease] or poison. Antimony would not [be likely to] cause it [this appearance]. My opinion is that he [deceased] died from tetanus, and that this tetanus was caused by medicine administered and [or] taken shortly before death. I believe that the pills on the Monday

Cross-examination continued. — Having given my evidence I returned to town, and soon afterwards heard that the prisoner had been committed on a charge of wilful murder.

And that his life depended in a great degree upon you? — No; I simply gave an opinion as to the poison, not as to the prisoner's case; I knew that I should probably be examined as a witness upon his trial.

Do you think it your duty to abstain from all public discussion of the question which might influence the public mind? — Yes. Did you write a letter to the *Lancet*? — Yes, to contradict several misstatements of my evidence which had been made.

This letter, which appeared in the *Lancet* of February 2, 1856, was put in by Mr. Serjeant Shee, and read by the clerk of arraigns. The principal part of the letter referred to the case of Mrs. Ann Palmer; the concluding paragraph, for which Mr. Serjeant Shee stated that he desired it should be read, was as follows:—

"During the quarter of a century which I have now specially devoted to toxicological inquiries I have never met with any cases like these suspected cases of poisoning at Rugeley. The mode in which they will affect the person accused is of minor importance compared with their probable influence on society. I have no hesitation in saying that the future security of life in this country will mainly depend on the judge, the jury, and the counsel who may have to dispose of the charges of murder which have arisen out of these investigations."[9]

---

night and the Tuesday night contained strychnia.

"I do not believe that the medicine administered [prescribed] by Dr. Bamford would have produced the effects I have heard [described] to-day. On the Monday night and the Tuesday night after the pills were taken, there was not the slightest indication [of the action] of morphia on the body. Further than this, we found no mercury in the liver or other parts of the body; and I do not think that mercury or calomel could have been taken on the Monday and Tuesday nights [as well as on the other nights] without our discovering [some] traces of it in the liver.

"The witness Mills has accurately described the symptoms produced by a small dose of strychnia such as would [might] be caused by pills [containing] strychnia given at half-past ten on Monday night; and the symptoms on the Tuesday night were those which would be produced by a larger dose of strychnia given in the pills taken on that night.

"There is an absence of any natural cause or disease to account for tetanus. The brain and spinal marrow were [found] healthy. There was no insensibility before death; perfect consciousness, and merely that effect of spasm on the muscular system which a poisonous dose of strychnia would cause."

[9] Here is the letter in its entirety.

"To the Editor of The Lancet.

"SIR,—I have great pleasure in replying to the inquiries contained in your leading article of January 19th.

"1. I stated that I had never known antimonial powder, when given in medicinal doses, (i.e., from five to eight grains at a dose,) to produce violent *vomiting and purging*.

"I am aware that experience differs on this point; that some have found this substance inert, while others have found it very active. From some recent experiments on antimonial preparations, I think it not unlikely that the powder may sometimes contain arseniate of lime. Dr. Pereira mentions that in the large dose of half a teaspoonful, it, on one occasion, produced violent vomiting, purging, and sweating; while in still larger doses (120 grains at a dose), prescribed by Dr. Elliotson, it occasioned in some instances only nausea. I have never met with any case in which serious symptoms could be referred to its operation; and in the case of Ann Palmer [Palmer's wife] this medicinal preparation would not account for the antimony found in her body.

"2. My statement as to the *cause of death* was, that the deceased died from the effects of tartar emetic, and from no other cause. That is the opinion which Dr. Rees and I formed from the result of our examination, and from the description of the symptoms under which the deceased laboured during the eight days which preceded her death. It is an opinion which I believe is now equally shared by the two medical attendants of the deceased. We are quite prepared to maintain this opinion on the trial. You will excuse me from entering into our reasons for this opinion on the present occasion, as this may form a very fair and proper subject for cross-examination at the trial. Possibly the defence may be, that tartar emetic in small doses is not a poison; that it cannot, under any circumstances, destroy life, and that it was the very best remedy for the disease (English cholera) under which it was stated the deceased was labouring.

"One other point connected with this inquiry may be here adverted to. The examination of the organs was made *fifteen month*s, not "fifteen weeks," after death, and the viscera examined were as well preserved as I have seen them in many cases of arsenical poisoning. They were in a better state of preservation than the viscera of Walter Palmer, whose body had been buried for a period of three months only, in a leaden coffin. The viscera in Ann Palmer's case were in such a state of preservation as to allow us to form an opinion of their condition.

"3. This inquiry refers to the elimination of antimony from the body. According to my experience, antimony is analogous to arsenic in the rapidity with which it enters into the blood and passes out of the system. These two metals are wholly different in this respect from mercury and lead, and probably from copper. I will be most happy after the trial to furnish you with facts and authorities, as far as I can, in reference to these interesting points. In the meantime, as this question may also form a fair subject for cross-examination, a detailed answer to it may be for the present reserved.

"4. The fourth inquiry involves, as you have justly suspected, an error of

Cross-examination continued. — That is my opinion now. It had been stated that if strychnia caused death it could always be found, which I deny. It had also been circulated in every newspaper that a person could not be killed by tartar emetic, which I deny, and which might have led to the destruction of hundreds of lives. I entertained no prejudice against the prisoner. What I meant, was that if these statements which I had seen in medical and other periodicals, were to have their way, there was not a life in the country which was safe.

Do you adhere to your opinion that "the mode in which they will affect the person accused," that is, lead him to the scaffold, "is of minor importance, compared with their probable influence on society?" — I have never suggested that they should lead him to the scaffold. I hope that, if innocent, he will be acquitted.

What do you mean by the mode in which they will affect the person accused being of minor importance? — The lives of 16,000,000 of people are, in my opinion, of greater importance than that of one man.

That is your opinion? — Yes. As you appear to put that as an objection to my evidence, allow me to state that in two dead bodies I find antimony. In one case death occurred suddenly, and in the other the body was saturated with antimony, which I never found before in the examination of 300 bodies. I say these were circumstances which demanded explanation.

You adhere to the opinion that, as a medical man and a member of an honourable profession, you were right in publishing this letter before the trial of the person accused? — I think I had a right to state that opinion in answer to the comments which had been made upon my evidence.

Had any comments been made by the prisoner? — No.

---

the press. What I said was to the effect, that if there were symptoms of fever, antimonial medicines might be fairly prescribed.

"In concluding this letter, I would observe that, during a quarter of a century which I have now specially devoted to toxicological inquiries, I have never met with any cases like these suspected cases of poisoning at Rugeley. The mode in which they will affect the person accused is of minor importance compared with their probable influence on society. I have no hesitation in saying that the future security of life in this country will mainly depend on the judge, the jury, and the counsel who may have to dispose of the charges of murder which have arisen out of these investigations.

"I am, Sir, your obedient servant,

"ALFRED S. TAYLOR, M.D., F.R.S.

"ST. JAMES'S-TERRACE, REGENT'S-PARK, JAN. 1856."

JOHN SMITH, ESQ., PALMER'S SOLICITOR

Or by any of his family? — Mr. [John] Smith, the solicitor for the defence,[10] circulated in every paper statements of "Dr. Taylor's inaccuracy." I had no wish or motive to charge the prisoner with this crime. My duty concerns the lives of all.

Do you know Mr. Augustus Mayhew, the editor of the *Illustrated Times*? — I have seen him once or twice.

Did you allow pictures of yourself and Dr. Rees to be taken for publication? — Be so good as to call them caricatures. No; I did not.

---

[10] Identified further by Fletcher as "John Smith, of Waterloo Street, Birmingham, generally known as "*Jack Smith of Brum*," a lawyer with a large practice and a great reputation for making the very most of his cases, and sparing no pains, no trouble, to win against any odds. He had defended many prisoners for all sorts of offences, and restored to Society some who had better have been under lock and key."

Mr. *Serjeant Shee* — There may be a difference of opinion as to that. I think it is very like.

Did you receive Mr. Mayhew at your house? — He came to me with a letter of introduction from Professor Faraday. I never received him in my laboratory.

Did you know that he called in order that you might afford him information for an article in the *Illustrated Times*? — I swear solemnly I did not. The publication of that article was the most disgraceful thing I ever knew. I had never seen him before, nor did I know that he was the editor of the *Illustrated Times*.

On your oath? — On my oath. It was the greatest deception that was ever practised on a scientific man. It was disgraceful. He called on me in company with another gentleman, with a letter from Professor Faraday. I received him as I should Professor Faraday, and entered into conversation with him about these cases. He represented, as I understood, that he was connected with an insurance company, and wished for information about a number of cases of poisoning which had occurred during many years. After we had conversed about an hour he asked if there was any objection to the publication of these details. Still believing him to be connected with an insurance-office, I replied that, so far as the correction of error was concerned, I should have no objection to anything appearing.

On that evening he went away without telling me that he was the editor of the *Illustrated Times*, or connected with any other paper. I did not know that until he called upon me on Thursday morning, and showed me the article in print. I remonstrated verbally with him. He only showed me part of a slip. I told him I objected to its publication, and struck out all that I saw regarding these cases. He afterwards put the article into the shape in which it appeared. I could not prevent his publishing the results of our conversation on points not connected with these cases.

You did permit him to publish part of the slip? — Nothing connected with the Rugeley cases.

Did he show you the slip of "Our Interview with Dr. A. Taylor"? — I do not remember seeing that. I will swear that, to the best of my judgment and belief, he did not. He showed me a slip containing part of what appeared in that article. I struck out all which referred to the Rugeley cases. I thought I had been deceived. A person came with a letter of introduction from a scientific man and extracted information from me.

Why did you not tell your servant to show him the door? — Until we had had the conversation, I did not know anything about the deception. It was not until the Thursday morning, that I knew he was connected with a paper. He told me it was an illustrated paper.

Did you correct what he showed you? — I struck out some portions.

And allowed the rest to be published? — I said I had nothing to do with it, but I objected to its publication.

Peremptorily? — No; I said, "I do not like this mode of putting the matter. I cannot, however, interfere with what you put into your journal."

Did you not protest as a gentleman, a man of honour, and a medical man, that it was wrong and objectionable to do it? — I told him that I objected to the parts which referred to the Rugeley cases. It was most dishonourable.

Did you not know that in the month of February an interview with Dr. Taylor on the subject of poison must be taken to apply to those cases? — I did not think anything about it. I thought it was a great cheat to extract from me that information. Mr. Mayhew was with me about twenty minutes or half an hour on the Thursday morning. I remonstrated with him. I was not angry with him in the sense of quarrelling.

Did you allow him to publish this — "Dr. Taylor here requested us to state that, although the practice of secret poisoning appeared to be on the increase, it should be remembered that by analysis the chemist could always detect the presence of poison in the body?" — I did not request him to state anything of the kind. I do not remember whether that was on the slip. Had I seen it I should have struck it out. I remember seeing on the slip, "And that when analysis fails, as in cases where small doses of strychnia had been administered, physiology and pathology would invariably suffice to establish the cause of death." I did not strike that out. I did not think of it circulating among the class of persons from whom jurors would be selected. I think the public ought to know that chemical analyses are not the only tests on which they can rely. I don't remember the passage — "Murder by poison could be detected as readily as murder in any other form, while the difficulty of detecting and convicting the murderer was felt in other cases as well as in those where poison was employed." The article has been very much altered. It was a disgraceful thing. I have not seen Mr. Mayhew since. Seeing in *The Times* an advertisement, stating that this information had been given by me, I wrote to him demanding its withdrawal, and that demand was complied with. That was on the Thursday or Friday.[11]

---

[11] The footnote from the 1856 edition stated that: "It is but fair to Mr. Mayhew to state that he has written a letter to *The Times* entirely denying the truth of Dr. Taylor's statements." Mayhew wrote that they told Taylor the interview would be published and confirmed Taylor's testimony that he had corrected the galley proof of the interview, which implied that the doctor did

Did you say to a gentleman named Cooke Evans that you would give them strychnia enough before they had done, or words to that effect? — No; I do not know the person.

Or to any one? — No. I never used any expression so vulgar and improper. You have been greatly misinstructed.

Or, "He will have strychnia enough before I have done with him?" — It is utterly false. The person who suggested that question to you, Mr. Johnson, has been guilty of other falsehoods. In the letter to Sir George Grey, and on other occasions, he has misrepresented my statements and evidence.

What did you do with the medical report to which you referred? — It was a private letter from Dr. Harland to Mr. Stevens.

Mr. Justice CRESSWELL — It was memoranda made by Dr. Harland at the time.

Cross-examination continued. — Cook's symptoms were quite in accordance with an ordinary case of poisoning by strychnia.

Can you tell me of any case in which a patient, after being seized with tetanic symptoms, sat up in bed and talked? — It was after he sat up that Cook was seized with those symptoms.

Can you refer to a case in which a person who had taken strychnia beat the body with his or her arms? — It is exactly what I should expect to arise from a sense of suffocation.

Do you know any case in which the symptoms of poisoning by strychnia commenced by this beating of the bed-clothes? — There have been only about 15 cases, and in none of those was the patient seized in bed. Beating of the bed-clothes is a symptom which may be exhibited by a person suffering from a sense of suffocation, whether caused by strychnia or other causes. A case has been communicated to me by a friend, in which the patient shook as though he had the ague.

Mr. *Serjeant Shee* objected to this last answer, but as the learned Serjeant had been questioning the witness as to the results of his reading,

The COURT ruled that the evidence was admissible.

Cross-examination continued. — I have known of no case of poisoning by strychnia in which the patient screamed before he was seized. That is common in ordinary convulsions. In cases of poisoning by strychnia the patient screams when the spasms set in; the pain is very severe. I cannot refer to a case in which the patient has spoken freely after the paroxysms had commenced.

Can you refer me to any case in an authentic publication in which the access of the strychnia paroxysm has been delayed so long

---

not object to its publication.

after the ingestion of the poison as in the case of Cook on the Tuesday night? — Yes, longer. In my book on medical jurisprudence, page 185 of the 5th edition, it is stated that in a case communicated to the *Lancet*, August 31, 1850, by Mr. Bennett, a grain and a-half of strychnia taken by mistake destroyed the life of a healthy young female in an hour and a-half. None of the symptoms appeared for an hour. There is a case in which the period which elapsed was two hours and a-half. It was not a fatal case, but that does not affect the question. A grain and a-half is a full, but not a very considerable dose.

In my book on poisons there is no case in which the paroxysm commenced more than half-an-hour after the ingestion of the poison. That book is eight years old, and since 1848 cases have occurred. There is a mention of one in which three hours elapsed before the paroxysms occurred.

Mr. *Serjeant Shee* then referred to this case, and called attention to the fact that the only statement as to time was that in three hours the patient lost his speech and at length was seized with violent tetanic convulsions.

Cross-examination continued. — I know of no other fatal case in which the interval was so long. In that case there was disease of the brain.

Referring to the *Lancet*, I find that in the case to which I referred, as communicated by Dr. Bennett, the strychnia was dissolved in cinnamon water. Being dissolved, one would have expected it to have a more speedy action. The time in which a patient would recover would depend entirely upon the dose of strychnia which had been taken. I do not remember any case in which a patient recovered in three or four hours, but such cases must have occurred. There is one mentioned in my book on medical jurisprudence. The patient had taken *nux vomica*, but its powers depend upon strychnia. In that case the violence of the paroxysms gradually subsided, and the next day, although feeble and exhausted, the patient was able to walk home. The time of the recovery is a point which is not usually stated by medical men.

I cannot mention any case in which there was a repetition of the paroxysms after so long an interval as that from Monday to Tuesday night, which occurred in Cook's case. I do not think that the attack on Tuesday night was the result of anything which had been administered to him on the Monday night.

In the cases of four out of five rabbits the spasms were continued at the time of death and after death. In the other the animal was flaccid at the time of death.

Are you acquainted with this opinion of Dr. Christison, that in these cases rigidity does not come on at the time of death, but comes on shortly afterwards? — Dr. Christison speaks from his experience, and I from mine.

Did you hear that Dr. Bamford said that when he arrived he found the body of Cook quite straight in bed? — Yes.

Can that have been a case of ophisthotonos?[12] — It may have been.

Are not the colour tests of strychnia so uncertain and fallacious that they cannot be depended upon? — Yes, unless you first get the strychnia in a visible and tangible form.

Is it not impossible to get it so from the stomach? — It is not impossible; it depends upon the quantity which remains there.

You do not agree that a fiftieth part of a grain might be discovered? — I think not.

Nor even half a grain? — That might be. It would depend upon the quantity of food in the stomach with which it was mixed.

Re-examined by the *Attorney-General*. In cases of death from strychnia the heart is sometimes found empty after death. That is the case of human subjects. There are three such cases on record. I think that emptiness results from spasmodic affection of the heart. I know of no reason why that should rather occur in the case of man than in that of a small animal like a rabbit. The heart is generally more filled when the paroxysms are frequent. When the paroxysm is short and violent, and causes death in a few moments, I should expect to find the heart empty.

The rigidity after death always affects the same muscles — those of the limbs and back. In the case of the rabbit, in which the rigidity was relaxed at the time of death, it returned while the body was warm. In ordinary death it only appears when the body is cold, or nearly so. I never knew a case of tetanus in which the rigidity lasted two months after death; but such a fact would give me the impression that there were very violent spasms. It would indicate great violence of the spasms from which the person died.

The time which elapses between the taking of strychnia and the commencement of the paroxysms depends on the constitution and strength of the individual. A feeling of suffocation is one of the earliest symptoms of poisoning by strychnia, and that would lead the patient to beat the bed clothes.

I have no doubt that the substances I used for the purpose of analysis were pure. I had tested them. The fact that three distinct processes each gave the same result was strong confirmation of each.

I have no doubt that what we found was antimony. The quantity

---

[12] A condition in which the body's muscles turn rigid. In extreme cases, the body forms into the shape of an arch. It can be caused by tetanus, severe cerebral palsy, brain injury, lithium intoxication, or strychnine.

found does not enable me to say how much was taken. It might be the residue of either large or small doses. Sickness would throw off some portion of the antimony which had been administered. We did not analyse the bones and tissues.

Why did you suggest questions to the coroner? — He did not put questions which enabled me to form an opinion. I think that arose rather from want of knowledge than from intention. There was an omission to take down the answers. I made no observation upon that subject.

At the time I wrote to Mr. Gardner, I had not learnt the symptoms which attended the attack and death of Cook. I had only the information that he was well seven days before he died, and had died in convulsions. I had no information which could lead me to suppose that strychnia had been the cause of death, except that Palmer had purchased strychnia. Failing to find opium, prussic acid, or strychnia, I referred to antimony as the only substance found in the body.

Before writing to the *Lancet*, I had been made the subject of a great many attacks. What I said as to the possibility or impossibility of discovering strychnia after death had been misrepresented. In various newspapers it had been represented that I had said that strychnia could never be detected, that it was destroyed by putrefaction. What I said was that when absorbed into the blood it could not be separated as strychnia. I wrote the letter for my own vindication.[13]

Dr. GEORGE OWEN REES,
examined by Mr. *E. James*, Q.C.

I am a lecturer on Materia Medica[14] at Guy's Hospital, and I assisted Dr. Taylor in making the *post-mortem* examination referred to by that gentleman; and he has most correctly stated the result. I was present during the whole time, and at the discovery of the antimony.

---

[13] Journalist Henry Mayhew did not appreciate Taylor's accusation of underhanded dealings. According to the memoirs of *Illustrated Times* editor Henry Vizetelly, he accompanied Mayhew during the next break to lodge a protest with Attorney General Alexander Cockburn:

"When the court adjourned for luncheon I accompanied him in search of Cockburn whom we found washing his hands in one of the upstairs lavatories. He listened to the explanation which appeared to perfectly satisfy him and laughingly remarked that the badgering Taylor had met with in the witness box had driven him to make a mountain out of a molehill."

[14] Latin for "medical materials," later renamed pharmacology. A teacher on the therapeutic properties of substances used for healing.

I am of the opinion that it may have been administered within a few days or a few hours of Mr. Cook's death. All the tests we employed failed to discover the presence of strychnia.

The stomach was in a most unfavourable state for examination; it was cut open, and turned inside out; its mucous surface was lying upon the intestines, and the contents of the stomach, if there had been any, must have been thrown among the intestines, and mixed with them. These circumstances were very unfavourable to the hope of discovering strychnia.

I agree with Dr. Taylor as to the manner in which strychnia acts upon the human frame, and I am of the opinion that it may be taken either by accident or design, sufficient to destroy life, and no trace of it be found after death.

I was present at the experiments made by Dr. Taylor upon the animals, and at the endeavour to detect it in the stomachs afterwards. We failed to do so in three cases out of four. The symptoms accompanying the deaths of the animals were very similar to those described in the case of Mr. Cook. I have heard the cases that have been mentioned in this Court, and the symptoms in every one of them are analogous to those in the case of Mr. Cook.

Cross-examined by Mr. *Grove*, Q.C. I did not see either of the animals reject any portion of the poison; but I heard that in one case the animal did reject a portion. I have no facts to state upon which I formed the opinion that the poison acts by absorption.

Professor WILLIAM THOMAS BRANDE, examined by Mr. *Welsby*.

I am Professor of Chymistry at the Royal Institution.[15] I was not present at the analysis of the liver and spleen, &c., of the deceased; but the report of Dr. Taylor and Dr. Rees was sent to me for my inspection afterwards. I was present at one of the analyses. We examined in the first place the action of copper upon a very weak solution of antimony, and we ascertained there was no action until the solution was slightly acidified by muriatic acid and heated. The antimony was then deposited, and I am enabled to state positively that that deposit was antimony.

By the *Attorney-General* — The experiment I refer to was made for the purpose of testing the accuracy of the test that had already been applied, and it was perfectly satisfactory.

---

[15] A group founded in 1799 for the purpose of scientific education and research.

Professor Christison, of Edinburgh

Professor ROBERT CHRISTISON examined.

I am a Fellow of the Royal College of Physicians, and Professor of Materia Medica to the University of Edinburgh; I am also the author of a work on the subject of poisons, and I have directed a good deal of attention to strychnia. In my opinion it acts by absorption into the blood, and through that upon the nervous system. I have seen its effect on a human subject, but not a fatal case. I have seen it tried upon pigs, rabbits, cats, and one wild boar. (A laugh.)

I first directed my attention to this poison in 1820, in Paris. It had been discovered two years before in Paris. In most of my experiments upon animals, I gave very small doses — a sixth of a grain; but I once administered a grain. I cannot say how small a dose would cause the death of an animal by administration into the stomach. I generally applied it by injection through an incision in the cavity of the chest. A sixth part of a grain so administered killed a dog in two minutes. I once administered to a rabbit, through the stomach, a dose of a grain. I saw Dr. Taylor administer three-quarters of a grain to a rabbit, and it was all swallowed except a very small quantity.

The symptoms are nearly the same in rabbits, cats, and dogs. The first is a slight tremor and unwillingness to move; then frequently the animal jerks its head back slightly; soon after that all the symptoms of tetanus come on which have been so often described by the previous witnesses. When the poison is administered by the stomach death generally takes place between a period of five minutes and five-and-twenty minutes after the symptoms first make their appearance. I have frequently opened the bodies of animals thus killed, and have never been able to trace any effect of the poison upon the stomach or intestines, or upon the spinal cord or brain, that I could attribute satisfactorily to the poison. The heart of the animal generally contained blood in all the cases in which I have been concerned. In the case of the wild boar the poison was injected into the chest. A third of a grain was all that was used, and in ten minutes the symptoms began to show themselves.

If strychnia was administered in the form of a pill it might be mixed with other ingredients that would protract the period of its operation. This would be the case if it were mixed with resinous materials, or materials that were difficult of digestion, and such materials would be within the knowledge of any medical man, and they are frequently used for the purpose of making ordinary pills. Absorption in such a case would not commence until the pill was broken down by the process of digestion.

In the present state of our knowledge of the subject, I do not think it is possible to fix the precise time when the operation of the poison commences on a human subject. In the case of an animal we take care that it is fasting, and we mix the poison with ingredients that are readily soluble, and every circumstance favourable for the development of the poison.

I have seen many cases of tetanus arising from wounds and other causes. The general symptoms of the disorder very nearly resemble each other, and in all the natural forms of tetanus the symptoms begin and advance much more slowly, and they prove fatal much more slowly, and there is no intermission in certain forms of natural tetanus. In tetanus from strychnia there are short intermissions.

I have heard the evidence of what took place at the Talbot Arms on the Monday and Tuesday, and the result of my experience induces me to come to the conclusion that the symptoms exhibited by the deceased were only attributable to strychnia, or the four poisons containing it. (The witness gave the technical names of the poisons he referred to.) There is no natural disease of any description that I am acquainted with to which I could refer these symptoms. In cases of tetanus consciousness remains to the very last moment.[16]

When death takes place in a human subject by spasm it tends to empty the heart of blood. When death is the consequence of the administration of strychnia, if the quantity is small, I should not expect to find any trace in the body after death. If there was an excess of quantity more than was required to cause the death by absorption, I should expect to find that excess in the stomach.

The colour tests for the detection of the presence of strychnia are uncertain. Vegetable poisons are more difficult of detection than mineral ones, and there is one poison with which I am acquainted for which no known test has been discovered.

The stomach of the deceased was sent in a very unsatisfactory state for examination, and there must have been a considerable quantity of strychnia in the stomach to have enabled any one to detect its presence under such circumstances.

Cross-examined by the *Attorney-General*. The experiments I refer to were made many years ago. In one instance I tried one of the colour tests in the case of a man who was poisoned by strychnia, but I failed to discover the presence of the poison in the stomach. I tried the test for the development of the violet colour by means of sulphuric acid and oxide of lead. From my own observation I should say that animals destroyed by strychnia die of asphyxia; but in my work, which has been referred to, it will be seen that I have left the question open.

Some further questions were put to the witness by the learned counsel for the prisoner in reference to opinions expressed by him in his work, and he explained that this work was written 12 years ago, and that the experience he had since obtained had modified some of the opinions he then entertained.

The trial was then again adjourned at six o'clock.

---

[16] With this, three of Britain's most eminent members of the medical profession — Brodie, Taylor, and Christison — agreed that Cook died from strychnine.

SIXTH DAY.—May 20, 1856.

The trial of William Palmer on the charge of poisoning John Parsons Cook was resumed this morning. The court was quite as much crowded as during the previous days. Among the gentlemen upon the bench were Mr. Horsman, M.P., Sir J. Ramsden, M.P., and Sir John Wilson, Governor of Chelsea Hospital.

The learned Judges, Lord Chief Justice Campbell, Mr. Baron Alderson, and Mr. Justice Cresswell, accompanied by the Recorder, the Sheriffs, Under-Sheriffs, and several members of the Court of Aldermen, came into court shortly before 10 o'clock, and took their seats upon the bench. The prisoner was immediately placed in the dock. His appearance and demeanour were in no respect changed.

Dr. John Jackson

JOHN JACKSON, examined by Mr. *James*.

I am a member of the College of Physicians. I have recently returned from India, where I have practised for 25 years. During that practice I have had my attention directed to cases of idiopathic and traumatic tetanus. In England idiopathic tetanus appears to be rare. In India it is comparatively frequent. The proportion of cases of idiopathic to traumatic tetanus is about one-third. I have seen not less than 40 cases in the hospital at Calcutta. That disease is not considered to be so fatal as traumatic tetanus, but I have found that it is equally so. It is commonly found in children both native and European. It takes place about the third day after birth. It will also be occasioned by cold in the climate of India. In infants there is a more marked symptom of lockjaw than in traumatic tetanus. In adults there is no difference between the symptoms of the two diseases.

I have always seen idiopathic tetanus preceded by premonitory symptoms. Those are a peculiar expression of the countenance and stiffness in the muscles of the throat and of the jaw. The period which usually elapses between the attack of idiopathic tetanus and the fatal termination of the disease is in infants 48 hours; in adults, if the disease arises from cold, it is longer, and may continue many days, going through the same grades as the traumatic form of the disease.

I have not heard the evidence of the attacks of the deceased Cook.

Cross-examined by Mr. *Serjeant Shee*. In idiopathic tetanus the patient is always uncomfortable for some time before the attack. The appetite is not much affected. He complains more of the muscles of his neck. He may within 12 hours of a serious attack preserve his relish for food. I never heard a patient complain of want of appetite. I have known cases of idiopathic tetanus in which the first paroxysm occurred in bed. I have known this disease occur to women after confinement or miscarriage. Sometimes one of the premonitory symptoms is a difficulty in swallowing.

Re-examined by the *Attorney-General*. In an infant not more than six hours will elapse between the premonitory symptoms and the commencement of the tetanic paroxysm; in an adult the interval will be from 12 to 24, sometimes more than that. The interval from the commencement of the tetanic convulsions to death will vary from three to ten days. Sometimes death may occur in two days, but that is an early termination. When the disease sets in the course of the symptoms is alike in both forms of tetanus. Both forms are much more common in India than in England. The symptoms in India are the same as in England. I have never seen a case in which the disease ended in death in 20 minutes or half-an-hour.

DANIEL SCULLY BURGEN,
re-examined by the *Attorney-General*.

I am the chief superintendent of police at Stafford. I attended the coroner's inquest on the body of Cook. After the verdict had been returned, I, on the night of Saturday, December 15, searched the house of the prisoner Palmer. I found a quantity of papers, the greater portion in the surgery and drawing-room, but some in Palmer's bedroom. I put them all into the drawing-room, locked the door, and put the key into my pocket.

On the following day (Sunday) I endeavoured to make a selection of them in the presence of Mr. George Palmer, the prisoner's brother, an attorney at Rugeley. Assisted by Inspector Crisp and Mr. Woollaston, I went through all the papers.

Eventually, on the Tuesday morning, I gave up the idea of selection and tied up all the papers, took them away in a black leather bag, and conveyed them to Stafford, where I delivered them to Mr. Hatton, the chief constable.

Some days afterwards, I believe on the 24th of December, the bag was opened in my presence, and the papers were gone through minutely by Mr. Deane, solicitor, acting for the prosecution. He classified them, and they were then again tied up. Mr. Deane copied a portion of them, but he kept none. They were all left at the office of the chief constable. When I examined the papers I saw what they were. I did not find a cheque on Messrs. Weatherby, purporting to bear the signature of Cook, nor any paper purporting to bear his signature respecting bills of exchange.

Some of the papers were afterwards returned to Mr. George Palmer. Mr. Deane selected a large number of letters and documents, private accounts, private letters, which were delivered to Inspector Crisp, with instructions to give them to Mr. George Palmer. William Palmer was arrested on the night of the 15th of December.[1]

Cross-examined by Mr. *Serjeant Shee*. The inquest was held at the Talbot Arms. It continued several days. The first meeting was merely to empanel the jury. The inquest lasted more than a fortnight. The prisoner was arrested by the sheriff on a civil process a day or two before the verdict was delivered. From the commencement of the inquest until that time he was at his house at Rugeley. He was never present at the inquest, nor did any one act professionally for him.

---

[1] In his biography, Fletcher adds that a friend went into Palmer's house after his arrest. Inside he found the packets of laudanum and prussic acid, but not the six grains of strychnine.

Some time before the death of Cook I heard of an Inspector Field, who I believe is not now a police-officer, being at Rugeley. I know that there are such persons as the Duttons, but I do not know anything about them, or their mother.

Mr. Deane, Solicitor

HENRY AUGUSTUS DEANE,
examined by Mr. *James*.

I am an attorney, and a member of the firm of Chubb, Deane, and Chubb, Gray's Inn.[2] I attended the inquest on the body of Walter Palmer, but not that on the body of Cook.

On the 24th of December, I saw Palmer's papers at Stafford. They

---

[2] One of the four professional associations remaining from the days when lawyers gathered to practice law and teach students the ways of the profession. The others are Lincoln's Inn, Inner Temple, and Middle Temple.

were in the custody of the last witness. The papers were in a black bag, which was unsealed in my presence. Bergen, Mr. Hatton, the chief constable, and myself were the persons present. I carefully examined all the papers, for the purpose of selecting those which it was necessary should be kept. I returned a considerable number of immaterial papers to George Palmer. Among the papers I found no cheque upon Messrs. Weatherby, purporting to be signed by the deceased Cook, nor any paper like that which the witness Cheshire stated that Palmer asked him to attest — an acknowledgment purporting to be signed by Cook that bills to the amount of some thousands had been accepted by Palmer for Cook's benefit. I saw George Palmer, the solicitor, after the papers which I had selected were returned to him.

Cross-examined by Mr. *Serjeant Shee*. I know Field, the detective officer. We were solicitors to the Prince of Wales Insurance Office. It was in our employment that Field went to Rugeley. He was at Rugeley only a part of one day. He was at Stafford for three or four days altogether. He

Inspector Field, the Detective Officer

did not see the prisoner Palmer. His visit had been preceded by that of another officer, named Simpson. Simpson went from Stafford to Rugeley with myself and Field. He told me he had seen Palmer. I think he went into Staffordshire in the first week in October.

Re-examined by Mr. *James*. Field was sent down to make inquiries as to the habits of life of Mr. Walter Palmer, of whose death the office had shortly before received notice, and also to inquire into the circumstances of a person named Bates, with reference to a proposal for an insurance of £25,000 upon his life.

JOHN ESPIN, examined by Mr. *James*.

I am a solicitor practising in Davies-street, Berkeley-square.[3] I am solicitor to Mr. Padwick. I produce a bill for £2,000 which was placed in my hands to enforce payment from the prisoner.

Mr. Strawbridge, manager of the bank at Rugeley, was called, and proved that the drawing and endorsement of this bill — a bill at three months for £2,000, drawn by William Palmer, and purporting to be accepted by Sarah Palmer — were in the handwriting of the prisoner, and that the acceptance was not in that of his mother.

John Espin continued — This bill would be due on the 6th of October, 1854. £1,000 had been paid off it. Judgment was signed on the 12th of December, and I had then had the bill only a day or two. The execution was issued on the 12th of December. I have here a letter from William Palmer addressed to Mr. Padwick on the 12th of November, and enclosing a cheque, and requesting that it should not be presented until the 28th of November. I produce the cheque for £1,000 enclosed in this letter of the 12th. The cheque is dated the 28th. That cheque was not paid. I produce another cheque, dated the 8th of December, 1855, payable to Mr. Padwick or bearer, for the sum of £600. [Mr. Strawbridge proved that the signature to this cheque was in the handwriting of the prisoner.] That was not paid. It was received a few days after the cheque for £1,000 was dishonoured. £1,000 still remained due. We issued a ca. sa.[4] against the prisoner's person. Upon that Palmer was arrested.

Cross-examined by Mr. *Serjeant Shee*. I believe all the documents were placed in my hands together about the 12th of December.

---

[3] A fashionable town square in London's West End consisting of a rectangular park surrounded by homes. It was named in the mid-18th century for the aristocratic Berkeley family, who lived there when they were not at their castle in Gloucestershire.

[4] Legal abbreviation for the Latin phrase "Capias ad satisfaciendu" or writ of execution.

THE TIMES REPORT

Dr. Bamford, of Rugeley

WILLIAM BAMFORD,
examined by the *Attorney-General*.

I am a surgeon and apothecary[5] at Rugeley, in Staffordshire. I first saw the deceased John Parsons Cook on Saturday, the 17th of November. Palmer, the prisoner, asked me to visit him. Palmer said that Cook had been dining with him the day before, and had taken too much champagne. I went with Palmer to see Cook. I asked Cook if he had taken too much wine the day before, and he assured me that he took but two glasses. I found no appearance of bile about Cook, but

---

[5] At 80 and in practice for more than five decades, Bamford was unqualified to practice medicine, as his testimony will show. It wouldn't be until the Medical Act of 1858 that a council would be formed to regulate doctors in Britain. But under the law, unqualified doctors would still be allowed to practice.

there was constant vomiting. I prescribed for him a saline effervescing draught and a six-ounce mixture. I never saw Cook take any of the pills which I had prescribed.

After I had prepared the pills on the Monday evening I took them to the Talbot Arms and gave them to a servant maid, who took them upstairs. On the Saturday, Sunday, and Monday, I prepared the same pills.

I saw Palmer on the Tuesday morning. I was going to see Cook when he met me. I asked him if he had seen Cook the night before. He said that he saw him between 9 and 10 o'clock, and was with him for half-an-hour. He requested that I would not disturb Cook, and I went home without seeing him. Between 12 and 1 o'clock Palmer begged I would not go, because he was still and quiet, and he did not wish him to be disturbed. At 7 o'clock in the evening Palmer came to my house, and requested me to go and see Cook again. I went and saw him. Having seen Cook, I left the room with Jones and Palmer. Palmer said he rather wished Cook to have his pills again, and that he would walk up with me for them. He did so, and stood by while I prepared them in my surgery. I had strychnia in a cupboard in my own private room. I put the pills in a box, and addressed it, "Night pills. John Parsons Cook, Esq." I wrote that direction on all the four nights. On the Tuesday night Palmer requested that I would put on a direction. After that I did not again see Cook alive.

Palmer took away the pills between 7 and 8 o'clock. I had wrapped the box up in paper, and had sealed it. There was no impression of a seal upon it. The direction was upon a separate paper, which I placed under the box, and between it and the outside paper. Nothing was written on the box or on the outside paper.

It was as near as could be 20 minutes past 12 at midnight when I saw Cook dead. I understood he was alive when they came to me, and I could not have been more than five or ten minutes in going up. I found the body stretched out, resting on the heels and the back of the head, as straight as possible, and stiff. The arms were extended down each side of the body, and the hands were clinched. I filled up the certificate, and gave it as my opinion that he died from apoplexy. Palmer asked me to fill up the certificate. I had forms of certificates in my possession. When Palmer asked me to fill up the certificate, I told him that, as Cook was his patient, it was his place to fill up the certificate. He said he had much rather I did it, and I did so.

I was present at the *post-mortem* examination. After it was over, Palmer said, "We ought not to have let that jar go." That was all he said.

Cross-examined by Mr. *Serjeant Shee*. My house is about 200 yards from that of the prisoner.

THE TIMES REPORT

MR. THOMAS PRATT, BILL DISCOUNTER

THOMAS PRATT, examined by Mr. *James*.

I am a solicitor, and practice in Queen-street, Mayfair.[6] I know the prisoner Palmer. My acquaintance with him commenced at the end of November, 1853. I obtained for him a loan of £1,000. That was repaid.

In October, 1854, I was employed by him to make a claim for two policies upon the life of Ann Palmer. I received upon the prisoner's account £5,000 from the Sun office, and £3,000 from the Norwich Union. The money was applied in payment of, I think, three bills, amounting to £3,500 or £4,000, which were due, and of loans obtained

---

[6] A wealthy area of central London bounded by Hyde Park on the west, Soho on the east, Oxford Street on the north and Piccadilly on the south. The district was largely residential in Palmer's time, although many homes have been converted to businesses.

after I had made the claims upon the policies. There was £1,500 not so applied. That was paid to Palmer, or applied to other purposes under his direction.

In April, 1855, Palmer applied to me for a loan of £2,000. He did not state the purpose for which he required the loan. I obtained it upon a bill for £2,000 drawn by himself, and purporting to be accepted by Sarah Palmer.

On the 28th of November of that year there were eight bills held by clients of mine or by myself. [These bills were produced and read; the total amount for which they were drawn was £12,500.] Two bills, dated July 22 and July 24, for £2,000 each, were the only bills which were overdue in November, 1855. Two bills, for £500 and £1,000, were held over from month to month. [These were bills dated June 5 and August 2, 1854.] The interest was paid monthly. With two exceptions, these bills were discounted at the rate of sixty per cent. On the 9th of November the interest for holding over the two bills, dated in 1854, was due.

I remember the death of Walter Palmer. That occurred in August, 1855. I was instructed by William Palmer to claim from the Prince of Wales Insurance Office £13,000 due upon a policy upon his life. The Sarah Palmer by whom these bills purport to be accepted is the mother of the prisoner. While holding these bills I from time to time addressed letters to her. I wrote to Palmer as follows:—

"If you are quite settled on your return from Doncaster, do pray think about your three bills, so shortly coming due. If I do not get a positive appointment from the office to pay, which I do not expect, you must be prepared to meet them as agreed. You told me your mother was coming up this month, and would settle them."

About a week afterwards I wrote to him. [This letter had no date, but bore a postmark, Sept. 24]:—

"You are aware there are three bills, of £2,000 each, accepted by your mother, Mrs. Sarah Palmer, falling due in a day or two. Now, as the £13,000 cannot be received from the Prince of Wales Insurance Office for three months, it will be necessary that those bills should be renewed; I will therefore thank you to send me up three new acceptances to meet those coming due; and which, when they fall due, I presume the money will be ready to meet, which will amount to £1,500 more than your mother has given acceptances for."

On the 2nd of October I wrote:—

"This, you will observe, quite alters arrangements,[7] and I therefore must request that you make preparations for meeting the two bills due at the end of this month. . . . . In any event bear in mind that you must be prepared to cover your mother's acceptances for the

---

[7] Pratt is referring to the refusal of the insurance companies to pay off the policy on Walter Palmer's death.

£4,000 due at the end of the month."

On the 6th of October I wrote to him another letter, containing this passage:—

"I have your note acknowledging receipt by your mother of the £2,000 acceptance, due the 2nd October. Why not let her acknowledge it herself? You must really not fail to come up at once, if it be for the purpose of arranging for the payment of the two bills at the end of the month. Remember I can make no terms for their renewal, and they must be paid."

I had received from Palmer a letter, dated October 5, acknowledging, on the part of his mother, the receipt of a bill of exchange for £2,000. On the 10th I wrote to Palmer a letter, from which the following is an extract:—

"However, not to repeat what I said in my last, but with the view of pressing on you the remembrance that the two bills due at the end of this month, the 26th and 27th, must be met, I say no more. The £2,000 acceptance of your mother, due the 29th of September, I sent her yesterday. It was renewed by the second of the three sent me up."

On the 18th of October I wrote to Palmer as follows:—

"I send copies of two letters I have received. As regards the first, it shows how important it is that you or your mother should prepare for payment of the £4,000 due in a few days. I cannot now obtain delay on the same ground I did the others, for then I could have no ground for supposing the claim would not be admitted."

On the 27th of October Palmer called and paid me £250. That was on account of the bills due on the 25th and 27th of that month. He said he would remit another sum of an equal amount before the following Wednesday, and would pay the remainder of the principal by instalments as shortly as possible.

In reply to a letter of mine of the 27th of October, I received the following letter from him, dated 28th of October:—

"I will send you the £250 from Worcester on Tuesday, as arranged. For goodness sake do not think of writs; only let me know that such steps are going to be taken and I will get you the money, even if I pay £1,000 for it; only give me a fair chance, and you shall be paid the whole of the money."

On the 31st of October I wrote to Palmer:—

"The £250 in registered letter duly received to-day. With it I have been enabled to obtain consent to the following:— That, with the exception of issuing the writs against your mother, no proceeding as to service shall be made until the morning of Saturday, the 10th, when you are to send up the £1,000 or £1,600. You will be debited with a month's interest on the whole of £4,000 out of the money sent up. I impress upon you the necessity of your being punctual as to the bills. You will not forget also the £1,500 due on the 9th of November."

On the 6th of November I issued writs against Palmer and his mother for £4,000. I sent them to Mr. Crabbe, a solicitor at Rugeley.

On the 10th of November Palmer called on me. I had received a letter from him on the 9th of November:— "I will be with you on Saturday next at half-past one."

He did call on me, and paid me £300, which, with the two sums I had before received made up £800. £200 was deducted for interest, leaving £600. He was to endeavour to let me have a further remittance, but nothing positive was said. It is possible that writs were mentioned, but I have no recollection of it. No doubt he knew of them. [A letter of November 13th from Pratt to Palmer was then read, in which, after giving some explanations with respect to the "Prince of Wales" policy, Pratt said, "I count most positively on seeing you on Saturday; do, for both our sakes, try and make up the amount to £1,000, for without it I shall be unable to renew the £1,500 due on the 9th."]

On the 16th of November Palmer wrote to me:— "I am obliged to come to Tattersall's on Monday to the settling, so that I shall not call and see you before Monday, but a friend of mine will call and leave you £200 to-morrow, and I will give you the remainder on Monday."

On the Saturday (November 17th) some one came from Palmer, and gave me a cheque of a Mr. Fisher for £200. On the 19th Mr. Palmer wrote to me:—

"All being well, I shall be with you to-morrow (Monday), but cannot say what time now. Fisher left the £200 for me."

On Monday, the 19th, which was the settling day at Tattersall's, Palmer called on me after 3 o'clock. This paper (produced) was then drawn up, and he signed it:—

"You will place the £50 which I have just paid you, and the £450 you will receive by Mr. Herring — together £500 — and the £200 you received on Saturday, towards payment of my mother's acceptance for £2,000 due on the 25th of October, making paid to this day the sum of £1,300."

He paid me £50 at the time, and said I should receive the £450 through the post, from Mr. Herring. I afterwards received a cheque from him for that amount, which was paid through my bankers. On the 21st of November Palmer wrote to me:—

"Ever since I saw you I have been fully engaged with Cook and not able to leave home. I am sorry to say, after all, he died this day. So you had better write to Saunders; but, mind you, I must have Polestar, if it can be so arranged; and, should any one call upon you to know what money or moneys Cook ever had from you, don't answer the question till I have seen you.

"I will send you the £75 to-morrow, and as soon as I have been to

Manchester you shall hear about other moneys. I sat up two full nights with Cook, and am very much tired out."

On the 22d of November I wrote to Palmer:—

"I have your note, and am greatly disappointed at the non-receipt of the money as promised, and at the vague assurances as to any money. I can understand, 'tis true, that your being detained by the illness of your friend has been the cause of not sending up the larger amount, but the smaller sum you ought to have sent. If anything unpleasant occurs you must thank yourself.

"The death of Mr. Cook will now compel you to look about as to the payment of the bill for £500 on the 2d of December."

On the 23rd of November I received a note from Palmer, saying that Messrs. Weatherby, of 6, Old Burlington-street, would forward a cheque for £75 in the morning. I saw him on the 24th when he signed the following paper:—

"I have paid you this day £100. £75 you will pay for renewal of £1,500 due the 9th of November for one month, and £25 on account of the £2,000 due the 25th of October, making £1,326 paid."

I had received a cheque for £75 on Messrs. Weatherby, but they refused to pay it. On the 26th of November Palmer wrote to me:—

"(Strictly private and confidential.)

"My dear Sir,— Should any of Cook's friends call upon you to know what money Cook ever had from you, pray don't answer that question or any other about money matters until I have seen you. And oblige yours faithfully,
"William Palmer."

There was a bill of sale on Polestar and another horse of Cook's called Sirius. I did not know Cook. I never saw him. The bill of sale was executed at the beginning of September. The prisoner had transacted the loan.

On the 26th of August Palmer wrote to me on the subject:—

"Now, I want, and must have it from somewhere, £1,000 clear by next Saturday without fail, and you can raise it on the policy (viz., the policy for £13,000 on the life of W. Palmer) if you like, and it must be had at a much less rate of interest than I have hitherto had, because the security is so very good, and if you cannot manage it you must let me have the policy, because you have plenty of security for your money."

On the 30th of August he again wrote:—

"I have undertaken to get the enclosed bill cashed for Mr. Cook. You had the £200 bill of his. He is a very good and responsible man. Will you do it? I will put my name to the bill." In this letter was enclosed Cook's acceptance for £500.

On the 6th of September Palmer wrote:—

"I received the cheque for the £100, and will thank you to let me have the £315 by return of post, if possible; if not, send it to me (certain) by Monday night's post, to the Post-office, Doncaster. I now return you Cook's papers signed, &c, and he wants the money on Saturday, if he can have it, but I have not promised it for Saturday. I told him he should have it on Tuesday morning at Doncaster; so please enclose it with mine, in cash, in a registered letter, and he must pay for it being registered. Do not let it be later than Monday night's post to Doncaster."

On the 9th of September he wrote:—

"You must send me for Mr. Cook, by Monday night's post (to the Post-office, Doncaster), £385 instead of £375, and the wine-warrant, so that I can hand it to him with the £375, and that will be allowing you £50 for the discount, &c. I shall then get £10, and I expect I shall have to take to the wine, and give him the money; but I shall not do so if you do not send £385, and be good enough to enclose my £315 with it, in cash, in a registered letter, and direct it to me to the Post-office, Doncaster."

I accordingly wrote to Palmer, at the Post-office, Doncaster, enclosing £300 in notes, and cheque for £375. I struck out the words "or bearer," so that it was payable to order. In the letter I said:—

"You know by this time that if I do what I can to accommodate you there is a limit to my means to do so, and more particularly as in this instance, you have been the means of shutting up a supply I could generally go to. I think also you had little reason to allude to the £10 difference after the trouble, correspondence, &c, I had with respect to a second insurance you know of, which, although it did not come off, arose not from any lack of industry on my part. I have no reply as yet from the Prince of Wales. When shall I see you about the three £2,000 bills coming due at the end of this month? I speak in time, in order that you may be prepared in case anything untoward happens with the Prince of Wales. I am obliged to send a cheque for Cook, as I have not received the money, which I shall do, no doubt, to-morrow."

The cheque for £375 and the wine warrant was the consideration for Cook's bill of sale for £500. The other £300 had nothing to do with Cook's transactions. [A letter from Palmer was then read, acknowledging the receipt of the previous letter, with the enclosures.]

I had one other transaction with Cook before this. It related to an acceptance of Cook for £200, which was paid. I had no other pecuniary transaction whatever with him.

The date of the first transaction was the end of April or early in May, 1855. The bill was drawn by Palmer on Cook, and was paid by Cook.

THE TIMES REPORT

Mr. Stevens was here recalled, and, having examined the endorsement on the cheque for £375, said — This endorsement is not in the handwriting of Cook. I never saw him write his name otherwise than "J. Parsons Cook," whereas this is written "J. P. Cook."

Mr. Strawbridge was shown some acceptances purporting to be by Mrs. Sarah Palmer, and said that none of them were in Mrs. Palmer's handwriting.

William Cheshire, who had been a clerk in the bank at Rugeley in September last, proved that Palmer had an account there, and that the cheque already in evidence had been received by him and carried to Palmer's credit.

Cross-examined by Mr. *Serjeant Shee.* — I did not know Cook; he never had any transactions with me.

Previous to May, 1855, I knew nothing at all about Cook. I then held a sum of £310, due to Palmer, and he wished me to add £190 to it, and to pay £500 to a Mr. Sargent. I declined to do that without further security. He then proposed the security of Cook's acceptances, and represented Cook to be a gentleman of respectability and substance. On his representation I agreed to accept a bill drawn by him on Cook for £200, and to make the advance. He thus got the £500. I wrote to Cook about the first transaction. I also wrote to him before his death, on the 13th of November, reminding him that £500 was due December 2. I sent the letter to him at Lutterworth.

Re-examined. The first £200 bill was due on the 29th of June, but was not then paid. I wrote about it, and Cook came up on the 2nd of July and paid it. I did not see him.[8]

---

[8] Pratt's greed led to his downfall. He accepted assurances that Palmer's mother was backing these loans, despite having never met her and seeing numerous signatures that did not match. He agreed to hold the £13,000 insurance policy on Walter Palmer's life after seeing Palmer cash in on his wife's death. This leads one to wonder just how much he closed his eyes to in the pursuit of profit. By the time Cook died, Palmer owed Pratt and Padwick about £25,000 and was four months behind in interest that averaged £1,250 a month.

Like the villain of a Victorian penny dreadful, Pratt suffered for his sins. At the Walter Palmer inquest, he screamed from the stand "How can you ask such questions of a man with three young children and a wife who will probably be ruined by this affair?" Testifying at the trial probably finished him off. Fletcher noted that "The cold, merciless manner in which he gave his evidence made a great impression at the trial." The press savaged him for his behavior and appearance. One reporter described him as "a sinister figure, tall and big, trying to be fashionable in his style of dress, enormous brown whiskers almost meeting at the chin, the face that of a small boy, the low, weak voice of a retiring female." It is believed that he went mad and died in an asylum within a year.

JOHN ARMSHAW, examined by Mr. *Welsby*.

I am an attorney, practising at Rugeley. About the 13th of November I was employed to apply to Palmer for payment of a debt of about £60, due to some mercers and drapers[9] at Rugeley. On the 19th of November I sent up to London instructions for a writ. On the next morning (the 20th) I went to Palmer's house. He gave me two £50 notes, and said he hoped he should not be put to the cost of the writ. One was a Bank of England, the other a local note. I took them to my employer to get the receipt and change, and to settle about the costs.

JOHN WALLBANK, examined by Mr. *Welsby*.

I am a butcher at Rugeley. On the Monday, in Shrewsbury race week, Palmer's man came to me and fetched me to Palmer's house. Palmer said, "I want you to lend me £25." I said, "Doctor, I'm very short of money, but I'll try if I can get it. He said, "Do, that's a good fellow; I'll give it you again on Saturday morning, as I shall then have received some money at Shrewsbury." On the Saturday I met him in the street, went to his house with him, and he paid me the money.

Cross-examined by Mr. *Serjeant Shee*. Palmer had lent me money sometimes when I had asked him. His mother lived in the town in a large house near the church. He was in the habit of going there.

JOHN SPILLBURY, examined by Mr. *Bodkin*.

I am a farmer, near Stafford, and have had dealings with Palmer. In November last he owed me £16 2s. On the 22nd of November (Thursday) I called on him, and he paid me that amount. He gave me a Bank of England note for £50. I called casually. I had not applied to him for the money. That was the first transaction I had with him.

Mr. THOMAS SMERDON STRAWBRIDGE, examined by the *Attorney-General*.

On the 19th of November Palmer had an account at the bank, and there was a balance of £9 6s. in his favour. Nothing was paid to his account after that. The 10th of October was the last date on which anything was paid to the account. The amount then paid was £50.

---

[9] Dealers in fabrics. Mercers tended to sell fine cloth, such as silk, that had to be imported, while drapers operated as retailers or wholesalers of all fabrics.

HERBERT WRIGHT, examined by Mr. *E. James*.

I am a solicitor, in partnership with my brother, at Birmingham. I have known Palmer since July, 1851. In November, 1855, he owed my brother £10,400. We had a bill of sale upon his property. [It was produced and read. It recited that Palmer was indebted to Edwin Wright in the sum of £6,500, on account of bills of exchange accepted by Sarah Palmer and endorsed by Palmer to Wright, and as security for that amount, and a further sum of £2,300, which had been advanced to him, a power of sale, subject to redemption, was given by Palmer over the whole of his property, including his horses.]

All the advances were made upon bills, together with other collateral security. All the bills are here. [The bills purporting to be accepted by Palmer's mother were produced; also an acceptance of Palmer's for £1,600.] In the early part of November I was pressing Palmer for payment. Many of the bills were overdue. Palmer always said the money would be paid after the Cambridgeshire races at Newmarket. I put the bill of sale in force in December, after the verdict of the coroner's jury was returned. I was present when the property was taken. I found no papers in the house.

Cross-examined by Mr. *Serjeant Shee*. Should you have objected to give Palmer more time for payment if you had been asked? — I hardly know; probably I should not. I was not hostile to him. I never accommodated Cook. I had offered to do so, but the transaction never assumed completion. (A laugh.)

Re-examined by the *Attorney-General*. These bills were discounted at 60 per cent, per annum, and would have been renewed probably at the same rate of interest.

Mr. Strawbridge proved that the acceptances produced by the last witness were not in the handwriting of Mrs. Palmer.

Cross-examined. — They are a bad imitation of her hand.

The *Attorney-General* said that Mr. Weatherby was the only remaining witness for the prosecution; and, as he was not now in court, he hoped their Lordships would allow him to be examined in the morning, before his learned friend opened the defence.

Mr. *Serjeant Shee* asked the Court to permit the witness Mills to be recalled, in order that he might examine her as to where she was now residing.

The *Attorney-General* — She was cross-examined upon that point.

Lord CAMPBELL — We are of the opinion that there is no ground for recalling her.

Mr. *Serjeant Shee* asked permission to put some further questions to Dr. Devonshire, with regard to his having been pushed by Palmer during the *post-mortem* examination.

Lord CAMPBELL — By all means.

Mr. Justice CRESSWELL observed, that he did not think it was a circumstance to which much importance could be attached; he had not taken a note of it.

Mr. Baron ALDERSON expressed a similar opinion. There was nothing extraordinary in a person who was interested in the examination being anxious to see all that was going on.

Mr. *Serjeant Shee*, after that intimation of their Lordships' would not press his request.

Lord CAMPBELL hoped that the jury would have an opportunity given them of breathing the fresh air that fine evening. — The Court adjourned at half-past 3.

SEVENTH DAY.—May 21, 1856.

The court was even more crowded this morning than it had been since the commencement of the trial. By 9 o'clock every available seat was occupied, and a great number of persons waited in the passages leading to the various entrances during the whole day without being able to obtain admission. Among the distinguished persons who were present we noticed the Lord Chief Baron, the Earl of Denbigh, Lord G. Lennox, Mr. Monckton Milnes, Mr. L. Gower, Mr. G.O. Higgins, Mr. Forster, and several other members of the House of Commons.

The learned Judges, Lord Campbell, Mr. Baron Alderson, and Mr. Justice Cresswell, entered the court at about 10 o'clock, accompanied by the Sheriffs, Sir R. W. Carden, and other Aldermen.

The prisoner was immediately placed at the bar. He listened with great attention to the address of his learned counsel, and maintained the same calmness and self-possession that he has exhibited since the first day of the proceedings.

Counsel for the Crown: the Attorney-General, Mr. E. James, Q.C., Mr. Welsby, Mr. Bodkin, and Mr. Huddleston; for the prisoner: Mr. Serjeant Shee, Mr. Grove, Q.C., Mr. Gray, and Mr. Kenealy.

CHARLES WEATHERBY,
examined by Mr. *Welsby*.

On the 21st of November I received a letter from Palmer, enclosing a cheque for £350. I produce that letter;—

"RUGELEY, NOV. 20, 1855.

"GENTLEMEN,— I will thank you to send me a cheque for the amount of the enclosed order. Mr. Cook has been confined here to his bed for the last three days with a bilious attack, which has prevented him from being in town. — Yours respectfully,

WM. PALMER."

On the morning of the 23rd I received another letter from him, which I also produce. [In this letter Palmer requested Messrs. Weatherby to send a cheque for £75 to Mr. Pratt, and a cheque for £100 to Mr. Earwaker, and deduct the same from Cook's draft.]

On the 23rd I sent a letter to Palmer, of which I produce a copy:—

MR. WEATHERBY, SECRETARY TO THE JOCKEY CLUB

"Nov. 23, 1855.

"SIR,— We return Mr. Cook's cheque, not having funds enough to meet it. When Mr. Frail called to-day to settle the Shrewsbury Stake account, he informed us that he had paid Mr. Cook his winnings there. We could not comply with your request as to paying part of the money even if we had had sufficient in hand to pay the sums you mention, which we have not. Be so good as to acknowledge the receipt of the cheque."

On the 24th the following notice, signed by Palmer, was left at my office:—

"Nov. 24, 1855.

"GENTLEMEN,—I hereby request you will not part with any moneys in your hands, or which may come into your hands, on account of John Parsons Cook, to any person, until payment by you to me or my order of the cheque or draft in my favour given by the said John Parsons Cook for the sum of £350 sent to you by me, and acknowledged in your letter received by me at Rugeley, on Wednesday morning, the 20th of this month of November. — Yours, &c,

"WM. PALMER.

"MESSRS. WEATHERBY, 6, OLD BURLINGTON-STREET."

On the 23rd I had sent a letter to Cook at Rugeley, which was subsequently returned to me through the dead-letter office.

Cross-examined by Mr. *Serjeant Shee*. The cheque for £350 was, as far as I recollect, signed by Cook.

The *Attorney-General* — Was it signed J.P. Cook, or J. Parsons Cook? — I did not observe.

By Lord CAMPBELL — I observed that the body of the cheque was not in Cook's handwriting, but that the signature was.

Mr. *Serjeant Shee* — When that cheque of Cook's was presented, you had not funds in hand to meet it? — No.

Were funds afterwards sent up by Mr. Frail, the clerk of the course at Shrewsbury? — They were to have been, but were not eventually.

In the ordinary course of things ought they to have been in your hands on the day you received the cheque? — I cannot positively say. Clerks of the course pay at different times. But Cook might reasonably have supposed that they would be in hand, as it was then a week after he had won the race. I informed Palmer when I did not pay his cheque, of my reason for not doing so.

JOHNSON ROGERSON BUTLER,
examined by the *Attorney-General*.

I attend races, and bet. I was at Shrewsbury races, and had an account to settle with Palmer. I had to receive £700 odd from him in respect of bets made at the Liverpool races. I had no money to receive in respect of the Shrewsbury races. I endeavoured to get my money at Shrewsbury and I got £40. I asked him for money several times, and he said he had none, but had some to receive. He did not say how much. He gave me a cheque for £250 upon the Rugeley Bank, which was not paid. I knew Cook's horse Polestar. After she had won the race at Shrewsbury she was worth about £700. She was worth more after than before she won.

Cross-examined by Mr. *Grove*. I won £210 on Polestar for Palmer, and kept it on account.

Mr. Stevens proved that Polestar was sold at Tattersall's, on the 10th of March, by auction, and fetched 720 guineas.

The *Attorney-General* — That is the case for the prosecution.

MR. SERJEANT WILLIAM SHEE

THE DEFENCE.

Mr. *Serjeant Shee* then rose to open the defence. He said,— In rising to perform the task which it now becomes my duty to discharge, I feel, gentlemen of the jury, an almost overwhelming sense of responsibility. Once only has it fallen to my lot to defend a fellow-creature charged with a capital offence. You can well understand that to take a leading part in a trial of this kind is sufficient to disturb the calmest temper and try the clearest judgment, even if the effort only last one day. But how much more trying is it to stand for six long days under the shade, as it were, of the scaffold, conscious that the least error in judgment may consign my client to an ignominious death and public indignation!

It is useless for me to conceal that which all your endeavours to keep your minds free from prejudice cannot wholly efface from your recollection. You perfectly well know that for six long months, under the sanction and upon the authority of science, an opinion has almost universally prevailed that the blood of John Parsons Cook has risen from the ground to bear witness against the prisoner; you know that a conviction of the guilt of the prisoner has impressed itself upon the whole population, and that by the whole population has been raised, in a delirium of horror and indignation, the cry of blood for blood. You cannot have entered upon the discharge of your duty — which, as I have well observed, you have most conscientiously endeavoured to perform — without, to a great extent, sharing in that conviction.

Before you knew that you would have to sit in that box to pass judgment between the prisoner and the Crown you might with perfect propriety, after reading the evidence taken before the coroner's jury, have formed an opinion with regard to the guilt or innocence of the prisoner. The very circumstances under which we meet in this place are of a character to excite in me mingled feelings of encouragement and alarm. Those whose duty it is to watch over the safety of the Queen's subjects felt so much apprehension lest the course of justice should be disturbed by the popular prejudice which had been excited against the prisoner — they were so much alarmed that an unjust verdict might, in the midst of that prejudice, be passed against him, that an extraordinary measure of precaution was taken, not only by her Majesty's Government, but also by the Legislature. An act of Parliament, which originated in that branch of the Legislature to which the noble and learned Lord who presides here belongs, and was sanctioned by him, was passed to prevent the possibility of an injustice being done through an adherence to the ordinary forms of law in the case of William Palmer.

The Crown, also, under the advice of its responsible Ministers, resolved that this prosecution should not be left in private hands, but that its own law officer, my learned friend the Attorney-General, should take upon himself the responsibility of conducting it. And my learned friend, when that duty was intrusted to him, did what I must say will for ever redound to his honour — he resolved that in a case in which so much prejudice had been excited, all the evidence which it was intended to press against the prisoner should, as soon as he received it, be communicated to the prisoner's counsel. I must therefore tell my unhappy client that everything which the constituted authorities of the land — everything which the Legislature and the law officers of the Crown could do to secure a fair and impartial trial has been done, and that if unhappily an injustice should on either side be committed, the whole responsibility will rest upon my Lords and upon the jury.

A most able man was selected by the prisoner as his counsel not many weeks ago, but, unfortunately, was prevented by illness from discharging that office. I have endeavoured to the best of my ability to supply his place; but I cannot deny that I labour under a deep feeling of responsibility, although the national effort, so to speak, which has been made to insure a fair trial is a great cause of encouragement to me. I am moved by the task that is before me, but I am not dismayed.

I have this further cause for not being altogether overcome in discussing the mass of evidence which has been laid before you. When the papers in the case came into my hands, I had formed no opinion as to the guilt or innocence of the prisoner. My mind was perfectly free to form what I trust will prove to be a right judgment upon the case, and — I say it in all sincerity — having read these papers, I commenced his defence with an entire conviction of his innocence. I believe that truer words were never pronounced than the words he uttered when he said "Not Guilty" to this charge, and if I fail in establishing his innocence to your satisfaction I shall have very great misgivings that my failure is attributable only to my own inability to do justice to his case, and not to any weakness in the case itself.

I will prove to you the sincerity with which I declare my conviction of the prisoner's innocence by meeting the case for the prosecution foot to foot, and grappling with every difficulty which has been suggested by my learned friend. You will see that I shall avoid no point which has been raised. I will deal fairly with you, and I know that I shall have your patient attention to an address which must, I fear, unavoidably be a long one, but in which no observation will be introduced which does not necessarily and properly belong to the case.

The proposition which my learned friend undertakes to establish entirely by circumstantial evidence may be shortly stated. It is that the prisoner, having in the second week in November made up his mind that it was in his interest to get rid of John Parsons Cook, deliberately prepared his body for the reception of a deadly poison by the slower poison of antimony, and that he afterwards despatched him by the deadly poison of strychnine.

Now, no jury will convict a man of the crime thus charged unless it be made clear, in the first place, that he had some motive for its commission — some strong reason for desiring the death of the deceased; in the second place, that the symptoms before death and the appearances of the body after death are consistent with the theory that he died by poison; and, in the third place, that they are inconsistent with the theory that death proceeded from natural causes. Under these three heads I shall discuss the vast mass of evidence which has been laid before you, and I must, by adhering to that order, exhaust the whole subject, and leave myself no chance of evading any difficulty without immediate detection.

Before, however, I proceed to grapple in these close quarters with the case for the Crown, allow me to restore to its proper place in the discussion a fact which although it was by no means concealed by my learned friend in that address by which he at once seized upon your judgments, appeared to me to be thrown too much into the shade, the fact, I mean, that strychnine was not found in the body of the unfortunate deceased. If he died of the poison of strychnine — if he died within a few hours or within a quarter of an hour or twenty minutes of the administration of a strong dose — if the *post-mortem* examination took place within six days of the death, there is not the least reason to suppose that between the time of the injection of the poison and the paroxysms of death there was any dilution of it, or any ejection of it by vomiting. Never, therefore, unless chemical analysis is altogether a failure in the detection of strychnine, were circumstances more favourable for its discovery. But, beyond all question, strychnine was not found.

Whatever we may think of the judgment and experience of Dr. Taylor, we have no reason to doubt that he is a very skilful chemist; we have no reason to believe — in fact, we know to the contrary — that he and Dr. Rees did not do all that the science of chemical analysis could enable men to do to detect the poison. They had a distinct intimation from the executor and near-relative of the deceased that he, for some cause or another, had reason to suspect that poison had been administered. They undertook an analysis of the stomach, which (without now going into details upon that point) was not on the whole in an unfavourable condition, with a firm expectation that if it was there it would be found, and without any doubt as to the efficiency of their tests. Then, in December they say:

"We do not find strychnine, prussic acid, or any trace of opium. From the contents having been drained away" (not drained out of the jar, you know) "it is now impossible to say whether any strychnine had or had not been given just before death, but it is quite possible for tartar emetic to destroy life if given in repeated doses; and, so far as we can at present form an opinion, in the absence of any natural cause of death, the deceased may have died from the effects of antimony in this or some other form."

But they afterwards attended the inquest, and having heard the evidence of Mills, of Mr. Jones, of Lutterworth, and of Roberts (who spoke to the purchase of strychnine on the morning of the death), they came to the conclusion that the pill administered to Cook on the Monday and the Tuesday night contained strychnine. Dr. Taylor came to that conclusion, notwithstanding his written opinion that Cook might have been poisoned by antimony, and notwithstanding the fact that no trace of strychnine was found in the body.

I call your attention now to this circumstance in order to claim for it its proper place in the discussion. The gentlemen who have come to the conclusion that strychnine may have been in the body, although it was not found, have arrived at that conclusion from experiments of a very partial kind indeed; they contend that when strychnine has once done its fatal work and become absorbed into the system it ceases to be the thing it was when taken into the system; it becomes decomposed, its elements are separated from each other, and therefore are no longer capable of responding to the tests which would certainly detect its presence if undecomposed. That is their case. They account for its not being found, and for their belief that it destroyed Cook, by that hypothesis.

Now, it is only an hypothesis. No authority for it can be drawn from experiments, and it is supported by the opinion of no eminent toxicologists but themselves. It is only fair to them and to Dr. Taylor in particular, to say that Dr. Taylor does propound that theory in his book. It is, however, only a theory of his own; he does not support it by the authority of any distinguished toxicologist; and when we recollect that his knowledge of the matter — good, humane man! — consists in having poisoned five rabbits 25 years ago, and five others since this question was raised, it cannot have much weight.

But I will call before you a number of gentlemen of high eminence in their profession as analytical chemists, who will state their utter renunciation of that theory. I will call Dr. Nunneley, a fellow of the Royal College of Surgeons and a professor of Chymistry, who attended the case at Leeds, which has been described to you, and Dr. Williams, professor of Materia Medica at the Royal College of Surgeons in Ireland, for 18 years surgeon to the City of Dublin Hospital. Dr. Letheby, one of the ablest and most distinguished men of science in this great city, professor of chymistry and toxicology in the Medical College of the London Hospital, and medical officer of the city of London, will tell you that he rejects the theory as a heresy unworthy of the belief of scientific men. Dr. Nicholas Parker, of the College of Physicians, London, and professor of medicine, Dr. Robinson, of the College of Physicians, and Mr. Rogers, professor of chymistry, concur with Dr. Letheby. Lastly, I will call Mr. William Herapath, of Bristol, probably the most eminent chemical analyst in this country, who also utterly rejects the theory.

All of those gentlemen contend that if not only half a grain of strychnine, but even one-fiftieth part or less has once entered into the human frame, it can and must be discovered by the tests known to chemists. They will tell you this, not as the result of a few experiments, for ever regretted, upon five rabbits, but from a large experience as to the operation of the poison upon the inferior animals, created as you know for the benefit of mankind, and many of them from their experience as to its effects upon the human system. I will satisfy you from their evidence that if you admit the correctness of the tests which were used, the only safe conclusion at which you can arrive is that, strychnine not having been found in the body, it could never have been there. They all agree, too, that no degree of putrefaction or fermentation in the human system could so decompose strychnine that it should no longer possess those qualities which cause it, in its undecomposed state, to respond to chemical tests.

I will now apply myself to a question which, in my judgment, is of equal, if not of greater importance — the question whether in the second week of November, 1855, the prisoner had a motive for the commission of this murder — a strong reason for desiring that Cook should die. I never will believe that, unless it were made clear that it was his interest to destroy Cook, you would come to the conclusion that he had committed such a crime. It seems to me abundantly clear upon the evidence that not only was it not the interest of Palmer that Cook should die, but that the death of Cook was the very worst calamity that could befall him, and that he could not possibly be ignorant that it would be followed by his own ruin. That it was followed by his immediate ruin we know.

We know that at the time when it is said he commenced to plot Cook's death he was in a condition of the greatest embarrassment — an embarrassment which, in its extreme intensity had come upon him but recently — an embarrassment, too, in some degree mitigated by the circumstances that the acceptances he is said to have forged were those of his mother — a lady of large fortune living in the town. My learned friend's hypothesis is, that not until he was in a state of the greatest embarrassment did he wish to destroy Cook. My learned friend stated to you, "That, being in desperate circumstances, with ruin, disgrace, and punishment staring him in the face, which could only be averted by means of money, he took advantage of his intimacy with Cook, when Cook had become the winner of a considerable sum, to destroy him, in order to obtain possession of his money."

Let us test this theory. Let us relieve our minds for a moment from the anxiety we must always feel when the life of a fellow-creature is at stake, and, looking at it as a mere matter of business, let us ask ourselves whether, in the second week in November, Palmer had any motive to commit this crime.

When a long correspondence is read to a jury, who are without the same means of testing its importance as the judge or the counsel, they frequently do not attach that weight to it which it deserves. But I watched the correspondence which was read to you yesterday with an anxiety which no words can express, because I firmly believed that in it the innocence of the prisoner lay concealed; that it proved not only that the prisoner had no motive to kill Cook, but that Cook's death was ruin to him.

Allow me to call your attention to the relation in which these men stood to each other. They had been intimate as racing friends for two or three years; they had had many transactions together; they were jointly interested in at least one racehorse, Pyrrhine; they generally stayed at the same hotels; they were seen together upon almost all the race-courses in the kingdom; they were known to be connected in adventures upon the same horses at the same races; and although, Cook being dead, the mouth of the prisoner being sealed, and transactions of this kind not being recorded in regular books, it is impossible to give you positive evidence as to their relations to one another; it is abundantly clear that they were very closely connected.

In August, 1855, money was wanted either by Cook or Palmer, and Palmer applied to Pratt for it. He seems to have wanted £200, to make up a larger sum, having already 190*l.*, in Pratt's hands; and he offered as security for the advance his friend Mr. Cook, whom he described as a gentleman of respectability and substance. We do not know the exact state of Cook's affairs at that time. Such a fortune as he had might have been thrown down in a week with the life he was leading; but a young man who is reckless as to the mode in which he employs his money and has only £13,000 may for a year or two pass before the world for a man of considerable means. It is not every one who will go to Doctors' Commons to ascertain the precise amount of property he has inherited.[1] Mr. Cook, of Lutterworth, kept his racehorses, lived expensively, was known to have inherited a fortune, and was altogether a person whose friendship was of considerable importance to a man like Palmer.

Recollect that I am not now defending Palmer against the crime of forgery, nor am I defending him against the imputation of reckless improvidence in obtaining money at an enormous discount. But as early as May, 1855, Palmer and Cook were thus circumstanced. What was their position in November? The evidence of Pratt, and the

---

[1] A legal institution that stored wills and last testaments. At a time when poverty was a real and frightful possibility, the deceased exerted a powerful influence on the living. Anyone learning that a relative had passed on could call for the will and learn what — if anything — was left to them. In "Picturesque Sketches of London, Past and Present" (1852), Thomas Miller described a young man sitting at one of the desks when he learned his fate:

"His fists . . . clenched, the nails of his fingers imbedded in the palms of his hands, his teeth set, his eyebrows knit: he strikes his hat as he places it on his head, closes the door with a loud slam, and curses the memory of the dead man, because he has left a reckless spendthrift just enough to live on all his life without working, yet so bequeathed it that he can but draw a given sum monthly. He is savage because he cannot have the whole legacy at once in his possession. If he could, he would be likely enough to squander it all away in a single night at some notorious gambling-house."

THE TIMES REPORT

correspondence which he proved, can leave no doubt on our minds upon that subject. Among a mass of bills, amounting altogether to £11,500, there were two, of £2,000. each, due the last week in October, two others, amounting to £1,500, having become due some time before, but being held over from month to month upon payment by Palmer, who was liable for them, of what was called interest at the rate of 60 per cent. These three sums — £2,000, £2,000, and £1,500 — were the embarrassments which were pressing upon him in the second week in November, and, be it observed, they were pressed upon him by a man who, although he would, doubtless, have been glad to get his principal, would also, upon anything like security, have been very well pleased to continue to receive interest. How can capital, if well secured, be better employed than in returning 40 or 60 per cent?

In this state of things Palmer, in answer to an urgent demand for money, came up to town on the 27th of October. Pratt then insisted that if Palmer could not pay one of the £2,000 bills which had just become due he should pay installments, in addition to the enormous interest charged upon it, and it was agreed that £250 should be paid down, £250 upon the 31st of October, and a further sum of £800 as soon afterwards as possible, making a total payment on account of that bill of £800, to "quiet" Pratt or his client, and to induce him to let the bill stand over.

On the 9th of November, the £300 was paid, and then a letter was written, to which I beg your particular attention. On the 13th of November, the day that Polestar won the race, Pratt wrote to Palmer that the case ("Palmer v. the Prince of Wales Insurance Company") had been laid before Sir F. Kelly, that in the opinion of several secretaries of insurance offices the company had not a leg to stand upon, and that the mere fact of the enormous premium would go a great way to get a verdict. The letter concluded,— "I count most positively on seeing you on Saturday. Do, for both our sakes, try and make up the amount to £1,000, for without it I shall be unable to renew the £1,500 due on the 9th." Pratt had threatened to issue a writ against Palmer's mother. Palmer had almost gone upon his knees to beg him not to do so, and this letter really meant, "Unless you give me £200 more and make up £1,000 a writ shall be served upon your mother." That letter is written on the 13th of November.

Palmer gets it at Rugeley, whither he had gone from the racecourse on the day that Polestar won. What does he do? He instantly returns to Shrewsbury, gets there on Wednesday, sees Cook. They say he doses him. We will see how probable that is presently.

Cook goes to bed in a state I will not describe, gets up next morning much more sensible than he went to bed, goes upon the racecourse, returns with Palmer to Rugeley on the Thursday, goes to bed, gets up next morning still uncomfortable, but able to go and dine with Palmer on that day (Friday). On that day, the 16th of November, Palmer writes to Pratt:—

"I am obliged to come to Tattersall's on Monday to the settling, so that I shall not call and see you before Monday, but a friend of mine will call and leave you £200 to-morrow, and I will give you the remainder on Monday."

The person who ordinarily settled Cook's accounts was a person named Fisher, a wine-merchant in Shoe Lane, who was called first in this case; and on that very day (the day on which Cook dined with Palmer) Cook writes to him:—

"It is of great importance, both to Mr. Palmer and myself, that a sum of £500 should be paid to a Mr. Pratt, of 5, Queen Street, Mayfair, to-morrow, without fail. £300 has been sent up to-night, and if you will be kind enough to pay the other £200 to-morrow on the receipt of this, you will greatly oblige me, and I will give it to you on Monday at Tattersall's."

There is a postscript, which I will read, but upon which I will at present make no observation— "I am much better."

What is the fair inference from these letters? I submit that the inference is, that at that date Cook was making himself very useful to Palmer. Pratt was pressing for an additional sum of £200. Palmer communicated his difficulty to Cook, who at once wrote to his agent to pay the £200.

More than this, — the £300 referred to in the letter, as having been paid "to-night" [The Attorney-General — "The other day"] means one of these things — it either means the £300. which had been sent up on the 9th of November (and if it did, then Cook knew all about it — probably had an interest in Palmer's transactions with Pratt); or it was a false representation, put forward merely for the purpose of putting a good face upon the matter to Fisher; or it means that on that day £300 had somehow or other come to their hands, and had been by Cook made applicable to the convenience of Palmer.

Whichever way you take it, it proves to demonstrate that Palmer and Cook were playing into each other's hands with respect to that heavy incumbrance upon Palmer, and that Palmer could rely upon Cook as his fast friend in any such difficulties. Although, when we take the sum total of £11,500, his difficulties sound large, yet the difficulty of the day was nothing like that, because, in the reckless spendthrift way in which they were living, putting on bills from month to month, and paying an enormous interest per annum, the actual outlay upon the day of putting on was not considerable.

I submit that this letter shows that on the day on which it is said that Palmer was poisoning Cook, the 16th of November, Cook was acting towards him in a most friendly manner, was acquainted with his circumstances, and willing to relieve his embarrassments, and actually did devote a portion of his earnings to Palmer's purposes. I will, however, make this plainer.

Part of the case of my learned friend is that Palmer, leaving Cook ill in bed at Rugeley, ran up to town on the Monday, and intending to despatch Cook that night obtained possession of his Shrewsbury winnings by telling Herring, who was not Cook's usual agent, that he was authorised by Cook to settle his Shrewsbury transactions at Tattersall's. On the Monday, as on the Tuesday, Cook, though generally indisposed, was during the greater part of the day quite well. He got up and saw his trainer and two jockeys. The theory of the case for the prosecution is that he was quite well, because Palmer was not there to dose him. You will see how grossly and contemptibly absurd that is presently.

Being well on Monday and Tuesday, do not you think that, had not Cook known that Palmer did not intend to go to his regular agent, Fisher, he would have been very much surprised that he on Tuesday morning received no letter from that gentleman, informing him of the settlement of his transactions? And could Palmer, as a man of business, have relied upon an absence of such surprise and alarm on the part of Cook? We have the evidence of Fisher, that he, at Cook's request, contained in the letter of the 17th November, advanced the £200, which he would, had he settled Cook's affairs, have been entitled to deduct from the money he would have received at Tattersall's on the Monday. He did not settle those affairs, and the money has never been paid.

That explains the whole transaction. Cook and Palmer understood each perfectly well. Accordingly, Cook said, "This settlement shall not go through Fisher's hands. We have got him to pay the £200 to Pratt, but it shall not be repaid to him on Monday. I will let Palmer go to London and settle the whole thing through Herring." That was done, and accordingly Fisher has never been paid.

There is a letter to which I will particularly call your attention. It is one sent by Palmer to Pratt on the 19th of November, 1855:—

"You will place the £50 which I have just paid you and the £450 you will receive by Mr. Herring — together £500 — and the £200 you received on Saturday." [That is the £200 which Fisher paid to Pratt at the express request of Cook,] "towards payment of my mother's acceptance for £2,000 due on the 25th of October, making paid to this day the sum of £1,300." Taking that letter with the one which Cook wrote to Fisher on Friday, the 16th, can you doubt that on that day

Cook was a most convenient friend to Palmer, who could not by possibility do without him?

It does not end there. Cook died at 1 o'clock on the morning of Wednesday, the 21st of November. If we want to know what influence that death had upon Palmer, we must take it from the letters. On the 22nd of November — and I am sure you will make some allowance for a day having elapsed from the death of Cook — Palmer writes to Pratt, "Ever since I saw you I have been fully engaged with Cook and not able to leave home." Unless he murdered Cook, that is the truest sentence that ever was penned.

He watched the bedside of his friend. He was with him night and day. He attended him as a brother. He called his friends around him. He did all that the most affectionate solicitude could do for a friend, unless he was plotting his death.

"Ever since I saw you I have been fully engaged with Cook and not able to leave home. I am sorry to say, after all, he died this day. So you had better write to Saunders; but, mind you, I must have Polestar, if it can be so arranged; and, should any one call upon you to know what money or moneys Cook ever had from you, don't answer the question till I have seen you.

"I will send you the £75 to-morrow, and as soon as I have been to Manchester you shall hear about other moneys. I sat up two full nights with Cook, and am very much tired out."

And did he not? Was it not true? It may not be true that he sat up the whole of the nights, but he was ready to be called if Cook should be ill. Elizabeth Mills says, that after the first serious paroxysm on the Monday night she left Palmer in the arm-chair sleeping by the side of the man whom the prosecution says he had attempted to murder. No; murderers do not sleep by their victims.

What was Pratt's answer to Palmer's letter? I will read it that you may see what quick ruin Cook's death brought upon Palmer. That answer, dated November 22, is as follows:—

"I have your note, and am greatly disappointed at the non-receipt of the money as promised, and at the vague assurances as to any money. I can understand, 'tis true, that your being detained by the illness of your friend has been the cause of not sending up the larger amount, but the smaller sum you ought to have sent. If anything unpleasant occurs you must thank yourself.

"The death of Mr. Cook will now compel you to look about as to the payment of the bill for £500 on the 2nd of December.

"I have written Saunders, informing him of my claim, and requesting to know by return what claim he has for keep and training. I send down copy of bill of sale to Crubble, to see it enforced."

So that the first effect of Cook's death was, in the opinion of Pratt, who knew all about it, to saddle Palmer with the sum of £500.

Now, I will undertake to satisfy you that the transactions out of which that bill for £500 arose were transactions for Cook's benefit, and in which Palmer lent his name to accommodate Cook, upon whose death he became primarily and alone responsible for the bill.

Let me state the view which my learned friend (the Attorney-General) takes of that transaction, because I intend to meet his case foot by foot, and I shall, I hope, convince him that, if he had had the option, he would never have taken up this case — the Crown would never have appeared in it. The universal feeling in the country was, however, such as to render it impossible that the case should not be tried, after the verdict of wilful murder had been obtained upon the evidence of Dr. Taylor; and the Crown felt that it would be neglecting its solemn duty to protect every one of the Queen's subjects, if it did not take care that a man, against whom there was so much prejudice — a man leading the life which Palmer has led, disgraced, as it is said, by forgeries to a large amount, and a gambler by profession, should have a fair trial.

There was no way of securing that, as my learned friend at once saw, no possibility of the prisoner's life being saved, except by giving to the counsel who defended him all the information which my learned friend himself possessed.

The view which my learned friend takes of the £500 transaction, the theory on which he thinks it probable that Palmer plotted the death of Cook, is this:—

"Pratt still declining to advance the money, Palmer proposed an assignment by Cook of two race-horses, one called Polestar, which won the Shrewsbury races, and another called Sirius. That was raised upon that security, which realised £375 in cash, and a wine warrant for £65. Palmer contrived, however, that the money and the wine warrant should be sent to him, and not to Cook. Mr. Pratt sent down his cheque to Palmer in the country on a stamp, as the act of Parliament required, and he availed himself of the opportunity now afforded by law of striking out the word 'bearer,' and writing 'order,' the effect of which was to necessitate the endorsement of Cook on the back of the cheque. It was not intended by Palmer that those proceeds should fall into Cook's hands, and accordingly he forged the name of John Parsons Cook on the back of that cheque. Cook never received the money, and you will see that, within ten days from that period when he came to his end, the bill in respect of that transaction, which was at three months, would have fallen due, when it must have become apparent that Palmer received the money, and that in order to obtain it, he had forged the endorsement of Cook."

OF THE TRIAL OF WILLIAM PALMER

That is the view which the prosecution take of the case, and I think I shall be able to satisfy you that it cannot possibly be a correct one. We know from Pratt exactly what took place. Palmer wrote to him, saying—

"I have undertaken to get the enclosed bill cashed for Mr. Cook. You had the £200 bill of his. He is a very good and responsible man. Will you do it? I will put my name to the bill."

So that it was represented to Pratt as a transaction for the accommodation of Cook. Pratt's answer to that is—

"If Mr. Cook chooses to give me security, I have no objection; but he must execute a bill of sale on his two horses, Polestar and Sirius; more, he must execute a power of attorney, and his signature to both must be witnessed by some solicitor in the country, so that I may be quite sure that it is a really valid security. If Cook will do that I will give him £375 in money, and a wine warrant for £65; which, charging £10 for expenses, and £50 for discount, will make £500."

There can be no doubt that Cook attached great value to Sirius and Polestar, which mare was probably then booked for the engagements in which she won so much money at Shrewsbury; and it is to the last degree improbable that he would have executed this bill of sale, with a power of attorney to enable the mortgagee or assignee to enforce it at once effectually, and yet have received no money. Would he, if such had been the case, have remained quiet to the day of his death, and never have written to Pratt to say that although he had sent him the required documents he had never received the money? Cook was as much in want of money as Palmer was; and would he thus have thrown away his money? Is it credible that if Palmer had misappropriated the cheque he could for three months have kept Cook in ignorance of the transaction? Is it not probable that Cook's name was written on the cheque with his full knowledge and consent? It is not suggested that there was any attempt to imitate his handwriting. Is it more probable that Cook, who I will prove to you from the letter, wanted ready money, and who would probably be put to inconvenience by receiving only a cheque which he would not get cashed for a day or two, took the ready money — £315, which Pratt sent at the same time to Palmer — and that Palmer took the cheque?

On the 6th of September Palmer wrote to Pratt:—

"I received the cheque for the £100, and will thank you to let me have the £315 by return of post, if possible; if not, send it to me (certain) by Monday night's post, to the Post-office, Doncaster. I now return to you Cook's papers signed, &c, and he wants the money on Saturday, if he can have it; but I have not promised it for Saturday. I told him he should have it on Tuesday morning at Doncaster; so please enclose it with mine in cash, in a registered letter, and he must pay for it being registered. Do not let it be later than Monday night's post to Doncaster."

So that Palmer asked that it should be sent like his own, Cook, according to the letter, wanting it in cash. Pratt replied to Palmer, acknowledging the receipt of the documents, and promising that he would send him his money to Doncaster on the Monday, and would endeavour to let Cook have his at the same time.

On the 9th of September Palmer wrote to Pratt:—

"You must send me, for Mr. Cook, by Monday night's post (to the Post-office, Doncaster), £385 instead of £375, and the wine warrant, so that I can hand it to him with the £375, and that will be allowing you £50 for the discount, &c. I shall then get £10, and I expect I shall have to take to the wine, and give him the money; but I shall not do so if you do not send £385, and be good enough to enclose my £315 with it, in cash, in a registered letter, and direct it to me to the Post-office, Doncaster."

In these letters there is an intimation that Cook wanted the money on the Saturday. He was inconvenienced by only getting a cheque upon London, which he could not immediately change; and, therefore, Palmer gave him the money and took the cheque. It is remarkable that, when we look to the banking account of Palmer at Rugeley, we find that the £375 is paid in by somebody to his account, but that the £315 is not paid in to his account at all. The bill was accepted for Cook's accommodation, Cook gave security for it, and he never, during the three months which elapsed before his death, complained to Pratt that he had not received the money for it.

I submit that the fair version of the transaction is that which is given in a letter from Palmer — that Palmer let Cook have the cash, and himself took the cheque, having Cook's authority to put his name at the back of it. How else can you account for the silence of Cook, and for the fact that the £375 is paid into the Rugeley Bank, but there is no trace of the £315? This being so, the result of Cook's death was to make Palmer liable for the £500 bill, on the back of which he had put his name.

Therefore, I submit to you, that on the second motive suggested by my learned friend (the Attorney-General), the case has entirely failed.

In addition to this, however, we find from these letters the difficulties which the death of Cook brought upon Palmer. We find the disappointment of Pratt that he could send no more money, the bill for £500, the danger of losing Polestar, which Palmer very much wanted to have, and which Pratt would, unless paid the £500, bring to the hammer in order to realise his security; and we find that inquiries were at once apprehended from Cook's friends as to the moneys which Pratt had paid to Cook, and the probable value which the latter had received for the endorsements and acceptances which he had given.

There is another, although not so strong a reason, why it is improbable that Palmer should have desired the death of Cook. Mr. Weatherby has told us to-day that, although it frequently happens that the moneys won at a race are sent up by the clerk of the course in a week after the race, yet that does not always happen. On Tuesday, November the 20th, on the night of which day he died, Cook, who was then perfectly sensible, perfectly comfortable and happy, and enjoying the society of his friend Mr. Jones, gave to Palmer a cheque for £350 upon Weatherby's. If Palmer killed Cook, and it happened that Fraill had not sent up the money so as to be there by Wednesday morning, Weatherby's would not pay the cheque, nor would they have cashed it if they had received information that Cook had died during the night. It actually happened that the cheque when presented was not paid, because Fraill did not send up the money. Was it probable that Palmer, having got from Cook a cheque for £380, would have run the risk of losing his money by destroying him the same night?

It is suggested that he obtained this cheque fraudulently, and then, lest Cook should detect the fraud, destroyed him. That was not likely to answer his purpose. He might be certain that directly the breath was out of Cook's body Jones would go to Mr. Stevens; that Stevens and Bradford, Cook's brother-in-law, would go down to Rugeley; that the death being sudden there would most likely be a *post-mortem* examination; and that, instead of settling for the £500 bill and the £350 cheque with Cook, he would have to settle with hard men of business, men who cared nothing for him, who would probably look upon him as a "leg" upon the turf, and would regard neither his feelings nor his interests, but would let him go to ruin any way he might, not stirring a finger to save him. Is it probable that a shrewd, intelligent man of business would make such a choice as that?

More than this, we know that at the very time Herring held one bill for £500, and three for £200 each, to which there were the names of both Palmer and Cook, and for all of which, either in the whole or in the part, Cook must, unless he rushed to his own ruin, provide. If Palmer put Cook to death he immediately became solely liable, not only for these bills, but for that as security for which the bill of sale was executed on Sirius and Polestar, which would not be so easily renewed as those for the large sums on which the enormous usury was paid. The bill would very likely soon find its way to his mother, and that it should do so would not suit Palmer, for his mother is a respectable and serious person, who, although she loved her son, did not like and gave no encouragement to his gambling; nor did that excellent and most honourable man who stands by him — his brother, who was estranged from him for a length of time until this calamity came upon him, simply because he disapproved of the gambling by which he lived.

Cook being dead there was, therefore, no one to save Palmer from ruin, for in all this voluminous evidence there is not the smallest trace that there was any one else in the world who would lend Palmer his name or would assist him to obtain money. If it be, as it is stated, a fact that he forged the name of his mother, is not that conclusive evidence that he had no other resource but the good nature — the easiness, perhaps the folly of Cook? Is it then credible that under such circumstances he would have desired to bring upon himself not merely the creditors and executors of Cook, but their solicitors — men who in the discharge of their duty to their clients can have no sympathy for any one, and with whom no arrangement is possible?

I have, therefore, I hope, shown you that Palmer had an interest in the life of Cook. But more than that, was it safe for him that Cook should die! Palmer was a man who had a shrewd knowledge of the world and a knowledge of his profession, and among other things, of chymistry. My learned friends have put in a book which was found in his house, and among other notes one in which there is this, "Strychnia kills by causing tetanic fixing of the respiratory muscles." In the same book there are many other notes.

Lord CAMPBELL. — The Attorney-General stated that he did not place much reliance upon that note.

Mr. *Serjeant Shee.* — My learned friend did not press this note, but he thought it was evidence which ought to be before you (the jury). I use it to satisfy you that Palmer had studied his profession sufficiently to know, and knew perfectly well, that if strychnine were administered it would in all probability kill the victim in horrible convulsions, in a very short time, and in a way so striking as to be the talk of a small neighbourhood like Rugeley for a month or more — time enough to alarm everybody and provoke inquiry into the circumstances of the death, which must certainly, in all probability, end in the detection of guilt.

If that is so, was he at that time so circumstanced as to render it safe for him to run the risk of such suspicions? His brother, Walter Palmer, had died in the month of August; and unless his mother forgave him, or recognised the acceptance, his only hope of extraction from his difficulties lay in getting from the Prince of Wales Office the money due to him as assignee of the policy on his brother's life. That his chance of getting that money was good is shown by the fact that he refused the offer of the office to return the premium, and that it was upon it that Pratt had obtained the discounts, and had resolved, under the direction of Palmer, to put it in suit. It was really the only unpledged property which he had, and how he was situated with regard to it appears from the letters and from the evidence.

The insurance company, annoyed at being called upon to pay so large a sum, were determined to do all they could to resist it. They accordingly sent Inspector Field and his man to Stafford to make inquiries. They could not do this without talking, and this had been going on for some time.

[To show that this had been the case the learned Serjeant read the deposition of the witness Deane, who was examined yesterday.]

So that just before the death of Cook, Palmer knew himself to be the subject of what he appeared from his actions to consider a most unfounded and unwarrantable suspicion. He put the policy into the hands of an attorney to enforce payment of the sum due upon it. The office met the claim by insinuations and inquiries which were of a nature to destroy his character and to bring upon his head the suspicion of a murder. The pressure by Pratt upon Palmer to meet the £2,000 bills did not commence until the office disputed the payment of that policy. All went as smooth as possible as long as Pratt held what he believed to be a good security, but when they began to dispute that, Pratt writes to Palmer and tells him that the state of things is changed. After saying that nothing can be done towards compelling the office to pay until the 24th, he says in his letter of the 2nd of October:—

"This, you will observe, quite alters arrangements, and I therefore must request that you make preparations for meeting the two bills due at the end of this month. ... In any event, bear in mind that you must be prepared to cover your mother's acceptances for the £4,000 due at the end of the month."

There was the pinch. The office would not pay, and bills for £4,000 were coming due. If anything occurred to increase the suspicions of the office — which was very unwilling to pay — all chance of the £13,000 was lost. That £13,000 is sure to be paid, unless that man (pointing to the prisoner) is convicted of murder. As sure as he is saved, and saved I believe he will be, that £13,000 will be paid. There is no defence — no pretence of a defence. The premium taken was an enormous one, and that £13,000 is good for him and will pay all his creditors.

This correspondence of which my learned friend must have taken a view different from any which I can take, but which I am sure he would have put in, whatever had been his view of it — this correspondence saves the prisoner if there is common sense in man.

Here is another letter from Pratt to Palmer, dated October the 6th:—

"I have your note, acknowledging receipt by your mother of the £2,000 acceptance, due the 2nd October. Why not let her acknowledge it herself? You must really not fail to come up at once, if it be for the purpose of arranging for the payment of the two bills at the end of the month. Remember I can make no terms for their renewal, and they must be paid. I will of course hold the policy for so much as it is worth, but in the present position of the affair, no one except your mother, who is liable upon the bills, can look upon it as a security. [That was because Simpson and Field were down there making inquiries.] Do not neglect attending to this, for under a recent act bills of exchange are now recovered in a few days. You know and can appreciate my conduct in avoiding all trouble and annoyance to your mother; but to that there is a limit. I cannot by any representation be a party to inducing anybody to believe that security exists where there is doubt upon the point. P.S. I cast no doubt upon the capability of the office to pay, but in the nature of things, with so large an amount in question, it is not to be surprised at, if they think they have grounds of objection, they should temporise by delay."

Does not this show that on the 6th of October suspicions were hanging over Palmer's head, which would come down with irresistible momentum and crush him if there were a suspicion of another violent and sudden death? Do you think that a man who had written in his manual what were the effects of strychnine, would risk such a scene as that poison would develop in the presence of the dearest and best friend of Cook, — a man whom he could not influence, — and a medical man, who loved Cook so well as to sleep in the same room with him, that he might be ready to attend him in case he needed assistance? Is that common sense?

Are you going to enforce such a theory as that which Dr. Alfred Taylor propounded as to the effects which strychnine produces upon rabbits? Impossible — perfectly impossible!

I will prove the position in which Palmer stood still more clearly. On the 10th of October Pratt, in a letter addressed to him, says:—

"I may add that I hear they (the insurance company) have been making inquiries in every direction."

To be sure, they had. Field, the detective officer, had been at Stafford, where he could make inquiries as well as at Rugeley.

"But on what they ground their dissatisfaction is as yet a mystery. In any event no step can be taken to compel payment until after the 4th of December."

It is plain that suspicions were then rife, or that attempts were made to excite suspicions against him with regard to the death of

OF THE TRIAL OF WILLIAM PALMER

Walter Palmer.

On the 18th of October Pratt enclosed to Palmer a letter from the solicitor of the company, stating that the directors had determined upon declining to pay the amount claimed; but that, although the facts disclosed in the course of their inquiries would have warranted their retention of the premiums which had been paid, they were prepared to refund them to any one who might be shown to be legally entitled to them. Palmer determined that the money should be paid; and a case was laid before Sir Fitzroy Kelly. If anything happened to Cook by foul play he had no more chance of receiving this £13,000 than of obtaining £130,000.

From all this I infer, not only that Palmer had no interest in Cook's death, but that he had a direct pecuniary interest in his living. I think it is impossible that I should be so much mistaken as that a considerable portion of what I have advanced should not be worthy of your attention; and I therefore submit to you, to the Court, and to my learned friend, that the case as to this supposed motive for the crime has failed.

We now proceed to the facts of the case, and in considering them it will be necessary to group them without entire reference to dates. I will first inquire whether the symptoms with which Cook was attacked, and the appearances presented by his body after death were consistent with the theory of his having died by strychnia poison, and inconsistent with that of his having died from some natural causes. It is under this head that I shall discuss, I hope not unduly, the medical evidence in this case, and present to you such observations as occur to me on the witnesses who have been called to support the view which the Crown takes of the effect of that medical testimony.

Cook died at 1 o'clock in the morning of Wednesday, Nov. 21, in the presence of Jones. It was no sooner light than Jones posted to town and saw his stepfather, Mr. Stevens. Mr. Stevens went down to Rugeley and was introduced to Palmer. Palmer went with him to the Talbot Arms, and uncovered the corpse — a bold thing to do if he had murdered him. The body was so little emaciated or affected by disease that Stevens wondered if he could be dead; but he observed some little rigidity about the muscles. Stevens's suspicions were roused; he asked Palmer to dinner, questioned him about the betting-book, got angry that it was not produced, dissembled with Palmer, cross-examined him, went up to town, met him at Euston-square, again at Wolverton, at Rugby, and at Rugeley. At last he gave him to understand that he suspected him and intended to probe the whole matter to the bottom. He resolved to have a *post-mortem* examination, and that examination took place.

The appearances presented by the body after death were such as might have been anticipated by those who were acquainted with his course of life, his general health, his pursuits, and, not to say anything hard of him, his vice, and the drinking, racing company which he kept. His father had died at 30 years of age, his mother about the same age, a few years after her second marriage; his sister was dead; and he himself was affected by a pulmonary disorder. Cook had been suffering for a long time from a sore throat, and bore about him all the signs and indications of having led a licentious life. Indeed, he appears to have been about as dissipated a young man as can well be imagined. I do not mean to say that he was utterly depraved, or that he was lost to all sense of honour and propriety; but it does not admit of doubt that his manner of living was wild, riotous, and extravagant. His complaints indicated his excesses, and he was avowedly addicted to pursuits the reverse of commendable.

When his body was opened there was evidences of a soreness of the tongue. I do not go the length of saying that there was anything to lead to the inference that there was an actual sore at the time of death, but there were follicles and symptoms, if not of a recent, certainly of a not very remote ulcer. The inside of the mouth had been ulcerated, and the skin taken off on both sides. There is abundant evidence to show that Cook was himself of the opinion that these symptoms were syphilitic. He could scarcely be persuaded to obey the instructions of Dr. Savage, the respectable and very competent physician whom he consulted, and, though it is admitted that he was not "fool enough to go to quack doctors," it is very certain that he was weak enough to follow the counsels of every medical man who would venture to give him advice when it coincided with his own opinion, that mercury was the best thing for his complaint. The spots which are the fatal characteristics of his dreadful malady had already made their appearance on his body, and he was haunted by the apprehension that some day, as he was running about the race-course, his face would be suddenly covered over with copper blotches, which would leave no doubt on the minds of those who saw them as to the true nature of his disease. Many a man similarly affected has retrieved his position, redeemed his character, and become a virtuous member of society. Far be it from me, then, to say one word that would press with undue severity on the memory of the dead; but no false delicacy shall deter me from the discharge of my duty; and I make these remarks not in an unkind or censorious spirit, but for the sake of truth, and because the state of Cook's health is a most important element in this inquiry.

It is certain that it was his own opinion that he was suffering from virulent syphilis, and in this opinion the medical men who originally attended him did not hesitate to concur. That he did not correct his habits is evident from the fact that within a recent period of his death he had again become diseased. When his body was opened on the second examination, there were found between the delicate membrane which the spinal marrow covers and is called the arachnoid,[2] and embedded to some extent in the next covering, not so delicate, termed the dura mater, granules about one inch in extent; and I will satisfy you, upon the evidence of witnesses whose authority will not be questioned, that if the body had been opened in the dead-house of any hospital in this metropolis, those granules would have been regarded as symptoms affording conclusive explanation of the cause of death.

Such, then, was the condition of Cook's health — a condition but partially and imperfectly revealed by the first *post-mortem* examination. That examination was not conducted with the same minuteness and precision that circumstances rendered necessary on a subsequent occasion, and the syphilitic disease was neither ascertained nor suspected.

The stomach was taken out, and you have heard the suggestion, which, were it not that the Court has ruled it to be of no significance, I should have been prepared to disprove, that Palmer attempted to interfere with the operation by shoving against the medical man engaged in it. The inference sought to be deduced was, that some of the stomach escaped from the jar; but we have the evidence of Dr. Devonshire himself that such was not the fact. None of it did escape, and it was sent up in its entirety to London, there to be analysed by Dr. Taylor and Dr. Rees.

Those gentlemen examined it with the knowledge that, owing to the report of Palmer having purchased a fatal drug from Mr. Roberts on the day of the death, there was a suspicion of foul play. Mr. Stevens talked of the fact to Dr. Taylor, and, with the consciousness of it on his mind, that gentleman wrote a letter attributing the death to antimony. [Dr. Taylor intimated dissent.] Well, if the letter is not to be so understood, it is at all events susceptible of this interpretation — that the death may have been caused by antimony.

Dr. Taylor attends the coroner's inquest, which, in all probability, is held in consequence of his own letter. He hears the evidence of Jones, Roberts, and Mills, and it is but natural to presume that these are the witnesses whose testimony has the greatest influence on his opinion. He forms his judgment on the evidence of chambermaids, waitresses, and housekeepers, and contrary to the opinion of the medical man who attended Cook in his last illness (for be it remembered he had no encouragement from Mr. Jones, the surgeon, of Lutterworth, a man of age and character to

---

[2] A membrane that surrounds the brain and the spinal cord. The layer between it and the skull is the dura mater.

form a sound decision on the case); he comes boldly and at once to the conclusion that his original notion about antimony having been the cause of death was a mistake, and then he has the incredible imprudence — an imprudence which has necessitated this trial, or at all events rendered it necessary that it should take place in this form and place — to declare upon his oath to the coroner's jury that he believes that the pills given to Cook on the Monday and Tuesday contained strychnine, and that Cook was consequently poisoned.

That evidence of his is carried on the wings of the press into every house in the United Kingdom. It becomes known throughout the length and breadth of the land that Dr. Taylor, a man who has devoted his life to science, a man of the highest personal character, and who stands well with his medical friends, has declared — not as a conjectural opinion, mark you, nor as a reserved opinion delivered in a private room to a few men whose discretion might be relied on — but, that in the public room of a public inn, in a little village where everything that occurs is known, he has declared upon his solemn oath that it is his belief that Cook died because pills containing strychnine were administered to him on the nights of Monday and Tuesday.

He had himself failed to discover the faintest traces of strychnine, yet, at the coroner's inquest he had the hardihood to declare his conviction that the pills contained strychnine, and that Cook died of them. His evidence is neither consistent with itself nor with the opinion of Mr. Jones. He takes upon him to pronounce positively, in the face of the world, that Cook's disease was nothing else than tetanus, and tetanus, too, of the kind that can be produced by poison only, and that poison strychnine. Such was Dr. Taylor's testimony; and on such testimony the coroner's jury returned their verdict.

But, merciful Heaven! in what position are we placed for the safety of our own lives and those of our families, if, on evidence such as this, men are to be put upon their trial for foul murder as often as a sudden death occurs in any household! If science is to be allowed to come and dogmatise in our courts — and not science that is successful in its operations or exact in its nature, but science that is baffled by its own tests, and bears upon its forehead the motto, "A little learning is a dangerous thing" — if, I say, science such as this is to be suffered to dogmatise in our courts, and to utter judgments which its own processes fail to vindicate, life is no longer secure, and there is thrown upon judges and jurymen a weight of responsibility too grievous for human nature to endure.

If Dr. Taylor had detected the poison by his own tests, he, with his long experience in toxicological studies, would have been an excellent witness for the Crown; that he has not found the poison, and not having seen the patient, and knowing nothing of his deathbed symptoms beyond what he gathered from the evidence of an ignorant servant girl and of Mr. Jones, whose testimony does not show that he agrees with him in opinion, Dr. Taylor thinks himself justified in declaring upon his oath in public court that the pills contained strychnine, and that Cook was poisoned.

If verdicts are to be moulded on testimony such as this, what medical practitioner is safe? On what ground does Dr. Taylor vindicate his opinion? He does not appear to have ever seen one solitary case of strychnine in the human subject, yet, with the full knowledge that the consequences of his assertion might be disastrous to the prisoner at the bar, he has the audacity to assert that the pills, which, for anything he knows to the contrary, were the same that Dr. Bamford prepared, contained strychnine, and that Cook was poisoned by it.

I have quoted the sentiment "A little learning is a dangerous thing," and assuredly to no science is that maxim so applicable as to the medical. Of all God's works there is no other which so eloquently attests our entire dependence on Him and our own utter nothingness as that mortal coil in which we live, and breathe, and have our being. We are struck with amazement as we contemplate it. We feel, we see, we hear; yet the instant that we attempt to give a reason for these sensations our path is crossed by the mystery of creation, and all we know is that God created man — that he is our Omnipotent Maker and we the work of His hands. Yet we fancy that we can penetrate all mysteries, and there are no bounds to our arrogance.

There has been much talk in this inquiry of the two kinds of tetanus — idiopathic and traumatic. Dr. Todd, urged by the Court to explain the former, described it as "constitutional." Perhaps "self-generating" would have done as well, but let that pass. But how is our knowledge advanced by translating "idiopathic" as constitutional? It is easy to give an English translation of that Greek compound, but the thing is to explain what the translation means. What is the meaning of the phrase "constitutional tetanus?"

Lord CAMPBELL. — Tetanus not occasioned by external injury.

Mr. *Serjeant Shee.* — Just so, my Lord, or in other words, tetanus not referable to any known cause. But, in truth, idiopathic means in a general sense "unaccountable." Not that constitutional tetanus is always and invariably so, but that cases of tetanus do continually occur of which you can only suspect the cause and attribute it by hypothesis to a "cold," or some other vague accident. In such cases you say that the disease is idiopathic, not traumatic.

The Crown will have it that Cook's was the tetanus of poison, but it is almost an assumption to say that it was tetanus at all. That he died of convulsions, or immediately after them, is certain, and that they were convulsions similar to those from which he suffered on the preceding night is beyond all doubt. But what pretence is there for positively asserting that they were tetanus at all? The evidence of Mr. Jones fairly interpreted cannot be construed otherwise than as intimating an impression that they were convulsions that partook of a tetanic character. That might be, and yet the malady might not be tetanus. It is bad reasoning — most defective logic — to argue without positive proof of the fact that the disease was tetanus, and no other tetanus in the world than that produced by poison.

Following the trail dragged for them by the toxicologists, the Crown have thought proper to impute the death of this man to the poison of strychnine. It is for them to prove the fact. We contest it, but it by no means follows that we should be bound to explain the death on other grounds. If we can satisfy you that this man was assailed by any one of the numerous kinds of convulsions to which humanity is liable, and that he was asphyxiated or deprived of life when writhing in some sudden spasm or paroxysm, we shall have done all that can in fairness be demanded of us, unless, indeed, the Crown shall be prepared to prove that Cook's symptoms were irreconcilable with any other doctrine than of death by strychnine. This they have not done and cannot do.

I propose to call your attention to the statements of the witnesses Mills and Jones with respect to the symptoms they observed in Cook on the evenings of Monday and Tuesday, and, having done so, I will submit to your candid judgment whether those symptoms may not be more naturally accounted for by attributing them to convulsions which are not tetanic at all, and most assuredly not tetanic in the distinctive character of strychnine, but which may rather be classed under those ordinary convulsions by means of which it constantly pleases Providence to strike men down without leaving upon their bodies the faintest indications from which the cause of death may be inferred.

You have it on the authority of medical men of the highest distinction that it sometimes occurs that men in the prime of life and full vigour of health are smitten to death by convulsions that leave no trace upon the body of the sufferer. The statements of Mills and Jones are such as to render it unnecessary to resort to the hypothesis of any kind of tetanus, much less to that of strychnine, in accounting for the death of Cook. Regard being had to the delicate state of his health, and to the continually recurring derangements of his constitution, it is far safer to conclude that he died of ordinary convulsions than of any description of tetanus, whether traumatic, idiopathic, or that produced by poison.

Nor must we omit to inquire into the state of his mind. He went to Shrewsbury races in the imminent peril of returning from them a ruined man. His father-in-law, Mr. Stevens, assured Palmer that there would not be four thousand shillings for those who had claims on his estate. From the necessity he was under of raising money at an enormous discount, we may easily infer that he was in desperate difficulties, and that, unless some sudden success on the turf should retrieve his fortunes, his case was hopeless. His health shattered, his mind distracted, he had long been cherishing the hope that Polestar would win, and so put him in possession of a sum amounting, in stakes and winnings, to something like a thousand guineas. The mare, it is true, was hardly his own, for she had been mortgaged, and if she should lose, she would become the property of another person.

Picture to yourselves what must have been the condition, mental and bodily, of that young man when he rose from his bed on the morning of the races. It is scarcely possible that, as he went down to breakfast, this thought must not have crossed his mind, "My fate is trembling in the balance; this is the crisis of my destiny; unless my horse shall win, and give me one chance more of recovering myself, to-night I am a beggar."

With these feelings he repairs to the race-course. Another race is run before Polestar is brought out. His impatience is extreme. He looks on in a state of agonising excitement. Will the minutes never fly? At last arrives the decisive moment. The time has arrived for his race. The flag is dropped; the horses start; his mare wins easily, and he, her master, has won a thousand guineas! For three minutes he is not able to speak, so intense is his emotion. Slowly he recovers his utterance, and then how rapturous is his joy! He is saved, he is saved! Another chance to retrieve his position, one chance more to recover his character! As yet, at all events, he will not be a disgrace to his family and his friends.

Conceive him to be, with all his faults, an honourable young man, and you may easily imagine what his ecstacy must have been. He loves the memory of his dead mother — he still reverences the name of his father — he is jealous of his sister's honour, and it may be that he cherishes silently in his heart the thought of some other being dearer still than all, to whom the story of his ruin would bring bitter anguish. But he is not ruined; he will meet his engagements like an honourable man. There is now no danger of his being an outcast, an adventurer, a black-leg. He will live to redeem his position, and to give joy to those who love him.

With such thoughts in his heart, he returns to his inn in a state of indescribable elation, and with a revulsion from despair that must have convulsed — though not in the sense of illness — every fibre of his frame.

His first idea is to entertain his friends, and he does so. The evidence does not prove that he drank to excess, but he gave a champagne dinner, and we all know that is a luxurious entertainment, at which there is no stint, and not much self-respect.

That evening he did not spend in the society of Palmer; indeed it is not clear in whose company he spent it. But we find him on the evening of Wednesday at the "Unicorn," with Saunders, his trainer, and a lady.

On Thursday he walks upon the course, and Herring remonstrates with him for doing so, as the day is damp and misty, and the ground wet. That night he is seized with illness, and he continues ailing until his death at Rugeley.

Arrived at Rugeley, it is but natural to suppose that a reaction of feeling may have set in. Then the dark side of the picture may have presented itself to his imagination. The chilling thought may have come upon him that his winnings were already forestalled, and would scarcely suffice to save him from destruction. It is when suffering from a weakened body, and an irritated and excited mind, that he is attacked by a sickness which clings to his system, leaves him without any rest, incapacitates him from taking food, distracts his nerves, and places him in imminent danger of falling a victim to any sudden attack of convulsions to which he may have a predisposition. He relished no society so much as that of Palmer, whose residence was immediately opposite the Talbot Arms Inn, where he was lying on his sick bed.

For two nights he had been taking opiate pills prescribed by Dr. Bamford. On Sunday night, at 12 o'clock, he started as from a dream in a state of the utmost excitement and alarm. He admitted afterwards that for two minutes he was mad, but he could not ascribe it to anything unless to his having been awakened by a squabble in the street. But do no such things happen to people of sound constitutions and regular habits? Do no such people awaken in agony and delirium because there is a noise under their windows?! No, these are the afflictions of the dissipated and the anxious, whose bodies are shattered and whose minds are distracted.

Next day, Monday, he was pretty well, but not so well as to mount his horse, or to take a walk in the fields. He could converse with his trainer and jockey, but he took no substantial food, and drank not a drop of brandy-and-water. You will bear in mind that Palmer was not with him that day. In the middle of the night he was seized with an attack similar in character to that of the night preceding, but manifestly much milder, for he retained his consciousness throughout it, and was not mad for a moment. The evidence of Elizabeth Mills is conclusive on the point. [The learned Serjeant read some passages from the deposition of the witness in question.]

At 3 o'clock on the following day (Tuesday) Mr. Jones, the surgeon of Lutterworth, arrived, and spent a considerable time —

probably from 3 to 7 o'clock — in his company. They had abundant opportunity for conversing confidentially, and they were likely to have done so, for they were very intimate, and Jones appears to have been on more familiar terms with Cook than was any other person, not even excepting Mr. Stevens. Nothing occurred, in the entire and unbounded confidence which must have existed between Mr. Cook and Mr. Jones, to raise any suspicions in the mind of Mr. Jones; and at the consultation which took place between 7 and 8 o'clock on Tuesday evening between Jones, Palmer, and Bamford, as to what the medicine for that evening should be, the fit of the Monday night was not mentioned.

That is a remarkable fact. The Crown may say that it is remarkable, inasmuch as Palmer knew it, and said not a word about it; but I think that it shows that the fit was so little serious in the opinion of Cook, that he did not think it worth mentioning to his intimate friend Jones. If Cook had not given to Elizabeth Mills a rather exaggerated description of what had occurred, would he not have said to Mr. Jones, when he came from Lutterworth to see him, "You can't judge of my condition from my appearance now, for I was in a state of perfect madness over night, and in fact I thought that I was going to die?" Evidently he would have said something of that sort, and if he had Mr. Jones would have mentioned it at the consultation.

My inference, then, that the first statement which was made by Elizabeth Mills, was the correct statement of what occurred. Palmer, in the presence of Jones, administered two pills to Mr. Cook, which it supposed poisoned him — which contained a substance which sometimes does its deadly work in quarter of an hour — which has done it in less, and which rarely exceeds half an hour; and we are asked to believe that, in spite of Cook's objecting in the presence of his friend to take the pills, Palmer positively forced them down his throat at the imminent peril of the man falling down in a few minutes in convulsions evidently tetanic.

As in the course of the examinations of Mr. Jones the word "tetanus" was used, it is right that I should say a word upon that subject. The word "tetanus" is not in his deposition; but I tell you what is in it, and it is one of the most remarkable features in this case, because it shows how people, when they get a theory into their heads, will fag that theory, how they will stretch it to the very utmost, and make it fit into the exact place in which they wish to put it.

We have it now in the evidence of Dr. Taylor that at the inquest he sat next to Mr. Deane, the attorney's clerk, and suggested the questions which it was necessary in his judgment to put in order to elicit the truth as to the symptoms of Mr. Cook's disease. Now, fancy Dr. Taylor, who had had a letter telling him that there was a suspicion of strychnine, and who had all but made up his mind at that time to state positively upon oath his opinion that the pills given on Monday and Tuesday nights contained strychnine; fancy —

The *Attorney-General.* — I am sorry that my learned friend should be misled upon a matter of fact; but I am told that Dr. Taylor was not present when Mr. Jones was examined.

Mr. *Serjeant Shee* continued. — Then the observations which I was about to make do not apply; and all I can say is, that Mr. Jones had probably in his mind's eye when he gave that evidence, a recollection of what he had seen on the Tuesday night.

He could not have seen very accurately, however, for he said that there was only one candle in the room, and that he had not light enough to see the patient's face, and that he could not tell whether there was much change in the countenance of the deceased — a very important fact when the doctors all say that Cook's disease cannot have been traumatic tetanus, because there is always a peculiar expression of the countenance in those cases, which was not observable in Cook.

However, Mr. Jones, who is a competent professional man, gave his evidence, and it is quite clear that the notion of tetanus must have entered into his mind, because I find in the depositions that the coroner's clerk first put down "tetanus;" and the probability, I think, is, that the disease did occur to Mr. Jones at the time, and that he used the word, because the clerk never could have invented it. Then "tetanus" is struck out; then the word "convulsions" is written, and also struck out; and, as the sentence stands, it is, "There were strong symptoms of violent convulsions."

What is the fair inference from that? Why, that the man who saw Cook in this paroxysm did not think himself justified in saying that it was a tetanic convulsion at all, though it was very like tetanus.

Now, I will just call your attention to the features of general convulsions as described in cross-examination by the medical witnesses, in order to show that the convulsions of which Cook died were not tetanic, properly speaking, but were of that strong and irregular kind which cannot be classed under the head of tetanus, either traumatic or idiopathic, but under the head of general convulsions. I propose upon this part of the case to read an extract from the work of Dr. Copland, which will enable you to judge whether Cook's complaint bears a greater resemblance to general convulsions than to traumatic tetanus or strychnine tetanus.

Before doing so, however, I would observe that the only persons who can be supposed to know anything of tetanus not traumatic are physicians, and that not one of that most honourable class of men (who see the attacks of patients in their beds, and not in the hospital) has been called by the Crown, with the exception of Dr. Todd, who is a most respectable man, and who gave his evidence in such a way as to command the respect of every one; but even his practice appears to be not so much that of a physician as of a surgeon.

I am instructed that I shall be able to show by the most eminent men in the profession that the description which I am about to read from Dr. [James] Copland's book, the *Dictionary of Practical Medicine*, is the true description of general convulsions. In that book I find the following, under the head of "Convulsions:"—

"Definition. — Violent and involuntary contractions of a part or of the whole of the body, sometimes with rigidity and tension (tonic convulsions), but more frequently with tumultuous agitations, consisting of alternating shocks (clonic convulsions) that come on suddenly, either in recurring or in distant paroxysms, and after irregular and uncertain intervals."

The article then goes on:—

"If we take the character of the spasm in respect of permanency, rigidity, relaxation, and recurrence as a basis of arrangement of all the diseases attended by abnormal action of voluntary muscles, we shall have every grade, passing imperceptibly from the most acute form of tetanus, through cramp, epilepsy, eclampsia, convulsions, &c., down to the most atonic states of chorea and tremor."

As to the premonitory symptoms, it says:—

"The premonitory signs of general convulsions are (*inter alia*), vertigo and dizziness, irritability of temper, flushings, or alternate flushing and paleness of the face, nausea, retching or vomiting, or pain and distension of stomach and left hypochondrium, unusual flatulence of the stomach and bowels, or other dyspeptic symptoms."

In further describing these convulsions the article says:—

"In many instances the general sensibility and consciousness are but very slightly impaired, particularly in the more simple cases, and when the proximate cause is not seated in the encephalon;[3] but in proportion as this part is affected primarily or consecutively, and the neck and face tumid and livid, the cerebral functions are obscured, and the convulsions attended by stupor, delirium, &c., or rapidly pass into, or are followed by these states."

Then, it adds:—

"The paroxysm may cease in a few moments or minutes, or continue for some or even many hours. It generally subsides rapidly, the patient experiencing at its termination, fatigue, headache, or stupor; but he is usually restored in a short time to the same state as before the seizure, which is liable to recur in a person once affected,

---

[3] The brain.

but at uncertain intervals. After repeated attacks the fit sometimes becomes periodic (the *convulsio recurrens* of authors)."

And, in detailing the origin of these convulsions it says:—

"The most common causes are (*inter alia*) all emotions of the mind which excite the nervous power and determine the blood to the head, as joy, anger, religious enthusiasm, excessive desire, &c., or those which greatly depress the nervous influence, as well as diminish and derange the actions of the heart, as fear, terror, anxiety, sadness, distressing intelligence, frightful dreams, &c. — the syphilitic poison and repulsion of gout or rheumatism."

Do you believe, if Dr. Taylor had read that before the inquest, that he would have dared to say that the man died from strychnine?

Is there one single symptom in the statement made in the depositions by Elizabeth Mills and Mr. Jones which may not be classed under one of the varieties of convulsions which Dr. Copland describes?

It is not for me to suggest a theory: but the gentlemen whom I shall call before you — men of the highest eminence in their profession, and not mere hospital surgeons, who have seen nothing of this nature but traumatic tetanus — will tell you that Mr. Cook's symptoms were those of general convulsions, and not of tetanus.

My belief is — and I hope you will confirm it by your verdict — that Mr. Cook's complaint was not tetanus at all, although it may well have been — according to the descriptions to which I shall call your attention — some form of traumatic or idiopathic tetanus, there being no broad, general distinction or certain confine between idiopathic, or self-generating tetanus, and many forms of convulsions. The tetanic form of convulsions is pretty much the same thing as idiopathic tetanus; and when we are told by medical witnesses that they never saw a case of idiopathic tetanus, my answer to that is that they must have had a very limited experience. It is not a disease of very frequent occurrence, it is true; but there are gentlemen here who have seen cases of idiopathic tetanus, and they are by no means of that rare occurrence which has been represented to you by the witnesses for the prosecution.

There is one gentleman here, of very large practice at Leeds, whom I shall call before you, who attended at the bedside of Mrs. Dove, who has himself seen four cases of idiopathic tetanus. Traumatic tetanus very frequently occurs in hospitals — in fact, it often supervenes upon the operations of the surgeon; but the persons to give you correct information upon idiopathic tetanus are the general practitioners who enjoy the confidence of families, and who have the opportunity of visiting at their dwellings, both rich and poor, when they are attacked by any of those convulsive diseases or fits which heads of families and brothers and sisters are so careful not to disclose to the world at large.

Dr. [Thomas] Watson is a general practitioner, and he says in his "Lectures on the Principles and Practice of Physic" [1855], that most cases of tetanus may be traced to one of two causes — which are, exposure to the cold, or sudden alternations of temperature, and bodily injury.

"It has been known to arise," he says, "from causes so slight as these,— the sticking of a fish-bone in the fauces, the air caused by a musket shot, the stroke of a whip-lash under the eye, leaving the skin unbroken, the cutting of a corn, the biting of the finger by a tame sparrow, the blow of a stick on the neck, the insertion of a seton, the extraction of a tooth, the injection of a hydrocele, and the operation of cupping."[4]

He goes on to say that when the disease arises from exposure to the cold or damp it comes on earlier than on other occasions — often in a few hours — so that if the exposure takes place in the night the complaint may begin to manifest itself next morning. He also says that although tetanus may be occasioned by a wound, independently of exposure to cold, or of exposure to cold without bodily injury, there is good reason for thinking that in many instances one of the causes would fail to produce it where both together would call it forth.

Dr. Watson adds that, although the pathology of tetanus is obscure, we may fairly come to the conclusion that the symptoms are the result of some peculiar condition of the spinal cord, produced and kept up by irritation of the substance, and that the brain is not involved in the disease; the modern French writers upon the disease hold that it is an inflammable complaint, and that it consists essentially of inflammation of the spinal marrow.

Now, who shall say that those symptoms which were spoken to on the day of the inquest by Elizabeth Mills and Mr. Jones may not be ranged under one of those forms of tetanus? Idiopathic tetanus is so like general convulsions that in many cases it cannot be distinguished from them; and to such an extent is this so that Dr. Copland states that convulsions frequently assume a tetanic appearance. It is true that traumatic tetanus begins in four cases out of five by a seizure of the lower jaw; but then in the fifth case it does not so commence; and Sir B. Brodie mentions two instances in which it began in the limb which was wounded.

Now, having gone so far, and having endeavoured to satisfy you that the symptoms which were spoken to by those two witnesses in their depositions may be, as I am told and instructed that they are, rather referable to a violent description of general convulsions than to

---

[4] The technique of heating a glass vessel, creating a partial vacuum, to draw blood to the surface of the skin. When the cup is removed, a small incision is made and blood drawn.

any form of tetanus, let us proceed to inquire whether or not the symptoms are consistent with what we know of tetanus produced by strychnine; because, if you shall be satisfied, upon full investigation, that they are not consistent with the symptoms which are the unquestionable result of strychia tetanus, then the hypothesis of the Crown entirely fails, and John Parsons Cook can't have died of strychnine poison.

Whether that be so or not will depend in a great degree, as it strikes me — although, of course, that will be for you to decide — upon what you think of the evidence of Elizabeth Mills; but, before I go to that evidence, I will call your attention to the description of strychnia tetanus as given by two very eminent gentlemen, Dr. Taylor and Dr. Christison, who were called for the Crown the other day; and, if you find from their description that strychnia tetanus is a different thing from the picture first given of the attack and paroxysms by Elizabeth Mills and Mr. Jones, you will, I think, have great difficulty in determining that Mr. Cook died from strychnine.

Let us first take Dr. Taylor's description of strychnia tetanus. I am not sure whether he stated that he had ever seen a case of strychnia tetanus in a human subject; but we must be just to Dr. Taylor. He has had large and extensive reading on the subject on which he writes, and it is not to be supposed that he has set down in his book what he has not found established upon respectable authority. Therefore, although we have it second hand in the book, we must suppose that Dr. Taylor knows something of the subject.

In his work upon strychnia poisoning, Dr. Taylor says, "that in from 5 to 20 minutes after the poison has been swallowed the patient is suddenly seized with tetanic symptoms affecting the whole of the muscular system, the body becoming rigid, the limbs stretched out, and the jaws so fixed that considerable difficulty is experienced in introducing anything into the mouth."

But according to the statement of the witnesses, Mr. Cook was sitting up in bed, beating the bedclothes, talking, frequently telling the people about him to go for Palmer, asking for "the remedy," and ready to swallow whatever was given him. There was no "considerable difficulty in introducing anything into the mouth," and the paroxysm, instead of beginning within "from 5 to 20 minutes after the poison was supposed to have been swallowed," did not begin for an hour and a-half afterwards.

Dr. Taylor further on states, "After several such attacks, increasing in severity, the patient dies asphyxiated." Now I submit, although there are some of these symptoms in this case, as there will be in every case of violent convulsions, that this is not a description of the case of John Parsons Cook.

The other medical authority, to whom I said I should refer, is Dr. Christison. He says that the symptoms produced by strychnine are very uncommon and striking — the animal begins to tremble, and is seized with stiffness and a starting of the limbs. Those symptoms increase, till at length the animal is attacked by general spasms. The fit is then succeeded by an interval of calm, during which the senses are impaired or are unnaturally acute; but another paroxysm soon sets in, and then another and another, until at last a fit occurs more violent than any that had preceded it, and the animal perishes suffocated.

Now, who can say that that description at all tallies with the account of Mr. Cook's symptoms? I know exactly what Dr. Christison means by this description, because I have had the advantage of having had several experiments performed in my presence by Dr. Letheby, which enable me to understand it.

One of those experiments was this:— A dog had a grain of strychnine put into his mouth, and for about 20 or 25 minutes he remained perfectly well. Suddenly he fell down upon his side, and his legs were stretched out in a most violent way. He was as stiff as it was possible to be. In that state the dog remained, with an occasional jerk, for two or three minutes. In a short time he recovered and got up, but he appeared to be dizzy and uncomfortable, and was afraid to move. If you touched him he shrunk and twitched, and after another minute down he went again. He got up again and fell down again, and at last he had a tremendous struggle, and then he died.

That is what Dr. Christison means by his description. If the dose had not been sufficient to kill the dog it would have been longer in producing an effect; the paroxysms would have occurred at more distant intervals, and they would have been less and less severe until the animal recovered. But if the dose be strong enough to kill, the interval between the paroxysms is short, and at last one occurs which is strong enough to kill.

Just before the animal dies the limbs become as supple and free as it is possible to conceive the limbs of an animal to be. Whichever way you put the limbs of the animal after it is quite dead, the *rigor mortis* comes on after a time, and they remain in any position in which they are placed.

I saw an experiment performed also upon two rabbits. The symptoms were substantially the same; the limbs of both of them were quite flaccid immediately upon death; and during the intervals between the paroxysms the animals shuddered and were extremely "touchy."

Now, gentlemen, I will give you my reasons for saying that, according to their own principles, as adduced in evidence by the

Crown, Mr. Cook's death cannot have resulted from strychnia poison. I object to the theory of it having resulted from strychnia poison — first, on the ground that no case can be found in the books in which, while the paroxysms lasted, the patient had so much command over the muscles of animal life and voluntary motion as Mr. Cook had upon Monday and Tuesday night. The evidence is that he was sitting up in his bed beating the bedclothes, calling out, and that so far from being afraid of people touching him, he actually asked to have his neck rubbed; and it was rubbed.

I now come to the next reason why we say that death in this case did not result from strychnia poison; and I assert that there is no authentic case of tetanus from strychnine in which the paroxysm was delayed so long after the ingestion of the poison as it was in Mr. Cook's case. Dr. Taylor says, in page 74 of his book, that in from 5 to 20 minutes after the poison has been swallowed the tetanic symptoms commence; and then, in support of this statement, he proceeds to cite a number of cases.

One young lady was "instantly deprived of the power of walking, and fell down."

In the next case, which was that of a girl, "tetanic symptoms came on in half an hour."

The next is a German case, taken from the *Lancet*, and there a young man, aged 17, was "attacked in about a quarter of an hour."

Then there is the case of Dr. Warner, who took half a grain of sulphate of strychnine, and died in 15 minutes.

Then there is the case of a young woman who took two or three drachms of *nux vomica*, and died in between 30 and 40 minutes.

Another case is given by Dr. Watson in his book, which he himself observed in the Middlesex Hospital, where strychnine pills intended for paralytic patients were taken by mistake. One-twelfth of a grain was intended to be administered every six hours; but unluckily a whole grain was given at one time, about 7 o'clock in the evening, and in half an hour it began to exhibit its effects. Dr. Watson says, that "any attempt at movement — even touching the patient by another person brought on a recurrence of the symptoms."

It is clear, then, from all these cases, that the interval which elapsed between the supposed ingestion of the poison and the commencement of the paroxysm was much too long — three times too long to warrant the supposition that strychnia poison had been taken in this case.

Thirdly, I submit — and I shall prove — that there is no case in which the recovery from a paroxysm of strychnine poison has been so rapid as it was in Cook's case upon Monday night, or in which a patient has endured so long an interval of repose or exemption from its symptoms afterwards. In this case of Mr. Cook, according to the theory of the Crown, the paroxysms would not have been repeated at all if a second dose had not been given. There was an end of it when Elizabeth Mills left Palmer sleeping by the side of his friend in an arm-chair; how easy would it have been then, if he had been so disposed, to administer another dose, and to have hurried into Elizabeth Mills's room and called out that Cook was in another fit?

Dr. Taylor says in his book that the patient is suddenly seized with spasms affecting the whole system, and that after several such attacks increasing in severity the patient dies asphyxiated. Dr. Christison holds precisely the same language; but I submit that here there is a broad distinction between the case of Cook and that which these gentlemen state to be the distinguishing feature of the disease.

I now come to the *post-mortem* examination. Dr. Letheby was good enough to dig up from his garden, in order that I might see it, an animal which had been killed by strychnine with a view to this inquiry a month before, and to examine the heart before me. The heart of that animal was quite full. The heart also of the dog that was killed in my presence was quite full, and so were the hearts of both the rabbits that I saw killed. Now, I am told by a gentleman whom I shall call before you, who is not afraid of dogs — and remember that this is rather a matter for experiment than of theory — I am told that the result of an enormously large proportion of such examinations — and, indeed, of all of them if they be properly conducted — is, that the heart is invariably full.

At the same time, I am told that if the examiners do the thing clumsily they may contrive to get an empty heart. If there be any doubt in your minds, however, as to the heart being full in these cases, I hope that some morning you will desire that a reasonable number of animals should be brought into one of the yards here, and that you will see them die by strychnine, and examine their hearts and form an opinion for yourselves.

I have now discussed what may be said to be the theory of these matters; but I have not yet met the strong point which was made by the Crown of the evidence of Elizabeth Mills. I, upon all occasions, am most reluctant to attack a witness who is examined upon his or her oath, and particularly if he be in a humble position of life. I am very reluctant to impute perjury to such a person; and I think that a man who has been as long in the profession as I have been, must, in most cases be put a little to his wits' end when he rushes upon the assumption that a person whose statements have, after a considerable lapse of time, materially varied, is therefore necessarily deliberately perjured.

The truth is, we know perfectly well that if a considerable

interval of time occurs between the first story and the second story, and if the intelligent and respectable persons who are anxious to investigate the truth, but who still have a strong moral conviction — upon imperfect information — of the guilt of an accused person, will talk to witnesses and say, "Was there anything of this kind?" or "anything of that kind?" the witnesses at last catch hold of the phrase or term which has been so often used to them, and having in that way adopted it, they fancy they may tell it in court.

This might have been the case with Elizabeth Mills; and let me point out to you what occurs to me to be the right opinion that you should form of that witness. I submit to you that in this case of life and death — or, indeed, in any case involving a question of real importance to liberty or to property — that young woman's evidence would not be relied on. In the ordinary administration of justice in the civil courts, if a person has upon material points told two different stories, juries are rarely willing to believe that person; and in criminal cases the learned judges, without altogether rejecting the evidence, point out to the jury the discrepancies which have taken place, and submit whether, under all the circumstances, it would be safe to rely upon the testimony last given, differing from the statement which was made when the impression was fresh upon the witness's mind.

It cannot be said in this case that Elizabeth Mills was not fully and fairly examined. I submit that my learned friend the Attorney-General really made a false point — the most unfortunate in the course of the prosecution — in attacking, upon this ground, the coroner, Mr. Ward.

Just place yourselves, gentlemen, for a moment in the position of the coroner; and to enable you the better to do so, just recollect what has passed in the course of this trial in this court; recollect, if you can, how many questions have been put by my learned friends and by me on account of which it has been necessary for counsel to interpose, and ask the learned judges whether the question was a proper one. Our rules of examination are strict, but they are most beneficial, because they exclude from the minds of the jury that loose and general sort of information, which in country towns especially, is the subject of pothouse stories and market gossip, and substitute for it the evidence of actual facts which have been seen and are deposed to by the witnesses.

Imagine the coroner in a large room at a tavern, just under the bed-room where poor Cook died — a crowd of excited villagers in the room, all full of suspicion produced by the inquiries of the Prince of Wales Insurance Office about Walter Palmer — and Inspector Field there and Inspector Simpson — and all impressed with the belief that whatever the London doctor said must be true, and that if Dr. Alfred Swaine Taylor had made up his mind that it was poison, poison it was. The whole town was in a state of uproar and excitement. Every question that occurred to every body must be put before the coroner — "Didn't you hear so and so?" "Didn't somebody tell you that someone had said so and so?" and so on.

How is it possible under such circumstances to conduct an inquiry with the dignity and decorum that are observed in the superior courts? There was a celebrated trial some years ago in France, in which I remember to have taken great interest, of the Ministers of Charles X. Upon that occasion one witness actually proved that he had read all the pamphlets that had been published on the subject, and he came forward to state what, upon the whole, was the result which those pamphlets had made upon his mind. It is true that that was in revolutionary times, but it shows to what extent the introduction of a loose system of questioning may go.

I don't say that Dr. Taylor suggested any but proper questions; but you must consider the difficulties under which the coroner had to labour, and I am told that he is an exceedingly good lawyer, and a most respectable man. Dr. Taylor said that the coroner's omission to ask questions arose, in his opinion, rather from want of knowledge than from intention. Of course the coroner would not be likely to know the proper questions to put in such a case, but when he did know them he seems to have put them. He was right in refusing to put irrelevant questions to gratify an inquisitive juryman: we are ourselves constantly being rebuked by the learned judges, and told to adhere to the rules and not to put questions which are irrelevant.

I have now pointed out such discrepancies in the evidence given by Mills before the coroner and before you as well, I think, make it clear to you that you cannot rely upon her testimony. Since she first gave her evidence she has had the means of knowing what is the case on the part of the Crown. I do not mean to say that she has been tutored by the Crown; I believe that my learned friend would not have called her if he thought she had; but she has had an opportunity of discovering by interviews with several different people that the case for the prosecution is, that Palmer, having first prepared the body of Cook for deadly poison by the poison of antimony, afterwards despatched him with the deadly poison of strychnine. Their case is, that there was an administration of something which had the effect of producing nausea, and irritation of the stomach. Those symptoms are therefore attributed to the persevering intention of the prisoner to reduce Cook to such a state of weakness that, when once ingestion of the deadly poison occurred, he was sure to be carried off.

In her evidence before the coroner she was asked whether she had tasted the broth? She said she had, and she thought it very good. She did not then say a word about any ill effects the broth had produced; but she has since learnt that it is part of the case of those out of whose hands the Crown has taken the prosecution, and that it is the theory of Dr. Taylor that all this retching and vomiting was the result of a constant dosing with antimonial poison. She has probably been frequently asked whether she was not sick after drinking the broth; perhaps she may have been sick on some Sunday or another, and she has persuaded herself — for I do not wish to impute perjury to her — that she was made sick by the two table-spoonfuls of broth which she drank.

Is it not to the last degree incredible that a shrewd, intelligent man like Palmer, should have exposed himself to such a chance of detection as sending broth which he had poisoned from his house, to stand by the kitchen fire of the Talbot Arms, when, sure as fate, the cook would taste it? Did you ever know a cook who would not taste broth sent by another person, and said to be particularly good? It is not in the nature of things. A cook is a taster, she tastes everything, and Palmer must have known that, as sure as ever he sent into the kitchen broth containing antimony, the cook would take it and be ill. Her statement is not credible, and cannot be relied on.

Then she said in her evidence before the coroner that on Saturday Cook had coffee and vomited directly he swallowed it, and that up to the time she gave him the coffee she had not seen Palmer. She was not then aware that the theory of the gradual preparation of the body by antimony was to fit into the theory of death from strychnine, but by the time she came here she had become acquainted with that part of the case. My learned friend stated that "Palmer ordered him coffee on Saturday morning; it was brought in by the chambermaid, Elizabeth Mills, and given to the prisoner, who had an opportunity of tampering with it before giving it to Cook."

There is all the difference between this statement of my learned friend and that first made by Mills before the coroner. But the young woman did not go quite so far as that. She went however to this extent:— "Palmer came over at eight o'clock and ordered a cup of coffee for Cook. I gave it to him. I believe Palmer was in the bedroom at the time. I did not see him drink it. I observed afterwards that the coffee had been vomited." Her statement was not so strong as that of my learned friend, but a great deal stronger than the one she made before the coroner. The two statements are essentially different, and the difference between them consists in this — the one supports the theory suggested by the prosecution, the other is totally inconsistent with it. Can you rely on a woman who makes such alterations in her testimony?

That is not all. The case suggested for the Crown now is, that

Cook expressed reluctance to take the pills ordered for him, and that his reluctance was overruled by Palmer. Mills's first statement was that Cook said the pills made him ill. Here she said that the pills which Palmer gave him made him ill. Before the coroner, too, she did not say that Palmer was in the bedroom between nine and ten on Monday night, as she has stated here. She makes him more about the bedside of the man, she gives him a greater opportunity of administering pills and medicine, she shows an *animus*, the result, according to the most charitable construction that can be put upon it, of a persuasion that Palmer must be guilty, but still an *animus* which shows that she is not to be relied on.

How easily may persons in her condition make mistakes without intending to deceive! It is the just punishment of all falsehood that when a lie has once been told it cannot be retracted without humiliation, and when once this young woman had been induced to vary her statements in a material particular she had not the moral courage to set herself right.

But the particulars I have mentioned are nothing to those to which I will now call your attention. I impeach her testimony on the ground that she here gesticulated and gave her evidence in such a manner that if it had been natural and she had adopted it at the inquest it must have attracted the attention of Dr. Taylor. The remarkable contortions into which she put her hands, her mouth, and her neck would, if they had been observed at the inquest, have been reduced to verbal expression, and recorded in the depositions. I am told by Dr. Nunneley, Dr. Robinson, and other gentlemen, that the symptoms she described are inconsistent with any known disease. There was an extraordinary grouping of symptoms, some of them quite consistent with tetanus produced by strychnine administered under peculiar circumstances, others quite inconsistent with it.

Now, in the last week in February a frightful case of strychnine occurred in Leeds.[5] A person having the means of access to the bedside of a patient was supposed to have administered small doses, day by day, and after keeping her sometime in a state of irritation, to have at last killed her. The person who attended the patient spoke of her symptoms for about a week before her death, and said she had "twitchings" in the legs, that she was alarmed at being touched in the intervals between the spasms.

I will now call your attention to the evidence of Mills. She states:— "Cook said, 'I can't lie down; I shall be suffocated if I lie down. Oh, fetch Mr. Palmer!' The last words he said very loud. I did not observe his legs, but there was a sort of jumping or jerking about his

---

[5] This is the Harriet Dove case referred to in the testimony of Elizabeth Mills, Jane Witham, and George Morley.

head and neck and his body. Sometimes he would throw back his head upon the pillow, and then raise it up again. He had much difficulty in breathing. The balls of his eyes projected very much. He screamed again three or four times while I was in the room. He was moving and knocking about all the time. He asked me to rub his hands. I did rub them, and he thanked me. I noticed him 'twitch.' I gave him toast-and-water. His body was still jerking and jumping. When I put the spoon to his mouth he snapped at it and got it fast between his teeth, and seemed to bite it very hard. In snapping at the spoon he threw forward his head and neck. He swallowed the toast-and-water, and with it the pills. Palmer then handed him a draught in a wineglass. Cook drank this. He snapped at the glass as he had done at the spoon. He seemed as though he could not exactly control himself."

The expressions she used, particularly the word "twitchings," are remarkable. It may well be that when this case became public she may have had her attention called to it, and then had questions put to her with regard to the symptoms of Cook which induced her to alter the evidence she had before given. I cannot otherwise account for the remarkable variance in her evidence.

From the time she left the Talbot Arms till she came here she seems to have been a person of remarkable importance. She went to Dolly's where Stevens visited her five or six times. What for? Stevens was unquestionably — and within proper limits he is not to be blamed for it — indignant at the circumstances of Cook's death. He is not in the same condition of life as Mills. Why did he call on her? Why did he converse with her in a private room? He came, she said, to inquire after her health and see how she liked London. Mr. Gardner also saw her in the street, but he only asked her how she was and talked of other things.

I do not say that these gentlemen went to her with the deliberate intention of inducing her to say what was false; but they did go with the deliberate intention of stimulating her memory upon points as to which they thought it required stimulating. Mr. Hatton, the police officer of Rugeley, also saw her a few times. They could have gone to her for no purpose but that of taking her evidence.

I may mention a circumstance which shows how differently minor matters may be stated by witnesses who do not wish to state what is false. When Palmer went into the bedroom, after being called up, he remarked, "I do not think I ever dressed so quickly in my life," and it is suggested that he never went to bed, but waited up for the commencement of the paroxysm. Mills answered the question I put to her upon that point pretty fairly; she said, "He came in his dressing-gown, and I do not recollect that there was anything like a day-shirt about his neck."

On the other hand, Lavinia Barnes, who gave her evidence in a most respectable manner, said that he was quite dressed; that he wore his usual dress. People get talking about what they have witnessed, the real image of what occurred becomes confused or altogether obliterated from their minds, and they at last unconsciously tell a story which is very different from the truth. Mills was examined three times before the coroner, and if that officer acted improperly on those occasions it was quite competent for the Crown to bring him here and give him an opportunity of vindicating himself, but he ought not to be blamed upon the evidence of a witness like her.

In the course of her examination, however, there came out a fact which is worthy of remark. Is there not something extraordinary in the periodicity of the attacks she described in their recurrence on the three nights nearly at the same hour. There are numerous cases in the books in which attacks of this kind occurred at the same distance of time after the patient had gone to bed.

Without going into unnecessary details, I will now state what I intend to prove upon this part of the case. I shall call a great number of most respectable medical practitioners and surgeons in general practice, with a large experience in great cities, who will support the theory that these fits of Cook were probably not tetanus at all, but violent convulsions, the result of a weak habit of body, increased by a careless mode of life — by at least a sufficient amount of disease to render violent mineral poisons, in their opinion, desirable, and by habits which led to a chronic ulceration of the tonsils and difficulty in swallowing. They will prove that men with constitutions weakened by indulgence have often, under the influence of strong mental excitement and violent emotion of any kind, been suddenly thrown into such a state of convulsions that symptoms have been exhibited in the voluntary muscles of violent disease, and that persons suffering from those symptoms have constantly died asphyxiated or of exhaustion, leaving no trace whatever as to the cause of death.

In addition, I will call several gentlemen who will speak to experiments they have made upon animals, and who will be ready to show you more experiments in any yard belonging to this building, if my Lords should think fit. They will tell you, on the authority of Orfila, that no degree of putrescence will decompose strychnine, and that if it is in the body they would be sure to find it even now.

Lord CAMPBELL said that the Court could not see the experiments made, but witnesses might be called to prove them.

Mr. *Serjeant Shee*. — I have now done with that branch of the case, and will proceed to the last matter to which I propose to direct your attention. I propose to discuss whether the circumstantial evidence is inexplicable on the supposition of the prisoner's innocence;

and, if I show you that in all its broad and salient features it is not so, I am sure that you will be only too happy to acquit him, recollecting that you represent the country, which is uninformed upon the case, which has no opportunity of hearing the witnesses on either side.

Lord CAMPBELL. — In the language of the law "which country you are."[6]

Mr. *Serjeant Shee.* — Which country you are. You are responsible not to render this kingdom liable to the charge of having, in a paroxysm of prejudice propagated by a professional man with no knowledge of his own upon the matter, condemned an innocent person. In discussing the circumstantial evidence, I will avoid no point that seems at all difficult; but not to waste time, I will not, after the intimation which I have received from the bench, trouble you with such matters as the pushing against Dr. Devonshire during the *post-mortem* examination or the cutting of a slit in the cover of the jar, which might be done accidentally with any of the sharp instruments which were being used, or the putting it at the further end of the room.

Lord CAMPBELL. — What was said referred only to the pushing.

Mr. *Serjeant Shee.* — I take leave to suggest that in an examination in the town of Rugeley, where Palmer was perfectly well known, the fact of there having been a little apparent shoving, which may for the moment have disturbed the operator, is not to be allowed to have weight against the prisoner, especially as Mr. Devonshire said nothing was lost. The matter was one in which all present took considerable interest, and a little leaning over might easily have produced the effect which was spoken to.

Then, as to the removal of the jar. It was not taken out of the room. It could not have been taken away without its removal being observed, and it would have been to the last degree foolish for any guilty person to attempt to remove it. That a man who knew himself to be innocent should be very unwilling that the jar should be removed out of the hands of persons upon whom he could rely for honest dealing is very probable. Palmer knew that there were some persons who did not want to pay him £13,000, and who had for a long time been doing all they could to undermine his character, and to impute to him most wicked conduct with regard to the death of a relation — suspicions in which none of his relatives had joined. It is clear from his observation, "Well, doctor, they won't hang us yet," that he knew that it was intended to ground a suspicion or a complaint upon the *post-mortem* examination, and it was exceedingly natural

---

[6] Lord Campbell is quoting a standard legal phrase from the indictment. It runs along the lines of, "To this indictment the defendant has pleaded not guilty, and has put himself on the country, which country you are, and you are now sworn to try the issue."

that he should like to have the jar kept in safe custody, even in the crowded room. All his conduct is consistent with this explanation.

To Dr. Harland, with whom he does not appear to have been particularly intimate, he says, "I am very glad you are come, because there is no knowing who might have done it." That is the conduct of a respectable man, who knew that his conduct would bear investigation if it were properly conducted I dare say there are in Rugeley many excellent and very serious people to whom the prisoner's habit of life, his running about to races and so on would not much recommend him, and who he had reason to know entertained prejudices against him.

As to his objection to the jar being taken to Mr. Frere's, there had, I believe, been some slight difference, arising out of Thirlby (Palmer's assistant) having come to him from Mr. Frere. I do not do Mr. Frere the injustice to think that this slight dispute would have led him to have put anything into the jar, but it may account for Palmer's caution.

Let us now come to those more prominent features of Palmer's conduct upon which, I in accordance with his instructions, my learned friend principally relied.

I will first call your attention to the evidence of Myatt, the postboy at the Talbot Arms. Mr. Stevens had come down from London, and had acted towards Palmer in such a way as would have induced some men to kick him. Assuming Palmer to be innocent, Stevens's conduct was most provoking. He dissembled with Palmer, cross-questioned him, pretended to take his advice, scolded him in a harsh tone of voice, almost insulted him, threatened a *post-mortem* examination, and acted throughout under the impression that some one had been guilty of foul play towards Cook, which ought to be brought to light and punished.

Stevens had been there during the whole of the *post-mortem* examination — a gloomy, miserable day it must have been, poring over the remains of that poor dead man; the jar was ready, and the fly was at the door to take himself and Boycott to Stafford, in order that this jar might be sent to London out of Palmer's ken and notice; so that if there was anybody base enough to do it either in support of a theory or to maintain a reputation — God forbid that I should suggest that to the prejudice of Dr. Taylor; I do not mean to do so — but if there was anybody capable of acting so great a wickedness it might be done; and it was but a reasonable concern that Palmer should be anxious that it should stop at Dr. Harland's. He did not like its going with Stevens to London. Stevens had been particularly troublesome; he had been vexatious and annoying to the last degree. The fly was ready, when Palmer met Myatt, the postboy, and learned that he was going to drive Mr. Stevens to Stafford. According to Myatt's evidence, Palmer then asked him if he would upset "them." That word was first used in this court to designate the jars; but as there was at that time but one jar, it must have been intended to apply to Mr. Stevens and his companion.

Palmer's conduct to Stevens had been most exemplary, and he must have been irritated to the last degree to find that he was suspected of stealing a paltry betting-book, which was of no use to anyone, and of having played foully and falsely with the life of his friend, the deceased. That he was much annoyed was proved by his observation to Dr. Harland in the morning — "There has been a queer old fellow down here making inquiries, who seems to suspect that everything is wrong. He thinks I have stolen a betting-book, which everyone who knows anything knows can be of no use to anyone now that poor Cook is dead."

This shows that Palmer's mind was impressed with a sense that Stevens had ill-treated him. He, no doubt, said to himself, "He (Stevens) has encouraged and brought back suspicions which have well nigh destroyed me already, and which if he proceeds in this course of bringing another charge against me will probably render it impossible to get the sum which would be sufficient to release me from my embarrassments." In this state of mind Palmer met the postboy who was ready to drive Mr. Stevens to Stafford. What occurred then was thus described by Myatt:

"He said he supposed I was going to take the jars. — What did you say then, or what did he say? — I said I believed I was. — After you said you believed you were, what did he say? — He says, 'Do you think you could upset them?' — What answer did you make? — I told him, 'No.' — Did he say anything more? — He said, if I could, there was a £10 note for me. — What did you say to that? — I told him I should not. — Did he say any more to you? — I told him that I must go, for the horse was in the fly waiting for me to start."

In cross-examination he was asked:—

"Were not these the words Palmer used,— 'I should not mind giving £10 to break Mr. Stevens's neck?' — I do not recollect him saying 'to break his neck.' — Were they not words to that effect, 'I should not mind giving £10 to break his neck?' — I do not recollect that. — Then '£10 to upset him?' — Yes. — Those were the words, were they? — Them were the words, to the best of my recollection. — Did he appear to have been drinking at the time? — I cannot say. — When he said 'to upset him,' did he use any epithet; did he describe him in any way such as 'upset the fellow?' — He did not describe him in any way. — Did he say anything about him at the time? — He did say something about it; 'it was a humbugging concern,' or something to that effect. — That he was a humbugging concern, was that it! — No. — That 'it was a humbugging concern,' or something to that effect? — Yes."

I submit to you that, after this evidence, you can only regard this expression about "upsetting them" in its milder and more innocent sense, as a strong expression used by a man vexed and irritated by the suspicious and inquisitive manner which Stevens had from the first exhibited. That this is the correct view of the matter is confirmed by the fact that at the time of the inquest nothing was known of this, and Myatt was not called. Myatt was engaged at the Talbot Arms, and must frequently have conversed about the death of Cook and the *post-mortem* examination with servants and other persons about that inn. Had any serious weight been attached to this offer of Palmer, it would have excited attention, and would have been given in evidence before the coroner.

On the other hand, it is to the last degree improbable that a medical man, knowing that he had given a large dose of strychnine, with the violent properties of which he was well acquainted, should have supposed that by the accidental spilling of a jar — the liver, spleen, and some of the tissues remaining behind — he could possibly escape detection.

I will next call your attention to the evidence of Charles Newton, who swore that he saw Palmer at Mr. Salt's surgery at 9 o'clock on Monday night, when he gave him three grains of strychnine in a piece of paper. He did not bring this to the knowledge of the Crown until the night before this trial commenced. He was examined before the coroner, but although then called to corroborate the statement of Roberts as to the presence of Palmer at Hawkins's shop, where he was said to have purchased strychnine, he then said nothing about the purchase on the Monday night. A man who so conducts himself, who when first sworn omits a considerable portion of what he tells three weeks afterwards, and again comes forward at the last moment and tells more than enough in his opinion to drive home the guilt to the person who is accused, that man is not to be believed upon his oath.

There are other circumstances which render Newton's statement in the highest degree improbable. That Palmer should once in a way purchase strychnine in Rugeley is not to be wondered at. It is sold to kill vermin, to kill dogs. And whatever the evidence as to the galloping of the mares and their dropping their foals, it shows that Palmer had occasion for it, and for other purposes. But that, having bought enough for all ordinary purposes, he should go and buy more the next day, and should purchase it at the shop of a tradesman with whom he had not dealt for two years, is in the highest degree incredible. Nobody would believe it. Nobody can or ought to believe it.

But observe this also. Palmer had been to London on the Monday, and in London there is no difficulty in procuring strychnine. It is sold to any one who, by writing down the technical description of what he wants, shows that he has had a medical education. Why did he not get it in London? And if he could not get it in London, why did he not get it in Stafford, or at any of the other places to which he had been? If he had bought it for this guilty purpose, would he not, as a wary man, have taken care that when his house was searched there should be found in it the paper containing the exact quantity of strychnine which he had purchased? What could have been easier to do than that? Newton's story, therefore, cannot be believed; but, in addition, I will show that Palmer, who is stated by Herring to have been in London at a quarter past 3 o'clock, could not have been in Rugeley at the time at which Newton says he was at Mr. Salts.

Palmer attended the *post-mortem* examination; and is it credible that he, a skilful medical man, who studied in a London hospital, and made a note upon one of his books of the effect of strychnine, would ask that stupid sort of fellow Newton anything about its action upon a dog; and would, when the answer was given, snap his fingers and say, "It is all right, then, it cannot be found." No one will believe it for a moment. The *animus* of Newton is shown by his omitting the word "poor," and representing Palmer as having said, "You will find this fellow suffering from a disease of the throat; he has had syphilis;" and then, when cross-examined upon the subject by my learned friend Mr. Grove, replying, "I don't know whether he said poor or rich," as if that had anything to do with the question.

I will now take you back to what occurred at Shrewsbury. The case for the Crown is, that as early as Wednesday, the 14th of November, the scheme of poisoning Cook began to be executed at Shrewsbury. It is suggested that Cook was dosed with something that was put into his brandy-and-water. You will remember that I read to you a letter from Cook to Fisher, dated the 16th of November, to which there is this postscript — "I am better." That must have referred to his illness at Shrewsbury. It is the postscript to a letter in which he speaks of the object he has in view, which is of great importance to himself and Palmer. Is his writing in that tone consistent with his having a belief that Palmer had drugged him with poison for the purpose of destroying his life at Shrewsbury? What did Palmer say about it? — "Cook says I have put something in his glass. I don't play such tricks." He treated it as though it had never been understood to be more than the expression of a man who, if not actually drunk, was very nearly so.

Palmer did not arrive at the Raven until after the dinner hour. We have no evidence how Cook fared there; but we shall be able to prove that he went from there to the Unicorn, where he arrived pretty flush, and where he sat drinking brandy-and-water with Saunders the trainer and a lady. Seven or eight glasses of brandy-and-water did this good young man drink, and the result was that his unfortunate syphilitic throat was in a very dreadful state, if not of actual laceration, at least of soreness and irritation.

[The learned Serjeant here read to the jury a long extract from an article which had appeared in some newspaper, which he did not mention, in which the occurrences at Shrewsbury were described in a style which seemed intended to be humorous, and in which Cook's sickness was attributed to his having taken too much brandy upon champagne, in order to "restore his British solidity."[7] The learned Serjeant said this entirely concurred with his own view of the case. He then continued.]

Cook's own conduct afterwards proved that his illness was owing to his having drunk too much. He got up in the morning, breakfasted with Palmer, was good friends with him, and went with him to Rugeley. At Rugeley they received Pratt's letter of the 13th, in consequence of which Palmer wrote to Pratt to say that some one would call upon him and pay him £200, and Cook wrote to Fisher and asked him to call on Pratt and pay this money. Does that look as though he thought there had been an attempt to poison him?

Mrs. Brooks, who gave her evidence in a most creditable manner, proved that there was much sickness among the strangers who were at Shrewsbury; and the rest of her evidence did not tell much against Palmer, who might, after Cook's complaint, very naturally have been looking at the tumbler to see if anything had been put into it.

Cook got worse, and at last had the good sense to put his money into Fisher's hands and go to bed. He was still very sick, and a doctor was sent for, who recommended an emetic. Cook made himself sick by drinking warm water and putting the handle of a toothbrush down his throat. He took a pill and a black draught, went to sleep, and next morning was quite well. This is really too ludicrous to receive a moment's consideration.

A person named [George] Myatt was in the room at the Raven all the evening. He has been put into the box, but I shall call him, and you will hear his account.

Palmer and Cook having got back to Rugeley, the history of the

---

[7] From the account published in several newspapers: "After indulging freely in the foreign wines of an English country town, the owner of Polestar took to brandy and water to restore his British solidity. Tossing off his glass, he complained that there was something in it, for it burned his throat. Perhaps those who have drunk strong brandy and water with similar haste, may have experienced the same sensation; perhaps also, like Mr. Cook, they may have vomited afterwards. That night he was very drunk, and very sick, and very ill. His dinner he cast up into a basin; his money he deposited with his friend, Mr. Ishmael Fisher, expressing his belief that Palmer had dosed him for the sake of his money. Next morning Cook looked very ill, but his drunken suspicions of Palmer had evaporated with the fumes of the brandy, and they were again friends and brother sportsmen."

slow poisoning continues. They went there together, and probably talked on the way of their difficulties and the mode of getting out of them, and of the small way that the winnings at Shrewsbury would go to effect that object, both seeing ruin staring them in the face unless the Prince of Wales Insurance Office could be made to pay the money which was due, and they could meanwhile remain free from all suspicion of insolvency or any sort of misconduct.

When they got to Rugeley they provided for the temporary difficulty by sending £200 to Pratt. They were then evidently on friendly terms, Cook's winnings being at Palmer's service, and probably both effecting their objects, because, as it would appear from what Palmer said, Cook had some interest in the bills which were outstanding. Probably his name might not be upon them, but as they were engaged in these racing transactions, were joint owners of one horse, and had the same trainer, they were very probably equally interested in these bills — were, in fact, what I remember to have once heard a nobleman well known upon the turf call "confederates."

The frequency of Palmer's visits to Cook during the illness of the latter at Rugeley, affords no ground of suspicion against the prisoner. On the contrary, it tells in his favour. Cook had no friend in the town but Palmer, with whom he may almost be said to have been on a visit; for though he did not sleep in Palmer's house, Palmer was in continual attendance on him; and, owing to the close proximity of his own residence, was enabled to bring him many little delicacies not easily attainable at an inn. Had he neglected the sick man, and only visited him occasionally, the inference of the Crown would probably have been that he was a black-hearted scoundrel, who only looked in now and then to give him his poison; but as he was zealously and laboriously attentive to him, the conclusion is that he must have murdered him!

It is said that Palmer was guilty of a falsehood in representing Cook as suffering from diarrhœa: but this is to put a very violent and a very uncharitable construction on his words; for you will remember, that Bamford swore to Cook having told him that his bowels had been affected twice or three times on Sunday.

But, leaving these minor points, I come to one which, in this case of circumstantial evidence, is of the very last importance, and should be deemed decisive of the prisoner's innocence. The supposition of the Crown is that Palmer intended to dose Cook with antimony — to keep his stomach in continual irritation by vomiting, in order that he might the more surely despatch him with strychnine; and that during Sunday, the day on which he insisted on his taking the broth, Cook was under the influence of this insidious treatment.

Now, supposing this to be true, and assuming it to be the fact that Palmer was indeed bent upon destroying Cook by this singular process, is it not manifest that there is one man who, of all the men in the world, would have been the very last whom he would have selected to be a witness of his proceedings? That man is a surgeon in the prime of life, a man intimately acquainted with Cook and very much attached to him — Mr. Jones, of Lutterworth. Yet this is the very man to whom, when he is about to set out for London, Palmer writes a letter, informing him that Cook is ill, and urging him to come over and see him without delay.

I entreat of you to appreciate the full importance of that fact. The more you think of it the more profound will become your conviction that it affords evidence irrefragable[8] of Palmer's innocence.

The imputation is that Palmer meant to kill Cook to possess himself of his winnings. Who was with Cook when the race was won? Who was by his side on Shrewsbury racecourse for the three minutes that he was speechless? Who saw him take out his pocketbook and count up his winnings? Who but Jones? — Jones, who was his bosom friend, his companion, his confidant, and who knew to the last farthing the amount of his gains. Jones was of all men living the most likely to be the recipient of Cook's confidence, and the man who was bound by every consideration of honour, friendship, and affection, to protect him, to vindicate his cause, and to avenge his death. Yet this was the man for whom Palmer sent, that he might converse with Cook, receive his confidences, minister to him in his illness, and even sleep in the same room with him!

How, if Palmer is the murderer they represent him, are you to account for his summoning Jones to the bedside of the sick man? If Cook really suspected — as we are assured he did — that Palmer was poisoning him, Jones was the man to whom he would most willingly have unbosomed himself, and in whose faithful ear he would have most eagerly disburdened the perilous stuff that weighed upon his own brain.

Palmer and Jones were both medical men, and it is not improbable that in the course of his studies the latter may have noted in his classbook the very passages respecting the operation of strychnine which also attracted the attention of the former. Is it conceivable, that if Palmer meant to slay Cook with poison in the dead of the night he would have previously ensured the presence, in his victim's bed-room, of a medical witness, who would know from the symptoms that the man was not dying a natural death? He brings a medical man into the room, and makes him lie within a few inches of the sick man's bed, that he may hear his terrific shrieks and witness those agonising convulsions which indicate the fatal potency of poison!

---

[8] Impossible to refute. From the Latin *irrefragabilis* for "to oppose."

Can you believe it? He might have despatched him by means that would have defied detection, for Cook was taking morphia medicinally, and a grain or two more would have silently thrown him into an eternal sleep. But instead of doing so he sends to Lutterworth for Jones.

You have been told that this was done to cover appearances. Done to cover appearances! No — no — no! You cannot believe it. It is not in human nature. It cannot be true. You cannot find him guilty — you dare not find him guilty on the supposition of its truth. The country will not stand by you if you believe it to be true. You will be impeached before the world if you say that it is true. I believe in my conscience that it is false, and that consistently with the rules that govern human nature it cannot possibly be true. [Sensation and murmurs of applause.]

With respect to the interviews and dialogues that took place between the prisoner and Mr. Stevens, I contend that, so far from telling against the former, they are in his favour. There is nothing but the evidence of a kind and considerate nature in the fact of his having ordered "a shell and a strong oak coffin" for the deceased; nor is it possible to torture into a presumption of guilt the few words of irritation that may have fallen from the prisoner in the course of a conversation in which Mr. Stevens treated him with scorn, not to say insolence.

With respect to the betting-book, many persons had access to Cook's room — servants, both men and women, undertaker's men, and barbers; and though I do not venture to mark out any particular person for suspicion, any one of them may have purloined the book and been afraid to return it. It is not fair in a case of this momentous importance to affix the opprobrium on a man who is not proved to have ever had it in his hand.

The Crown had no doubt originally intended to rely upon the prisoner's medical books as affording damning proof of his guilt; but I will refer to those volumes for evidences that will speak eloquently in his favour.

In youth and early manhood there is no such protection for a man as the society of an innocent and virtuous woman to whom he is sincerely attached. If you find a young man devoted to such a woman, loving her dearly, and marrying her for the love he bears her, you may depend upon it that he is a man of a humane and gentle nature, little prone to deeds of violence.

To such a woman was Palmer attached in his youth, and I will bring you proof positive to show that the volumes cited against him were the books he used when a student, and that the manuscript passages are in the handwriting of his wife. His was a marriage of the heart. He loved that young and virtuous woman with a pure and generous affection; he loved her as he now loves her first-born, who awaits with trembling anxiety the verdict that will restore him to the arms of his father, or drive that father to an ignominious death upon the scaffold. [The prisoner here covered his face with his hands, and shed tears.]

Here in this book I have conclusive evidence of the kind of man that Palmer was seven years ago. I find in its pages the copy of a letter addressed by him while still a student to the woman whom he afterwards made his wife. It is as follows:—

"MY DEAREST ANNIE,— I snatch a moment from my studies to write to your dear, dear little self. I need scarcely say that the principal inducement I have to work is the desire of getting my studies finished, so as to be able to press your dear little form in my arms. With best, best love, believe me, dearest Annie,
"YOUR OWN WILLIAM."

Now this is not the sort of letter that is generally read in courts of justice. It was no part of my instructions to read that letter, but the book was put in to prove that this man is a wicked, heartless, savage desperado; and I show you what he was seven years ago,— that he was a man who loved a young woman for her own sake — loved her with a pure and virtuous affection — such an affection as would, in almost all natures, be a certain antidote against guilt. Such is the man whom it has been my duty to defend upon this occasion, and upon the evidence that is before you, I cannot believe him to be guilty.

Don't suppose, gentlemen, that he is unsupported in this dreadful trial by his family and his friends. An aged mother, who may have disapproved of some part of his conduct, awaits with trembling anxiety your verdict; a dear sister can scarcely support herself under the suspense which now presses upon her; a brave and gallant brother stands by him to defend him, and spares neither time nor trouble to save him from an awful doom.

I call upon you, gentlemen, to raise your minds to a capacity to estimate the high duty which you have to perform. You have to stem the torrent of prejudice; you have to vindicate the honour and character of your country; you have, with firmness and courage, to do your duty, and to find a verdict for the Crown, if you believe that guilt is proved; but, if you have a doubt upon that point, depend upon it that the time will come when the innocence of that man will be made apparent, and when you will deeply regret any want of due and calm consideration of the case which it has been my duty to lay before you.

The speech of the learned Serjeant occupied exactly eight hours in its delivery. There were some slight indications of an attempt to applaud at its conclusion, but they were instantly repressed.

The Court then adjourned till 10 o'clock this day.

EIGHTH DAY.—May 22, 1856.

On the resumption of this case this morning the court was, as usual, densely crowded, and all its avenues were beset by eager applicants for admission. His Royal Highness the Duke of Cambridge[1] was among the distinguished persons who were accommodated with seats upon the bench.

The learned Judges, Lord Campbell, Mr. Baron Alderson, and Mr. Justice Cresswell, took their seats at 10 o'clock. The prisoner was at once placed at the bar. His demeanour was, as on the previous days of his trial, calm and attentive, but betrayed no additional anxiety.

Immediately after the learned Judges took their seats,

Lord CAMPBELL said, before the proceedings commenced, I must express a most earnest hope that until this trial is concluded the public journals will continue to abstain from any comments upon the merits of the case, or upon any part of the evidence. The propriety of this course is so obvious as to need no explanation. This warning ought to extend to the insertion of letters as much as to that of editorial articles.

THOMAS NUNNELEY, examined by Mr. *Grove*.

I am a Fellow of the College of Surgeons, and Professor of Surgery at the Leeds School of Medicine. I am also a member of several medical and learned societies, foreign and English, and have been in practice between twenty and thirty years. I have a large practice, and have seen cases of both traumatic and idiopathic tetanus. Of the latter disease I have seen four cases. They did not all commence with lockjaw. One did not commence so, nor did lockjaw become so marked in it as to prevent swallowing once during the course of the disease.

I have heard the evidence as to the symptoms of Cook, and had previously read the depositions as to that part of the case. Judging from those symptoms, I am of the opinion that death was caused by some convulsive disease. I found that opinion upon the symptoms described in the depositions and the evidence before the Court.

Lord CAMPBELL said that the witness could only be examined as

---

[1] Prince George, 2nd Duke of Cambridge (1819-1904), King George III's grandson and Queen Victoria's cousin, became the commander-in-chief of the British Army this year. Resistant to reforms, the army stagnated under his leadership, and he was blamed for their failures during the Second Boer War. The title became extinct upon his death and was revived in 2011 when Queen Elizabeth II awarded the title to her grandson, Prince William.

MR. NUNNELEY, PROFESSOR OF SURGERY AT LEEDS

to his opinion founded upon the *viâ voce*[2] evidence before the Court.

Mr. *Grove* said that his object was to distinguish between the opinion founded on the *viâ voce* evidence, and that founded on the depositions.

Examination continued. — From the symptoms described by the witnesses in court I am of the opinion that death was caused by some convulsive disease. Looking at Cook's general state of health.—

Mr. Baron ALDERSON. — You have nothing to do with that. You must only give an opinion upon the symptoms described in evidence.

Examination continued by Mr. *Serjeant Shee*. — I have been in court during the whole of the trial. I have heard the evidence as to the symptoms of Mr. Cook's health previous to his final attack at Rugeley, the description of the actual symptoms during the paroxysms, and the appearance of the body on the *post-mortem* examination.

---

[2] By word of mouth. From the medieval Latin for "with the living voice."

Do you remember the account of the syphilitic sores?

The *Attorney-General* objected to this mode of putting the question, because it was an assumption that these sores existed. A medical man ought to be asked his opinion on the supposition only that certain symptoms existed.

Mr. Justice CRESSWELL. — Let the witness describe what he assumes to have been the state of Cook's health, and you will then see whether he is justified in his assumption.

Examination continued. — I assume that Cook was a man of very delicate constitution — that for a long period he had felt himself to be ailing, for which indisposition he had been under medical treatment; that he had suffered from syphilis; that he had disease of the lungs; and that he had an old standing disease of the throat; that he led an irregular life; that he was subject to mental excitement and depression; and that after death appearances were found in his body which show this to have been the case.

There was an unusual appearance in the stomach. The throat was in an unnatural condition. The back of the tongue showed similar indications. The air vessels of the lungs were dilated. In the lining of the aorta[3] there was an unnatural deposit, and there was a very unusual appearance in the membranes of the spinal marrow. One of the witnesses also said that there was a loss of substance from the penis. That scar on the penis would only have resulted from an ulcer. A chancre is an ulcer, but an ulcer is not necessarily a chancre. The symptoms at the root of the tongue and the throat I should ascribe to syphilitic inflammation of the throat.

Supposing these symptoms to be correct, I should infer that Cook's health had for a long time not been good, and that his constitution was delicate. His father and mother died young. Supposing that to have been his state of health, it would make him liable to nervous irritation. That might be excited by moral causes. Any excitement or depression might produce that effect. A person of such health and constitution would be more susceptible of injurious influence from wet and cold than would one of stronger constitution. Upon such a constitution as that which I have assumed Cook's to have been convulsive disease is more likely to supervene. I understand that Cook had three attacks on succeeding nights, occurring about the same hour. As a medical man, I should infer from this that the attacks were of a convulsive character. I infer that in the absence of other causes to account for them.

According to my personal experience and knowledge from the study of my profession, convulsive attacks are as various as possible

---

[3] The large artery that moves blood from the heart into the body.

in their forms and degrees of violence. It is not possible to give a definite name to every convulsive symptom. There are some forms of convulsion in which the patient retains his consciousness. Those are forms of hysteria, sometimes found in the male sex. It is also stated that there are forms of epilepsy in which the patient retains consciousness.

By Lord CAMPBELL. — I cannot mention a case in which consciousness has been retained during the fit. No such case has come under my notice.

Examination continued. — I know by reading that that, although rarely, does sometime occur. The degree of consciousness in epilepsy varies very much. In some attacks the consciousness is wholly lost for a long time. Convulsive attacks are sometimes accompanied by violent spasms and rigidity of the limbs. Convulsions, properly so called, sometimes assume a tetanic complexion.

I heard the passage from the works of Dr. Copland read to the Court yesterday. I agree with what he states. Convulsions arise from almost any cause — from worms in children, affections of the brain in adults, hysteria, and in some persons the taking of chloroform. Adults are sometimes attacked by such convulsions. Affections of the spinal cord or eating indigestible food will produce them. I know no instance in which convulsions have arisen from retching and vomiting. I agree with Dr. Copland that these convulsions sometimes end immediately in death. The immediate proximate cause of death is frequently asphyxia.

By Lord CAMPBELL. — Death from a spasm of the heart is often described as death by asphyxia.

Examination continued. — I have seen convulsions recurring. I have seen that in various cases. The time at which a patient recovers his ease after a violent attack of convulsions varies very much. It may be a few minutes, or it may be hours. From an interval between one convulsion and another I should infer that the convulsions arise from some slight irritation in the brain or the spinal cord. When death takes place in such paroxysms there is sometimes no trace of organic disease to be found by a *post-mortem* examination.

Granules between the dura mater and the arachnoid[4] are not common at any age. I should not draw any particular inference from their appearance. They might or might not lead to a conjecture as to their cause and effect. I do not form any opinion upon these points. They might produce an effect upon the spinal cord. There are three preparations in museums where granules are exhibited in the spinal cord, in which the patients are said to have died from tetanus. Those

---

[4] Two of the three membranes inside the skull that surround the brain and the spinal cord. The third is the pia mater.

are at St. Thomas's Hospital. To ascertain the nature and effect of such granules the spinal cord ought to be examined immediately after death. Not the most remote opinion could be formed upon an examination made two months after death, more especially if the brain had been previously opened. Independently of the appearance of granules, it would not after that period be possible to form a satisfactory opinion upon the general condition of the spinal cord.

If there were a large tumour, or some similar change, it might be exhibited; but neither softening nor induration of the structure could be perceived. The nervous structure changes within two days of death. To ascertain minutely its condition it is necessary to use a lens or microscope. That is required in an examination made immediately after death.

I have attended cases of traumatic tetanus. That disease commonly begins with an attack upon the jaw. One of the four cases of idiopathic tetanus that I have seen was my own child. In three of those cases the disease began with lockjaw. The fourth case commenced in the body, the facility of swallowing remaining.

I have within the last twelve months made *post-mortem* examinations of two persons who had died from strychnia. I did not see the patients before death. In both cases I ascertained by chemical analysis that death had been caused by strychnia. In both I found the strychnia.

In one case — that of a lady aged twenty-eight years — I made my examination forty-two hours after death, and in the other thirty hours. In the former case the body had not been opened before I commenced my examination.

[The witness read a report of this examination, in which it was stated that the eyelids were partially open and the globes flaccid, and the pupils dilated. The muscles of the trunk were not in the least rigid; indeed, they were so soft that the body might be bent in any direction. The muscles at the hip and shoulder joints were not quite so flaccid, but they allowed these joints to be easily moved; while those of the head and neck, fore-arms, &c, were rigid. The fingers were curved, and the feet somewhat arched. All the muscles, when cut into, were found soft and dark in colour. The membranes of the liver were exceedingly vascular. The membrane of the spinal cord was much congested. There was bloody serum in the pericardium; the lungs were distended, and some of the air-cells were ruptured. The lining membrane of the trachea and bronchial tubes were covered with a layer of dark bloody mucus of a dark chocolate colour. The thoracic vessels and membranes were much congested, and the blood was everywhere dark and fluid.]

After reading this report the witness continued:— In the second case I made my examination thirty hours after death. I first saw the body about twelve hours after death. It was a woman somewhere near twenty years of age. [The witness also read the report of the examination in this case. The appearances of the body were substantially similar to those presented in the previous case.]

In two other cases I have seen a patient suffering from overdoses of strychnia. Neither of those cases was fatal. In one case I had prescribed the twelfth of a grain, and the patient took one-sixth. That was for a man of middle age. Strychnia had been given in solution. In a few minutes the symptoms appeared. They were a want of power to control the muscles, manifested by twitchings, rigidity, and cramp, more violent in the legs than in any other part of the body. The spasms were not very violent. They continued six hours before they entirely disappeared. During that time they were intermittent at various intervals. As the attack passed off the length of the intervals increased. At first their length was but a few seconds. The spasms were not combated by medical treatment. The other case was a very similar one. The quantity taken was the same — double what I had prescribed.

I have experimented upon upwards of sixty animals with strychnia. Those animals were dogs, cats, rats, mice, guinea pigs, frogs and toads. The symptoms of the attack in all animals present great resemblances. Some animals are, however, much more susceptible of its influence than others are. The period elapsing between the injection of the poison and the commencement of the symptoms has been from two minutes to thirty, — more generally five or six.

I administered the poison occasionally in solution, but more generally in its solid state. It was sometimes placed dry upon the back of the tongue, and some fluid poured down the throat; sometimes it was enclosed between two portions of meat, sometimes mixed up with butter or suet, and sometimes rolled up in a small piece of gut. To frogs and toads it was administered by putting them into a solution of strychnia. I have also applied it direct to the spinal cord, and in other cases to the brain.

The first symptom has been a desire to be quite still; then hurried breathing; then slaverirg at the mouth (when the poison had been given through that organ); then twitching of the ears, trembling of the muscles, inability to walk, convulsions of all the muscles of the body, the jaws being generally firmly closed; the convulsions attended by a total want of power in the muscles, which on the least touch were thrown into violent spasms with a galvanic-like shock. Spasms also come on if the animal voluntarily attempts to move; that is usually the case, but occasionally the animal is able to move without inducing a recurrence of the spasms. These spasms occur at various periods, but do not always increase in violence. The animals die after periods varying from three hours to three hours and a half. In the cases where the animals live longest the paroxysms occur at the longest intervals. In all cases in the interval before death the rigidity ceases (I know no exception to this) and the muscles become quite soft, powerless, and flaccid. The limbs may be put in any position whatever. There is but little difference from ordinary cases of convulsive death in the time at which the *rigor mortis* comes on. I have destroyed animals with other poisons, and there is very little difference between the rigidity in their cases and that in the cases of death from strychnia.

In the two women I have mentioned the *rigor mortis* was much less than is usual in cases of death from natural disease. I have known fatal cases of poisoning animals by strychnia in which there has between the first and the second paroxysm been an interval of about half an hour, but that is not common.

I have examined the bodies of upwards of forty animals killed by strychnia. I have invariably found the heart full on the right side; very generally the left ventricle firmly contracted, and the blood usually dark, and often fluid. There is no particular appearance about the spine.

I have experimented with other poison upon upwards of 2,000 animals, and have written upon this subject. It very often happens that in the case of animals dying suddenly from poisoning, the blood is fluid after death. That also happens in cases of sudden death from other causes.

I have attended to the evidence as to the symptoms exhibited by Cook on the Sunday, Monday, and Tuesday nights. The symptoms on Sunday night I assume to have been caused by great excitement. Cook described himself as having been very ill, and in such a state that he considered himself mad for a few minutes. He stated that the cause of this was a noise in the street. These symptoms, in the three nights I have mentioned, do not resemble those which I have seen following the administration of strychnia. Cook had more power of voluntary motion than I have observed in animals under the influence of this poison. He sat up in bed, and moved his hands about freely, swallowed, talked, and asked to be rubbed and moved, none of which, if poisoned by strychnia, could he have done. The sudden accession of the convulsions is another reason for believing that they were not produced by strychnia.

Other reasons for believing that the convulsions were not produced by strychnia are their sudden accession without the usual premonitory symptoms, the length of time which had elapsed between their commencement and taking of the pills which are supposed to have contained poison, and the screaming and vomiting. I never knew an animal which had been poisoned with strychnia to vomit or scream voluntarily. I apprehend that where there is so much spasm of the heart there must be an inability to vomit. In the cases related in which attempts were made to produce vomiting they did not succeed. There is such a case in the 10th volume of the *Journal de Pharmacie*, in which an emetic was given without success.

The symptoms exhibited after death in animals poisoned by strychnia differ materially from those presented by the body of Cook. In his case the heart is stated to have been empty and uncontracted.

Lord CAMPBELL. — I do not remember that. I think it was said that it was contracted.

Mr. Baron ALDERSON. — According to my note, Dr. Harland said that the heart was contracted, and contained no blood.

Examination continued. — The lungs were not congested, nor was the brain. In the case of animals which have recovered the paroxysms have subsided gradually. I never knew a severe paroxysm followed by a long interval of repose. I have experimented upon the discovery of strychnia in the bodies of animals in various stages of decomposition, from a few hours after death up to the forty-third day, in which latter case the body was quite putrid. It has never happened to me to fail to discover the poison. I have experimented in about fifteen cases.

Supposing a person to have died under the influence of strychnia poison in the first paroxysm, and his stomach to have been taken out and put into a jar on the sixth day after death, must strychnia have, by a proper analysis, been found in the body? — Yes. If the strychnia be pure, such as is almost invariably found among medical men and druggists, the test is nitric acid, which gives a red colour, which in a great measure disappears on the addition of protochloride of tin. If the strychnia be pure, it does not undergo any change on the addition of sulphuric acid, but on the addition of a mixture of bichromate of potash, with several other substances it produces a beautiful purple, which changes to varying shades until it gets to be a dirty red.

There are several other tests. In this case the stomach was not, in my opinion, in an unfavourable condition for examination. The circumstances attending its position in the jar and its removal to London would give a little more trouble, but would not otherwise affect the result. If the deceased had died from strychnia poison it ought to have been found in the liver, spleen, and kidneys. I have seen this poison found in similar portions of animals which had been killed by it. I have also seen it found in the blood; that was by Mr. Herapath, of Bristol.

Could the analyses be defeated or confused by the existence in the stomach of any other substance which would produce the same colours? — No. Supposing that pyroxantine and silicine were in the parts examined, their existence would not defeat the analysis.[5] Pyroxantine is very unlikely to be found in the stomach. It is one of the rarest and most difficult to be obtained. The distinction between pyroxantine and strychnia is quite evident. Pyroxantine changes to a deep purple on the addition of sulphuric acid alone, and the bichromate of potash spoils the colour. In strychnia no change is produced by sulphuric acid. It requires the addition of bichromate to produce the colour.

Supposing the death to have been caused by a dose of strychnia, not more than sufficient to destroy the animal, would it be so diffused by the process of absorption that you would not be able by these tests to detect it in any portion of the system? — No; I believe it would not.

Had that question occupied your attention before you were called upon to give evidence upon this trial? — It had.

What is your reason for stating that strychnine, when it has done its work, continues as strychnine in the system? — Those who say that some change takes place argue that as food undergoes a change when taken into the body, so does the poison; it becomes decomposed. But the change in food takes place during digestion, consequently its traces are not found in the blood. Substances like strychnine are absorbed without digestion, and may be obtained unchanged from the blood. They may be administered in various ways.

In your judgment will any amount of putrefaction prevent the discovery of strychnine? — To say that it is indestructible would be absurd, but within ordinary limits, no. I have found it at the end of forty days.

---

[5] Pyroxantine is a yellow, crystalline substance obtained from creosote, which was used to treat coughing. Silicine (or salicine) is a bitter compound derived from willow bark. It is related to aspirin and was used to relieve pain. The question arose during the testimony of Alfred Swaine Taylor, omitted by the *Times* reporter, about substances used in medicine that could be mistaken for strychnine by the Marsh test. Here is the relevant question and answer according to the Old Bailey transcript:

Q. Are there, in your opinion, other vegetable matters to which, if these colouring tests were applied, similar results as to colour might be obtained?

A. There are a variety of substances — a mixture of sugar and bile will produce the purple and red tint, and a substance called pyroxanthine — that substance is a product of the distillation of wood — it produces precisely similar colours to those caused by strychnia, so that I have known persons deceived — in my laboratory, in performing the experiments, they have said, 'You have got strychnia there,' when it has been a mixture of pyroxanthine with a small quantity of salicine added to it."

What is the probable relative rapidity of action of strychnine in an empty and a full stomach? — The emptier the stomach the quicker the action.

Cross-examined by the *Attorney-General*. — I am a lecturer on surgery. Mr. Morley, who was called for the prosecution, is a lecturer on chymistry. Part (perhaps half) of the experiments on the sixty animals were made by me and Mr. Morley jointly. There was nothing to distinguish the experiments which I made alone from those which I made jointly with him. I state the apparent results of the whole. My experiments were spread over a period of thirty years. Many of them have been made since the Leeds case. I can't say how many.

Now, don't put yourself in a state of antagonism to me, but tell me how many of your experiments were made in reference to this particular case? — I cannot answer that question. The great bulk certainly were not. I was first concerned in this about the time of the death of the person at Leeds.[6] I was applied to. I was in correspondence with the attorney for the defence. The details of the Leeds case was forwarded to him by me, and I called his attention to them.

The general dose in these experiments was from half a grain to two grains. Half a grain is sufficient to destroy life in the larger animals. I have seen both a dog and cat die from that dose, but not always. Some animals as a species are more susceptible than others. The symptoms in the experiments I have mentioned did not appear after so long a period as an hour. We have had to repeat the dose of poison in some instances when half a grain has been given. That happened in the case of a cat. Symptoms of spasm were produced, but the animal did not die. She had not, however, swallowed the doses. I think I have known animals of the cat species killed with half a grain.

Have you any doubt about it? — Yes.

Half a grain, then, is the *minimum* dose which will kill a cat? — I think it would be the minimum dose in the case of an old strong cat. If administered in a fluid state I think a smaller dose would suffice.

Hurried breathing is one of the first symptoms, afterwards there are twitching and tremblings of the muscles, then convulsions.

Is there any diversity, as in the intervals and the order of symptoms, in animals of the same species? — They certainly don't occur after the same intervals of time, but I should say they generally occur in the order I have described. There is some difference in the periods at which the convulsions take place. Some animals will die after less convulsion than others, but an animal generally dies after four or five. In one or two instances an animal has died after one convulsion. In those instances a dose has been given equal in amount

---

[6] A reference to the Harriet Dove poisoning case that surfaced in Elizabeth Mills' testimony.

to another dose which has not produced the same effect. The order in which the muscles are convulsed varies to some extent. The muscles of the limbs are generally affected first. The convulsions generally occur simultaneously.

Do you know any case of strychnine in which the rigidity after death was greater than the usual *rigor mortis*? — I think not. I don't think there is any peculiar rigidity produced by strychnine.

Have you never found undue rigidity in a human subject after death from strychnine? — Considerably less.

In the anonymous case to which we have referred [e.g., the Dove case] were not the hands curved and the feet arched by muscular contraction? — Not more than is unusual in cases of death from ordinary causes. The limbs were rigid, but not more than usual.

In the face of the medical profession, I ask you whether you signed a report stating that "the hands were curved and the feet decidedly arched by muscular contraction," and whether you meant by those words that there was no more than the ordinary rigidity of death? — Certainly; I stated so at the time.

Where? In the report? — No; in conversation. Allow me to explain that a distinction was drawn between the muscles of the different parts of the body. I heard Mr. Morley's evidence with regard to experiments on animals, and his statement that "after death there was an interval of flaccidity, after which rigidity commenced more than if it had been occasioned by the usual *rigor mortis*."

You don't agree with that statement? — I do not. I generally found the right side of the heart full.

Does the fact of the heart in Cook's case having been found empty lead you to the conclusion that death was not caused by strychnine? — Among other things it does. I heard the evidence of Dr. Watson as to the case of Agnes Sennet, in which the heart was found distended and empty; also, that of Mr. Taylor as to the *post-mortem* examination of Mrs. [Sarjantson] Smyth. No doubt he stated that the heart in that case also was empty.

And do those facts exercise no influence on your judgment? — They would not unless I knew how the *post-mortem* examination had been made. If it was commenced at the head, the blood being fluid, the large drains would be opened, and the blood, from natural causes, would drain away.

Do you know how the *post-mortem* examination was made in this case? — No. Excuse me, I do. The chest and the abdomen, not the head, were first opened.

The heart, then, was not emptied in the first instance? — No.

Then what occasioned the contraction of the heart? — When the heart is emptied it is usually contracted.

But how do you account for its contraction and emptiness? — I cannot account for it.

Lord CAMPBELL. — Would the heart contract if there was blood in it? — No.

Lord CAMPBELL. — When you find the heart contracted you know, then, that it was contracted at the moment of death? — It is necessary to draw a distinction between the two cavities. It is very common to find the left ventricle contracted and hard, while the right is uncontracted.

Lord CAMPBELL. — That is death by asphyxia? — Precisely.

By the *Attorney-General*. — In Cook's case the lungs were described as not congested. Entosthema[7] is of two kinds; one of them consists of dilation of the cells, the other of a rupture of the cells. When animals die from strychnine entosthema occurs. I do not know the character of the entosthema in Cook's case. It did not occur to me to have the question put to the witnesses who described the *post-mortem* examination.

To what constitutional symptoms about Cook do you ascribe the convulsions from which he died? — Not to any.

Was not the fact of his having syphilis an important ingredient in your judgment upon his case? — It was. I judge that he died from convulsions, by the combination of symptoms.

What evidence have you to suppose that he was liable to excitement and depression of spirits? — The fact that after winning the race he could not speak for three minutes.

Anything else? — Mr. Jones stated that he was subject to mental depression. Excitement will produce a state of brain which will be followed, at some distance, by convulsions. I think Dr. Bamford made a mistake when he said the brain was perfectly healthy.

Do you mean to set up that opinion against that of Dr. Devonshire and Dr. Hurland, who were present at the *post-mortem*? — My opinion is founded in part on the evidence taken at the inquest, in part on the depositions. With the brain and the system in the condition in which Cook's were I believe it is quite possible for convulsions to come on and destroy a person. I do not believe that he died from apoplexy. He was under the influence of morphia. I don't ascribe his death to morphia, except that it might assist in producing a convulsive attack. I should think morphia was not a very good treatment, considering the state of excitement he was in.

Do you mean to say, on your oath, that you think he was in a state of excitement at Rugeley? — I wish to give my evidence honestly. Morphia, when given in an injured state of the brain, often disagrees with the patient.

---

[7] The anonymous *Times* transcriber misheard the word "emphysema," a lung disease.

But what evidence have you as to the injured state of the brain? — Sickness often indicates it. I can't say whether the attack of Sunday night was an attack of convulsions. I think that the Sunday attack was one of a similar character, but not so intense, as the attack of Tuesday, in which he died. I don't think he had convulsions on the Sunday, but he was in that condition which often precedes convulsions. I think he was mistaken when he stated that he was awoke by a noise. I believe he was delirious. That is one of the symptoms on which I found my opinion. Any intestinal irritation will produce convulsions in a tetanic form. I have known instances in children. I have not seen an instance in an animal. Medical writers state that such cases do occur. I know no name for convulsions of that kind.

Have you ever known a case of convulsions of that kind, terminating in death, in which the patient remained conscious to the last? — I have not. Where epilepsy terminates in death consciousness is gone. I have known four cases of traumatic, and five or six of idiopathic tetanus.

You heard Mr. Jones make his statement of the symptoms of Cook after the commencement of the paroxysms: — "After he swallowed the pills, he uttered loud screams, threw himself back in the bed, and was dreadfully convulsed. He said, 'Raise me up! I shall be suffocated.' The convulsions affected every muscle of the body, and were accompanied by stiffening of the limbs. I endeavoured to raise Cook with the assistance of Palmer, but found it quite impossible, owing to the rigidity of the limbs. When Cook found we could not raise him up he asked me to turn him over. He was then quite sensible. I turned him on to his side. I listened to the action of his heart. I found that it gradually weakened, and asked Palmer to fetch some spirits of ammonia, to be used as a stimulant. When he returned the pulsations of the heart were gradually ceasing, and life was almost extinct. Cook died very quietly a very short time afterwards. When he threw himself back in bed he clinched his hands, and they remained clinched after death. When I was rubbing his neck his head and neck were unnaturally bent back by the spasmodic action of the muscles. After death his body was so twisted or bowed that if I had placed it upon the back it would have rested upon the head and the feet?" Now, I ask you to distinguish in any one particular between those symptoms and the symptoms of tetanic convulsions? — It is not tetanus at all; not idiopathic tetanus.

I quite agree with you that it is not idiopathic tetanus, but point out any distinction that you can see between these symptoms and those of real tetanus. — I do not know that there is any distinction, except that in a case of tetanus I never saw rigidity continue till death and afterwards.

Can you tell me of any case of death from convulsions in which the patient was conscious to the last? — I do not know of any; convulsions occurring after poison has been taken are properly called tetanic.

We were told by Sir B. Brodie that while the paroxysms of tetanic convulsion last there is no difference between those which arise from strychnine and those which arise from tetanus properly so called, but the difference was in the course the symptoms took. Now, what do you say is the difference between tetanus arising from strychnine and ordinary tetanus? — The hands are less violently contracted; the effect of the spasm is less in ordinary tetanus. The convulsion, too, never entirely passes away. I have stated that tetanus is a disease of days, strychnine of hours and minutes; that convulsive twitchings are in strychnine the first symptoms, the last in tetanus; that in tetanus the hands, feet, and legs are usually the last affected, while in strychnine they are the first. I gave that opinion after the symptoms in the case of the lady at Leeds, which were described by the witness [Jane] Witham, and I still adhere to it. I never said that Cook's case was one of idiopathic tetanus. I do not think it was a case of tetanus in any sense of the word. It differed from the course of tetanus from strychnine in the particulars I have already mentioned.

Repeat them. — There was the sudden accession of the convulsions.

Sudden — after what? — After the rousing by Jones. There was also the power of talking.

Don't you know that Mrs. [Sarjantson] Smyth talked and retained her consciousness to the end; that her last words were "turn me over?" — She did say something of that kind. No doubt those were the words she used.

I believe that in poison tetanus the symptoms are first observed in the legs and feet. In the animals upon which I have experimented twitchings in the ears and difficulty of breathing have been the premonitory symptoms.

When Cook felt a stiffness and a difficulty of breathing, and said that he should be suffocated on the first night, what were those but premonitory symptoms? — Well, he asked to be rubbed; but, as far as my experience goes with animals —

The *Attorney-General* — They can't ask to have their ears rubbed, of course. (A laugh.)

Mr. *Serjeant Shee* said the witness was about to explain the effect of being rubbed upon the animals.

Cross-examination continued. — In no single instance could the animals bear to be touched.

Did not Mrs. [Sarjantson] Smyth ask to have her legs and arms rubbed? — In the Leeds [Dove] case the lady asked to be rubbed before the convulsions came on, but afterwards she could not bear it, and begged that she might not be touched.

Can you point out any one point, after the premonitory symptom, in which the symptoms in this case differ from those of strychnine tetanus? — There is the power of swallowing, which is taken away by the inability to move the jaw.

But you have not stated that lockjaw is the last symptom that occurs in strychnine tetanus? — I have. I don't deny that it may be. I am speaking of the general rule. In the Leeds case it came on very early, more than two hours before death, the paroxysms having continued about two hours and a half.

In that case we believed that the dose was four times repeated. Poison might probably be extracted by chemical process from the tissues, but I never tried it except in one case of an animal. I am not sure whether poison was in that case given through the mouth. We killed four animals in reference to the Leeds case, and in every instance we found strychnine in the contents of the stomach. In one case we administered it in two processes, and one failed and the other succeeded.

Re-examined. — In making reports upon cases such as that which has been referred to we state ordinary appearances; we state the facts without anything more.

Mr. WILLIAM HERAPATH,
examined by Mr. *Grove*.

I am a professor of chymistry and toxicology at the Bristol Medical School. I have studied chymistry for more than 40 years, toxicology for 30. I have experimented on the poison of strychnine. I have seen no case of a human subject during life, but I have examined a human body after death. In one case I examined the contents of the stomach and I found strychnine about three days after death. There are several tests — sulphuric acid and bichromate of potash, sulphuric acid and puce-coloured oxide of lead, sulphuric acid, and peroxide of lead, sulphuric acid and peroxide of manganese, &c. The lower oxides of lead would not succeed. These are all colour tests, and produce a purple colour, passing to red. Another class of tests gives a different colour with impure, but not with pure, strychnia. The process used previous to these tests is for the purpose of producing strychnia. I obtained evidence of strychnia by the colour tests in the case I have mentioned.

MR. WILLIAM HERAPATH, PROFESSOR OF TOXICOLOGY

I have experimented upon animals with regard to strychnine in eight or nine cases. I have analysed the bodies in two cases in which I destroyed the animals myself. Both of them were cats. I gave the first one grain of strychnia in a solid form. The animal took the poison at night, and I found it dead in the morning. It was dreadfully contorted and rigid, the limbs extended, the head turned round — not to the back, but to the side — the eyes protruding and staring, the iris expanded so as to be almost invisible. I found strychnine in the urine, which had been ejected; and also in the stomach, by the tests I have mentioned.

I administered the same quantity of strychnine in a solid form to another cat. It remained very quiet for fifteen or sixteen minutes, but seemed a little restless in the eyes and in breathing. In thirty-five minutes it had a terrible spasm, the extremities and the head being drawn together, and the feet extended. I watched it for three hours.

The first spasm lasted a minute or two. The saliva dropped from its mouth, and it forcibly ejected its urine. It had a second spasm a few minutes afterwards. It soon recovered and remained still, with the exception of a trembling all over. It continued in that state for three hours. During nearly two hours and a-half it was in a very peculiar state; it appeared to be electrified all through, blowing upon it or touching the basket in which it was placed produced a kind of electric jump like a galvanic shock.

I left it in three hours, thinking it would recover, but in the morning I found it dead, in the same indurated and contorted condition as the former animal. I examined the body thirty-six hours after death, and found strychnia in the urine, in the stomach and upper intestine, in the liver, and in the blood of the heart.

I have discovered strychnia in all other cases by the same tests, but I took extraordinary means to get rid of organic matter. In all cases in which strychnia has been given I have been able to find it, and not only strychnia, but also the *nux vomica* from which it is taken. I have found *nux vomica* in a fox and in other animals.

The detection of *nux vomica* is more complicated than that of strychnia. In one case the animal had been buried two months. I have experimented with strychnia not in a body, but mixed purposely with organic putrefying matter. I have found it in all cases, whatever was the state of decomposition of the matter.

Are you of the opinion that where strychnia has been taken in a sufficient dose to poison it can and ought to be discovered? — Yes; unless the body has been completely decomposed; that is, unless decomposition has reduced it to a dry powder. I am of the opinion, from the accounts given by Dr. Taylor and the other witnesses, that if it had existed in the body of Cook it ought to have been discovered. I am aware of no cause for error in the analyses, if the organic matter had been properly got rid of.

The experiments I have mentioned were made in Bristol. I have made experiments in London, and found strychnia in the stomach, liver, and blood of an animal.

Cross-examined by the *Attorney-General*. I don't profess to be a physiologist. I have principally experimented on the stomach until lately. I tried my chymical process on the 8th of this month with a view to the present case. The experiment here was on a dog. I experimented on the tissues of a cat at Bristol and of a dog in London. I found strychnia in the blood, the heart, and the urine of the cat, besides the stomach. One grain was given to the dog. It was a large dog. I have seen a cat killed with a quarter of a grain. I have said that Dr. Taylor ought to have found strychnia.

Have you not said that you had no doubt strychnia had been taken, but that Dr. Taylor had not gone the right way to find it? — I may have said so. I had a strong opinion from reading various newspaper reports — among others the *Illustrated Times* — that strychnia had been given. I have expressed that opinion, no doubt, freely. People have talked a great deal to me about the matter, and I can't recollect every word I have said, but that was my general opinion.[8]

Re-examined by *Mr. Grove*. — What is the smallest quantity of strychnia that your process is capable of detecting? — I am perfectly sure I could detect the 50,000th part of a grain if it was unmixed with organic matter. If I put ten grains in a gallon or 70,000 grains of water, I could discover its presence in the 10th part of a grain of that water. It is more difficult to detect when mixed with organic matter.

If a person had taken a grain a very small quantity would be found in the heart, but no doubt it could be found. I made four experiments with a large dog to which I had given the eighth part of a grain. I have discovered it by the change of colour in the 32nd part of the liver of a dog.

Mr. Grove said he believed his Lordship was of the opinion that the experiments could not be shown.

Lord CAMPBELL. — We have intimated that that is our clear opinion.

Mr. JULIAN EDWARD DISBROWE ROGERS,
examined by *Mr. Gray*.

I am professor of chymistry at St. George's School of Medicine, in London. I have made experiments upon one animal, a dog poisoned by strychnia. The experiments commenced at the close of last December, and ended about ten days since. I gave it two grains of pure strychnia in meat. Three days after death I removed the stomach and contents, and some of the blood. The blood became putrid in about ten days, and I then analysed with a view to find strychnine. I separated the strychnine by colour tests. I cannot say how much it was by weight. In a month or five weeks, when the matter had putrefied, I analysed the stomach and its contents. I treated it with acidulated distilled water, and succeeded in discovering strychnia in large quantities about ten days ago.

I never analysed a human subject with a view to find strychnia,

---

[8] Herapath's testimony haunted Taylor for the rest of his life. Decades later, Palmer biographer George Fletcher heard Taylor lecture on strychnine at Guy's Hospital in London. Most of the session focused on the Palmer case, he wrote, and Taylor's "animosity against Professor Herapath was very evident and *would* come out, off and on, all through the lecture."

but I have many times done so to find other poisons. Strychnia must unquestionably have been discovered in this case if it had been present and the proper tests had been used.

Cross-examined by the *Attorney-General*. I have only made one experiment. If the contents of the stomach were lost it would make a difference, but not if they were only shaken up. The operation would then be more difficult. I am a medical man. I did not analyse the tissues of the body of the dog. If I had tried the tissues of Cook's body it might have been found if it was there, notwithstanding the time that had elapsed since he died. I don't say that the time would prevent its discovery if there.

Re-examined by *Mr. Gray*. — If strychnia were in the stomach a portion would probably be smeared over the mucous membrane, and then I should expect to find it on the surface.

Dr. Letheby, Medical Officer of Health to the City of London

Dr. HENRY LETHEBY,
examined by Mr. *Kenealy*.

I am a bachelor of medicine, professor of chymistry and toxicology in the London Hospital of Medicine, and Medical Officer of Health to the City of London. I have been engaged for a considerable time in the study of poisons and their action on the living animal economy. I have also been frequently engaged on behalf of the Crown in prosecutions in cases of this nature during the last fourteen years. I have been present during the examination of the medical witnesses, and have attended to the evidence as to the symptoms which have been described as attending the death of Cook. I have witnessed many cases of animals poisoned by strychnine, and many cases of poisoning by *nux vomica* in the human body, one of which was fatal.

The symptoms described in this case do not accord with the symptoms I have witnessed in the case of those animals. They differ in this respect:— In the first place I never witnessed the long interval between the administration of the poison and the commencement of the symptoms which is said to have elapsed in this case. The longest interval I have known has been three-quarters of an hour, and then the poison was administered under most disadvantageous circumstances. It was given on a very full stomach and in a form uneasy of solution. I have seen the symptoms begin in five minutes. The average time in which they begin is a quarter of an hour.

In all cases I have seen the system has been in that irritable state that the very lightest excitement, such as an effort to move, a touch, a noise, a breath of air, would send the patient off in convulsions. It is not at all probable that a person, after taking strychnia, could pull a bell violently. Any movement would excite the nervous system, and bring on spasms. It is not likely that a person in that state could bear to have his neck rubbed. When a case of strychnia does not end fatally, the first paroxysm is succeeded by others, gradually shaded off, the paroxysms becoming less violent every time, and I agree with Dr. Christison that they would subside in twelve or sixteen hours.

I have no hesitation in saying that strychnine is of all poisons, either mineral or vegetable, the most easy of detection. I have detected it in the stomach of animals in numerous instances, also in the blood and in the tissues. The longest period after death in which I have detected it is about a month. The animal was then in a state of decomposition.

I have detected very minute portions of strychnia. When it is pure the 20,000th part of a grain can be detected. I can detect the tenth part of a grain most easily in a pint of any liquid, whether pure or putrid. I gave one animal half a grain, and I have the strychnia here now within a very small trifle. I never failed to detect strychnine where it had been administered. I have made *post-mortem* examinations on various animals killed by it. I have always found the right side of the heart full. The reason is that the death takes place from the fixing of the muscles of the chest by spasms, so that the blood is unable to pass through the lungs, and the heart cannot relieve itself from the blood flowing to it, and therefore becomes gorged. The lungs are congested and filled with blood.

I have administered strychnia in a liquid and a solid form; I agree with Dr. Taylor that it may kill in six or eleven minutes when taken in a solid state in the form of a pill or bolus. I also agree with him that the first symptom is that the animal falls on its side, the jaws are spasmodically closed, and the slightest touch produces another paroxysm. But I do not agree with him that the colour tests are fallacious. I do not agree that it is changed when it is absorbed into the blood, but I agree with its absorption, I think it is not changed when the body is decomposed.

The shaking about of the contents of the stomach with the intestines in a jar would not prevent the discovery of strychnia if it had been administered. Even if the contents of the stomach were lost the mucous membrane would, in the ordinary course of things, exhibit traces of strychnia.

I have studied the poison of antimony. If a quantity had been introduced into brandy-and-water, and swallowed at a gulp, the effect would not be to burn the throat. Antimony does not possess any such quality as that of immediate burning. I have turned my attention to the subject of poison for seventeen or eighteen years.

Cross-examined by the *Attorney-General*. I am not a member of the College of Physicians or of Surgeons. I do not now practise. I have been in general practice for two or three years. I gave evidence in the last case of this sort, tried in this court in 1851. I gave evidence of the presence of arsenic. The woman was convicted. I stated that it had been administered within four hours of death. I was the cause of her being respited, and the sentence was not carried into effect, in consequence of a letter I wrote to the Home Office. Other scientific gentlemen interfered, and challenged the soundness of my conclusions before I wrote that letter. I have not since been employed by the Crown.[9]

---

[9] To protect his reputation, Letheby rearranged the facts surrounding the trial — in 1850, not '51 — of Ann Merritt, who was convicted of poisoning her husband, James, with arsenic. Somehow, the arsenic she had bought, packaged in two bags marked "POISON" by the chemist, had been transferred to an unmarked bag and placed near her husband's stomach

By Mr. Justice CRESSWELL. — I was present at the trial. I perfectly remember it.

Cross-examination continued. — I detected the poison. I said in my letter that I could not speak as to possibilities, but merely as to probabilities. I have experimented on animals for a great number of years. On five recently. I have never given more than a grain, and it has always been in a solid form — in pills or bread. In the case where poison was administered under disadvantageous circumstances it was kneaded up into a hard mass of bread.

Mr. Baron *Alderson*. — Did the animal bolt it or bite it?

Witness. — I opened the mouth and put it into the throat. About half an hour elapsed before the symptoms appeared in one case in which half a grain had been given. In another case death took place within thirteen minutes. I have noticed twitching of the ears, difficulty of breathing, and other premonitory symptoms. There are little variations in the order in which the symptoms occur. I have known frequent instances in which an animal has died in the first paroxysm.

I heard the evidence of Mrs. [Sarjantson] Smyth's death, and I was surprised at her having got out of bed when the servant answered the bell. It is not consistent with the cases I have seen. That fact does not shake my opinion. I have no doubt that Mrs. [Sarjantson] Smyth died from strychnine. Cook's sitting up in bed and asking Jones to ring the bell is inconsistent with what I have observed in strychnine cases.

If a man's breath is hurried is it not natural for him to sit up? — It is. I have seen cases of recovery of taking strychnine. There is a great uniformity in its effects — that is, in their main features, but there is a small variation as to the time in which they are produced.

What do you attribute Cook's death to? — It is irreconcileable with everything with which I am acquainted.

---

powder. Letheby testified that he had found 8.5 grains of white arsenic in the thick gruel found in James's stomach. More damning, some had been administered less than three hours before he died, at a time when he was too ill to have taken the poison himself. As the only person with him at the time was his wife, she was convicted and condemned.

But several doctors challenged Letheby's testimony. They pointed out that James's digestion could have been slow and that the thick substance in the stomach could have been remnants of food. It also came out that in another trial, Letheby claimed that arsenic burned with a blue flame. Elemental arsenic does, but not the white arsenic commonly available. Letheby stood his ground against his critics, even when medical men hired by the authorities disputed his conclusions. Eventually he gave in. Since his letter to the Home Office saying he might be wrong led to Merritt's reprieve from the gallows, he should receive some credit for saving her life, just not as much as he implied he deserved. As for Mrs. Merritt, her sentence was commuted to life imprisonment, and she was transported to Australia.

Is it reconcileable with any known disease you have ever seen or heard of? — No.

Re-examined by Mr. *Serjeant Shee*. We are learning new facts every day, and I do not at present conceive it to be impossible that some peculiarity of the spinal cord, unrecognisable at the examination after death, may have produced symptoms like those which have been described. I, of course, include strychnia in my answer; but it is irreconcileable with everything I have seen or heard of. It is as irreconcileable with strychnia as with everything else; it is irreconcileable with every disease that I am acquainted with, natural or artificial.

Touching an animal during the premonitory symptoms will bring on a paroxysm. Vomiting is inconsistent with strychnia. The Romsey case was an exceptional one, from the quantity of the dose.[10] The ringing of the bell would have produced a paroxysm. I am still of the opinion that the evidence I gave on the trial in 1851 is correct. I am not aware that there is any ground for an imputation upon me in respect of that evidence. I have no reason to think Government was dissatisfied with me. I have not been since employed in Crown prosecutions. After that case Dr. Pereira came to my laboratory and asked me, as an act of mercy, to write a letter to him to show to the Home Office, admitting the possibility of the poison which I found in the stomach having been administered longer than four hours before death. I wrote the letter, drawing a distinction between what was possible and probable, and the woman was transported for life.

Mr. ROBERT EDWARD GAY,
examined by Mr. *Serjeant Shee*.

I am a member of the Royal College of Surgeons. I attended a person named Forster for tetanus in October, 1855. He had sore throat, muscular pains in the neck, and in the upper portion of the cervical vertebras. He was feverish, and had symptoms ordinarily attending catarrh.[11] I put him under the usual treatment for catarrh, and used embrocations[12] externally to the muscles of the neck and throat, and also gargles.

About the fourth day of my attendance the muscular pains extended to the face, difficulty of swallowing came on, the pains in the cervical

---

[10] This is the accidental strychnine death of Mrs. Sarjantson Smyth. See the testimony, above, of Caroline Hickson.
[11] Inflammation of the mucus membrane in which the nose and air passages become filled with mucus.
[12] Liniments rubbed on the skin to relieve muscle pain.

vertebrae increased, also those of the muscles of the face, particularly the lower jaw. In the evening of the same day the jaw became completely locked, the pains came on in the muscles of the bowels, the legs, and the arms. He became very much convulsed throughout the entire muscular system, had frequently involuntary contractions of the arms, and hands, and legs, his difficulty of swallowing increased, and not a particle of food, solid or liquid, could be introduced into the mouth. Attempting to swallow the smallest portions brought on violent convulsions; so strong were they throughout the system that I could compare him to nothing but a piece of warped board. The head was thrown back, the abdomen thrust forward, and the legs frequently drawn up and contracted; the attempt to feed him with a spoon, the opening of a window, or placing the fingers on the pulse, brought on violent convulsions. While the patient was suffering in this manner he continually complained of great hunger, and repeatedly exclaimed that he was hungry, and could not eat.

He was kept alive to the 14th day entirely by injections of a milky and farinaceous[13] character. He screamed repeatedly, and the noises that he made were more like those of a wild man than anything else. On the 12th day he became insensible, and continued in that state until he died, which was in the 14th day from the commencement of the attack of lockjaw.

The man was an omnibus driver,[14] and when I first attended him he had been suffering from sore throat for several days. There was no hurt or injury of any kind about his person that would account for the symptoms I have mentioned. His body was not opened after death, because it was considered unnecessary.

I consider his disease was inflammatory sore throat from cold and exposure to the weather, and that the disease assumed a tetanic form on account of the patient being a very nervous, excited, and anxious person. His condition in life was that of an omnibus conductor. He was a hard-working man, and had a large family dependent upon him, and this no doubt, acting upon his peculiar temperament, tended to produce the tetanic symptoms.

The witness, in conclusion, said he had not heard all the evidence in this case, but he thought it right to communicate to the prisoner's solicitor the particulars of the case to which he had now referred, as he

---

[13] Rich in starch. The patient was being fed by injections of food into his stomach.

[14] A driver of a large horse-drawn wagon used to haul passengers through cities. The idea for mass transit originated in France, where the first omnibuses hit the streets in 1828. The name was derived from the Latin word for "for all." As motorized transport began to replace horse-drawn vehicles in the 1900s, the word was shortened, first to 'bus (with the apostrophe, as it appears in Dorothy L. Sayers' "Whose Body?") and then just bus.

considered it had an important bearing upon the charge against the prisoner.

Cross-examined by the *Attorney-General*. The case I have mentioned was undoubtedly one of idiopathic tetanus. It is the only one of the kind I ever had to deal with. It arose from exposure to cold, acting upon a nervous and irritable temperament. I have a good many patients who are nervous and irritable, but I never met with such another case. The disease was altogether progressive from the first onset, and, although there was a remission of the symptoms, they invariably recurred. The locking of the jaw was one of the very first symptoms that made their appearance.

CONDEMNED CELL IN NEWGATE

Mr. *Serjeant Shee* then addressed the Court, and said that the next witness he proposed to call would occupy some time in examination, and, as it was now nearly six o'clock, he suggested that it would be better to adjourn the examination to the next day.

The Lord CHIEF-JUSTICE said he had no objection to the course proposed by the learned Serjeant, and he then inquired of him how much time the case for the defence was likely to occupy.

Serjeant Shee said he hoped to conclude the defence to-morrow; and he should endeavour to do so if he possibly could.

The Lord CHIEF-JUSTICE said there was no desire to hurry him. It was most essential in so important an inquiry that the most ample opportunity should be allowed for a full and satisfactory investigation.

The Court then adjourned to this morning at ten o'clock.

NINTH DAY.—May 23, 1856.

There was a great crowd as usual in court this morning, long before the commencement of the proceedings.

The Duke of Wellington,[1] the Earl of Albemarle, Lord Donoughmore, Lord Dufferin, Lord Feversham, Sir J. Pakington, Mr. Harcourt Vernon, General Peel, Mr. Tollemache, Mr. S. Warren, and other members of Parliament were present.

The learned Judges, Lord Campbell, Mr. Baron Alderson, and Mr. Justice Cresswell, took their seats upon the bench at about 10 o'clock, and, the prisoner having been placed at the bar, the examination of witnesses for the defence was resumed. No alteration has taken place in the prisoner's demeanour.

Counsel for the Crown: the Attorney-General, Mr. E. James, Q.C., Mr. Welsby, Mr. Bodkin, and Mr. Huddleston; for the prisoner: Mr. Serjeant Shee, Mr. Grove, Q.C., Mr. Gray, and Mr. Kenealy.

Mr. JOHN BROWN ROSS,
examined by Mr. *Grove*.

I am house-surgeon to the London Hospital. I recollect a case of tetanus being brought into the hospital on the 22nd of March last. A man, aged 37, was brought in about half-past seven in the evening. He had had one paroxysm in the receiving-room; his pulse was rapid and feeble, his jaws were closed and fixed, there was an expression of anxiety about the countenance, the features were sunken, he was unable to swallow, and the muscles of the abdomen and the back were somewhat tense.

After he had been in the ward about ten minutes he had another paroxysm, and his body became arched; it lasted about a minute. He was afterwards quieter for a few minutes, and then had another attack and died. The whole lasted about half an hour.

There was an inquest held on the body. It was examined, and no poison was found. I think tetanus was the cause of death. There were three wounds on the body, two at the back of the right elbow, each about the size of a shilling, and one on the left elbow, about the size of a sixpence. The man had had those wounds for twelve or sixteen years. They were old chronic indurated ulcers, circular in outline, the edges thickened and rounded, and covered with a white coating, without any granulation. I am unable to say what was the origin of those ulcers, but I have seen other wounds like them. I have seen old

---

[1] This is second duke, Arthur Wellsley (1807–1884), the son of the general who commanded the Anglo-Prussian forces at Waterloo.

chronic syphilitic wounds like them in other places. Those wounds were the only things which would account for tetanus.

Cross-examined by the *Attorney-General.* I ascertained that poultices[2] had been applied to the wounds a day or two before, but I am not certain as to the exact time. The man's wife had objected to their application. They were made of linseed meal. The man's jaws were fixed so as to render him perfectly incapable of swallowing anything. He said he had first been taken with symptoms of lockjaw at 11 o'clock — as he told me, at dinner, but, as he told my colleague, at breakfast. He was able to speak, but could not open the jaw. That is a symptom of tetanus. There were symptoms of rigidity about the abdominal and lumbar muscles. He did not say how long he had felt that rigidity. I gathered that some other medical man, a surgeon, had seen him in the afternoon before he came to the hospital, but I am not certain as to that; he was a labouring man.

Have you any doubt that the disease had been coming on since the morning? — No doubt at all. The sores were ugly sores of a chronic character — ulcers. There was an integument[3] which connected the two on the right arm, so that they would be likely to run into one another. The wounds continued under the skin, and there were no signs of healing. They had the appearance of old neglected sores. They were at the seat of the ulnar nerve — a very sensitive nerve — that which is commonly called the "funny-bone." I believe he had successive paroxysms all the afternoon before he came to the hospital.

I think his attack arose from tetanus. My opinion is founded upon the facts that he had had wounds, that he had died of spasms, that he had lockjaw, that the muscles of the abdomen and back were rigid, and that he complained of pain in the stomach. I did not hear the account of the symptoms of Cook's death. An affection of the ulnar nerve was peculiarly liable to produce tetanus.

Re-examined by Mr. *Grove.* — Strychnine was suspected in this case. The nerves of the tongue are very delicate, as are also those of the throat and fauces. I have read descriptions of tetanus in the books. The case described by Mr. Gay was idiopathic, having been caused by a cold. An injury to any delicate nerve would decidedly be a cause of tetanus.

Mr. RYNERS MANTELL,
examined by Mr. *Gray.*

---

[2] A soft mass of material held against the body with a bandage to ease soreness and inflammation.

[3] A tough outer layer. From the Latin *integer* for "to cover."

I am a house-surgeon at the London Hospital. I saw the case mentioned by Mr. Ross, and his statement with respect to the symptoms is correct. In my judgment, the disease of which the patient died was tetanus, produced by the sores on the arms.

Dr. FRANCIS WRIGHTSON,
examined by Mr. *Kenealy*.

I was a pupil of Liebig at Giessen.[4] I am a teacher of chymistry in a school at Birmingham. I have studied the nature and acquired a knowledge of poisons, and I have been engaged by the Crown in the detection of poison in a prosecution. I have experimented upon strychnia. I have found no extraordinary difficulties in the detection of strychnia. It is certainly to be detected by the usual tests.

I have tested and discovered both pure and mixed with impure matter after decomposition has set in. I have detected it in a mixture of bile, bilious matter, and putrefying blood. Strychnia can be discovered in the tissues. I have discovered it in the viscera of a cat, in the blood of one dog, and in the urine of another dog, both of them having been poisoned by strychnia.

I am of the opinion that strychnia does not undergo decomposition in the act of poisoning or in entering into the circulation. If it underwent such a change, if it were decomposed, I should say it would not be possible to discover it in the tissues; it might possibly be changed into a substance, in which, however, it would still be detectable.

It can be discovered in extremely minute quantities indeed. When I detected it in the blood of a dog I had given the animal two grains. To the second dog I gave one grain, and I detected it in the urine. Half a grain was intended to be administered to the cat, but a considerable portion of it was lost.

Assuming that a man was poisoned by strychnine, and if his stomach were sent to me for analysation within five or six days after death, I have no doubt that I should find it, generally. If a man had been poisoned by strychnine I should certainly expect to detect it.

Cross-examined by the *Attorney-General*. — Supposing that the whole dose were absorbed into the system, where would you expect to find it? — In the blood.

Does it pass from the blood into the solids of the body? — It does; or I should rather say it is left in the solids of the body. In its progress

---

[4] Justus von Liebig (1803-1873), a German chemist and innovative teacher. His discovery that nitrogen was an essential plant nutrient helped create the fertilizer industry. He taught at the University of Giessen, where he established the world's first school of chemistry.

towards its final destination, the destruction of life, it passes from the blood, or is left by the blood in the solid tissues of the body. If it be present in the stomach, you find it in the stomach; if it be present in the blood, you find it in the blood; if it be left by the blood in the tissues, you find it in the tissues? — Precisely so.

Suppose the whole had been absorbed? — Then I would not undertake to find it.

Suppose the whole had been eliminated from the blood, and had passed into the urine, should you expect to find any in the blood? — Certainly not.

Suppose that the minimum dose which will destroy life had been taken, and absorbed into the circulation, then deposited in the tissues, and then a part of it eliminated by the action of the kidneys, where should you search for it? — In the blood, in the tissues, and in the ejections; and I would undertake to discover it in each of them.

Re-examined by Mr. *Serjeant Shee*. — Suppose you knew a man to have been killed by strychnia administered to him one and a half hours before he died, in your judgment would that strychnia certainly be detected in the stomach in the first instance? — Yes.

Suppose it to have been administered in the shape of pills and completely absorbed and got out of the stomach, would it still be found? — I can't tell. If it were found it would be in the liver and kidneys.

Could it be detected under those circumstances in the coats of the stomach? — Not knowing the dose administered and the power of absorption, I cannot say that it could certainly be detected, but probably it could.

When death has taken place after one paroxysm, and an hour and a half after ingestion of the poison, can you form an opinion as to whether the dose was considerable or inconsiderable? — I cannot.

Mr. Baron ALDERSON. — How do you suppose strychnine acts when taken into the stomach? — I cannot form an opinion.

Mr. Baron ALDERSON. — It goes, I suppose, from the stomach to the blood, and from the blood somewhere else; and, arriving at that somewhere else, it kills.

Lord CAMPBELL. — I cannot allow this witness to leave the box without expressing my high approbation[5] of the manner in which he has given his evidence.

Mr. *Serjeant Shee* requested to be allowed to ask the witness whether a strong dose was likely to pass through all the stages his Lordship had mentioned.

Mr. Baron ALDERSON. — That depends on where the killing takes place.

---

[5] Praise or approval.

Professor RICHARD PARTRIDGE, examined by Mr. *Grove*.

I have been many years in extensive practice as a surgeon, and I am a Professor of Anatomy in King's College. I have heard the evidence as to Cook's symptoms and *post-mortem* examination. I have heard the statements as to the granules that were found on his spine. They would be likely to cause inflammation, and no doubt that inflammation would have been discovered if the spinal cord or its membranes had been examined shortly after death. It would not be likely to be discovered if the spinal cord was not examined until nine weeks after death. I have not seen cases in which this inflammation has produced tetanic form of convulsions, but such cases are on record. It sometimes does, and sometimes does not produce convulsions and death.

Can you form any judgment as to the cause of death in Cook's case? — I cannot. No conclusion or inference can be drawn from the degree or kind of the contractions of the body after death.

Lord CAMPBELL. — Can you not say from the symptoms you heard whether death was produced by tetanus, without saying what was the cause of tetanus? — Hypothetically, I should infer that he died of that form of tetanus which convulses the muscles. Great varieties of rigidity arise after death from natural causes. The half-bent hands and fingers are not uncommon after natural death. The arching of the feet in this case seemed to me rather greater than usual.

Cross-examined by the *Attorney-General*. — Granules are sometimes, but not commonly, found about the spine of a healthy subject — not on the cord itself; they may exist consistently with health. No satisfactory cases of the inflammation I have described have come under my notice without producing convulsions. It is a very rare disease. I cannot state from the recorded cases the course of the symptoms of that disease. It varies in duration, sometimes lasting only for days, sometimes much longer. If the patient lives it is accompanied with paralysis. It produces no effect on the brain which is recognisable after death. It would not affect the brain prior to death. I do not know whether it is attended with loss of sensibility before death. The size of the granules which will produce it varies, this disease is not a matter of months, unless it terminates in palsy. I never heard of a case in which the patient died after a single convulsion. Between the intervals of the convulsions I don't believe a man could have twenty-four hours' repose. Pain and spasms would accompany the convulsions. I cannot form a judgment as to whether the general health would be affected in the intervals between them.

You have heard it stated that from the midnight of Monday till Tuesday Cook had complete repose. Now, I ask you, in the face of the medical profession, whether you think the symptoms which have been described proceeded from that disease? — I should think not.

Did you ever know the hands completely clinched after death except in case of tetanus? — No.

Have you ever known it even in idiopathic or traumatic tetanus? — I have never seen idiopathic tetanus. I have seen the hands completely clinched in traumatic tetanus. A great deal of force is often required to separate them.

Have you ever known the feet so distorted as to assume the form of a club foot? — No.

You heard Mr. Jones state that if he had turned the body upon the back it would have rested on the head and the heels. Have you any doubt that that is an indication of death from tetanus? — No; it is a form of tetanic spasm. I am only acquainted with tetanus resulting from strychnine by reading. Some of the symptoms in Cook's case are consistent, some are inconsistent with strychnine tetanus. The first inconsistent symptom is the intervals that occurred between the taking of the supposed poison and the attacks.

Are not symptoms of bending of the body, difficulty of respiration, convulsions in the throat, legs, and arms perfectly consistent with what you know of the symptoms of death from strychnine? — Perfectly consistent. I have known cases of traumatic tetanus. The symptoms in those cases had been occasionally remitted, never wholly terminated. I never knew traumatic tetanus run its course to death in less than three or four days. I never knew a complete case of the operation of strychnine upon a human subject.

Bearing in mind the distinction between traumatic and idiopathic tetanus, did you ever know of such a death as that of Cook according to the symptoms you have heard described? — No.

Re-examined by Mr. *Grove.* — Besides the symptom which I have mentioned as being inconsistent with the theory of death by strychnine there are others — namely, sickness, beating the bedclothes, want of sensitiveness to external impressions, and sudden cessation of the convulsions and apparent complete recovery. There was apparently an absence of the usual muscular agitation. Symptoms of convulsive character arising from an injury to the spine vary considerably in their degrees of violence, in their periods of intermission, and in the muscles which are attacked. Intermission of the disease occurs, but is not frequent, in traumatic tetanus.

I don't remember that death has ever taken place in fifteen hours; it may take place in forty-eight hours during convulsions. Granules about the spine are more unusual in young people than in old. I don't know of any case in which the spine can preserve its integrity, so as to be properly examined, for a period of nine weeks. I should not feel justified in inferring that there was no disease from not finding any at the end of that time. The period of decomposition varies from a few hours to a few days. It is not in the least probable that it could be delayed for nine weeks.

By the *Attorney-General.* — Supposing the stomach were acted on by other causes, I do not think sickness would be inconsistent with tetanus.

JOHN GAY, examined by Mr. *Gray*.

I am a Fellow of the Royal College of Surgeons, and I have been a surgeon to the Royal Free Hospital.[6] A case of traumatic tetanus in a boy came under my observation in that hospital in 1843. The patient was brought in during the time he was ill. He was brought on the 28th of July and died on the 2nd of August. He had met with an accident a week before. During the first three days he had paroxysms of unusual severity. His mother complained that he could not open his mouth, and he complained of stiff neck. During the night he started up and was convulsed.

On the following night he was again convulsed. At times the abdominal muscles, as well as those of the legs and back, were rigid; the muscles of the face were also in a state of great contraction.

On the following (the third) day he was in the same state. At two o'clock there was much less rigidity of the muscles, especially those of the abdomen and back.

On the following morning the muscular rigidity had gone, he opened his mouth and was able to talk; he was thoroughly relieved. He had no return of spasms till half-past five o'clock the following day. He then asked the nurse to change his linen, and as she lifted him up in the bed to do so violent convulsions of the arms and face came on, and he died in a few minutes. About thirty hours elapsed between the preceding convulsion and the one which terminated his life. Before the paroxysm came on the rigidity had been completely relaxed. I had given the patient tartar emetic (containing antimony) in order to produce vomiting on the second day; it produced no effect. I gave a larger dose on the third day, which also produced no effect. I gave no more after the third day.

Cross-examined by the *Attorney-General*. — The accident which had happened to him was that a large stone had fallen upon the

---

[6] A teaching hospital in the Hampstead area of London. It was founded in 1828 by surgeon William Marsden to provide free care to the poor.

middle toe of the left foot, and completely smashed it. The wound had become very unhealthy. I amputated the toe. The mouth was almost closed up when I first saw him. The jaw remained closed until the 1st of August, but I could manage to get a small quantity of tartar emetic into the mouth. The convulsions were intermitted during the day, but the muscles of the body, chest, abdomen, back, and neck were all rigid, and continued so for the two days on which I administered tartar emetic. Rigidity of the muscles of the chest and stomach would no doubt go far to prevent vomiting.

The symptoms began to abate on the morning of the 1st of August (the fourth day), and gradually subsided until the rigidity entirely wore off. I then thought he was going to get well. The wound might have been rubbed against the bed when he was raised, but I don't think it probable. Some peculiar irritation of the nerves would give rise to the affection of the spinal cord. No doubt the death took place in consequence of something produced by the injury to the toe.

Re-examined by Mr. *Gray*. — There may be various causes for that irritation of the spinal cord which ends in tetanic convulsions. It would be very difficult merely from seeing symptoms of tetanus, and in the absence of all knowledge as to how it had been occasioned, to ascribe it to any particular cause.

Dr. WILLIAM MACDONALD, examined by Mr. *Kenealy*.

I am a licentiate of the Royal College of Surgeons of Edinburgh. I have been in practice for fourteen years, and have had considerable experience, practical and theoretical, of idiopathic and traumatic tetanus. I have seen two cases of idiopathic tetanus, and have made that disease the subject of medical research.

Tetanus will proceed from very slight causes. An alteration of the secretions of the body, exposure to cold or damp, or mental excitement would cause it. Sensual excitement would produce it. The presence of gritty granules in the spine or brain might produce tetanic convulsions. I have seen cases in which small gritty tubercles[7] in the brain were the only assignable cause of death, which had resulted from convulsions. I believe that in addition to the slight causes which I have named tetanic convulsions result from causes as yet undiscoverable by human science.

In many *post-mortem* examinations of the bodies of persons who had died from tetanus no trace of any disease could be discovered

---

[7] Small protuberances or lumps.

beyond congestion or vascularity[8] of some of the vessels surrounding the nerves. Strychnia, however, is very easily discoverable by a scientific man.

I remember the case of a woman, Catharine Watson, who is now present, and who was attacked with idiopathic tetanus on the 20th of October, 1855.

[The witness read a report of the circumstances attending this case, the subject of which was a young woman twenty-two years of age, who, after going about her ordinary occupation during the day, was attacked with tetanus at 10 o'clock at night. By the administration of chloroform the violence of the spasms was gradually diminished and she recovered. After her recovery she slept for thirty-six hours.]

In that case there was lockjaw, which set in about the middle of the attack. It is generally a late symptom.

I had a patient named Coupland who died of tetanus. It must have been idiopathic, as there was no external cause. The patient died in somewhat less than half an hour, before I could reach the house.

I have made a number of experiments upon animals with reference to strychnia poison. I have found the *post-mortem* appearances very generally to concur. The vessels of the membranes of the brain have generally been highly congested. The sinuses gorged with blood. In one case there was hemorrhage from the nostrils. That was a case of very high congestion. In some cases there has been an extravasation of blood at the base of the brain. I have cut through the substance of the brain, and have found in it numerous red points.

The lungs have been either collapsed or congested. The heart has invariably been filled with blood on the right side, and very often on the left side also. The liver has been congested, the kidneys and spleen generally healthy. The vessels of the stomach on the outer surface, have been congested, and on the mucous or inner surface highly vascular. The vessels of the membranes of the spinal cord have been congested, and sometimes red points have been displayed on cutting it through.

From a *post-mortem* examination you may generally judge of the cause of death. I have in a great many cases experimented for the discovery of strychnia. You may discover in the stomach the smallest dose that will kill. If you kill with a grain you may discover traces of it. By traces I mean evidences of its presence. You can discover the

---

[8] Vascular is defined as anything relating to blood vessels or ducts in the body, so what he meant by "vascularity of some of the vessels" is unknown. According to the Old Bailey transcript, Mr. Kenealy had asked "In addition to the slight causes you have mentioned, do you believe that tetanic convulsions arise from causes that are as yet quite undiscoverable by human science?"

fifty-thousandth part of a grain, I have actually experimented so as to discover that quantity.

The decomposition of strychnia is a theory which no scientific man of eminence has ever before propounded. I first heard of that theory in this court. In my opinion, there is no well-grounded reason for it. I have disproved the theory by numerous experiments. I have taken the blood of an animal poisoned by two grains of strychnia, about the least quantity which would destroy life, and have injected it into the abdominal cavities of smaller animals, and have destroyed them, with all the symptoms and *post-mortem* appearances of poisoning by strychnia.

Strychnia being administered in pills would not affect its detection. If the pills were hard they would keep it together, and you might find its remains more easily. I do not agree with Dr. Taylor that colour tests are fallacious. I believe that such tests are a reliable mode of ascertaining the presence of strychnia.

I have invariably found strychnia in the urine which has been ejected. Strychnia cannot be confounded with pyrozanthe. After strychnia has been administered there is an increased flow of saliva. In my experiments that has been a very marked symptom. Animals to which strychnia had been given have always been very susceptible to touch. The stamp of a foot or a sharp word would throw them into convulsions. Even before the paroxysms commenced, touching them would be likely to throw them into tonic convulsions.

Lord CAMPBELL. — As soon as the poison is swallowed? — No; it would be after a certain time the first symptoms of poisoning must have been developed.

Examination continued. — I do not think rubbing them would give them relief. It is extremely improbable that a man who had taken a dose of strychnia sufficient to destroy life could after the symptoms had made their appearance pull a bell violently.

I have attended to the evidence as to Cook's symptoms. To the symptoms I attach little importance as a means of diagnosis, because you may have the same symptoms developed by many difference causes. A dose of strychnia sufficient to destroy life would hardly require an hour and a-half for its absorption. I think that death was in this case caused by epileptic convulsions with tetanic complications. I form that opinion from the *post-mortem* appearances being so different from those that I have described as attending poisoning with strychnia, and from the supposition that a dose of strychnia sufficient to destroy life in one paroxysm could not, so far as I am aware, have required even an hour for its absorption before the commencement of the attack. If the attack were of an epileptic character, the interval between the attacks of Monday and Tuesday would be natural, as epileptic seizures often recur at about the same hours of successive days.

Assuming that a man was in so excited a state of mind that he was silent for two or three minutes after his horse had won a race, that he exposed himself to cold and damp, excited his brain by drink, and was attacked by violent vomiting, and that after his death deposits of gritty granules were found in the neighbourhood of the spinal cord, would these causes be likely to produce such a death as that of Cook's? — Any one of these causes would assist in the production of such a death.

As a congeries[9] would they be still more likely to produce it? — Yes.

Cross-examined by the Attorney-General. — I am a general practitioner, and am parochial medical officer.[10] I have had personal experience of two cases of idiopathic tetanus. What I have said about mental and sensual excitement and so on has not come within my own observation. In the case of Catherine Watson I saw the patient at about half-past ten at night. She had been ill nearly an hour, and had five or six spasms. She had gone about her usual duties up to evening. She felt a slight lassitude for two days previous to the attack. It was only by close pressing that I ascertained that lockjaw came on about an hour or two after I was called in.

The case of Coupland was that of a young child between three and four years old. I was attending the mother, and saw the child in good health half an hour before it came on. It was seized with spasm, what I conjectured to be of the diaphragm, and died in about half an hour. I had seen the child asleep, but I did not examine it. I don't know whether I saw the face of the child, but it was in bed. I judged that it was asleep.

Is that the same as seeing it asleep? — Sometimes a medical man can form a better judgment than a lawyer. Mr. [John] Smith applied to me to be a witness in this case. I communicated to him the case of Catherine Watson, as resembling the case of Cook. I furnished my notes to be copied the night before last. I have been here since the commencement of the trial. I have been at all the consultations.

I began the experiments for this case in January. I had made experiments before. That was eight or ten years ago. I then found out that strychnia could be discovered by chemical and physiological tests. I killed dogs, cats, rabbits, and fowls. The doses I administered were from three-quarters up to two grains. To dogs the smallest quantity

---

[9] A collection or jumble.
[10] The parish's medical officer, responsible for overseeing the health of paupers and children seeking apprenticeships, and the committing of lunatics to asylums.

administered was a grain. In four cases I killed with one grain, five with a grain and a half, one with a grain and a quarter, and two with two grains. I never killed a dog with half a grain of strychnia, and therefore never experimented to find that quantity after death.

I have always found the brain and heart highly congested. The immediate cause of the fulness of the heart is that the spasm drives the blood from the small capillaries into the large vessels. The spasm of the respiratory muscles prevents the expansion of the lungs. The congestion of the brain is greatest when the animal was young and in full health. It does not depend upon the frequency of the spasms.

I have seen cases of traumatic tetanus. I have had two in my own practice. One lasted five or six days, the other six or seven days, and the patient recovered. I have never seen a case of strychnia in the human subject.

So far as I can judge, Cook's was a case of epileptic convulsions with tetanic complications. Nobody can say from what epilepsy proceeds. I have not arrived at any opinion in which a patient dying from epilepsy has preserved his consciousness to the time of death.

You have been reading up on this subject? — I am pretty well up in most branches of medicine. (A laugh.) I know of no case in which a patient dying from epilepsy has been conscious. My opinion is that Cook died of epileptic convulsions with tetanic complication.

By Lord CAMPBELL. — That is a disease well known to physicians. It is mentioned in Dr. Copland's Dictionary.

Examination continued. — I believe that all convulsive diseases, including the epileptic forms and the various tetanic complications, arise from the decomposition of the blood acting upon the nerves. Any mental excitement might have caused Cook's attack. Cook was excited at Shrewsbury, and wherever there is excitement there is consequent depression. I think Cook was afterwards depressed. When a man is lying in bed and vomiting he must be depressed.

This gentleman was much overjoyed at his horse winning, and you think he vomited in consequence? — It might predispose him to vomit.

I am not speaking of "mights." Do you think that the excitement of the three minutes on the course at Shrewsbury on the Tuesday accounts for the vomiting on the Wednesday night? — I do not. I find no symptoms of excitement or depression reported between that time and the time of his death.

The white spots found in the stomach of the deceased might, by producing an inflammatory condition of the stomach, have brought on the convulsions which caused death.

The *Attorney-General.* — But the gentlemen who made the *post-mortem* examination say that the stomach was not inflamed. —

There were white spots, which cannot exist without inflammation. There must have been inflammation.

The *Attorney-General*. — But these gentlemen say that there was not. — I do not believe them. (A laugh.) Sensual excitement might cause epileptic convulsions, with tetanic complications. The chancre and syphilitic sores were evidence that Cook had undergone such excitement. That might have occurred before he was at Shrewsbury.

Might sexual intercourse produce epilepsy a fortnight after it occurred? — There is an instance on record in which epilepsy supervened upon the very act of intercourse.

Have you any instance in which epilepsy came on a fortnight afterwards? (A laugh.) — It is within the range of possibility.

Do you mean, as a serious man of science, to say that? — The results might.

What results were there in this case? — The chancre and the syphilitic sores.

Did you ever hear of a chancre causing epilepsy? — No.

Did you ever dream of such a thing? — I never heard of it.

Did you ever hear of any other form of syphilitic disease producing epilepsy? — No; but tetanus.

The *Attorney-General*. — But you say this was epilepsy; we are not talking of tetanus? — You forget the tetanic complications. (Roars of laughter.)

The *Attorney-General*. — If I understand right then, it stands thus — the sexual excitement produces epilepsy, and the chancre superadds tetanic complications? — I say that the results of sexual excitement produce epilepsy.

Mr. Baron ALDERSON said he had heard some person in court clap his hands. On an occasion on which a man was being tried for his life such a display was most indecent.

Examination continued. — I cannot remember any fatal case of poisoning by strychnia in which so long a period as an hour and a-half intervened between the taking of the poison and the appearance of the first symptoms.

What would be the effect of morphia given a day or two previously? Would it not retard the action of the poison? — No; I have seen opium bring on convulsions very nearly similar.

What quantity? — A grain and a half. From my experience, I think that if morphia had been given a day or two before it would have accelerated the action of the strychnia. I have seen opium bring on epileptic convulsions. If this were a case of poisoning by strychnia, I should suppose that as both opium and strychnia produce congestion of the brain, the two would act together, and would have a more speedy effect. If congestion of the brain was coming on when morphia was given to Cook on the Sunday and Monday night, it might have increased rather than allayed it.

But the gentlemen who examined the body say that there was no congestion after death? — But Dr. Bamford says there was.

You stick to Dr. Bamford? — Yes, I do, because he was a man of experience, could judge much better than younger men, and was not so likely to be mistaken.

But Dr. Bamford said that Cook died of apoplexy; do you think this was apoplexy? — No.

What, then, do you think of Dr. Bamford, who certified that it was? — That was a matter of opinion, but the existence of congestion in the brain he saw.

The *Attorney-General.* — The other medical men said there was none.

Lord CAMPBELL. — That is rather a matter of reasoning than of evidence.

Re-examined by Mr. *Serjeant Shee.* — I have seen a great many children asleep, and can tell whether they are so without seeing their faces. In the case of the child who died of tetanus the mother had told me that it was asleep.

Dr. Mason Good[11] is a well known author upon convulsions. From my reading of his works and others I have learnt that there are convulsions which are not, strictly speaking, epilepsy, although they resemble it in some of its features. I also know the works of M. Esquirol.[12] From reading those and other works I know that epileptic convulsions sufficiently violent to cause death frequently occur without the patient entirely losing his consciousness.

Epilepsy, properly so called, is sudden in its attack. The patient falls down at once with a shriek. That disease occurs very often at night, and in bed. It sometimes happens that its existence is known to a young man's family without his knowing anything about it. Convulsions of an epileptic character are sometimes preceded by premonitory symptoms. It sometimes happens that during such convulsions actual epilepsy comes on, and the patient dies of an internal spasm. It often happens that if a patient has suffered from epilepsy and convulsions of an epileptic kind during the night, he may be as well next day as if nothing had happened, more especially when an adult is seized for the first time. In such cases it often happens that such fits succeed each other within a short period.

---

[11] John Mason Good (1764-1827) was a surgeon and writer on religious and medical subjects.

[12] Jean-Etienne Esquirol (1772-1840) was a psychiatrist who advocated government-supported treatment of the mentally ill. He also founded an asylum devoted to the study and treatment of insanity.

I heard the deposition of Dr. Bamford. If it were true that the mind of the deceased were distressed and irritable the night before his death, I should say that he was suffering from depression. From what Cook said about his madness in the middle of the Sunday night I should infer that he had been seized by some sudden and mental excitement. There might be some disturbance of the brain.

I do not believe that inflammation can be absent while spots on the stomach are present. About eighteen months ago I examined the stomach of a person who had died from fever, in which I found white spots. I consulted various authors. In an essay on the stomach by Dr. Sprodboyne, a medical man who practiced in Edinburgh, I found mention of similar spots on the stomach of a young woman who had died suddenly.

Dr. JOHN NATHAN BAINBRIDGE, examined by Mr. *Grove*.

I am a doctor of medicine, and medical officer to the St. Martin's workhouse. I have had much experience of convulsive disorders. Such disorders present a great variety of symptoms. They vary as to the frequency of the occurrence and as to the muscles affected. Periodicity, or recurrence at the same hours, days, or months, is common.

I had a case in which a patient had an attack on one Christmas night, and on the following Christmas night, at the same hour, he had a similar attack. The various forms of convulsions so run into each other that it is almost impossible for the most experienced medical men to state where one terminates and the other begins. In both males and females hysteria is frequently attended by tetanic convulsions. Epileptic attacks are frequently accompanied by tetanic complications.

Cross-examined by the *Attorney-General.* — Hysteric convulsions very rarely end in death. I have known one case in which they have done so. That occurred within the last three months. It was the case of a male. It occurred in St. Martin's workhouse. The man had been for years subject to this complaint. On the occasion on which he died he was ill only for a few minutes. I did not make a *post-mortem* examination. I was told he was seized with sudden convulsions, fell down on the ground, and in five minutes was dead. There was slight clinching of the hands, but I think no locking of the jaw. The man was about thirty-five years of age. He was the brother of the celebrated aëronaut, Lieutenant Gale.[13]

---

[13] George Gale (1797?-1850), an actor and balloonist. He assumed the title of lieutenant as a result of an appointment, obtained with the help of influential

In many cases of this description consciousness is destroyed. It is not so in all. I have met with violent cases in which it has been preserved. I never knew a case in which during the paroxysm the patient spoke. Epilepsy is sometimes attended with opisthotonos.[14] I have seen cases of traumatic tetanus. In such cases the patient retains his consciousness. I have known many cases of epilepsy terminating in death. Loss of consciousness — not universally, but generally — accompanies epilepsy. I never knew a case of death from that disease where consciousness was not destroyed. I have known ten or twelve such fatal cases.

Re-examined by Mr. *Grove*. — Persons almost invariably fall asleep after an epileptic attack.

The *Attorney-General*. — And after taking opium? — Yes.

EDWARD AUSTIN STEDDY,
examined by Mr. *Gray*.

I am a member of the Royal College of Surgeons, and am in practice at Chatham. In June, 1854, I attended a person named Sarah Ann Taylor for trismus and pleuro-tothonos.[15] When I first saw the patient she was bent to one side. The convulsions came on in paroxysms. The pleuro-tothonos and trismus lasted about a fortnight. The patient then so far recovered as to be able to walk about.

About a twelvemonth afterwards, on the 3rd of March, 1855, she was again seized. That seizure lasted about a week. She is still alive. The friends of the patient said that the disease was brought on by depression arising from a quarrel with her husband.

Cross-examined by Mr. *James*. — I do not know how long before the attack this quarrel occurred. During it the woman received a blow upon her side from her husband. During the whole fortnight the lockjaw or trismus continued. In March, 1855, she was under my care about a week, during the whole of which the trismus continued.

---

friends, as a coast blockade inspector in Ireland. When his career on the stage failed, he bought a balloon and made his first ascent at Peckham in 1848. Over the next two years, he made more than a hundred ascents. For his 114th attempt, he ascended aboard a pony attached to the balloon. After it landed, the pony was unslung, but the peasants let loose the balloon, leaving Gale holding onto the ropes. His body was found several miles away the next day.

[14] The condition in which the body is rigid, with the back arched and the head thrown backward.

[15] *Trismus:* Lockjaw. *Pleura-tothonos:* A condition in which the spine flexes involuntarily so that the person is leaning. Also called Pisa syndrome, named for the Leaning Tower of Pisa.

Dr. GEORGE ROBINSON,
examined by Mr. *Kenealy*.

I am a licentiate of the Royal College of Physicians, and physician to the Newcastle-on-Tyne Dispensary and Fever Hospital. I have devoted considerable attention to the subject of pathology. I have practised as a physician for ten years. I have heard the whole of the medical evidence in this case.

From the symptoms described I should say that Cook died of tetanic convulsions, by which I mean, not the convulsions of tetanus, but convulsions similar to those witnessed in that disease. The convulsions of epilepsy sometimes assume a tetanic appearance. I know no department of pathology more obscure than that of convulsive diseases.

I have witnessed *post-mortem* examinations after death from convulsive diseases, and have sometimes seen no morbid appearances whatever, and in other cases the symptoms were applicable to a great variety of diseases. Convulsive diseases are always connected with the condition of the nerves. The brain has a good deal to do with the production of convulsive diseases, but the spinal cord has more. I believe that gritty granules in the region of the spinal cord would be very likely to produce convulsions, and I think they would be likely to be very similar to those described in the present case. I think that from what I have heard described of the mode of life of the deceased it would have predisposed him to epilepsy.

I have witnessed some experiments with strychnia, and have performed a few. I have also prescribed it in cases of paralysis.

By the *Attorney-General*. — I have seen 20 cases where epilepsy has been attended by convulsions of a tetanic character. I have never seen the symptoms of epilepsy proceed to anything like the extent of the symptoms in Cook's case. I never saw a body in a case of epilepsy so stiff as to rest upon the head and the heels. I never knew such symptoms to arise in any case except tetanus. When epilepsy presents any of these extreme forms it is always accompanied by unconsciousness. In almost every case of epilepsy the patient is unconscious at the time of the attack.

In cases of epilepsy I have found gritty granules on the brain, and any disturbing cause in the system, I think, would be likely to produce convulsions. I believe that the granules in this case were very likely to have irritated the spinal cord, and yet that no indication of that irritation would have remained after death. I think that these granules might have produced the death of Mr. Cook.

The *Attorney-General*. — Do you think that they did so? — Putting aside the assumption of death by strychnia I should say so.

The *Attorney-General.* — Are not all the symptoms spoken to by Mr. Jones indicative of death by strychnia? — They certainly are.

The *Attorney-General.* — Then, it comes to this — that if there were no other cause of death suggested you would say that the death in this case arose from epilepsy? — Yes.

Mr. *Serjeant Shee.* — Epilepsy is a well-known form of disease which includes many others.

DR. BENJAMIN WALL RICHARDSON,
examined by Mr. *Serjeant Shee.*

I am a physician, practising in London. I have never seen a case of tetanus, properly so-called, but I have seen many cases of death by convulsions. In many instances they have presented tetanic appearances without being strictly tetanus. I have seen the muscles fixed, especially those of the upper part of the body. I have observed the arms stiffened out, and the hands closely and firmly clinched until death. I have also observed a sense of suffocation in the patient. In some forms of convulsions I have seen contortions both of the legs and the feet, and the patient generally expresses a wish to sit up.

I have known persons die of a disease called angina pectoris.[16] The symptoms of that disease, I consider, resemble closely those of Mr. Cook. Angina pectoris comes under the denomination of spasmodic diseases. In some cases the disease is detectable upon *post-mortem* examination; in others it is not.

I attended one case. A girl 10 years old was under my care in 1850. I supposed she had suffered from scarlet fever. She recovered so far that my visits ceased. I left her amused and merry in the morning; at half-past 10 in the evening I was called in to see her, and I found her dying. She was supported upright at her own request, her face was pale, the muscles of the face rigid, the arms rigid, the fingers clinched, the respiratory muscles completely fixed and rigid, and with all this there was combined intense agony and restlessness, such as I have never witnessed. There was perfect consciousness. The child knew me, described her agony, and eagerly took some brandy-and-water from a spoon. I left for the purpose of obtaining chloroform from my own house, which was 30 yards distant. When I returned her head was drawn back, and I could detect no respiration; the eyes were then fixed open, and the body just resembled a statue; she was dead.

On the following day I made a *post-mortem* examination. The brain was slightly congested; the upper part of the spinal cord seemed

---

[16] A pain in the chest due to an obstruction or spasm of the coronary arteries.

healthy; the lungs were collapsed; the heart was in such a state of firm spasm and solidity and so emptied of blood that I remarked that it might have been rinsed out. I could not discover any appearance of disease that would account for the death, except a slight effusion of serum in one pleural cavity. I never could ascertain any cause for the death. The child went to bed well and merry, and immediately afterwards jumped up, screamed, and exclaimed, "I am going to die."

Cross-examined by the *Attorney-General*. — I consider that the symptoms I have described were those of angina pectoris. It is the opinion of Dr. Jenner that this disease is occasioned by the ossification of some of the small vessels of the heart. I did not find that to be the case in this instance. There have been cases where no cause whatever was discovered. It is called angina pectoris from its causing such extreme anguish to the chest.

I do not think the symptoms I have described were such as would result from taking strychnia. There is this difference — that rubbing the hands gives ease to the patient in cases of angina pectoris. I must say there would be great difficulty in detecting the difference in the cases of angina pectoris and strychnia. As regards symptoms I know of no difference between the two.

I am bound to say that if I had known so much of these subjects as I do now in the case I have referred to I should have gone on to analyse to endeavour to detect strychnia.

In the second case I discovered organic disease of the heart, which was quite sufficient to account for the symptoms. The disease of angina pectoris comes on quite suddenly, and does not give any notice of its approach. I did not send any note of this case to any medical publication. It is not at all an uncommon occurrence to find the hands firmly clinched after death in cases of natural disease.

Re-examined by Mr. *Serjeant Shee*. — There are cases of angina pectoris in which the patient has recovered and appeared perfectly well for a period of twenty-four hours, and then the attack has returned. I am of the opinion that the fact of the recurrence of the second fit in Cook's case is more the symptom of angina pectoris than of strychnia poison.

Dr. *Wrightson* was re-called, and in answer to a question put by Serjeant Shee he said it was his opinion that when the strychnia poison was absorbed in the system it was diffused throughout the entire system.

Cross-examined by the *Attorney-General*. — The longer time that elapsed before the death would render the absorption more complete. If a minimum dose to destroy life were given, and a long interval elapsed to the death, the more complete would be the absorption and the less the chance of finding it in the stomach.

Re-examined by *Serjeant Shee*. — I should expect still to find it in the spleen and liver and blood.

CATHERINE WATSON,
examined by Mr. *Grove*.

I live at Garnkirk, near Glasgow. I was attacked with a fit in October of last year. I had no wound of any kind on my body when I was attacked. I did not take any poison.

Cross-examined by the *Attorney-General*. — I was taken ill at night. I had felt heavy all day from the morning, but had no pain till night. The first pain I felt was in my stomach, and then I had cramp in my arms, and after that I was quite insensible. I have no recollection of anything after I was first attacked, except that I was bled.

Serjeant Shee then said that he was now about to enter into another part of the case for the defence, and probably the Court would think it a convenient period to adjourn.

The Lord CHIEF JUSTICE said that the Court had no objection to adjourn if the learned Serjeant thought it would be a convenient time to do so.

The *Attorney-General* requested that before the Court was formally adjourned a witness named Saunders, whose name was upon the back of the bill, and who was not in attendance, and who he believed had not made his appearance during the trial, should be called on his recognizances. He added that he believed this witness was also subpoenaed on behalf of the prisoner, but he (the Attorney-General) intended to have called him for the Crown.

The Court directed that the witness should be called upon his recognizances, and this was done, but he did not appear.

The Court then adjourned until 10 o'clock on Saturday morning.

GALLERY LEADING FROM NEWGATE TO THE CENTRAL CRIMINAL COURT

TENTH DAY.—May 24, 1856.

The trial of William Palmer for the murder of John Parsons Cook was resumed this morning. At the opening of the proceedings and during the whole day the court was densely crowded. Several noble lords and members of the House of Commons were accommodated with seats upon the bench.

The learned judges, Lord Campbell, Mr. Baron Alderson, and Mr. Justice Cresswell, took their seats at 10 o'clock, and the prisoner was immediately placed at the bar. Although to any one who had not seen him since the commencement of the trial he might have appeared considerably altered, yet the change was no greater than might naturally arise from the length of these proceedings, and did not indicate any increase of anxiety as to the result of his trial. To the speech of the Attorney-General he listened with a fixed attention, which scarcely permitted a single change of position; but during the whole time the expression of his countenance was unaltered.

Counsel for the Crown: The Attorney-General, Mr. E. James, Q.C., Mr. Bodkin, Mr. Welsby, and Mr. Huddleston; for the prisoner: Mr. Serjeant Shee, Mr. Groves, Q.C., Mr. Gray, and Mr. Kenealy.

OLIVER PEMBERTON,
examined by Mr. *Serjeant Shee*.

I am lecturer on anatomy at Queen's College, Birmingham, and surgeon to the General Hospital in that town. I was present at the examination of the body of Cook after its exhumation in January last. I observed the spinal cord. It was not in such a state as to enable me to say what had been its condition immediately after the death of the deceased. The upper part, where the brain had been separated, was green in colour from the effects of decomposition. The remaining portion, though fairly preserved for a body which had been buried two months, was so soft that I could not form any opinion as to its state immediately after death.

Cross-examined by the *Attorney-General*. — It was the day after the long canal had been opened that I saw the spinal cord. The opening of that canal would expose the cord to the atmosphere, but it was still to a certain extent protected by a strong membrane. It is my impression that the dura mater or outer membrane was not opened until I was present. I am not certain of that. I attended on behalf of the prisoner, as also did Mr. Bolton, a professor of Queen's College, Birmingham.

Mr. *Serjeant Shee* intimated that this concluded the medical evidence on behalf of the prisoner.

HENRY MATTHEWS, examined by Mr. *Grove*.

I am an Inspector of Police at the Euston-square railway station. I was stationed there on Monday, the 19th of November last. The last train from London to the north, which stops at Rugeley, leaves London, and left on that day, at 2 o'clock in the afternoon. The express train left at 5 o'clock in the afternoon. It is due at Stafford at 8.42 p.m.; but on the night I have mentioned did not arrive until 8.45 p.m. The distance from Stafford to Rugeley is by railway nine miles; by road I don't know how far. The quickest mode of getting to Rugeley after the 2 o'clock train has left London is by express train to Stafford, and thence by road to Rugeley.

JOSEPH FOSTER, examined by Mr. *Gray*.

I am a farmer and grazier at Sibbertoft, Northamptonshire.[1] Up to Lady-day[2] last I kept the George Hotel, at Welford, in that county. I knew Cook for many years before his death. I have met him on the hunting field, at dinner, and in various other places. I think he was of a weak constitution. I form this opinion from the fact that, when I have been out with him, he has often had bilious attacks. Those are the only circumstances from which I form that opinion.

Cross-examined by Mr. *James*. — I had known Cook many years. For the last two years he hunted regularly in Northamptonshire. Sometimes he kept two horses, and sometimes three. I have known him to hunt three days a-week, and that pretty regularly, when he was well. I know Mr. George Pell [an attorney at Northampton]. There is a cricket club at Welford. I have seen Cook play, but not for these last three or four years.

I last saw Cook at Lutterworth about the middle of October last. I should think it is a year and a half since he last had a bilious sick headache. That occurred at my own house. He could not hunt that day. He had come to my house to meet the hounds, but did not go out.

---

[1] A county in central England, southeast of Rugeley.
[2] March 25. The traditional name for the Feast of the Annunciation of the Blessed Virgin, when the angel Gabriel visited the Virgin Mary to tell her that she would be the mother of Jesus. This is one of four traditional quarter days on the calendar, on which servants are hired, school terms started and rents come due.

He stayed two or three hours, and then went home. I will not swear that I did not see him in the hunting field within a week.

Re-examined by Mr. *Gray.* — I never saw him sick on any other occasion except at a cricket match seven years ago. It was after dinner.

GEORGE MYATT, examined by Mr. *Grove.*

I am a saddler, and reside at Rugeley. I was at Shrewsbury Races on the Tuesday, the day that Polestar won. I was at the Raven Hotel on the Wednesday. I saw Cook and Palmer there that evening about 12 o'clock. I was waiting in the room when they came in. I considered Cook the worse for liquor. They proposed to have a glass of brandy-and-water each before they went to bed. We each had a glass of that liquor. While we were drinking it Cook made some remark that he fancied it was not good. He drank off the best part of his glass, and then said he thought there was something in it, and gave it to some one who was standing by to taste. Cook proposed to have some more, but Palmer said he would not have any more unless Cook drank his up. No more brandy came in, and we all went to bed. I slept in the same room as Palmer. The brandy was brought in in a decanter. Mine was poured out, but I don't know by whom. I did not leave the room after Cook and Palmer came in until we went to bed. I never saw anything put into the brandy-and-water. It could not have been put in without my seeing it. Palmer and I went to bed together, I believe we left Cook in the sitting-room. Nothing more occurred during the night. When we went to bed I locked the bed-room door, and Palmer did not leave the room during the night.

When we got up in the morning Palmer asked me to go and call Cook. I did so. I went to the door of Cook's bedroom, rapped at it, and he told me to come in. I went in, and he told me how ill he had been during the night. He said that he had been obliged to send for a doctor. He asked me what was put in the brandy-and-water, and I told him that I did not think anything was. He asked me to send "the doctor," meaning Palmer, to him. I did so.

I next saw Cook when he came into the room to breakfast. Palmer was then in the room. Palmer and I had breakfasted before Cook came in. He breakfasted in the same room. At night we all three went to Rugeley. We dined together at the Raven first. We left Shrewsbury about 6 o'clock by the express train. Palmer paid for the three tickets. On their way to Rugeley Palmer was sick, and he and Cook said they could not account for it. Palmer vomited. This was on the road between Stafford and Rugeley. We had left the train at Stafford, and were then in a fly. They said they could not account for the vomiting unless the dinner had been cooked in a brass vessel,[3] or there was something the matter with the water; and that there had been a great many people sick at Shrewsbury Races. I had heard other people say that they had been ill, and could not account for it. The distance by the road from Stafford to Rugeley is nine miles.

Cross-examined by Mr. *James*.— I have known Palmer all his life. He deals with me for saddlery. I have not recently been in the habit of going to races with him. I have gone occasionally. I have never been at Doncaster with him. I was at Wolverhampton Races with him in August last. We went there together. We did not sleep in the same room there. We did not stop at the same hotel. I stopped with a brother-in-law. I was at Wolverhampton a couple of days. I never dined nor breakfasted with Palmer.

I also attended Lichfield Races with him in September last. The course is within 10 miles of Rugeley. We did not sleep at Lichfield. I did not go with Palmer nor did I return home with him. I think that is about all the races that I was at last year. Except at Shrewsbury I never slept in a double-bedded room with Palmer at any races. I never was at Worcester in my life. Palmer paid my hotel expenses at Shrewsbury. He has never paid my expenses at other races. I dare say that I was at races with Palmer the year before last. I was at two or three, but cannot say how many.

I had an interview with Palmer in Stafford Gaol. I was with him about a couple of hours. It is a month or five weeks ago. I cannot say whether it was since the Stafford Assizes or before. Mr. [John] Smith said he was going, and I thought I should like to see Palmer. Now and then I have stood half-a-sovereign or a sovereign on Palmer's horses. I did not bet at Shrewsbury. I did not back Cook's mare Polestar. I have stood a sovereign or so with Palmer upon a horse.

It was as near as possible 12 o'clock when I first saw Cook and Palmer at the Raven. I had dined at Rugeley. I arrived at Shrewsbury between 8 and 9 o'clock. I went to the Raven. I knew the room which Palmer generally had, and I went up to it to see if he was in. Near the door (out-side) I saw Cook, who said, "Holloa! what brings you here?" I told him I had come to see how they were getting on. Palmer had gone out, so I went into the town.

I returned to the Raven in about an hour, and went into Palmer's room. Palmer was not there, but a man named Shelley — a betting man — was. I waited about a couple of hours — that is, till about 12 o'clock, when Palmer and Cook came in. Cook was the worse for liquor, but not very drunk. He was so much the worse for it that I could easily see that he was so. The brandy-and-water was brought in

---

[3] It was believed that food cooked or stored in brass vessels would be infused with enough copper to cause a poisonous reaction.

directly. The brandy was brought in in a decanter, but I cannot say how the water was brought. It might have been upon the table. I should say that the tumblers were brought up with the brandy. I do not remember Mrs. Brooks coming or Palmer being called out of the room. A gentleman came in, whom I now know to be Mr. Fisher. Palmer had not left the room before that. That I will swear. He never left the room until we went to bed.

When Fisher came in, Cook asked Palmer to have some more brandy-and-water. Palmer said he would not have any more unless Cook drunk his. Palmer sat close to me. Cook drunk his brandy off at a draught. Directly he had drunk it he said there was something in it. I will swear that he did not say "It burns my throat." He said nothing of that kind. He gave it to some one to taste, but made no other observation. I believe it was Fisher to whom he gave it to be tasted. I will not swear whether it was Palmer or Cook who gave it to Fisher. When Cook drank the brandy-and-water there were only four persons in the room. I can't say whether any one but Fisher came in afterwards. When Cook drunk it he as nearly as possible emptied the glass. There was a little left in it. I will not swear whether or not Palmer touched the glass. I believe he tasted what was left in the glass, and said he could not taste anything that was the matter with the brandy-and-water. I believe he handed the glass to Fisher. I do not recollect that Fisher said "It is of no use giving me the glass, it is empty." I will not swear that he did not.

About 20 minutes or half an hour elapsed before Palmer and I went to bed. Cook did not leave the room before we did. Palmer and I went straight up to bed. We left Cook in the sitting-room. I did not that night hear of Cook's vomiting, or of his being ill. I only drank one glass of brandy-and-water. We drank our brandy with cold water.

On the following day (Thursday) I dined with Palmer at the Raven. Cook carved. During the first two days of the inquest on Cook's body I was at home at Rugeley. I did not go to the inquest.

Re-examined by Mr. *Grove*. — I was not subpoenaed for the Crown. I was examined, but not summoned. There was an officer of the gaol present during the whole of my interview with Palmer at Stafford. We did not talk about this case.

The *Attorney-General*. — Did not you tell Mr. Gardner that you knew nothing about the brandy-and-water at Shrewsbury? — No.

Did you not tell Mr. Crisp and Mr. Sweeting that you knew nothing about it? — No; I told them what I knew about it.

Will you swear you did not tell them anything about it? — I do; I told them exactly what I tell you now.

JOHN SERJEANT,
examined by Mr. *Serjeant Shee*.

I am of no business. I attend almost every race in the kingdom. I knew Cook intimately. I also know the prisoner Palmer. During the Shrewsbury Races I received a letter from Cook. I was subpoenaed on the part of the Crown, but had no notice to produce the letter. I have not got it. I searched for it, but I found I had sent it to Saunders the trainer. I applied to him for it by letter, to which I received no answer. I have taken all means to obtain Cook's letter. I have no copy of it.

Mr. *Serjeant Shee* submitted to their lordships that he had now proved sufficient to enable him to give secondary evidence as to the contents of this letter; but as there was a possibility that Saunders (the witness who was on the previous day called upon his recognizances, but did not attend), might be examined, the Court ruled that secondary evidence could not be received.

Examination continued. I was not at Shrewsbury, and I don't know what Palmer and Cook won or lost there beyond what Cook told me.

Shortly before Cook's death I had an opportunity of noticing the state of his throat. I was with him at Liverpool on the week previous to the Shrewsbury Races; we slept in adjoining rooms, and in the morning he called my attention to the state of his throat. I looked at it, and saw that it was full of ulcers and very much inflamed. His tongue was swollen. I told him I was surprised that he could eat and drink with his mouth and throat in such a state. He said it had been in that state for weeks and months, and now he did not take notice of it. That was all which then passed between us about the sore throat. He had shown me that his throat was in this state previously, at almost every one of our meetings.

On the platform at Liverpool, after the races, I saw him take a gingerbread nut, with cayenne in it, by mistake. He told me afterwards that it was very nearly killing him.[4] He did not say more particularly than that what effect it produced upon him.

---

[4] Practical jokes were popular in an era in which people had to entertain themselves and would do anything to relieve the tedium of a rainy Sunday afternoon in the country. Francis Jacox's "Scripture Proverbs" (1876) condemned practical jokes such as having your chair pulled out from under you as you're sitting, throwing detonating balls at the feet of old ladies, or passing out "ginger bread nuts made of cayenne pepper." Jacox was particularly harsh on the pranks of the Duke of Montague (1690-1749), who, "in order to divert himself and two or three chosen friends at another's expense, used sometimes to invite to dine with him six stammerers and stutterers, or three men six feet four high and three men scarcely four feet six, or a half-dozen sufferers from some nervous affliction, or the St. Vitus's dance order, wherewith to make merry."

At Liverpool, the week before the Shrewsbury races, Cook was very poor. He owed me £25, and he gave me £10 on account. He said he had not sufficient to pay his expenses at Liverpool, but that I should have the rest on the Shrewsbury week.

Cook and Palmer were in the habit of "putting on" horses for each other. They did so at the Liverpool meeting. I "put on" money for Palmer at Liverpool, and he told me that Cook stood it along with him. I have heard Cook, a short time before his death, apply to Palmer to supply him with a lotion called "black wash." [It was admitted that this was a mercurial lotion.] I never saw his throat dressed by any one.

Cross-examined by Mr. *James*, Q.C. — The black wash was not to be drunk. That happened at the Warwick meeting in the spring of 1855. Cook was at Newmarket before the Warwick meeting. He was at nearly all the autumnal races of last year. At Liverpool his appetite was pretty good. I was surprised at seeing him eat so much. The cayenne was mixed up for a trick in one nut, which was mixed with other nuts. Of course cayenne nuts are stronger than other nuts.

JEREMIAH SMITH,
examined by Mr. *Serjeant Shee*.

I am an attorney at Rugeley. I am acquainted with Palmer, and I also knew the late Mr. Cook. I saw Cook at the Talbot Arms on Friday, the 16th of November, in his bedroom, about 10 o'clock. I was present at his breakfast. He breakfasted in bed. He took a cup of tea with a wineglass of brandy in it.

On the same day I dined in his company at Palmer's house. I am not sure whether I saw him in the interval. We had a rumpsteak, and we drank champagne at dinner and port wine after dinner. We drank three bottles altogether, and Cook drank his share. There were only Cook, Palmer, and myself. Dinner was over about half past 2, and we rose from table between 5 and 6. Cook and I left the house towards 6. We went to my house, and from there to the Albion Hotel. We had a glass of cold brandy-and-water each, and Cook left me there. He said before he went that he felt cold, and warmed himself at the fire. He also said that he would go home and read in bed. He had borrowed a book. He left me between 7 and 8.

In the afternoon, after dinner, we were talking about racing, and I asked Cook for money — for £50. He gave me £5. When he took the note out of his case, I said — "Why you can pay me all." He said, "No; there is only £41 10s. due to you. I cannot let you have it, because I have given Palmer money, but I will pay you the remainder when I return from Tattersall's on Monday."

On the next night (Saturday) Cook was not well, and I slept in his room. It was late (about 12) when we went to bed. In the early part of the night he was unwell. He got some toast-and-water and was washing his mouth; he was sick, and he gargled his throat. I did not leave my bed. About 2 o'clock I went to sleep, being tired, as I had been out shooting, and I slept until Palmer and Bamford came in the morning.

I heard a conversation between the doctors and Cook as I lay in the bed. Bamford said, "Well, Mr. Cook, how are you this morning?" Cook said, "I am rather better. I slept from about 2 or 3 o'clock after the house had become quiet." Bamford said, "I will send you some medicine." I don't recollect that there was any further conversation, and I got up and left the house.

I know Mrs. Palmer, the prisoner's mother. In consequence of what passed between me and her on the Monday evening, I went about nine o'clock to the prisoner's house to see if he had arrived. I did not find him. About ten minutes past ten I saw him. He was coming from the direction of Stafford in a car. He said, "Have you seen Cook to-day?" I said, "No. I have been to Lichfield on business." He said, "We had better run up and see him before I go to my mother's, or it will be too late." We then went up to Cook's room together. Cook said, "You are late to-night, doctor; I did not expect you to look in. I have taken the medicine which you gave me." We did not stay more than two or three minutes. I think he asked me why I had not called in earlier, and I told him I had been to Lichfield on business. He said he had taken the pills which Bamford had sent, intimating, as I thought, that he should not have taken them if Palmer had called in.[5]

Did Palmer when he entered the room make inquiries of the nature which a medical man usually makes to his patient?

---

[5] Fletcher was shown two letters Palmer wrote to Smith from Stafford jail that hinted about what the lawyer was supposed to say on the stand. Here's a portion from one of them:

"Now as there is a God in Heaven (I am sure you can't have forgotten it) you know that you were waiting for my coming and when I got out of the Fly you told me that my mother wanted to see me particularly, and after bidding Cook good night we walked together down to the YARD [Mrs. Palmer's house], and got a good brushing from the old Lady about a writ of Brown's that Arminshaw had sent for; that Arminshaw told to George and George to my mother — and if you recollect she was very cross.

"We then walked back to my house and you said, 'Well, let me have a glass of spirit.' I went to the cupboard and there was none—you said 'Never mind' and bid me good night. This must have been after 11 o'clock—now I should like to know how I could get to Mr. Salt's shop at 9 o'clock on that night."

THE TIMES REPORT

BENJAMIN THIRLBY, PALMER'S LATE PARTNER

The *Attorney-General* objected to this question.

Mr. *Serjeant Shee*. — What inquiries were made? — Cook told Palmer that he had been up, talking with Saunders and Ashmall part of the day. Palmer said, "You ought not to have got up." I don't remember that anything else passed. We left the room together and went straight to Palmer's mother, whose house is 400 or 500 yards from the Talbot Arms. We were there about half an hour. We left together and went then to Palmer's house. I asked him for some refreshment (a glass of grog), but could not get it. I left Palmer in the house and went home.

The day after we had dined at Palmer's I asked Cook and Palmer to dine with me. Cook sent me a message on that day, that he was not well enough to leave his room and that he could not come to dinner. I had a boiled leg of mutton for dinner, and I sent part of the broth from the Albion by a charwoman (I think her name was Rowney) to Cook. I borrowed £200 for Cook shortly before his death, and I also negotiated a loan with Pratt for £500 for him. I borrowed £100 from Mrs. Palmer, and £100 from William Palmer to make up the £200.

When Cook's horse was going to run, Palmer "put on" for him, and when Palmer's ran, Cook "put on" for him. I have seen Thirlby, Palmer's former assistant, dress Cook's throat with caustic. I think this was chiefly before the races at Shrewsbury.

I have some signatures of Cook's which I know to be in his handwriting. The two notes with instructions to negotiate the loan of £500, I saw Cook sign. [The notes were put in.] One of them is signed "J.P. Cook," the other "J. Parsons Cook." I knew from Cook that he was served with a writ, but I don't think that I was present when he was served. I do not remember whether I received any instructions to appear for him.

The letters put in were read by the Clerk of Arraigns. The first was signed "J. Parsons Cook," Monday; and was in the following terms:—

"My dear Sir,— I have been in a devil of a fix about the bill, but have at last settled it at the cost of an extra two guineas, for the 'd———d' discounter had issued a writ against me. I am very much disgusted at it."

Witness continued. — The letter was sent to me, but I have destroyed the envelope. The next letter bore the date 25th of June, 1855, and was as follows:—

"Dear Jerry,— I should like to have the bill renewed for two months. Can it be done? Let me know by return. I have scratched Polestar for the Nottinghamshire and Wolverhampton stakes. I shall be down on Friday or Saturday. Fred tells me Arabas will win the Northumberland stakes."

The memorandum put in and read was signed "J.P. Cook," and the following is a copy:—

"Polestar three years, Sirius two years; by way of mortgage to secure £200 advanced upon a bill of exchange for £500, dated 29th of August, 1855, payable three months after date."

Cross-examined by the *Attorney-General*. — Are you the gentleman who took Mr. Myatt to Stafford Gaol? — I am.

Have you known Palmer long? — I have known him long and very intimately, and have been employed a good deal as an attorney by Palmer and his family.

In December, 1854, did he apply to you to attest a proposal of his brother Walter Palmer for £13,000 in the Solicitors and General Insurance Office? — I cannot recollect; if you will let me see the document I will tell you.

Will you swear that you were not applied to? — I will not swear either that I was not applied to for that purpose or that I was. If you will let me see the document I shall recognise my writing at once.

In January, 1855, were you applied to by Palmer to attest a proposal of his brother for £13,000 in the Prince of Wales Office? — I don't recollect.

Don't recollect! Why £13,000 was a large sum for a man like Walter Palmer, wasn't it, who hadn't a shilling in the world? — Oh, he had money, because I know that he lived retired and carried on no business.

Didn't you know that he was an uncertificated bankrupt?[6] — I know that he had been a bankrupt some years before, but I did not know that he was an uncertificated bankrupt. I know that he had an allowance from his mother, but I do not know whether he had money from any other source. I believe that his brother William (the prisoner) gave him money at different times.

Where, in the course of 1854 and 1855, were you living — in Rugeley? — In 1854 I think I resided partly with William Palmer, and sometimes at his mother's.

Did you sometimes sleep at his mother's? — Yes.

When you did that where did you sleep? — In a room.

Did you sleep in his mother's room — on your oath were you not intimate with her — you know well enough what I mean? — I had no other intimacy, Mr. Attorney, than a proper intimacy.

How often did you sleep at her house, having an establishment of your own at Rugeley? — Frequently. Two or three times a week.

Are you a single or a married man? — A single man.

How long did that practice of sleeping two or three times a week at Mrs. Palmer's continue? — For several years.

Had you your own lodgings at Rugeley at the time? — Yes, all the time.

How far were your lodgings from Mrs. Palmer's house? — I should say nearly a quarter of a mile.

Explain how it happened that you, having your own place of abode within a quarter of a mile, slept two or three times a week at Mrs. Palmer's? — Sometimes her son Joseph or other members of her family were on a visit to her, and I went to see them.

And when you went to see those members of her family was it too far for you to return a quarter of a mile in the evening? — Why we used to play a game of cards, and have a glass of gin-and-water, and smoke a pipe perhaps; and then they said "It is late — you had better stop all night;" and I did. There was no particular reason why I did not go home that I know of.

---

[6] A person who owes debts and is liable to be imprisoned for them until payment could be arranged. The law allowed a debtor to become a certificated bankrupt by seeking protection from the court. This gave the debtor the right to be freed on bail if he's arrested and to borrow money to pay back those debts.

Did that go on for three or four years? — Yes; and I sometimes used to stop there when there was nobody there at all — when they were all away from home, the mother and all.

And you have slept there when the sons were not there and the mother was? — Yes.

How often did that happen? — Sometimes for two or three nights a-week, for some months at a time, and then perhaps I would not go near the house for a month.

What did you stop for on those nights when the sons were not there; there was no one to smoke and drink with then, and you might have gone home, might you not? — Yes; but I did not.

Do you mean to say on your oath that there was nothing but a proper intimacy between you and Mrs. Palmer? — I do.

Now, I will turn to another subject. Were you called upon to attest another proposal for £13,000 by Walter Palmer in the Universal Office? — I cannot say; if you will let me see the proposal I shall know.

I ask you, sir, as an attorney and a man of business, whether you cannot tell me whether you were applied to by William Palmer to attest a proposal for an assurance for £13,000 on the life of Walter Palmer? — I say that I do not recollect it. If I could see any document on the subject I dare say I should remember it.

Do you remember getting a £5 note for attesting an assignment by Walter Palmer to his brother of such a policy? — Perhaps I might. I don't recollect positively.

The *Attorney-General* (handing a document to witness). — Is that your signature? — It is very like my signature.

Have you any doubt about it? — (After considerable hesitation) I have some doubt.

Read the document, and tell me, on your solemn oath, whether it is your signature? — I have some doubt whether it is mine.

Read the document, sir. Was it prepared in your office? — It was not.

I will have an answer from you on your oath one way or another. Isn't that your handwriting? — I believe that it is not my handwriting. I think that it is a very good imitation of my handwriting.

Baron ALDERSON.— Did you ever make such an attestation? — I don't recollect, my Lord.

The *Attorney-General*. — Look at the other signature there, "Walter Palmer," is that his signature? — I believe that is Walter Palmer's.

Look at the attestation and the words "signed, sealed, and delivered;" are they in Mr. Pratt's handwriting? — They are.

Did you receive that from Mr. Pratt? — Most likely I did; but I can't swear that I did. It might have been sent to William Palmer.

Did you receive it from William Palmer? — I don't know; very likely I did.

Did William Palmer give you that document? — I have no doubt he did.

If that be the document he gave you, and those are the signatures of Walter Palmer and of Pratt, is not the other signature yours? — I'll tell you, Mr. Attorney —

Don't "Mr. Attorney" me, sir! Answer my question. Isn't that your handwriting? — I believe it not to be.

Will you swear that it isn't? — I believe that it is not.

Did you apply to the Midland Counties Insurance Office in October, 1855, to be appointed their agent at Rugeley? — I think I did.

Did you send them a proposal on the life of Bates for £10,000 — you yourself? — I did.

Did William Palmer apply to you to send that proposal? — Bates and Palmer came together to my office with a prospectus, and asked me if I knew whether there was any agent for that company in Rugeley? I told them I had never heard of one, and they then asked me if I would write and get the appointment, because Bates wanted to raise some money.

Did you send to the Midland Office and get appointed as their agent in Rugeley, in order to effect that £10,000 insurance on Bates's life? — I did.

Was Bates at that time superintending William Palmer's stud and stables? — He was.

At a salary of £1 a-week? — I can't tell his salary.

After that did you go to the widow of Walter Palmer to get her to give up her claim on the policy of her husband? — I did.

Where was she at that time? — At Liverpool.

Did you receive a document from Pratt to take to her? — William Palmer gave me one which had been directed to him.

Did the widow refuse? — She said she should like her solicitor to see it; and I said, "By all means."

Of course! Didn't she refuse to do it — didn't you bring it back? — I brought it back as I had no instructions to leave it.

Didn't she say that she had understood from her husband that the insurance was for £1,000?

Mr. *Serjeant Shee* objected to this question. What passed between the widow and witness could be no evidence against the prisoner.

The *Attorney-General* said, that the question was intended to affect the credit of the witness, and with that view it was most important.

The Court ruled that the question could not be put.

The *Attorney-General*. — Do you not know that Walter Palmer obtained nothing for making that assignment? — I believe that he ultimately did get something for it.

Don't you know that what he got was a bill for £200? — Yes; and he had a house furnished for him.

Don't you know that he got a bill for £200? — Yes.

And don't you know that that bill was never paid? — No, I do not.

Now, I'll refresh your memory a little with regard to those proposals (handing witness a document). Look at that, and tell me whether it is in your handwriting? — It is.

Refreshing your memory with that, I ask you were you not applied to by William Palmer in December, 1854, to attest a proposal on the life of his brother Walter for £13,000 in the Solicitors and General Insurance Office? — I might have been.

Were you or were you not, sir! Look at that document, and say have you any doubt upon the subject? — I do not like to speak from memory with reference to such matters.

No; but not speaking from memory in an abstract sense, but having your memory refreshed by a perusal of that document, have you any doubt that you were applied to? — I have no doubt that I might have been applied to.

Have you any doubt that in January, 1855, you were called on by William Palmer to attest another proposal for £13,000 on his brother's life in another office; look at the document and tell me? — I see the paper, but I don't know; I might have signed it in blank.

Do you usually sign attestations of this nature in blank? — I have some doubt whether I did not sign several of them in blank.

On your oath, looking at that document, don't you know that William Palmer applied to you to attest that proposal upon his brother's life for £13,000? — He did apply to me to attest proposals in some offices.

Were they for large amounts? — One was for £13,000.

Were you applied to to attest another for the like sum in the Universal Office? — I might be.

They were made much about the same time, were they not? You did not wait for the answers to come back to the first application before you made the second? — I do not know that any answers were returned at all.

Will you swear that you were not present when Walter Palmer executed the deed assigning the policy upon his life to his brother

William Palmer? Now, be careful, Mr. Smith, for depend upon it you shall hear of this again if you are not. — I will not swear that I was, I think I was not? I am not quite positive.

(Very few of the answers to these questions of the Attorney-General were given without considerable hesitation, and the witness appeared to labour under a sense of embarrassment which left a decidedly unfavourable impression upon the minds of the audience.)

Do you know that the £200 bill was given for the purpose of enabling William Palmer to make up a sum of £500? — I believe it was not; for Cook received absolutely from me £200. If I am not mistaken, he took it with him to Shrewsbury races — not the last races.

In whose favour was the bill drawn? — I think in favour of William Palmer. I don't know what became of it. I have never seen it since. I cannot state with certainty who saw me on the Monday; but I called at the Talbot Arms, and went into Cook's room. One of the servants gave me a candle. As well as I can remember, the servant who did so was either Bond, Mills, or Lavinia Barnes, I can't say which.

Re-examined by Mr. *Serjeant Shee*. — I have known Mrs. Palmer, the prisoner's mother, for twenty years. It is upwards of twenty years since her husband died. I should think she must be about sixty years of age. William Palmer is not her eldest son. Joseph is the eldest. He resides at Liverpool, and is a timber merchant. He is 45 or 46 years of age. I think George is the next son. He lives at Rugeley. He was frequently at his mother's house. There is another son, a clergyman of the Church of England. He resided with his mother until within the last two years, except when he was at college. There is a daughter. She lives with her mother. There are three servants. Mrs. Palmer's family does not visit much in the neighbourhood of Rugeley. Her house is a large one, and there are many spare bedrooms in it. I slept in the room nearest the old church.

Mr. *Serjeant Shee*. — Is there any pretence for saying you have ever been charged with any improper intimacy with Mrs. Palmer?

Witness. — I hope not.

Mr. *Serjeant Shee*. — Is there any pretence for saying so?

Witness. — There ought not to be.

Mr. *Serjeant Shee*. — Is there any truth in the statement or suggestion that you have had any improper intimacy with Mrs. Palmer?

Witness. — They might have said so, but they had no reason for saying so.

Mr. *Serjeant Shee*. — Is there any truth in the statement?

Witness. — I should say not. (Laughter.)

William Joseph Saunders, a witness, subpoenaed both by the Crown and the prisoner, was then called upon his recognisance, but did not appear.

The *Attorney-General* said, he should be extremely sorry to commence his reply if there were any chance of the witness making his appearance.

Lord CAMPBELL. — There does not appear to be the slightest chance. He has been called repeatedly.

Mr. *Serjeant Shee* said he should now ask for the production of a letter written by Cook to Palmer on the 4th of January, 1855. The letter, of which the following is a copy, was then put in and read:—

"LUTTERWORTH, JAN. 4, 1855.

"MY DEAR SIR,— I sent up to London on Tuesday to back St. Hubert for £50, and my commission has returned 10s. 1d. I have, therefore, booked 250 to 25 against him, to gain money. There is a small balance of £18 due to you, which I forgot to give you the other day. Tell Will to debit me with it on account of your share of training Pyrrhine. I will also write to him to do so, and there will be a balance due from him to me.

"YOURS FAITHFULLY,

"W. PALMER, ESQ.

"J. PARSONS COOK."

Mr. *Serjeant Shee* contended that he was entitled to reply on the part of the evidence. The course taken by the Attorney-General in getting at the contents of the cheque, the contents of an assignment of the policy on Walter Palmer's life, and the contents of the proposals to various offices for the insurance, he submitted entitled him to a reply on those points.

The LORD CHIEF JUSTICE. — We are of the opinion that you have no right to reply.

Mr. Baron ALDERSON. — That is quite clear.[7]

The *Attorney-General* said, he had been taken somewhat by surprise yesterday by the evidence of Dr. Richardson with respect to the disease known as angina pectoris. Dr. Richardson adverted to several books and authorities. He had now those books in his possession, and he was desirous of putting some questions arising out of that part of the evidence.

The Court decided against the application.

---

[7] "I wish there was two and a half grains of strychnia in old Campbell's acidulated draught," Palmer wrote in a note to his counsel, "solely because I think he acts unfairly."

THE TIMES REPORT

The Prisoner in the Dock.

The case for the defence here concluded.[8]

The *Attorney-General* rose to reply on the part of the Crown, and spoke as follows:—

May it please your lordships and gentlemen of the jury, the case for the prosecution and that for the defence are before you, and it now becomes my duty to address to you such observations upon the whole of the evidence as suggest themselves to my mind.

I feel that I have a most solemn and important duty to perform. I wish that I could have answered the appeal made to me the other day by my learned friend, Serjeant Shee, and say that I am satisfied with the case which he submitted to you for the defence; but standing here as the instrument of public justice, I feel that I should be wanting in the duty I have to perform if I did not revert to my original position, and again solicit at your hands a verdict of guilty against the accused.

I approach the consideration of the case in what, I hope, I may term a spirit of fairness and moderation. My business is to convince you, if I can, by facts and legitimate arguments, of the prisoner's guilt; and if I cannot establish it to your satisfaction, no man will rejoice more than I shall in a verdict of acquittal.

Gentlemen, in the mass of evidence which has been brought before you two main questions present themselves prominently for your consideration. Did the deceased man, into whose death we are now inquiring, die a natural death, or was he taken off by the foul means of poison? And if the latter proposition be sanctioned by the evidence, then comes the important question, whether the prisoner at the bar was the author of his death? I will proceed with the consideration of the subject in the order I have mentioned.

Did John Parsons Cook die by poison? I again assert the affirmative of that proposition. The case submitted to you on behalf of the Crown is this — that, having been first practised upon by antimony, Cook was at last killed by strychnine.

The first question to be considered is — what was the immediate and proximate cause of his death. The witnesses for the prosecution have told you, one and all, that, in their judgment he died of tetanus, which signifies a convulsive spasmodic action of the muscles of the body. Can there be any doubt that their opinion is correct? Of course it does not follow that, because he died of tetanus, it must be the tetanus of strychnine. That is a matter for after consideration. But, inasmuch as strychnine produces death by tetanus, we must see, in the first place, whether it admits of doubt that he did die of tetanus.

I have listened with great attention to every form in which that disease has been brought under your consideration — whether by the

---

[8] Courts did not allow defendants to testify in their defense until the 1880s.

positive evidence of witnesses, or by reference to the works of scientific writers — and I assert deliberately that no case, either in the human subject or in the animal, has been brought under your notice in which the symptoms of tetanus have been so marked as in this case.

From the moment the paroxysms came on in which the unhappy man died, the symptoms were of the most marked and striking character. Every muscle, says the medical man who was present at the time, was convulsed — he expressed the most intense dread of suffocation — he entreated them to lift him up lest he should be suffocated — every fibre of his body, from the crown of his head to the soles of his feet, was contracted — the flexibility of the trunk and of the limbs was gone — and you could only have raised him up as you would have lifted a corpse. In order that he might escape from the sense of suffocation they turned him over, and then, in the midst of that fearful paroxysm, one mighty spasm seems to have seized his heart, to have pressed from it the life-blood, and the result was death. And when he died his body exhibited the most marked symptoms of this fearful disease. He was convulsed from head to foot. You could have rested him on his head and heels — his hands were clasped with a grasp that it required force to overcome, and his feet were twisted so as to resemble a natural malformation.

Then, if it was a case of tetanus — into which fact I will not waste your time by inquiring — the question arises, was it a case of tetanus produced by strychnine? I will confine myself for a moment to the exhibition of the symptoms as described by the witnesses. Tetanus may proceed from natural causes as well as from the administration of poisons, and while the symptoms last they are the same. But in the course of the symptoms, and before the disease reaches its consummation in the death of the patient, the distinction between the two is marked by characteristics which enable any one conversant with the subject to distinguish between them.

We have been told that the distinctions are these — natural tetanus is a disease not of minutes, not of hours, but of days. It takes — say several witnesses — from three to four days; and will extend to a period of even three weeks before the patient dies. Upon that point we have the most abundant and conclusive evidence. We have examined Sir Benjamin Brodie, a man, I need scarcely say, of the most exalted eminence in his profession, Mr. Curling, Dr. Todd, Dr. Daniel, a gentleman who has seen between twenty-five and thirty cases of natural tetanus in India, and all these distinguished witnesses give exactly the same description of the course which the case invariably takes.

Idiopathic or natural tetanus, therefore, is out of the question. Traumatic tetanus is out of the question for a different reason. That description of disease is brought on by the lesion of some part of the body. But what is there in this case to show that there was anything like lesion at all?

We have had several representations of the death of Cook by witnesses who appear to have come into court — I say it with the deepest sorrow — for the express purpose of studiously misconceiving and misinterpreting the facts of this case. We have called before you an eminent physician who had Cook under his care. It seems that, in the spring of the year 1855, Cook, having found certain small spots in one or two parts of his body, and having something of an ulcerated tongue and a sore throat, conceived that he was labouring under symptoms of a particular character. He addressed himself to Dr. Savage, who found that the course of medicine he had been pursuing was an erroneous one. He enjoined the discontinuance of mercury. His injunction was obeyed, and the result was that the patient was suffering neither from disease nor wrong treatment. But lest there should be any possibility of mistake, Dr. Savage made him come to him again and again to see that all was going on well, and this medical witness assures us that long before the summer advanced every unsatisfactory symptom had entirely disappeared; there was nothing wrong about Cook except that affection of the throat to which thousands of people are subject.

In other respects the man was better than he had been, and might be said to be convalescent. On the very day that he left London to go into the country, a fortnight before the races, his stepfather, who accompanied him to the station, congratulated him upon his healthy and vigorous appearance; and the young man, conscious of restored health, struck his breast and said, "I am well, very well."

Then he goes to Shrewsbury, and shortly afterwards arose those matters to which I am about to call your attention. I want to know in what part of the evidence there is the slightest pretence for saying that this man had an affection which might bring on traumatic tetanus? It is said that he had exhibited his tongue to witnesses and applied for a mercurial wash, but it is clear that, although he had at one time adopted that course, he had, under the recommendation of Dr. Savage, got rid of it, and there is no justification for saying he was suffering under syphilitic affection of any kind. The statement has been negatived by a man of the highest authority and distinction. There is not a shadow of foundation for it, and I should be false to my duty if I did not denounce it as utterly undeserving of your attention. There was nothing about the man to give even a colour of probability to the supposition that there was in any part of his body any mark, wound, or lesion — syphilitic or otherwise — that could result in traumatic tetanus.

THE TIMES REPORT

One or two cases of traumatic tetanus have been adduced in the evidence which has been brought forward for the defence. One is the case of a man in the London Hospital, who was brought into that institution one evening and died the same night. But what are the facts? The facts are, that before he had been brought in he had had a paroxysm early in the morning, and that he was suffering from ulcers of the most aggravated description. The symptoms had run their course rapidly, it is true, but the case was not one of minutes, but of hours.

Another case has been brought forward in which a toe was amputated, but there we have disease existing some time before death. But then it is suggested that this may be a case of idiopathic tetanus proceeding from — what?

They say that Cook was a man of delicate constitution, subject to excitement; that he had something the matter with his chest; that in addition to having something the matter with his chest he had a diseased condition of throat; and, putting all these things together, they say that if the man had taken cold he might have got idiopathic tetanus.

We are here launched into a sea of speculations and possibilities. Dr. Nunneley, who comes here for the purpose of inducing you to believe there was something like idiopathic tetanus, goes through supposed infirmities, and talks about his excitability, his delicacy of chest, his affection of the throat, and he says these things would predispose to idiopathic tetanus if he took cold.

But what evidence is there that he did take cold? Not the slightest in the world. There is not the smallest pretence that he ever complained of a cold or was treated for a cold.

I cannot help saying that it is a scandal upon a learned, distinguished, and liberal profession that men should come forward with speculations and conjectures such as these, and that they should misinterpret facts and extract from them sophistical[9] and unwarrantable conclusions with the view of deceiving a jury. I have the greatest respect for science. No man can have a greater. But I cannot repress my indignation and abhorrence when I see it perverted and prostituted to the prejudice of truth in a court of justice. A medical witness has talked to you about certain excitements being the possible causes of idiopathic tetanus. You remember the sorts of excitement of which he spoke. They are unworthy of your notice. They were topics discreditable to be put forward by a witness as worthy of your consideration.

But suppose for a single moment that excitement at the time

---

[9] A plausible argument that contains an error that could deceive or mislead.

could produce any such effect, where is the excitement manifested by Cook as leading to the supposed disease? They say that the man when his horse won at Shrewsbury was for a moment excited. And well he might be. His fortunes depended upon the result of the race, and I will not deny that he was overpowered with emotions of joy. But those emotions subsided, and we have no further trace of them from that time to the moment of his death. The man passed the rest of the day with his friends in ordinary conversation and enjoyment. No symptom of emotion was exhibited. He is taken ill. He goes to Rugeley. He is taken ill there again. But is there the slightest symptom of excitement about him, or of depression? Not the least.

When he is ill, like most people, he is low-spirited. As soon as he gets a little better he is cheerful and happy. He invites his friends and converses with them. On the night of his death his conversation is full of merriment and joy; he is mirthful and happy; little thinking, poor wretch, of the awful fate that is hanging over him. He is cheerful and talks of the future, but not in language of frantic excitement.

What pretext, then, is there for this idle story about excitement so intense and convulsive as possibly to have excited idiopathic tetanus? There is not a shadow of a pretext for any such theory.

But even if there were excitement or depression — if these things were capable of producing idiopathic tetanus, the tetanus of disease is so unlike the tetanus of poison it is impossible to mistake the two. What are the cases which they attempt to set up against us? They brought all the way from Scotland a girl named Watson who deposed that, though she had not taken any poison, and had no wound of any kind on her body, she was attacked with a violent paroxysm in the month of October last year.

But in cross-examination it appeared that she had been ill all day, was taken worse at night, had a pain in her stomach and cramps in her arms, was for a while quite insensible, but soon recovered, and went about her business.

This is the case they have brought forward as a parallel for that mortal anguish — the spasms — the convulsions — the death agony of this unhappy man! This is the sort of evidence with which they attempt to meet the appalling case that now engages your attention.

Gentlemen, I venture, upon the evidence which has been brought before you, to assert boldly that the cases of idiopathic and traumatic tetanus are masked by clear and obvious characteristics — distinguishing them from the tetanus of strychnine; and I say that the tetanus which accompanied Cook's death is not referable to either of these forms of tetanus. It was the tetanus not of disease, but of poison.

You have upon this point the evidence of men of the highest

competency and most unquestionable integrity, and upon their testimony I am satisfied you can come to no other conclusion than that this was not a case of either idiopathic or traumatic tetanus.

But, then, various attempts have been made to set up various causes as capable of producing this tetanic disease. First, we have the theory of general convulsions; and Dr. Nunneley, having gone through the bead-roll[10] of the supposed infirmities of Cook, says, "Oh, this may have been a case of general convulsions — I have known general convulsions assuming a tetanic character." Therefore I asked him this question, "Have you ever seen one single case in which convulsions marked by tetanic symptoms were not also accompanied by entire unconsciousness on the part of the patient?" He replied, "No; I have never seen any such case, but I am told that in the books some such case is reported." And then he went on to cite Dr. Copland's book as an authority for the theory that general convulsions may be accompanied by tetanic symptoms.

Now, Dr. Copland, I apprehend, would stand higher as an authority than the man who quotes him. Dr. Copland might have been called, but was not called, notwithstanding the challenge that I threw out, because it is, unfortunately, easier to gather together from the east and from the west practitioners of more or less celebrity, than to bring to bear on the subject the light of science as treasured in the breasts of eminent practitioners.

But I say, as regards general convulsions the distinction is plain. If they destroy the patient they previously destroy his consciousness. But here we have no such state of facts. It is beyond all controversy that from the first moment of Cook's attack till his bursting heart ceased to beat consciousness remained.

But then comes another supposed condition, from which it is conjectured that death in this particular form may have resulted. It appears from the evidence that at the *post-mortem* examination certain granules were discovered in the spinal marrow of Cook, and it is attempted to be shown, upon authority of Mr. Partridge, — a surgeon, I admit, of the highest eminence and the most unblemished honour — that these granules may have occasioned tetanic convulsions. Mr. Partridge was called to prove that this may have been a case of what is called arachnitis,[11] arising from granules.

I asked him to explain the symptoms which he would find in such a case. I called his attention to what it had evidently not been called to before, namely, the symptoms in Cook's case, and I asked

---

[10] A list of names, derived from the practice begun in medieval times, of reading in church the names of parishioners for whom prayers should be said.
[11] An inflammation of the membrane protecting the central nervous system, including the spinal cord.

him in simple terms, whether, looking at the symptoms, he would pledge his reputation, in the face of the medical world and in the face of this Court, that this was a case of arachnitis? He would not do so, and the case of arachnitis went.

Then we had a gentleman from Scotland to inform us as the next proposition, that Cook's was a case of epileptic convulsions with tetanic complications. Well, I asked him this question, "Did you ever know of epilepsy, with or without tetanic complications, in which consciousness was not destroyed before the patient died!" His reply was, "No, I cannot say that I ever did, but I have read in some book that such a case has occurred." — "Is there anything to make you think this was epilepsy?" — "It may have been epilepsy, because I don't know what else it was." "But you must admit that epilepsy is characterised generally by loss of consciousness; what difference would the tetanic complications have made?" That he was unable to explain.

I remind you of this species of evidence that you may perceive that you have had before you witnesses who have resorted to the most speculative reasoning, and put forward the barest possibilities, in support of theories for which there is little if any foundation. But this I undertake to assert, that there is not a single case to which they have spoken from their experience, or as the result of their own knowledge, in which there were the formidable and decisive symptoms of marked tetanus which existed in the present case.

Having gone through these four sets of diseases — general convulsions, arachnitis, epilepsy proper, and epilepsy with tetanic complications, I supposed we had pretty nearly exhausted the whole of their scientific theories. But we were destined to have another, and that assumed the formidable name of angina pectoris. It must have struck you when my learned friend opened his case, that he never ventured to assert the nature of the disease to which they refer the death of Cook; and it strikes me as most remarkable that no less than five distinct and separate theories are set up by the witnesses who have been called — general convulsions, arachnitis, epilepsy proper, epilepsy with tetanic complications, and, lastly, angina pectoris. My learned friend had an advantage in not stating to you what his medical witnesses would set up, because I admit that one after another they took me by surprise.

The gentleman who was called yesterday, and who talked of angina pectoris, would not have escaped so easily if I had been in possession of the books to which he referred; for I should have been able to expose the ignorance or the presumption of the assertions he dared to make. I say the ignorance or the presumption, or, what is worse, the deliberate intention to deceive. I lay to his charge one or other of these three, and, in the presence of this Court, and in the face of the whole medical profession, I assert that one or other of these charges I should have been able to substantiate. The medical witnesses for the defence differ one and all in their views; but there is a remarkable coincidence between the opinions of some of them and the opinions of those who have been examined on the other side. All the medical men brought forward by the defence — Partridge, Robinson, and Letheby, concur with Sir B. Brodie and the other Crown witnesses in declaring that, in the whole course of their experience, and in the whole range of their learning and observation, they know of no disease to which the symptoms in Cook's case can be referred.

When such men as these agree upon any point it is impossible to exaggerate its importance. If it be the fact that there is no known disease which can account for such symptoms as those in Cook's case, and that they are referable to poison alone, can you have any doubt that that poison was strychnia? The symptoms, at all events, from the time the paroxysms set in, are precisely the same.

Distinctions are sought to be made by the sophistry of the witnesses for the defence between some of the antecedent symptoms and some of the others. I think I shall show you that these distinctions are imaginary, and that there is no foundation for them. I think I may say that the witnesses called for the defence admit this, that, from the time the paroxysm set in of which Cook died, until the time of his death, the symptoms are precisely similar to that of tetanus by strychnine. But then they say — and this is worthy of most particular attention — there are points of difference which have led them to the conclusion that these symptoms could not have resulted from strychnine.

In the first place, they say that the period which elapsed between the supposed administration of the poison and the first appearance of the symptoms is longer than they have observed in the animals on which they have experimented. The first observation which arises in this: that there is a known difference between animal and human life, in the power with which certain specific things act upon their organisation. It may well be that poison administered to a rabbit will produce its effect in a given time. It by no means follows that it will produce the same effect in the same time on an animal of a different description. Still less does it follow that it will exercise its baneful influence in the same time on a human subject.

The whole of the evidence on both sides leads to establish this fact, that not only in individuals of different species, but in individuals of the same species, the same poison and the same influence will produce effects different in degree, different in duration, different in power. But again, it is perfectly notorious that the rapidity with which the poison begins to work depends mainly upon the mode of its administration. If it is administered in a fluid state it acts with great rapidity. If it is given in a solid state its effects come on more slowly. If it is given in an indurated[12] substance it will act with still greater tardiness.

Then what was the period at which this poison began to act after its administration, assuming it to have been poison? It seems, from Mr. Jones's statement, that Palmer came to administer the pills somewhere about 11 o'clock, but they were not administered on his first arrival, for the patient, as if with an intuitive sense of the death that awaited him, strongly resisted the attempts to make him take them; and no doubt these remonstrances, and the endeavours to overcome them, occupied some period of time.

The pills were at last given. Assuming — which I only do for the sake of argument — that the pills contained strychnine, how soon did they begin to operate? Mr. Jones says he went down to his supper, and came back again about 12 o'clock. Upon his return to the room, after a word or two of conversation with Cook, he proceeded to undress and go to bed, and had not been in bed ten minutes before a warning came that another of the paroxysms was about to take place. The maidservant puts it still earlier, and it appears that as early as ten minutes before twelve the first alarm was given, which would make the interval little more than three-quarters of an hour. When these witnesses tell us that it would take an hour and a half, or two hours, we see here another of those exaggerated determinations to see the facts only in the way that will be most favourable to the prisoner.

I find in some of the experiments that have been made that the duration of time, before the poison begins to work has been little, if anything, less than hour. In the case of a girl at Glasgow it was stated that it was three-quarters of an hour before the pills began to work. There may have been some reason for the pills not taking effect within a certain period after their administration. It would be easy to mix them up with substances difficult of solution, or which might retard their action. I cannot bring myself to believe that if in all other respects you are perfectly satisfied that the symptoms, the consequences, the effects, were analogous, and similar in all respects to those produced by strychnine, you will conclude that in this case strychnine was not administered, and found your conclusion on the simple fact that a quarter of an hour more than usual may have elapsed before the pills operated.

---

[12] A substance that is made harder by the introduction of fibrous elements. In other words, the attorney general is saying that if the pill was made harder to dissolve, it will delay the effects of the poison.

But they say the premonitory symptoms were wanting. They assert that in the case of animals the animal at first manifests some uneasiness, shrinks, and draws itself into itself, as it were, and avoids moving; that certain involuntary twitchings about the head come on, and that there were no such premonitory symptoms in Cook's case.

I utterly deny the proposition. I say there were premonitory symptoms of the most marked character. He is lying in his bed; he suddenly starts up in an agony of alarm. What made him do that? Was there nothing premonitory there — nothing that warned him the paroxysm was coming on? He jumps up, says, "Go and fetch Palmer — fetch me help! I am going to be ill as I was last night!" What was that but a knowledge that the symptoms of the previous night were returning, and a warning of what he might expect unless some relief were obtained?

He sits up and prays to have his neck rubbed. What was the feeling about his neck but a premonitory symptom, which was to precede the paroxysms that were to supervene? He begs to have his neck rubbed, and that gives him some comfort.

But here they say this could not have been tetanus from strychnine, because animals cannot bear to be touched, for a touch brings on a paroxysm — not only a touch, but a breath of air, a sound, a word, a movement of any one near will bring on a return of the paroxysm.

Now, in three cases of death from strychnine we have shown that the patient has endured rubbing of the limbs, and received satisfaction from that rubbing. In Mrs. [Sarjantson] Smyth's case, when her legs were distorted, she prayed and entreated that she might have them straightened. The lady at Leeds, in the case which Dr. Nunneley himself attended, implored her husband between the spasms to rub her legs and arms in order to overcome the rigidity. That case was within his own knowledge, and yet in spite of it, although he detected strychnine in the body of the unhappy woman, he dares to say that Cook's having tolerated the rubbing between the paroxysms is a proof that he had not taken strychnine.

Then there is the case of Clutterbuck. He had taken an overdose of strychnine, and suffered from the reappearance of tetanus, and his only comfort was to have his legs rubbed.

Therefore, I say that the continued endeavour to persuade a jury that the fact of Cook's having had his neck rubbed proves that this is not tetanus by strychnine, shows nothing but the dishonesty and insincerity of the witnesses who have so dared to pervert the facts.

But they go further, and contend that Cook was able to swallow. So he was before the paroxysms came on. But nobody has ever pretended that he could swallow afterwards. He swallowed the pills, and, what is very curious, and illustrates part of the theory is this — that it was the act of swallowing the pills, a sort of movement in raising his head, which brought on the violent paroxysm in which he died. So far from militating against the supposition that this was a case of strychnine, the fact strongly confirms it.

Then they call our attention to the appearances after death, and they say there are circumstances to be found which go against this being a case of strychnine. They say the limbs became rigid either at the time of death or immediately after, and that ought not to be found in a case of strychnine.

Dr. Nunneley says, "I have always found the limbs of animals become flaccid before death, and I have not found them become rigid after death."

Now, I can hardly believe that statement. The very next witness who got into the box told us that he had made two experiments upon cats and killed them both, and he described them as indurated and contracted when he found them some hours after death. And yet the presence of rigidity in the body immediately after death is put forth by Dr. Nunneley as one of his reasons for saying that this is not a death by strychnine, although Dr. Taylor told us that, in the case of one of the cats, the rigidity of the body was so great that he could hold it out by the leg in a horizontal position. Notwithstanding that evidence Dr. Nunneley has the audacity to say that he does not believe this is a case of strychnine, because there was rigidity of the limbs, because the feet were distorted, the hands clinched, and the muscles rigid.

This shows what you are to think of the honesty of this sort of evidence, in which facts are selected because they make in favour of particular hypotheses of the person advancing them.

The next point relied on is that the heart was empty, and that in the animals operated upon by Dr. Nunneley and Dr. Letheby the heart was full. I don't think that applies to all cases. But it is a remarkable fact connected with the history of the poison that you never can rely upon the precise form of its symptoms and appearances. There are only certain great, leading, marked characteristic features. We have here the main, marked, leading characteristic features; and we have what is more — collateral incidents, similar to the cases in which the administration and the fact of death have been proved beyond all possibility of dispute.

Why, in two cases which have been mentioned — that of Mrs. [Sarjantson] Smyth and the Glasgow girl — the heart was compressed and empty. We know that in no cases of tetanus death may result from more than one cause. All the muscles of the body are subject to the exciting action of the poison. But no one can tell in what order these muscles may be affected, or where the poisonous influence will put forth. When it arrests the play of the lungs and the breathing of the atmospheric air, the result will be that the heart is full; but if some spasm seizes on the heart the heart will be empty. You have never any perfect certainty as to the mode in which the symptoms will exhibit themselves.

This is brought forward as a conclusive fact against death by strychnine, and yet the men who make this statement under the sanction of scientific authority have heard both cases spoken to by the gentlemen who examined the bodies.

Then, with regard to congestion of the brain, and other vessels, the same observation applies. Instead of being killed by action on the respiratory muscles of the heart, death is the result of a long series of paroxysms, and you expect to find the brain and other vessels congested by that series of convulsive spasms. As death takes place from one or other of these causes, so will the appearances be. There is every reason to believe that the symptoms in this case were symptoms of tetanus in the strongest and most aggravated form.

Looking at the peculiar sufferings which attended this unhappy man, setting aside the theory of convulsions, of epilepsy, of arachnitis, and angina pectoris, and excluding idiopathic and traumatic tetanus, what remains? The tetanus of strychnine, and the tetanus of strychnine alone.

And I pray your attention to the cases in which there was no question as to strychnine having been administered in which the symptoms were so similar — so analogous — that I think you cannot hesitate to come to the conclusion that this death was death by strychnine. Several witnesses of the highest eminence, both on the part of the Crown and for the defence, agree that in the whole range of their experience, observation, and knowledge, they have known of no natural disease to which these remarkable symptoms can be attributed. That being so, and there being a known poison which will produce them, how strong, how cogent, how irresistible is the conclusion that it is that poison, and that poison alone to which they are to be traced?

On the other hand, I am bound in candour to admit that the case is not without its difficulties. Strychnine was not found in this body, and we have it, no doubt, upon strong evidence, that in a great variety of experiments upon the bodies of animals killed by strychnine, strychnine has been detected by tests which science places at the disposal of scientific men. If strychnine had been found of course there would have been no difficulty in the case, and we should have had none of the ingenious theories which medical gentlemen have been called here to propound. But the question for your consideration is whether the absence of its detection leads conclusively to the conclusion that this death was not caused by the administration of strychnine?

Now, in the first place, under what circumstances was the examination made by Dr. Taylor and Dr. Rees? They have told us that the stomach of the man was brought to them for analysation under the most unfavourable circumstances. They state that the contents of the stomach had been lost, and that, therefore, they had no opportunity of experimenting upon them. It is true that they who put the portions of the body into the jar make statements somewhat different. But there appear to have been by accident some spilling of the contents, and there is the most undeniable evidence of considerable bungling in the way in which the stomach had been cut and placed in the jar. "It was cut," says Dr. Taylor, "from end to end, and it was tied up at both ends." It had been turned among the intestines, and placed among a mass of feculent matter, and was altogether in the most unsatisfactory condition for analysation.

It is very true that Dr. Nunneley, Mr. Herapath, and Dr. Letheby say that whatever impurities there may have been, if strychnine had been in the stomach they would have found strychnine there, no matter how decomposed or putrescent the organic matter might be. Bearing in mind Mr. Herapath's eminence in his profession, I should have had much confidence in his testimony were it not for the active and zealous feeling of partisanship which he has manifested on repeated occasions in the course of this inquiry.

It had come to my knowledge that he had been heard to assert that this was a case of death by strychnine, but that Dr. Taylor had not gone the right way to find out the poison. I pressed him urgently on this point, and I am sure you will be of the opinion with me that his explanation of his having formed his judgment merely from the newspaper reports, was anything but satisfactory. There can be no doubt that in his conscience Mr. Herapath believes this to be a case of death by poison — indeed he has said as much; and yet we have seen him mixing himself up in this case with all the enthusiasm of a partisan, and suggesting to my learned friend questions with a view to the protection of a man whom he feels to be guilty of murder.

I reverence the man who from a sense of justice and an innate love of truth, comes forward on behalf of any accused person who is in danger of being swept to destruction by the torrent of prejudice; but I have no language to express my abhorrence for that traffic testimony which from professional pique, or for the sustentation of a particular theory, men of science — I grieve to say it — occasionally are led to offer.

But assuming all that they say on the question of detecting

strychnine to be true, is it certain that the poison can be found in all cases? Dr. Taylor says, "No," and that it would be a most mischievous and dangerous proposition to assert that the poison must in all cases be detected, for such a theory might enable many a guilty man to escape who would take care to administer only such quantities as being large enough to destroy would not be large enough to admit of subsequent detection by analysis in the stomach.

What have these gentlemen done? They have given large doses in the experiments they have made for the purposes of this case, in which they have been "retained" — I use the word "retained" for it is the proper word — in all these cases, I say, they have given doses large enough to be detected. But the gentlemen who made the experiments in Cook's case failed in detecting strychnine in two cases out of four in which they had administered it to animals. The conclusion I draw is that there is no positive mode of detection.

But this case does not rest here. Alas, I wish it did! I must now draw your attention to one part of the case which has not been met or attempted to be disputed in the slightest degree by my learned friend. My learned friend said that he would contest the case for the prosecution step by step. Alas! we are now upon ground upon which my friend has not even ventured a word in explanation.

Was the prisoner at the bar possessed of the poison of strychnine? This is a matter with which it behoved my learned friend to deal, and to exhaust all the means in his power in order to meet this part of the case. The prisoner obtained possession of strychnine on the Monday night.

It may have been that Dr. Taylor did not go the right way to work. It may have been that Mr. Herapath would have found the strychnine, but the man who did experiment failed in two cases out of four to reproduce the poison with a similar test; and, although I cannot have the advantage which the positive detection of strychnine would have afforded, there is no room for the opposite conclusion, the converse of the proposition for which my learned friend and his witnesses contend, that the fact of strychnine not having been discovered affords negative conclusive proof that there was no strychnine there. I have no positive proof; but on the other hand my learned friend is in the same predicament. He cannot say that he has negative conclusive proof that this gentleman was not poisoned with strychnine.

But is there no other proof? Do I ask you to come to the conclusion that the prisoner administered strychnine to his friend simply because the symptoms are reconcileable with no form of disease with which the most enlarged experience and knowledge are acquainted? No, gentlemen, it does not rest there. Or, because these symptoms are precisely those which show themselves in cases of poisoning by strychnine?

No, the case does not rest there. I wish it did. I must draw your serious attention to a part of the case which has not been met or grappled with. My learned friend said that he would contest the ground with the prosecution foot by foot. Alas! we are now upon ground which is, as it were, entirely abandoned by the defence. Alas! with this part of the case my learned friend has not grappled at all. When death reached its dread manifestation was the prisoner at the bar possessed of that poison? Did he obtain it upon the eve of the death!

These are matters of fearful moment. They are matters upon which it behoved my learned friend to comment with all the vigour of which he is capable and all the means which this case afforded to him. Yet this part of the case he has left entirely untouched.

The prisoner at the bar obtained strychnine on the Monday night. He got it again on Tuesday morning. The fact of his having got it on Monday night rests, it is true, upon the evidence of a person whose statement, as I told you on the outset, and as I now repeat, requires at your hands the most careful and anxious attention before you convict the prisoner. This man, Newton, tells us, that on that night, after Palmer came back from London, he obtained from him three grains of the poison, which, had it been administered would have produced just the symptoms with which Cook was that night attacked.

Is Newton speaking the truth, or is he not? It is open to observation — I said so in the beginning, and my learned friend has done no more than to repeat the warning which I gave to you. It is open to serious observation that Newton never made that statement until the day previous to the commencement of this trial. He has explained to you the reasons which induced his silence. His employer had for a long time been upon unpleasant terms with Palmer. The young man, who appears to have been on more or less intimate terms with him, did not hesitate to give him three grains of strychnine. Palmer was a medical man, and there was, therefore, nothing extraordinary, at a time when the shops might be expected to be shut, in his asking for this strychnine. Newton gave it to him, and probably thought little more about it.

But when afterwards this question of the mode in which Cook's life had been taken away became rife in Rugeley, when suspicion of poisoning by strychnine arose, when Roberts came forward and said that on the Tuesday morning Palmer had purchased strychnine of him, when this young man was called to confirm the statement of Palmer having been at the shop, and heard that there was a question about strychnine, it seemed to him that it might seriously implicate him with his employer, and even cast a shadow of doubt and suspicion upon himself if he came forward voluntarily, and stated that he had supplied Palmer with poison on the night of Monday. Therefore he locked this secret in his breast.

When, however, the trial came on, and he knew that he would be subjected to examination here, he felt oppressed by this concealment, and voluntarily came forward and made the statement which he has repeated here.

It is for you to say whether you are satisfied with that explanation. It is unquestionably true that this long concealment detracts from the otherwise perfect credibility of this witness; but, on the other hand, there is a consideration which I cannot avoid pressing upon your attention. What possible conceivable motive, except a regard for truth, can this young man have had for coming forward on this occasion? My learned friend has, with justice and propriety, asked your most attentive consideration to the question of motives involved in this case. Before you convict a man of having taken away the life of another, it is important to see whether there were motives which could operate upon him.

But does that not equally apply to this witness? Even the odious crime of taking life by poison is not so horrible to contemplate as the notion of a judicial murder effected through a false witness. Can you suppose that this man Newton can have the remotest shadow of a motive for coming forward on an occasion like this, and, under the solemn sanction of an oath, taking away the life of a fellow man; for, alas! if you believe this evidence, it must take away life.

If you believe that on the night of Monday, without any conceivable or assignable purpose, except the deed of darkness which was to be done that night upon the person of Cook, the prisoner at the bar obtained from Newton a fatal and deadly instrument whereby life might be destroyed, it is impossible for you to come to any other conclusion than that the prisoner is guilty, and that conclusion you are bound to express in your verdict. What says my learned friend? He says that Newton does not speak the truth — firstly, because he did not make that statement until the last minute, and, secondly, because he fixes the time of his interview with the prisoner at 9 o'clock, the fact being that the prisoner was not at Rugeley until 10.

Now, in the first place, I must remark that the young man does not say "9 o'clock," he says, "about 9," and every one knows how easy it is to make a mistake of half an hour, three-quarters of an hour, or even of an hour, if your attention is not called to the circumstances until a week, a fortnight, or three weeks afterwards. A man may be reading in his study or his surgery, having no clock before him, and nothing occurring to impress upon his mind the precise hour at which the circumstance occurs; and to say that if he afterwards, when speaking under the sanction of an oath, makes a slight mistake as to time, he must therefore be taken to be speaking untruly as to all the circumstances, appears to me to be a most unsatisfactory and most untenable position.

It is true that my learned friend has sought to meet this part of the case. He has to-day produced a witness, of whom all I can say is, that I implore you, for the sake of justice, not to allow the man who stands at the bar to be prejudiced by that most unworthy and most discreditable witness. Of this I am sure, that to not one word which that man said will you attach the slightest value.

Before I come to him, however, I must make this remark. If Newton could not have been mistaken as to the time how is it possible that the prisoner should be so? That he was; because, on Tuesday morning, he told Dr. Bamford that he visited Cook between nine and ten o'clock the night before; and now there comes a witness who tells us that at ten minutes after ten o'clock he had not alighted from the car which brought him from Stafford, and therefore it must have been nearly half-past ten o'clock before he went to the Talbot Arms. The prisoner says that he saw Cook between nine and ten o'clock, and Lavinia Barnes, to whose testimony there is not attached the slightest shadow of discredit, asserts that he came to the hotel before nine o'clock. It is clear she must have been mistaken. He could not have been there much before ten o'clock. I am told that it takes about an hour to go from Stafford to Rugeley, and the prisoner therefore arrived at the latter place shortly before ten o'clock.

Of the statement of the witness who was called this morning, that he saw Palmer alight from the car, that they went together to see Cook, and afterwards went to Palmer's mother's and stayed there a certain time, so as to cover the whole evening, I ask you not to believe a single word, and I do so because I do not believe one single word of it to be true.

It is a remarkable fact, which perhaps has not escaped your attention, that my learned friend never opened one single word of that evidence. He said that he hoped, and believed that he should be able, to cover the period by evidence from Rugeley. Did he tell us who the witness was whom he was about to call and what he would prove; that Mr. Jeremiah Smith had been upstairs, and had been seen by some of the people at the inn going upstairs to Cook's room? No! He did not, for if he had, we should have had plenty of time to ascertain the truth or falsehood of this, and to meet Mr. Jeremiah Smith with evidence.

It is well when you are uncertain what a witness will say, or what case you can get up, not to disclose too much, because if you do you will be met with conflicting evidence — evidence better than that of the miserable man who to-day exhibited a spectacle which, in the whole course of my experience I have never seen surpassed in a court of justice. He calls himself a member of the legal profession. I blush for that profession that it numbers such a man upon its rolls. There was not one who heard him to-day who was not satisfied that that man came here to tell a false tale. There cannot be one who is not convinced that he has been mixed up in many of the villanies which, if not perpetrated, have been attempted to be perpetrated, and that he came now to save, if he can, the life of his companion and friend, the son of the woman with whom he has that intimacy which he to-day sought in vain to disguise.

Looking at all these circumstances, balancing the evidence on both sides, and seeing that Newton cannot possibly have any motive for coming here to give false evidence (which must be fatal to a man whom, if that evidence be not true, he must believe to be innocent) — and to suppose that he would do so without a motive is to suppose human nature to be a hundred times more wicked and perverse than in its worst and most repulsive form experience has ever found it to be, — I cannot but submit to you that you ought to believe that evidence. If you believe it, it is conclusive.

But the case does not stop there. We have the clearest and most unquestionable evidence that on the morrow of that day Palmer bought six grains more strychnine at Hawkins's shop.

The circumstances attending that purchase are peculiar. He comes to the shop and gives an order for prussic acid. Having got the prussic acid he gives an order for strychnine. Before the strychnine is put up, Newton — the man from whom he had got the strychnine on the previous night — came into the shop.

What does the prisoner do? He immediately takes Newton by the arm, says that he has something particular to say to him, and leads him to the door. What was it he had to say? Was it anything particular? Was it anything of the slightest importance? Was it anything which might not have been said in the presence of Roberts?

Certainly not. It was to ask Newton when young Mr. Salt was going to a farm which he had taken. In that question there was nothing to prevent its being put in the presence of anybody whatever.

At the same time a person named Brassington comes up, who has something to say to Newton about some bills which Mr. Salt owed him. Brassington and Newton get into conversation a short distance from the door; the prisoner immediately takes advantage of their being engaged in conversation, goes back and completes the purchase of the strychnine. While the strychnine is being made up, however, he stands in the doorway with his back to the shop and his face to the street, so as to have a perfect command of the persons of Newton and Brassington, and to be in such a position that, if their conversation had ended and Newton had been returning to the shop, he might have taken positive steps to prevent his going in until the strychnia had been safely put up.

I ask you whether, having this description of the transaction given to you by Roberts, and confirmed by Newton, you can have any reasonable doubt that the prisoner was anxious to prevent Newton knowing that he was purchasing strychnia. You can very well understand why he should have that desire; because, if it be true that Newton let him have three grains the night before, his attention would naturally have been roused by so strange a circumstance as the purchase of six grains on the following day. Three grains were sufficient to kill three, perhaps six people. What could a man want with nine within so short a space of time? Therefore it would attract Newton's attention; and it did, for he immediately asked what Palmer had wanted there? — for he was, in the first place, surprised that Palmer, who had two years before withdrawn his custom from Mr. Hawkins, and given it to his former assistant, Thirlby, should have been at the shop at all. It was remarkable that he should, on this occasion, go to Hawkins's shop to get the strychnia. Why did he not go to Thirlby?

I will tell you. Thirlby would have known perfectly well that he would have no legitimate use for such an article. Thirlby had taken his practice. Palmer no longer practised, except in a small circle of his relatives and particular friends; and if he had gone to Thirlby for strychnia, Thirlby would naturally have asked what he was going to do with it? Therefore he did not go to Thirlby.

I agree with my learned friend that it is one of the mysteries of the case why he should have purchased strychnia on two successive days; but that he did so is undeniably true; and if some little difficulty arise from this, is it not infinitely more difficult to account for the motive which could have induced him to purchase strychnia either on the Monday night or the Tuesday? If it were for professional use — for the benefit of some patient to whom small doses might be advantageous, where is that patient? why is he not produced? My learned friend did not in his powerful address even advert to the question of the second day's purchase of strychnia. He passed it over in mysterious but significant silence. Account for that six grains of strychnia, the purchase of which is an undoubted and indisputable fact!

Throw doubt if you please — I blame you not — upon the story of the previous night, but it is unquestionably true that on the Tuesday six grains of strychnia were purchased by the prisoner. Purchased for whom — purchased for what? If for any patient, who is that patient? Produce him. If for any other purpose, at least let us have it explained. Has there been the slightest shadow of an attempt to explain it? Alas! I grieve to say none — none.

At the outset of the case something was said about some dogs which had been troublesome in the paddocks where the mares and foals were kept, but that proved to have been in September. If there had been any recurrence of such a thing, where are the grooms who had the charge of these horses? Why are they not here to state the fact? If this poison was used to destroy dogs, some one must have assisted Palmer in the attempts which he made for that purpose. Where are they? Why are they not called? Not only are they not called, they are not even named. My learned friend does not venture to go into the question.

I ask you, gentlemen, what conclusion can we draw from all these things, save one? Death in all the convulsive throes and agonies which that fatal poison produces in the frame of man — death with all the appearances which follow upon such an end, and mark how it has come to pass; these things leading in the minds of those who can discuss and consider them with calm and dispassionate attention, who do not mix themselves up with the case as advocates or partisans — leading to one and but one conclusion; and then the fact of strychnia having been purchased by the prisoner on the day of this horrible death — even if it were not, as sworn to, obtained by him also on the previous night — and this part of the case left wholly uncovered, wholly unmet, without a shadow of explanation! Alas! is it possible that you can come to any other conclusion than the one dreadful one of guilt? I protest I can suggest none.

But, said my learned friend, why should Palmer have purchased strychnia in Rugeley when he might have got it in London? I feel the force of the observation; and if he could have shown that he had done anything with the strychnia which he undoubtedly did purchase — if he could have shown any legitimate purpose to which it was intended to be applied, then I should say that that would be a matter worthy of our gravest and most attentive consideration.

But let us see how the facts stand. He was in town on the Monday, and had the opportunity, as my learned friend suggests, of purchasing strychnia there. On the other hand, he had much to do on that day. He had the train to catch at a certain hour, and, in the meantime, he had his pecuniary embarrassments to solve if he could. Time may have flown too fast to permit him to purchase this strychnia. Even if it had not, I do not believe that strychnia is sold in chemists' shops without the requisite of some name or voucher; and it would have been worse to have bought strychnia in London than at home. I do not say that this is not a difficulty in the case — a matter well worthy of your consideration; but, on the other hand, I say that there is proof of the purchase of strychnia under circumstances which cannot fail to lead to the conclusion that he shrunk from the observation of Newton at the time that he was buying it; and there is a total absence of all proof — nay, of all suggestion, of any legitimate purpose to which that fatal poison was intended to be, or was, in point of fact, afterwards applied.

But it is said that there are other circumstances in the case which make strongly in favour of the prisoner, and negative the presumption of a guilty intention. One of these facts is, that he called in two medical men. I admit that this is a matter to which all due consideration ought to be given. He called in Mr. Bamford on Saturday, and on Sunday he wrote to Mr. Jones, desiring his presence with his sick friend. It is quite true that, as medical men, they would be likely to know the symptoms produced by strychnia, and to suspect that death had been caused by it.

But here I am struck by one of the single inconsistencies in which the witnesses for the defence involved my learned friend. If all these were not exclusively the symptoms of strychnia, if they were referrible to that multiform variety of diseases of which these witnesses have spoken, why should the prisoner have the credit of having selected medical men who would be likely to know that these were symptoms of poisoning by strychnia?

But I pass that by; it was matter of minor importance. It is true that he did have these two medical men. He called in old Mr. Bamford. I speak of that gentleman in terms of perfect respect, but I think I do him no injustice if I say that the vigour of his intellect and his power of observation have been impaired — as all human powers are liable to be impaired — by the advance of life. I do not think that he was a person likely to make very shrewd observations upon any symptoms that might be exhibited to him either immediately after death, or upon a *post-mortem* examination. The best proof of this is to be found in that which he has done and written.

To Mr. Jones the same observation does not apply. He was a young man, in the full possession of his intellect and professional knowledge, yet the prisoner appears to have selected his man well; for what has come to pass shows how wisely he judged what was likely to be the case. This death occurred in the presence of Mr. Jones with all those fearful symptoms which you have heard described, yet Mr. Jones suspected nothing, and if Mr. Stevens had not come down — if he had not exhibited that sagacity and firmness which he did manifest — if Palmer had succeeded in getting the corpse hastily introduced into the strong oak coffin which he had had made for it, the body would have been consigned to the grave, and nobody would have been the wiser; the presence of Mr. Jones and the attendance of Mr. Bamford would not have led to detection — would not have frustrated the designs which I shall presently contend before you that this death was to accomplish.

On the other hand, the matter is, perhaps, capable of this explanation. It may have been that a man whose skill was equal to his boldness may have thought that the best course to adopt to avoid suspicion, and to prevent its possibility, was to take care that medical men should be called in, and should be present at the death; nor is there anything to show that he (Palmer) had the slightest information that Mr. Jones intended to sleep in Cook's room. Had he not done so, his friend would have been found dead in the morning; he would have gone through his mortal struggle; of intense and fearful agony — would have died alone and untended — and would, next morning, have been found dead in bed. The old man would have said it was apoplexy; the young man that it was epilepsy. If any one had whispered suspicion, the same argument would have been used which has been used now with so much power and force by my learned friend — "Can you suspect a man who called in medical men to be witnesses of the death?"

But, gentlemen, if pills were on the Monday night administered to Cook by Palmer — and that I believe will be your conclusion, notwithstanding the statement made by the witness to-day, that he heard Cook say to Palmer that he had taken the pills already because he was so late; for the witness Mills told you that when next morning Cook reminded her of the agony which she had seen him go through the night before, he said that he ascribed it to the pills which Palmer had given him at half-past 10 o'clock — If you believe that statement that the pills were given to him at half-past 10 o'clock, if you find that a few short minutes before, Palmer had purchased poison, and if you find that on that first night there were paroxysms, which, though not so violent, were analogous in character to those of Tuesday night, can you doubt that on that evening Palmer administered this poison? For what purpose I know not; I can only speculate. It may be that he intended by some minute dose to bring about convulsions which should not have the complete character of tetanus, which should resemble natural convulsions, and which should justify his afterwards saying that those of the next evening were merely a succession of similar fits, and that the man has died of convulsions. It may be that he on the Monday night attempted to carry out his fatal purpose to its fullest extent, but that the poison did not take effect. We hear that an inferior form of this poison called brucia is occasionally sold, and it may have been — but this is only speculation. I cannot tell.

I only know that Palmer purchased poison on the Tuesday, and that on that night Cook died with all the symptoms of that poison; that the poison is not now in any way accounted for; that the symptoms, though greater in intensity were the same in character on the Tuesday as on the Monday night; and I cannot avoid the conclusion to which my reasoning power irresistibly compels me, that the poison was administered on the first night, but failed, and that on the second it took fatal effect.

Alas! it does not stop there. There is another part of this case, which although it does not immediately refer to the cause of death, is still of considerable importance. We have had witnesses — medical men and analytical chymists — and they have told us a great deal about strychnine, but not one word about antimony.

On the Wednesday night, at Shrewsbury, this man drinks a glass of brandy-and-water, fancies there is something in it that burns his throat, exclaims at the time and is immediately seized with vomiting. On the same night Mrs. Brooks sees the prisoner shaking something in a glass, evidently dissolved in some fluid. A man has been called to-day — the boon-companion, chosen associate, and racing confederate of the prisoner — to come and tell you that all that was nothing — the woman never came, Palmer never carried out the brandy-and-water; there is not a word of fact in it; Palmer and Cook only came in at 12 o'clock, and this Mr. Myatt had been waiting for them two hours. This story is, according to him an entire invention from beginning to end, and he swears that if anything had been put into the brandy-and-water he must have seen it, and that nothing was.

I think you will be more ready to believe Mrs. Brooks than people who have been the associates of the prisoner and the partners in his transactions. It is a remarkable fact that Cook drinks this brandy-and-water, and is immediately taken ill. Other people were taken ill at Shrewsbury, and it may be that this illness of Cook's was only some form of the same complaint. I do not want to press it further than I ought; but it is remarkable that a man should be seen holding a tumbler to the light, and immediately afterwards one who is drinking at the same table with him, and who, if Myatt is telling the truth, was then somewhat in liquor, and therefore ought not to have been pressed by Palmer to take any more, is told by him as an inducement to drink, that he (Palmer) will not take any more until he has drunk his glassful, and afterwards that man is taken ill. These are circumstances which are not incapable of exciting suspicion; but I will pass from them to what occurred at Rugeley.

THE TIMES REPORT

From the Saturday until the Monday morning this poor man suffered from vomiting. It is clear that could not have been the Shrewsbury disease. He had got rid of that, and was well upon the Thursday and Friday. It was not until the Saturday morning, the day after he had been dining with Palmer, that he was taken ill.

Then we have Palmer administering remedies and sending over toast-and-water and broth, and whenever these are taken Cook is seized with incessant vomiting. The broth is said to-day, by Mr. Jeremiah Smith, to have been sent by him from the Albion; but it is taken, not to the Talbot Arms, but to the prisoner's kitchen. What is done with it there? Instead of leaving it, as one would have expected, to the woman who was to take it to the Talbot Arms, Palmer himself takes it from the fire, puts it into a cup, and gives it to her to take over; it is taken over, and as soon as Cook has drunk it he vomits and is ill for the whole day.

On Sunday the same thing occurs again. Broth is brought from the same quarter, and attended by the same results. Of that broth a woman took a couple of spoonfuls; and with what results? She is sick for some hours, vomits twenty times, and is unable to leave her bed for five or six hours.

It is urged by my learned friend that she did not state this before the coroner. Perfectly true, she did not. Nevertheless, it is the fact, because it is sworn to by the other servant, who perfectly remembers her being ill. I quite understand why she did not at first mention it, and to me it shows the honesty and simplicity of the woman's character. It did not at first occur to her to connect the sickness from which she suffered with the taking of the broth; but afterwards, when the question of antimony came up, and Cook's sickness was connected with it, she remembered perfectly well, after her evidence had been given, how she had taken the broth and immediately afterwards became ill.

The fact is not now capable of dispute. It may be that she did not mention it at the inquest, but it is undoubtedly the fact as she states it, and I think you will deem it to be an important and significant fact.

On Monday Palmer is absent and Cook is better. On Tuesday he vomits again, though not to the same extent. After the death — now comes the important fact — antimony is found in the tissues of his body and in his blood. Its presence in the blood shows that it must have been taken recently — within the last forty-eight hours before his death. How came it there? The small quantity that is found does not afford the slightest criterion of the quantity that had been administered to him. Part of it would be thrown up by the act of vomiting, and part would pass away by other means; but none would be there unless he had taken it.

Now, what did he take it for? I find that he is suffering from vomiting for days before his death; the prisoner is constantly administering things to him, and after taking these he vomits; the prisoner sends over a basin of broth for his especial use, and a woman servant taking two spoonfuls of it is for many hours reduced to the same condition as himself; antimony is an irritant which will produce vomiting and retching.

To what other conclusion, then, can you come than that antimony must have been given to him by some one, and who is there but the prisoner at the bar who could have given it? My learned friend says that he might have taken some at a former time — he might have taken James's powder. Is there the slightest trace of his having, during the whole period over which this evidence extends, ever taken that medicine? Moreover, as I have just said, the antimony was in the blood, and therefore must have been taken within 48 hours before death. I ask you to form your own judgment, but I submit that the conclusion is irresistible.

For what purpose was it administered? It is difficult to say with anything like precision. We can only speculate. It may have been to produce an appearance of natural disease and to account for the calling in of the medical men, and for the catastrophe which was then in contemplation; but it may also have had a different object. If we are right as to the motive which impelled the prisoner to commit this great crime, it was, at all events, in part that he might possess himself of the money which Cook was to receive on the Monday at Tattersall's. Cook intended to go himself to receive it. If he had done so the prisoner could not have obtained the money; but by making Cook ill at Shrewsbury he got him to go to Rugeley instead of to London or anywhere else; and the making him ill and keeping him ill at Rugeley, at all events over Monday, might be part of a cleverly contrived scheme.

It might have been with one or other of these designs, or it might have been with both that the antimony was administered, but that sickness was produced and antimony was afterwards found in the body are facts incapable of dispute.

If you are satisfied that antimony was given to Cook to produce vomiting and sickness, then I say that there is no one who can have given it to him within the period within which it must have been taken, except the prisoner at the bar. Neither the doctor at Shrewsbury, nor the doctor at Rugeley ever gave him one fraction of antimony. If you are satisfied that the prisoner gave him the antimony which produced these natural effects, can it have been given with any other view than that of paving the way for the more important act which was to follow? You cannot arrive at any conclusion but that the antimony was given for the purpose I have stated.

See the important influence which this circumstance exercises upon the case. Antimony can have been given with no legitimate object, it can have been given by no one but the prisoner at the bar; the conclusion therefore is that, in order to carry out the purpose he had in his mind, he administered that antimony of which the effects have been proved.

It is important, next, to consider the conduct of the prisoner in the after stages of the transaction, and I fear that if you look at it in all its circumstances you will find but too cogent reason to believe his guilt.

Let us begin with a remarkable incident that took place on Tuesday, the day of the death. The deceased has had what every one admits to have been a most severe fit the night before, and Dr. Bamford comes in, but not a word does the prisoner say to him about it; he is even very solicitous that Dr. Bamford should not see Cook, for twice in the course of the morning, when the doctor expressed a desire to go to him, he says, "No; he is tranquilly dozing, don't disturb him." If Dr. Bamford had seen the young man, possibly he would have told him what had happened the night before.

In the meanwhile Mr. Jones arrives. One would expect Mr. Jones having been invited to come by the prisoner for the express purpose of seeing Cook, that the first thing the prisoner would mention would be how he had found the unfortunate man that morning. Instead of that, he talks of nothing but bilious symptoms; "bilious," at Shrewsbury, "bilious," to Dr. Bamford, "bilious" to Mr. Jones, and yet all the medical men agree that there were no bilious symptoms, no fever, no unnatural pulse!

The moment Jones sees him, he says, referring to the letter he had received from the prisoner, "This is not a bilious attack; here is no diarrhœa." The answer is, "You should have seen him before." Not one single word is said about the fit of the night before.

The three medical men consult at the patient's bedside, and the only remarkable circumstance which then occurs is, that the patient turns round and says, "Mark, I'll have no more pills or medicine to-night," thus intimating that he ascribed his suffering on the previous night to the pills and medicine he had taken. No observation is even then made by Palmer as to the nature of the night attack.

They go into the lobby and converse about what is the best thing to be done. The man has declared his strong aversion to take pills or medicine, and Palmer proposes that Bamford should make up some pills like those of the night before, but says to Jones — "Don't tell him their contents, for he has a strong objection to them."

Then it is arranged that these pills shall be made up, and Palmer, instead of waiting, although it is early in the evening, accompanies Bamford home. I cannot for the life of me understand what necessity there was for Bamford to make up those pills. The prisoner might have made them up himself in two minutes; instead of which he goes with Bamford and gets him to make them up and write a direction on them. He then takes them away, and an interval of an hour or two occurs, during which he has abundant opportunity of going to his surgery and substituting others for them. He then goes to Cook, but before administering the pills he calls the attention of Jones to the handwriting on the direction as being remarkable for a man at such an advanced age as Bamford.

Was it not, think you, part of the scheme, in case a question should afterwards arise as to the cause of the man's death, that he should say — Why you know the pills were Bamford's. Were you not present at the bedside when I administered them? Did I not call your attention to the handwriting on the direction? Who knows that such a circumstance might not have prevented suspicion from being excited?

No one of these circumstances in itself, gentlemen, could be, I venture to submit to you, conclusive as to the guilt or innocence of the prisoner; but I ask your attention to the series of facts following closely one upon the other — facts of the most remarkable character — facts which can, I think, lead you but to one conclusion.

Death having taken place after a short interval, the father-in-law arrives. What is now the conduct of the prisoner? The father-in-law applies to him for information on the subject of the son's attack, and hearing that he had died in comparative poverty something is said as to burying him. "Well," says Mr. Stevens, "rich or poor, poor fellow, he must be buried."

Palmer interposes — "If that is all, I'll bury him myself." The brother-in-law also expresses a desire to bury him; but Stevens says, "No, I will do it."

Now, Palmer may have most innocently made the offer to bury his friend, but this remarkable circumstance follows:— Mr. Stevens expresses his regret at putting the people of the inn to inconvenience, but says that he wishes the body to remain there two or three days, so that it may be taken to London and laid in the mother's grave. "Oh, there is no harm in that," says Palmer, "the body can stay as long as you like, but it ought to be put in a coffin immediately." Mr. Stevens then gets into a conversation with his son-in-law, during which Palmer slips away. He returns in about half-an-hour, and Mr. Stevens, upon asking him for the name of an undertaker, finds that Palmer has taken on himself, without any authority, to order a shell and a strong oak coffin, in order that the body might be immediately enclosed. Why should he meddle in a matter that did not concern him, but that he had made up his mind that the body should be consigned to its last resting place and be removed as soon as possible from the sight of man?

You have heard what further conversation took place on that occasion, and I now come to the Saturday when Palmer and Mr. Stevens met upon the railway and had some conversation at various stations between London and Stafford. Mr. Stevens having seen the corpse with its clinched hands, that and other circumstances had engendered suspicions in his mind which he was determined to satisfy, and he made known to Palmer his resolution to have the body opened and examined. It is but fair to Palmer to observe that he did not flinch from the trying ordeal of Mr. Stevens's scrutizing glance when the *post-mortem* examination was mentioned.

But what does he do afterwards? He is anxious to know who is to perform the operation, but Mr. Stevens will not inform him. It is to take place on the Monday, and on the Saturday occurs that remarkable conversation with Newton which was not stated by him before the coroner, but which had been in possession of the Crown for some time. He did not state it before the coroner because he was only called to corroborate the evidence of Roberts with regard to the purchase of strychnine, and no questions were put to him except upon that point, but he afterwards communicated it to the Crown.

What is his statement? He is sent for by Palmer, he goes to Palmer's house, he is treated with brandy-and-water, and suddenly Palmer says, "What strychnine would you give if you wanted to kill a dog?" — "From half a grain to a grain," is the reply.

"Would you expect to find any appearance in the stomach after death?" — "No."

Upon which there is a kind of half ejaculation from Palmer, accompanied with a motion of the hand, "That's all right!"

Do you believe that conversation? It may have proceeded from two causes. It may be that the prisoner was in a state of great anxiety with regard to the *post-mortem* examination, and wished to know whether the views of another medical man as to the appearance of a body after death from strychnine coincided with his own. It may be that he meditated some jugglery which involved the total destruction of the body; it may be that he contemplated an attempt to poison a dog in order to account for the purchase of strychnine which he knew could be proved against him.

Whether any such attempt was made I know not. I surmised that some evidence to that effect would have been brought forward, but it has not — not the slightest account has been given as to how the strychnine that was purchased was disposed of. Has it been found among the prisoner's effects? If not what has become of it? This and many other matters remain enveloped in mystery, but in no aspect can I look at it in which it does not reflect light on the darkness in which the whole transaction is involved.

But I will now leave that conversation and the other matters of a similar kind in your hands. It is for you to say whether you entertain any doubt that the death of Cook was caused by strychnine, or that strychnine was administered by the prisoner from the quantity he bought either on the Monday or the Tuesday.

But my learned friend says that the man had no motive to take away Cook's life. If, gentlemen, I have satisfied you beyond the reach of reasonable doubt that the death was caused by strychnine, if the evidence for the defence has failed to neutralise that evidence, and to show that it was not so caused, if I have also shown that strychnine could have been administered by no one but Palmer, the question of motive becomes a matter of secondary consideration.

It is often difficult to dive into the breast of man, to discover the motives working there, and by them account for actions. If facts are proved against a man beyond the possibility of reasonable doubt, it is not because we may not have sufficient scrutinising power to ascertain his motives that we are to doubt these facts. Nevertheless, the question of whether there was a motive for the commission of the crime is no doubt an important element in the case. But we must recollect that that which to the good would appear no motive at all — that which would not exercise the remotest influence in inducing them to commit a crime, will often exercise a strong influence upon the bad.

Palmer, as I have before said, was in circumstances of the direst embarrassment, with ruin actually staring him in the face, which nothing could avert save pecuniary means at once procured. The proofs I have offered fully come up to my opening statement upon that point. In November, 1854, it appears that Palmer was in this position, — He owed upon bills, all of them forged, the sum of £19,000. Of this, £12,500 was in the hands of Pratt; £6,500 was in the hands of Wright, and two of the bills (£2,000 each) held by Pratt were overdue.

It is quite clear that the prisoner looked to the £13,000 which he hoped to obtain on Walter Palmer's policy as the means of relieving himself. He was disappointed, the Insurance-office, for reasons that I will not now discuss, declining payment, and Pratt then gave him to understand in distinct terms that the bills must be met. Bills for £4,000 were becoming due at the end of the month, and it was necessary immediately to obtain the sum of £5,500. Pratt gave notice that he could grant no longer delay inasmuch as the office had resolved to dispute the policy, and it was no longer a valid security, and he could not represent it as such to his clients who, he said, had discounted the bills.

Palmer pays two sums of £250, and one of £300 — in the whole £800. But £200 goes for the renewal of the bills, leaving only £600 applicable to the principal. He is told at once that he must do a great deal more, or writs will be issued against his mother and himself.

He knows that this must bring matters to a termination, he entreats that the writs may not be served, and obtains the concession that they shall not be served until May, he undertaking to make further payments in the interval.

On the 13th of November, Pratt presses for further payments. On that day Polestar won. Cook was in an ecstacy of delight feeling that his difficulties were overcome for the time, and he should now have cash to carry him through the winter until the spring races.

Little did he think what was about to take place! If the accusation against the prisoner be true, the winning of that mare, and his becoming entitled to a large sum of money, was the most fatal accident that could possibly have befallen him.

Alas, how great is the shortsightedness of mortal man! Where we deem we have the greatest cause for joy we often find the destruction of our prosperity and happiness, while calamities which for the moment seem fatal may produce in the end the most beneficial results. From that fatal day, if the prisoner be guilty, was the poor young man doomed.

It became perfectly clear to Palmer at that moment that an important crisis was approaching. What was he to do? He had no source to which to turn for money. He could not go to his mother; that source had clearly been long since exhausted, or he need not have forged her name. How could he satisfy Pratt's demands? Pratt is a kind, indulgent man as long as he is certain of payment, as long as his security is satisfactory; but let that once become doubtful, you may as well ask for pity from the rabid tiger, as well seek for mercy from a stone as from him. He gives fair warning that the bills must be met or instalments paid to keep them down. Where is the money to come from?

My learned friend says, Cook was Palmer's best friend, and as long as he kept Cook alive there was a friend in need to whom he could resort for assistance. But in what way could Cook assist him? Would Cook give acceptances to Pratt? Would Pratt accept Cook's acceptances unless the instalments of principal and interest were paid to the day? Clearly he would not, for he had refused to take Cook's personal security for the £500 without the further security of an assignment of the horses. Cook had already assigned the whole of his property as security for £500, and all that he possessed in the world was his winnings upon the races, part of which he had received at Shrewsbury and part he was to receive at Tattersall's. Yet you are asked to believe that he would still be useful to Palmer as a resource.

On the other hand, just see what interest Palmer had in his death. My learned friend says they were mixed up in various transactions, they were confederates on the turf; but "putting on" horses for one another would not make Cook responsible for Palmer's liabilities. Can anyone suppose that Cook ever intended to find means to enable Palmer to meet Pratt's insatiable demands — to leave himself destitute in order to secure his friend? Yet that is the proposition which my learned friend has to establish before he can contend that it was Palmer's interest that Cook should live rather than that he should die.

My learned friend says that proof of their being mixed up in several transactions is to be found in Cook's letter to his agent, Fisher (written on the Friday after dining with Palmer):—

"It is of great importance, both to Mr. Palmer and myself, that a sum of £500 should be paid to a Mr. Pratt, of 5, Queen-street, Mayfair, to-morrow, without fail. £300 has been sent up to-night, and if you will be kind enough to pay the other £200 to-morrow, on the receipt of this, you will greatly oblige me, and I will give it to you on Monday at Tattersall's."

I submit that this transaction is fatal to my learned friend's arguments. Its explanation is to me as clear as the sun at noonday. Cook had brought with him £600 or £700 from Shrewsbury. He had not had time to spend it since it was seen in his possession. There was only one transaction with Pratt in which he and Palmer could have had a common interest, and that was the £500 loan raised by the assignment of Polestar. The £200 was advanced by Fisher, but who knows that the £300 ever was sent up that night? It was not sent up. Then where is it to be found? Where has Cook's money gone? I can understand his handing over £300 to Palmer to pay Pratt, and requesting Fisher to make up the other £200, but on account of what transaction? Why, on account of the loan raised by the assignment of the mare which had just won at Shrewsbury, and which he naturally wished to redeem, knowing that the bill was becoming due and that he had money to receive on Monday at Tattersall's. That is the only transaction with Pratt in which they had a common interest. Except with regard to this £500, Pratt had nothing to do with Cook.

How then does this letter apply? It shows that Cook sent to Fisher, asking him to advance £200 for the purpose of redeeming the mare, that he gave another £300 for the same purpose, and that the £300 was not applied to that purpose.

What was done with it? Was it carried to the joint account? No such thing. It went towards the payments from Palmer to Pratt, and it is a false pretence to say that Cook was in any way responsible for any bills besides the one of £500, although it might be intended to represent that he was so responsible when he was no more.

The matter does not stop there. I now come to the transaction of the Monday when £1,020 of Cook's money was applied to the prisoner's use. He goes to London and ascertain by some means the amount Cook has to receive. Probably Cook had desired him to hand the account to Fisher, who was to go to Tattersall's and receive the money. We know that he did not do it; but, says my learned friend, Cook, in concert with Palmer, meditated a fraud; they intended to apply the £200 which ought to have been repaid to Fisher to their own use. That is nothing but a surmise, and there is no reason to believe that Cook would have consented to be a party to any such transaction.

Observe, that if the prisoner's representation to Cheshire was true, he had a genuine cheque of Cook's for the whole sum he was to receive from Messrs. Weatherby on account of the Shrewsbury stakes. Is it a reasonable proposition that he would hand over to the prisoner the whole £1,020 he was to receive?

However, he goes to London, and instead of proceeding to Fisher, Cook's regular agent, who would have repaid himself his advance of £200 out of the money to be received at Tattersall's, and who would not have parted with the balance except on Cook's authority, he takes the account to a stranger, who had never before acted as Cook's agent, and who therefore has no hesitation in paying the money according to the directions of the man who had authorised him to receive it. He gives Mr. Herring the list of bets Cook has to receive at Tattersall's, and how does he direct him to dispose of them? He says to Herring, "Pay yourself £200, pay Pratt £450, and pay Padwick £350."

It is clear that this £450 was a debt from Palmer to Pratt, and it is untrue that Cook had anything to do with it. With regard to Padwick's debt, there is evidence that Palmer treated it as his own. Both Pratt and Padwick were getting impatient for their money, and Padwick would no doubt have resented the non-payment of a debt of honour, which no doubt this was, by enforcing the early payment of Palmer's £1,000 bill.

That event did actually come to pass, for in consequence of Mr. Herring not having received all the money he had expected to receive at Tattersal's, Padwick was not paid, and put the law in motion to recover the amount of his bill. A large portion, if not the whole £350, was a debt of Palmer's, the £450 was a payment on account of

Palmer's liabilities, and the £200 was a payment in respect of one of Palmer's acceptances. Thus he had a clear interest in the appropriation of the money; it was his only means of staving off the evil hour.

The degree of motive must not be measured by this alone. He knew that not only might process be, at any moment, issued against him on account of the bills, but that the moment the law was put in motion, the crimes of which he had been guilty — fraud and forgery — would come to light, and he would be exposed to the consequences of a violation of the law — transportation or penal servitude. It is said that he had a cheque from Cook which entitled him to receive the amount of the winnings. But no suggestion is made as to Cook's reason for giving it to him, and it is not produced. It is clear that it is in the prisoner's hands. It is proved that it was returned to him. Why is it not produced that we may see whether it is genuine or not? Let us look at the circumstances under which he presents it for payment.

He asks Cheshire to fill up the body of the cheque, and when Cheshire expresses his surprise, he says, "Cook, poor fellow, is ill, and I am apprehensive that if I fill it up Messrs. Weatherby will know my handwriting." Why should they not know it if the transaction was an honest one? Some fraud was going on here, too, which he was afraid might be detected. Why on earth should he send for Cheshire, who was busily engaged at the post-office, at seven in the evening, at the very time when he had to meet Bamford and Jones in consultation upon the patient's case, and when, if he had not wished to write the cheque, and Cook had wished to give it, he might have asked Cook's intimate friend Jones to fill it up? Does not this transaction bear fraud upon the face of it?

Before the prisoner was finally arrested on civil process, which, unluckily for him, took place before the verdict of the coroner's jury secured his person to answer a criminal charge, he had undisputed possession of his own papers, and it is clear, since this cheque has not since been found, that he must have dealt with it in some way or other. The inference from its non-production is that the transaction will not bear inspection.

That is not all. It is clear that he meditated another fraud of a different kind. Almost as soon as the breath is out of the poor man's body he intimates that he has a claim of £3,000 or £4,000 for bills for which he was liable, but which had, in fact, been negotiated for Cook's benefit. He had before taken Cheshire a document with the signature of John Parsons Cook, purporting to be an acknowledgment that certain large bills had been negotiated for him, and that Palmer had derived no benefit from them.

There were no such bills in existence. If there were, who knows better than the prisoner at the bar that there would be no difficulty in satisfying you of the fact, and removing this great stumbling-block from his case? But he asks Cheshire to attest this document, and on the same day, the day following the poor man's death, he writes to Pratt, "Mind, I must have Polestar." Having got every shilling of the man's money, his purpose was to secure his remaining property — Polestar, the value of which he may have considerably exaggerated, or with which he may have intended to speculate in future races. His intention, if the document had been attested, was doubtless to force Cook's executors to purchase some of the bills out of the estate. If Cheshire had had the weakness to comply with his request he would have had the man in his power, and have brought him trembling and reluctant into the witness-box to swear that he had seen the dead man sign the paper. If that document is genuine, not a forgery, produce it, and let us test it!

Here again I must remind you that the prisoner's papers were in his own possession until the time of his arrest. Who can doubt that the document taken to Cheshire has been destroyed because if it had been found it would have exposed some meditated fraud to the completion of which Cook's death was necessary?

I have now gone through that part of the case which relates to the motive. It is for you to say whether, if you are satisfied that strychnine was the cause of the man's death, and that the prisoner had the opportunity of administering pills to him containing strychnine, you do not in this state of things find sufficient motive to account for the act.

Another part of the prisoner's conduct throws, I think, great light upon the question you have to determine. What has become of Cook's betting-book? What has been the language and conduct of the prisoner with regard to that betting-book? On the very night when Cook dies, ere the breath be well parted from the poor man's body, the prisoner was rummaging his pockets and searching among his papers. He might have done that innocently, but what comes next? He tells Jones, that it is his duty, as the nearest friend of the deceased, to take possession of his watch and other effects; Jones does so.

My learned friend endeavours to explain this awkward part of his case by saying that other persons, the undertaker's men, the women, and the servants, had access to the bedroom. But even before the women came to lay out the corpse, Jones seeks for the book. The prisoner is asked about it, and he says it is of no use. The father-in-law comes down, and shortly afterwards requests Jones to seek for it. They go upstairs — Jones and Palmer — but, of course, they do not find it, and they return to inform Stevens.

"You can't find it," says Stevens, "how is that?" — "Oh," says Palmer, "the betting-book is of no use." — "No use," replies Stevens, "I am the best judge of that. Why is it of no use?" — "Because," he is told, "dead men's bets are void, and Cook received some of his money on the course."

Dead men's bets are void! True; but they are not void when they have been received. Who received the dead man's bets? The prisoner at the bar. Who appropriated the proceeds of the bets? The prisoner at the bar. Who was answerable for the bets? The prisoner at the bar. Who was interested in concealing the amount of the bets? The prisoner at the bar. The executor of the deceased wanted to know what he was entitled to receive. The prisoner tells him the record is of no use. If it had been found Stevens would have seen that he was entitled to receive £1,020. Does this throw no light upon the case?

There is more yet in the conduct of the prisoner on which I must say a few words. Mr. Stevens determined on having a *post-mortem* examination. Observe the conduct of the prisoner in respect to that most important proceeding. He is on the watch for Mr. Stevens and for the local medical men wherever they go, and when Dr. Harland says to him, as was natural enough, speaking to a brother medical man, "What is this case; I hear there is a suspicion of poison?" — "No," says Palmer, "the man had two epileptic fits on Monday and Tuesday, and you'll find old disease of the head and heart." There was no disease, however, either of the head or heart.

That very man had gone to Dr. Bamford on the day before, and had asked him to certify to the cause of Cook's death. "No," said Dr. Bamford, "he is your patient; you certify." Palmer says, however, that he had rather that Dr. Bamford should certify, and he does so accordingly. The very next day Palmer tells Dr. Harland that Cook died of epilepsy.

The *post-mortem* examination then takes place, and the contents of the stomach, or a portion of them, are put into a jar. It is fastened with a parchment covering doubled over it and sealed, and Dr. Harland discovers that the prisoner has removed the jar from the spot where it was placed. The prisoner has, in fact, taken it to the other end of the room, near the door, and he says, "I thought that it would have been more convenient for you as you were going out."

That is possible; but is it not strange and remarkable that the jar containing the contents of the dead man's body should be found in the hands of the person against whom rests the suspicion of having deprived the deceased of life?

Still, the proceeding might have been an innocent one. We are left in conjecture upon this point, but I am afraid that there is no conjecture which is consistent with the innocence of the prisoner. It might have been done in order to put something into the jar, which it was supposed would neutralise and destroy the evidence of poison. I can't say what was the motive; but he is restless and uneasy as to what is to be done with the jar, and he remonstrates with Dr. Bamford, as if he had any interest in the matter; as if Dr. Bamford had any concern in Cook's death.

The jar is taken away; and we know well, because it must have made a painful impression upon your minds, that Palmer went to the postboy Myatt, who was to drive the fly, and asked him to upset those who were to take the jar to Birmingham or to London for examination.

My learned friend endeavoured to explain that matter, and told you that the bribe of £10 to upset the man who had charge of the jar arose simply out of resentment against that "officious, meddling stepfather, who had dared to interfere;" that he had been guilty, in return for the consideration and courtesy and kindness with which he had been treated by the prisoner, of prying, meddling, and insolent curiosity.

Surely the man who saw his stepson, to whom he was tenderly attached, lying dead, under circumstances which naturally excited grave suspicion, was justified in insisting upon inquiry; and one would have thought that the matter was of sufficient weight to protect him against the suggestion of insolent curiosity. It was known that Mr. Stevens insisted upon an inquiry. Was that a reason or a motive which, operating upon the mind of Palmer, should have induced him to entertain anger or resentment, and have made him offer £10 to the postboy to upset Mr. Stevens on the road? No; but if he had upset Mr. Stevens he would have upset the jar; the contents would have been lost or rendered unfit for analysis; and that was all that the prisoner wanted.

Then again we find the prisoner sending presents to that important officer the coroner, during the time that the inquest was sitting, presents, unquestionably, of game and of things of that description; and, if the evidence has not much misled us, of money also. For what purpose was all that done?

Then, again, there is his obtaining a knowledge of the communication which is sent by the eminent chemist who is employed to analyse the contents of the stomach to Mr. Gardner, the attorney at Rugeley, who was instructed on behalf of Mr. Stevens — is that the conduct of innocence or guilt? Why should he be desirous of knowing whether strychnine, above all things, had been found in the stomach? Look at his letter to the coroner, in which he states that he has seen it in black and white, that Dr. Taylor has been unable to discover strychnine, and adds, "I hope the verdict to-morrow will be that death resulted from natural causes, and that there the matter will end." But the verdict was not so; and it did not end there.

Now, gentlemen, it is for you to say whether, upon a review of the whole of this evidence, you can come to any other conclusion than that the death of the deceased was occasioned by poison administered by the prisoner at the bar. Look to all this restless anxiety. It might possibly be compatible with innocence if it stood by itself alone; but you must remember that it is one of a series of things which, though small perhaps in their individual capacity, do, when grouped together, lead to the inevitable and irresistible conclusion that the prisoner was the cause of this man's death.

This is the case which you have to decide. You have in the prisoner a man labouring under a pressure almost overwhelming, with pecuniary liabilities which he is utterly unable to meet, involving penalties of the law which must bring down disaster and ruin upon him. The only mode by which he can prevent those consequences is by obtaining money; and under such circumstances we know that a comparatively small amount, if it will meet the exigencies of the moment and will avert the impending catastrophe of ruin, will operate with immense power.

You then find that he had access to the bedside of the man whose death you have now to inquire into.

You find that he has means of administering poison to him, and that within 48 hours of the death he has twice acquired possession of the poison which we suppose him to have administered to the deceased.

Then you have the death itself in its terrible and revolting circumstances, all of which are characteristic only of death by that poison — strychnine — and no other.

You have then the fact that to the utmost of his ability the prisoner realises the purpose for which it is suggested to you that the death was accomplished.

Whether these facts, coupled with the undoubted and undisputed fact that a subsidiary poison — antimony was used, of which traces were found, although none were found of the principal poison, justify you in returning a verdict of "guilty" against the prisoner, it is for you to determine; and you must take all these circumstances into your consideration.

You have indeed had introduced into this case one other element, which I own I think had better have been omitted. You have had from my learned friend the unusual — I think I may say almost unprecedented, assurance of his conviction of the innocence of his client. I can only say upon that point that I think it would have been better if my learned friend had abstained from giving such an assurance. What would he think of me if, imitating his example, I should at this moment declare to you, on my honour, as he did, what is the intimate conviction which has followed from my own conscientious consideration of this case?

My learned friend also, in his address, of which all admired the power and ability — adopting a course which is sometimes resorted to by advocates, but which, in my mind, involves more or less a species of insult to the good sense or good feeling of the jury — endeavoured to intimidate you, by an appeal to your consciences, from discharging firmly and honestly the great and solemn duty which you are called upon to perform.

My learned friend told you that if your verdict in this case should be "guilty," the innocence of the prisoner would one day be made manifest, and that you would never cease to regret the verdict which you had given.

If my learned friend were sincere in that — and I know that he was, for there is no man in whom the spirit of truth and honour is more keenly alive — if he said what he believed, I can only answer that it shows how, when a man enters upon the consideration of a case with a strong bias on his mind, he is liable to be led into error. I think, then, that my learned friend had better have abstained from making any assurance which involved his conviction of the prisoner's innocence.

I think, further — in justice and consideration to you — that he should have abstained from representing to you that the voice of the country would not sanction the verdict which you might give. I say nothing of the inconsistency which is involved in such a statement, coming from one who but a short hour before had complained in eloquent terms of the universal torrent of passion and of prejudice by which he said that his client would be borne down; but in answer to my learned friend I say this to you:— Pay no regard to the voice of the country, whether it be for condemnation or for acquittal; pay no regard to anything but to the internal voice of your own consciences, and to that sense of duty which you owe to God and man upon this occasion, seeking no reward except the comforting assurance that when you look back to the proceedings of this day, you will feel that you have discharged to the utmost of your ability and to the best of your power the duty which it was yours to perform.

If on a review of this whole case, comparing the evidence on one side and on the other and weighing it in the even scales of justice, you can come to the conclusion of innocence, or can even entertain that fair and reasonable amount of doubt of which the accused is entitled to the benefit, in God's name acquit him; but if, on the other hand, all the facts and all the evidence lead your minds, with satisfaction to yourselves, to the conclusion of his guilt, then — but then only — I ask for a verdict of "Guilty" at your hands. For the protection of the good, for the repression of the wicked, I ask for that verdict by which alone — as it seems to me — the safety of society can be secured, and the demands, the imperious demands of public justice, can be satisfied.

The learned Attorney-General concluded his address shortly before half-past 6 o'clock.[13]

The LORD CHIEF JUSTICE then informed the jury that, inasmuch as he felt it due to the cause of justice to read over nearly the whole of the evidence in this important case, he could not think of attempting to discharge that duty at so advanced a period of the day. He feared, therefore, that he must for another Sunday sequester the jury from their family and friends.

The Court was then adjourned till 10 o'clock on Monday.

---

[13] The law at the time did not permit Shee an opportunity to respond to the attorney general, giving the prosecution an undeniable advantage in summing up the evidence. This would change with the passing of the Criminal Procedure Act in 1865.

The Jurors Attending Divine Service in the Chapel at Newgate.

ELEVENTH DAY.—May 26, 1856.

The proceedings in this protracted case were resumed this morning at the Old Bailey. The public interest which it has excited from the first appears in no degree to have abated, and the Court was again densely crowded. The prisoner was placed at the bar punctually at 10 o'clock, and we were unable to trace any change in his appearance or demeanour, although he naturally listened with marked attention, in which one might occasionally detect a shade of anxiety, to the summing up of the Lord Chief Justice. Still it must be admitted that he looked as little concerned as any one in Court.

Several persons of distinction were present during portions of the day, and among them we noticed Mr. Gladstone, M.P.[1], General Fox, Mr. Milnes Gaskell, M.P., Mr. C. Forster, M.P., Mr. Oliveira, M.P., Lord G. Lennox, M.P., the Recorder, the Common Serjeant, Alderman Sir R. W. Carden, the Sheriffs, and other gentlemen officially connected with the administration of justice in the city.

LORD CHIEF JUSTICE CAMPBELL

Silence having been proclaimed,

The LORD CHIEF JUSTICE (CAMPBELL) proceeded to sum up the case to the jury; but spoke in so low a tone that some part of his

---

[1] There were two Gladstones serving in Parliament in 1856: William Ewart (1809-1898), the future prime minister, and his older brother, John Neilson (1807-1863).

THE TIMES REPORT

address was not audible in the reporters' inconvenient box. He said,— Gentlemen of the Jury, we have at length arrived at that stage in this solemn and important case when it becomes the duty of the Judge to explain to you the nature of the charge brought against the prisoner, and the questions and considerations upon which your verdict ought to be given.

Gentlemen, I must begin by conjuring you to banish from your minds all that you may have heard before the prisoner was placed in that dock. There is no doubt that a strong prejudice elsewhere did prevail against the prisoner at the bar. In the county of Stafford, where the offence for which he has to answer was alleged to have been committed, that prejudice was so strong that the Court of Queen's Bench made an order to remove the trial from that county. The prisoner, by his counsel, expressed a wish that the trial might take place at the Central Criminal Court; and to enable that wish to be accomplished, an Act has been passed by the Legislature, authorising the Court of Queen's Bench to direct the trial to be held in this Court, so as to secure to the prisoner that he shall have a fair and impartial trial.

Gentlemen, I must not only warn you against being influenced by what you have before heard, but I must also warn you not to be influenced by anything but by the evidence which has been laid before you with respect to the particular charge for which the prisoner is now arraigned. It is necessary that I should so warn you in this case, because the evidence certainly implicates the prisoner in transactions of another description which are very discreditable. It appears that he has forged a great many bills of exchange, and that he had entered upon transactions which were not of a creditable nature. Those transactions, however, must be excluded from your consideration altogether. By the practice in foreign countries it is allowed to raise a probability of the prisoner having committed the crime with which he is charged by proving that he has committed other offences — by showing that he is an immoral man, and that he is not unlikely, therefore, to have committed the offence with which he is charged.

That is not the case in this country. You must presume that a man is innocent until his guilt be established, and his guilt can only be established by evidence directly criminating him on the charge for which he is tried.

Gentlemen, it gives me great satisfaction that this case has been so fully laid before you. Everything has been done that could have been accomplished for the purpose of assisting the jury in arriving at a right conclusion. The prosecution has been taken up by the Government, so that justice may be duly administered, the Attorney-

General, who is the first law officer of the Crown, having conducted it in his capacity of a minister of justice. The prisoner also appears to have had ample means for conducting his defence; witnesses have very properly been brought from all parts of the kingdom to give you the benefit of their information; and he has had the advantage of having his case conducted by one of the most distinguished advocates of the English bar.

Gentlemen, I must strongly recommend you to attend to everything that fell from that advocate, so eloquently, so ably, and so impressively. You are to judge, however, of the guilt or innocence of the prisoner from the evidence, and not from the speeches of counsel, however able or eloquent those speeches may be. When a counsel tells you that he believes his client to be innocent, remember that that is analogous to the mere form by which a prisoner pleads "Not Guilty." It goes for nothing more; and the most inconvenient consequences must follow from regarding it in any other light.

I will now say a few words in order to call to your minds what are the allegations in this case on one side and on the other. On the part of the prosecution it is alleged that the deceased, John Parsons Cook, was first tampered with by antimony, that he was then killed by the poison of strychnia, and that his symptoms were the symptoms of poisoning by strychnia. Then it is alleged that the prisoner at the bar had a motive for making away with the deceased, that he had an opportunity of administering poison, that suspicion could fall upon no one else, and that a few days before the time when the poison is supposed to have been administered he had purchased strychnia at two different places. It is also alleged by the prosecution that his conduct, during that transaction and after it, was that of a guilty and not of an innocent man.

The prisoner at the bar, on the other hand, puts forward these allegations — that he had no interest in procuring the death of John Parsons Cook, but, on the contrary, that it was his interest to keep him alive; that the death was not occasioned by strychnia, but by natural disease, and that the symptoms were those of natural disease, and were by no means consistent with the supposition of death by strychnia.

Those are the allegations which are urged upon one side and the other, and it is for you to say upon the evidence which of those allegations you believe to be founded on truth.

Gentlemen, you have a most anxious duty to perform. The life of the prisoner is at stake; if he be guilty, it is necessary that he should expiate his crime; if he be innocent, it is requisite that his innocence should be vindicated. If his guilt be proved to you on satisfactory evidence, it is your duty to society and to yourselves to convict him;

but unless his guilt be fully sustained by the evidence it is your duty to acquit him.

You must bear in mind that in a case of this sort you cannot expect that witnesses should be called to state that they saw the deadly poison mixed up by the prisoner, and by him openly administered. Circumstantial evidence of the fact is all that can be expected; and if there be a series of circumstances leading to the conclusion of guilt, a verdict of guilty may be satisfactorily pronounced.

With respect to the motive, it is of great importance in cases of this description that you should consider whether there was any motive for committing the crime with which a prisoner is charged, for if there be no motive there is an improbability of the offence having been committed.

If, on the other hand, there be any motive which can be assigned for the commission of the deed the adequacy of that motive becomes next a matter of the utmost importance.

The great question which you will have to consider is whether the symptoms of Cook's death are consistent with poisoning by strychnia. If they are not, and you believe that the death arose from natural causes, the prisoner is at once entitled to your verdict of not guilty. If, on the other hand, you think that the symptoms are consistent with poisoning by strychnia, you have another and important question to decide — namely, whether the evidence which has been adduced is sufficient to convince you that death was effected by strychnia, and, if so, whether such strychnia was administered by the prisoner.

In cases of this sort the evidence has often been divided into the medical and the moral, or circumstantial, evidence. They cannot be separated, however, in the minds of a jury, because it is by a combination of those two species of evidence that their verdict ought to be given.

In this case you must look at the medical evidence, to see whether the deceased died from strychnia or from natural causes; and you must look to what is called the moral evidence, to consider whether that shows that the prisoner not only had the opportunity, but that he actually availed himself of that opportunity, and administered the poison to the deceased.

Now, gentlemen, with these preliminary observations, I will proceed to read over the evidence which has been given in the course of this long trial, praying you most earnestly to weigh that evidence carefully, and to be guided entirely by it in the verdict at which you may arrive.

I begin with that part of the case which was first raised by the

Attorney-General with respect to the motive which the prisoner is supposed to have had for taking away the life of John Parsons Cook. Now, I think that that arises out of certain pecuniary transactions which must be fresh in the minds of all of you. It appears that the prisoner had borrowed large sums of money upon bills of exchange, which he drew, and which purported to be accepted by his mother — a lady, it seems, of considerable wealth, residing at Rugeley. Those acceptances were forged, and the lady was not aware of them until a recent period, when they became due, and proceedings were taken upon them.

One of those acceptances, for £2,000, was in the hands of a gentleman named Padwick; £1,000 had been paid, and £1,000 remained due to Mr. Padwick upon that bill. A solicitor named Pratt, of Queen-street, Mayfair, had advanced large sums of money to the prisoner upon similar bills — to the amount, I think, of £12,500. Several of those bills had been renewed without the knowledge of the mother; but there were two which remained unrenewed — one, for £2,000, became due on the 25th of October, 1855, and another, for £2,000, became due on the 27th of October, 1855. Besides these, Mr. Pratt held one bill for £500, and another for £1,000, which were overdue, but not renewed, and which Pratt held over, charging a very high rate of interest upon them.

In addition to these large sums, which had been advanced by Pratt to the prisoner, it appears that upon similar bills Palmer had contracted a very large debt with an attorney at Birmingham, named Wright, to whom he owed £10,400. It had been stated by Palmer that he should be able to liquidate those bills by the proceeds of a policy of assurance which had been effected on the life of his brother, Walter Palmer.

Gentlemen, the law of this country wisely forbids an insurance being effected by one person upon the life of another who has no interest in that life; but, unfortunately, it does not prevent a man from insuring his own life to any amount, however large, and whatever his position may be, and assigning the policy of that insurance to another person. It has been proved in evidence that there had been an insurance for £13,000 effected on the life of Walter Palmer, who was a bankrupt, without any means except such as were furnished to him by his mother; and that the policy had been assigned by Walter Palmer to the prisoner at the bar. It was expected that the £13,000 insured upon the life of his brother would be the means of enabling the prisoner to meet the acceptances to which I have referred, but the directors of the Prince of Wales Insurance office denied their liability upon that policy, and refused to pay it.

Hence arose the most pressing embarrassments; claimants were urging the payment of their accounts, and it was evident that, unless they were immediately paid, the law would be put in force against the prisoner and his mother, and that the system of forgeries which had been so long carried on would be made apparent.

Now I begin with the evidence of Mr. John Espin, a solicitor practising in Davies-street, Berkeley-square. [The learned Judge then read the evidence of Mr. Espin with respect to the £2,000 bill held by Mr. Padwick, the dishonouring of the cheque for £1,000, and the final issuing of a ca. sa.[2] against the person of the prisoner on the 12th of December.] This, continued the noble Lord, is certainly strong evidence to show the desperate state of the prisoner's circumstances at that time; but we now come to the evidence of Mr. Thomas Pratt, who had advanced money to the prisoner upon bills of exchange, which bore the forged acceptance of the prisoner's mother, to the amount of £12,500.

[The learned judge then proceeded to read the whole of the evidence of Mr. Pratt, together with the voluminous correspondence between that gentleman and the prisoner, detailing the entire history of the transactions which had taken place between them from the date of their first acquaintance in November, 1853, down to the period of the apprehension of the prisoner upon the present charge. They will be found previously detailed.]

With regard to the letter subjoined, and marked "strictly private and confidential,"—

"MY DEAR SIR. — Should any of Cook's friends call upon you to know what money Cook ever had from you, pray don't answer that question or any other about money matters until I have seen you,

"And oblige yours faithfully,

"WILLIAM PALMER."

the learned judge observed that the jury would recollect that when that letter was written Mr. Stevens, the step-father of Cook, was making inquiries of a nature which were certainly very disagreeable to Palmer.

[Having first disposed of that portion of the correspondence respecting money due from Palmer to Pratt, and with regard to which Cook was supposed to have no interest, the learned Judge next

---

[2] Legal abbreviation for the Latin phrase "Capias ad satisfaciendu" or writ of execution.

proceeded to read that branch of the correspondence relating to the assignment of the two racehorses, Polestar and Sirius, and to some other occurrences to which Cook was supposed to have been a party.]

With respect to the cheque for £375 sent by Pratt to Palmer for Cook, from which the words "or bearer" had been struck out, his Lordship observed:— Now, it is rather suggested on the part of the prosecution, upon this evidence, that Cook had been defrauded of this money by Palmer, and certainly the endorsement was not in Cook's handwriting; but, as was very properly argued on the part of Palmer, it is very possible that Cook may have authorised Palmer or some one else to write his name. Cheshire, a clerk in the bank, is then called, and says that the cheque was carried to Palmer's account. Now, all this may have happened with the consent of Cook, in pursuance of some agreement between him and Palmer.

[His Lordship then read the cross-examination of Pratt, the bill of £500 drawn by Palmer on Cook, and payable on the 2nd of December, and also the evidence of Armshaw, who proved that on the 13th of November, Palmer was in a state of embarrassment, and that on the 20th he received from him two £50 notes.]

It is for you, gentlemen, to draw your own inference from this evidence. Having before the races been pressed for money, on the night of the Tuesday on which Cook died he had two £50 notes in his possession.

[His Lordship next read the evidence of Spillbury, who on the 22nd of November received a £50 note from Palmer, and of Strawbridge, who proved that on the 19th of November his balance at the bank was only £9 6s.]

This evidence certainly shows that the finances of the prisoner were at the lowest ebb, and he had no means of meeting his bills.

[His Lordship next read Wright's evidence as to the large debts due to his brother from Palmer, and the bill of sale given by Palmer, as security, upon the whole of his property; Strawbridge's evidence as to the forgery of Mrs. Palmer's name to acceptances; and the further evidence of Mr. Weatherby, particularly calling the attention of the jury to the fact of the cheque purporting to be signed by Cook having been returned to Palmer by Mr. Weatherby, when he refused payment of it.]

A great deal, said his Lordship, turns upon the question of whether that cheque was really signed by Cook or not, as, if not, it shows that Palmer was dealing with Cook's money and appropriating it to his own use.

Mr. *Serjeant Shee* observed that Mr. Weatherby expressed an opinion that the cheque was Cook's.

Lord CAMPBELL. — Mr. Weatherby said that the body of the

cheque was not in Cook's handwriting, and he had paid no attention to the signature.

You, gentlemen, must consider all the evidence with regard to this part of the case. The cheque is not produced, although it was sent back by Mr. Weatherby to Palmer and notice to produce it has been given. If it had been produced we could have seen whether Cook's signature was genuine. It is not produced!

[His Lordship then read the evidence of Johnson Rogerson Butler, to whom Palmer owed money in respect of bets, and of Bergen, an inspector of police, who had searched Palmer's house for papers after the inquest.]

It might have been expected that the cheque which was returned by Mr. Weatherby to Palmer, who professed to set store upon it and to have given value for it, and who required Mr. Weatherby not to pay away any money until it had been satisfied, would have been found, but it is not forthcoming. It is for you to draw whatever inference may suggest itself to you from this circumstance.

We then come to the arrest of Palmer. Now, as it strikes my mind, the circumstance that Palmer remained in the neighbourhood after suspicion had arisen against him is of importance, and ought to be taken into consideration by you, although he may, perhaps, have done so thinking that from the care he had taken nothing could ever be discovered against him.

It seems, however, that he was imprisoned on civil process before the verdict of the coroner's jury rendered him amenable to a criminal charge. Besides the cheque purporting to be signed by Cook the prisoner also had in his possession a document purporting that certain bills had been accepted by him for Cook, but neither that document nor any such bills have been found. All the papers which were not retained were returned to the prisoner's brother, and notice has been given to produce them, but neither the bills nor the document are produced.

With regard to this witness's statement, that Field was at Rugeley, I know not how it is connected with the present investigation. If Field was employed to inquire into the health of Walter Palmer at the time the insurance was effected on his life, and into the circumstances of his death, I know not what he can have to do with the question you are to determine.

This, then, is the conclusion of the evidence upon one branch of the case, and now begins the evidence relating to the health of Cook and the events immediately preceding his death.

[His Lordship then read the evidence of Ishmael Fisher, observing in the course of it that one of the most mysterious circumstances in the case was that after Cook had stated his suspicion as to Palmer having put something in his brandy he remained constantly in Palmer's company; he appeared to have entire confidence in Palmer, and during the few remaining days of his life he sent for Palmer whenever he was in distress; in fact, he seemed to be under the influence of Palmer to a very great extent. His Lordship also directed the attention of the jury to the circumstance of the £700 which Cook had intrusted to the care of Fisher having been returned to him on the morning of the day on which he went with Palmer to Rugeley. His Lordship then read Fisher's statement that he had been in the habit of settling Cook's account.]

And now, he continued, comes the very important letter of the 16th of November. Certainly if Cook induced Fisher to make an advance of £200 on the security of his bets, and then employed another person to collect these bets, there was a fraud on his part. In the letter of the 16th of November Cook says—

"It is of great importance, both to Mr. Palmer and myself, that a sum of £500 should be paid to Mr. Pratt, of 5, Queen-street, Mayfair, to-morrow, without fail. £300 has been sent up tonight, and if you will be kind enough to pay the other £200 to-morrow, on the receipt of this, you will greatly oblige me, and I will give it to you on Monday at Tattersall's."

Mr. *Serjeant Shee.* — There is a postscript, my lord.

Lord CAMPBELL. — Yes. "I am much better."

Now, the signature to this letter is undoubtedly genuine, and it shows, first, that Cook at that time intended to be in London on the Monday; and, secondly, that he desired an advance of £200 to pay Pratt. How he came to alter his intention as to going to London, and how Herring came to be employed for him instead of Fisher, you must infer for yourselves. But if he authorised the employment of Herring in order to prevent Fisher from reimbursing himself, he was a party to a fraud. You must infer whether he did so or not.

[His Lordship then read the remainder of Fisher's evidence, and also the evidence of Mr. Jones, the law stationer, of Gibson, and of Mrs. Brooks.]

This, he said, ends the history of Cook's illness at Shrewsbury. Taken by itself it amounts to very little, but in connection with what follows it deserves your serious consideration.

Then with regard to what took place at the Talbot Arms, at Rugeley, where Cook lodged, you have a most important witness — Elizabeth Mills.

[His Lordship then read the evidence of Mills, observing that the events of Monday and Tuesday, the 19th and 20th of November, and the symptoms which immediately preceded the death of Cook, formed a most material part of the case.]

It has been suggested, continued the learned Judge, by the counsel for the defence, that Elizabeth Mills may have been bribed by Mr. Stevens, the father-in-law of Cook, to give evidence prejudicial to the prisoner; but, in justice both to Mr. Stevens and to Elizabeth Mills, I am bound to declare that not one fact has been adduced to warrant us in believing that there is the slightest foundation for any such statement. It has also been alleged that Mr. Stevens called upon Elizabeth Mills, and read to her an extract from a newspaper, with the view, it is to be presumed, of influencing her evidence or guiding it in a particular direction; but this, too, is a gratuitous assertion, and, so far from being supported by the evidence, it is distinctly denied.

As regards the manner in which Palmer was dressed when he ran over from his own house to the Talbot Arms on the night of Cook's death, there is, no doubt, a difference between the testimony of Elizabeth Mills and that of her fellow-servant, Lavinia Barnes, the former asserting that he wore a plaid dressing-gown, and the latter a black coat; but it is for you to decide whether the point is of sufficient significance to justify a suspicion dishonourable to the veracity of either witness. It has been asserted also that there are certain discrepancies between the evidence given by Elizabeth Mills before the coroner and that which she gave in your presence. That you may the more accurately estimate the importance of those differences it is competent for the prisoner's counsel to require that the depositions shall be read. What say you, brother Shee?

Mr. *Serjeant Shee.* — With your Lordship's permission, we desire to have them read.

Lord CAMPBELL. — Then let them be read by all means.

The Clerk of Arraigns then read the depositions of Elizabeth Mills, as taken before the coroner.

Lord CAMPBELL. — You have now heard the depositions read, and you will decide for yourselves whether her statements before the coroner are not substantially the same as those which she made before you in the course of her examination. You will have to determine whether there is any material discrepancy between them. Her own explanation of her omission to state before the coroner that she was sick after partaking of the broth prepared for Cook is that she was not asked the question; but that she was sick the evidence of another witness goes distinctly to prove, and it is for you to say whether, corroborated as it thus is, the testimony of Elizabeth Mills is worthy of being believed, and, if so, what inference should be drawn from it.

The next witnesses are Mr. James Gardner, attorney, of Rugeley, and Lavinia Barnes, fellow-servant of Elizabeth Mills at the Talbot Arms Inn.

[The learned Judge, having read his notes of the evidence of the witnesses in question, observed the testimony of Lavinia Barnes corroborates that of Mills as to the latter having been seized with illness immediately after she had taken two spoonfuls of the broth.]

There is some little difference of evidence as to the exact time when Palmer was seen at Rugeley on the Monday night after his return from London, but you have before you the statements of all the witnesses, and you will decide whether the point is one of essential importance.

[The learned Judge then read over without comment his notes of the evidence given by the witnesses Anne Rowley and Sarah Bond, and then proceeded to recapitulate the facts deposed to by Mr. Jones, surgeon of Lutterworth.]

Your attention [he observed] has been very properly directed to the letter written by the prisoner on Sunday evening to Mr. Jones, summoning the latter to the sick bed of his friend Cook. The learned counsel for the defence interprets that document in a sense highly favourable to the prisoner, and contends that the fact of his having insured the presence of such a witness is conclusive evidence of the prisoner's innocence. You will say whether you think that it is fairly susceptible of such a construction.

It is important, however, to consider at what period of Cook's illness Jones was sent for, and in what a condition he was when Jones arrived. Palmer's assertion in his letter to Jones was that Cook had been suffering from diarrhœa, but of this statement we have not the slightest corroboration in the evidence.

When Jones, looking at Cook's tongue, observed that it was not the tongue of a bilious attack, Palmer's reply was, "You should have seen it before." What reason could Palmer have had for using these words, when there is not the slightest evidence of Cook's having suffered from such an illness? It is a matter for your consideration.

[The deposition of Jones taken before the coroner having been read at the instance of Mr. Serjeant Shee, the learned Judge remarks,—]

It is for you to say whether, in your opinion, this deposition at all varies from the evidence given by Mr. Jones when examined here; I confess that I see no variation and no reason to suppose that Mr. Jones's evidence is not the evidence of sincerity and of truth.

[After observing that the evidence of Dr. Savage (which he read) went to show that down to the hour of the Shrewsbury races and the attack on the Wednesday night, Cook was in perhaps better health than he had enjoyed for a long time, the learned Judge called the attention of the jury to the evidence of Charles Newton, who deposed to having furnished three grains of strychnia to Palmer on the

Monday night and to having seen him at the shop of Mr. Hawkins on the Tuesday. Having read the evidence of this witness and his deposition before the coroner, his Lordship said,—]

This is the evidence of Newton, a most important witness. It certainly might be urged that he did not mention the furnishing of the strychnia to Palmer on the Monday night before the coroner; he did not mention it until the Tuesday morning, when he was coming up to London. That certainly requires consideration at your hands; but then you will observe that in his deposition, which has been read to you, although there is an omission of that which is always to be borne in mind, there is no contradiction of anything which he has said here.

Well, then, you are to consider what is the probability of his inventing this wicked lie — a most important lie, if lie it be. He had no ill-will towards the prisoner at the bar; he had never quarrelled with him, and had nothing to gain by injuring him, much less by betraying him to the scaffold. I cannot see any motive that he could have for inventing a lie to take away the life of the prisoner. No inducement was held out to him by the Crown; he says himself that no inducement was held out to him, and that he at last disclosed this circumstance from a sense of duty.

If you believe him his evidence is very strong against the prisoner at the bar; but we will now turn to the next witness, Charles Joseph Roberts, whose evidence is closely connected with that of Newton.

[Having read the evidence of Roberts, Mr. Hawkins's assistant, who stated that on the Tuesday he sold to the prisoner, at his master's shop, six grains of strychnia, his Lordship continued,—]

This witness was not cross-examined as to the veracity of his testimony, nor is he contradicted in any way. It is not denied that on this Tuesday morning the prisoner at the bar got six grains of strychnia from Roberts. If you couple that with the statement of Newton — believing that statement — you have evidence of strychnia having been procured by the prisoner on the Monday night before the symptoms of strychnia were exhibited by Cook, and, by the evidence of Roberts, undenied and unquestioned, that on the Tuesday six grains of strychnia were supplied to him. Supposing you should come to the conclusion that the symptoms of Cook were consistent with death by strychnia — if you think that his symptoms are accounted for by merely natural disease, of course the strychnia obtained by the prisoner on the Monday evening and the Tuesday morning would have no effect; but if you should think that the symptoms which Cook exhibited on the Monday and Tuesday nights are consistent with strychnia, then a case is made out on the part of the Crown.

OF THE TRIAL OF WILLIAM PALMER

After the most anxious consideration, I can suggest no possible solution of the purchase of this strychnia. The learned counsel for the prisoner told us in his speech that there was nothing for which he would not account. He quite properly denied that Newton was to be believed. Disbelieving Newton, you have no evidence of strychnia being obtained on the Monday evening; but, disbelieving Newton and believing Roberts, you have evidence of six grains of strychnia being obtained by the prisoner on the Tuesday morning, and of that you have no explanation. The learned counsel did not favour us with the theory which he had formed in his own mind with respect to that strychnia. There is no evidence — there is no suggestion how it was applied, what became of it. That must not influence your verdict, unless you come to the conclusion that the symptoms of Cook were consistent with death by strychnia.

If you come to that conclusion, I should shrink from my duty, I should be unworthy to sit here, if I did not call your attention to the inference that if he had purchased that strychnia, he purchased it for the purpose of administering it to Cook.

[The evidence next read by the learned Judge was that of Mr. Stevens, the stepfather of Cook. Upon this the noble Lord observed,—]

The learned counsel for the prisoner, in the discharge of his duty, made a very violent attack upon the character and conduct of Mr. Stevens. It will be for you to say whether you think it deserved that censure. In the conduct of that gentleman I cannot see anything in the slightest degree deserving of blame or reprobation. Mr. Stevens was attached to this young man, who was his step-son, and who had no one else to take care of him; and, whatever the result of this trial may be, I think there were appearances which might well justify suspicion.

I know nothing which Mr. Stevens did which he was not perfectly justified in doing. Having been to Rugeley and seen the body of the deceased, he goes to his respectable solicitors in London, who recommended him to a respectable solicitor, Mr. Gardner, at Rugeley.

Under his advice Mr. Stevens acts; a conversation ensues between himself and the prisoner Palmer, but I see nothing in the proceedings which he took at all deserving of animadversion.[3] Whether Palmer had any right to complain of what was said about the betting-book, and whether Mr. Stevens could be blamed for suspecting that Palmer had taken it, it is for you to say.

[Having read the evidence of the woman Keeling, who laid out the body of Cook, and of Dr. Harland, who spoke to the circumstances

---

[3] Criticism or censure.

attending the *post-mortem* examinations, to the pushing of Mr. Devonshire, who operated, and the removal of the jar on the first occasion, the learned Judge continued,—]

From that push no inference unfavourable to the prisoner can be drawn, as it might easily be the result of accident. In the removal of the jar there would be nothing more than in the pushing, were it not coupled with the evidence afterwards given, which may lead to the inference that there was a plan to destroy the jar and prevent the analysis of its contents.

[The learned Chief Justice then read the evidence of Mr. Devonshire, the surgeon, of Rugeley; Dr. Monckton, the physician; of Mr. John Boycott, the clerk to Messrs. Landor, Gardner, and Landor, the Rugeley attorneys; and of James Myatt, the postboy of the Talbot Arms, who swore that Palmer had offered him £10 to upset the fly containing Mr. Stevens and the jar with the contents of the deceased's stomach. Remarking upon the evidence of this last witness, the Chief Justice said,—]

In cases of circumstantial evidence you must look to the conduct of the person charged, and you must consider whether that conduct is consistent with innocence or is compatible with guilt. I see no reason to doubt the evidence of that postboy. An attempt was made upon cross-examination to show that the offer of £10 was not made in reference to the jar, but as an inducement, to upset Mr. Stevens. It was suggested, you will remember, that Stevens had wantonly provoked Palmer, and that Palmer might be excused, therefore, if he wished him to be upset. I see no ground for supposing that Stevens gave Palmer any such provocation, and, if you believe the postboy, that bribe was offered to him to induce him to upset the jar. That is not indeed a decisive proof of guilt, but it is for you to say whether the prisoner did not enter upon that contrivance in order to prevent an opportunity of examining the contents of the jar, which, might contain evidence against him.

We have next the evidence of Samuel Cheshire, formerly postmaster at Rugeley.

[The learned Judge read the evidence, remarking upon the circumstance of Palmer calling upon him to witness a document said to have been signed by Cook as if he had been present and had seen Cook sign it; upon the remarkable fact of Palmer endeavouring to obtain information from Cheshire as to the contents of the letter from Dr. Taylor to Mr. Gardner; and upon the impropriety of the following letter addressed by the prisoner to the coroner, Mr. Ward, during the progress of the inquest:—

"My dear Sir,— I am sorry to tell you that I am still confined to my bed. I don't think it was mentioned at the inquest yesterday that Cook was taken ill on Sunday and Monday night, in the same way as he was on the Tuesday, when he died. The chambermaid at the Crown Hotel (Masters's) can prove this. I also believe that a man by the name of Fisher is coming down to prove he received some money at Shrewsbury. Now, he could only pay Smith £10 out of £41 he owed him. Had you not better call Smith to prove this? And, again, whatever Professor Taylor may say to-morrow, he wrote from London last Tuesday night to Gardner to say, 'We (and Dr. Rees) have this day finished our analysis, and find no traces of either strychnia, prussic acid, or opium.' What can beat this from a man like Taylor, if he says what he has already said, and Dr. Harland's evidence? Mind you, I know and saw it in black and white what Taylor said to Gardner; but this is strictly private and confidential, but it is true. As regards his betting-book I know nothing of it, and it is of no good to any one. I hope the verdict tomorrow will be that he died of natural causes, and thus end it.

"Ever yours,

"W. P."]

Palmer says in that letter that he had seen it in black and white. Cheshire states he had not shown him the letter. However that might be, there can be no question that this was a highly improper letter for the prisoner to write; and, speaking as the chief coroner of England, and being desirous for the due administration of justice and of the law, I have no hesitation in saying that it was not creditable in Mr. Ward to receive such a letter without a public condemnation of its having been written.

You will say, gentlemen, whether the conduct of the prisoner in that respect — suggesting to the coroner the verdict which he should obtain from the jury — is consistent with innocence.

[The noble and learned lord then read the evidence of Ellis Crisp, the police inspector at Rugeley, who produced a medical book, which had been found in the prisoner's house, and in which the following passage occurred in the prisoner's handwriting:— "Strychnia kills by causing tetanic fixing of the respiratory muscles;" and, remarking that this was a book which was in the possession of the prisoner seven years ago, when he was a student, he said that there was nothing in it which ought to weigh for a moment against the prisoner at the bar. Having read without comment the evidence of Elizabeth Hawkes, the boardinghouse keeper, with respect to the sending of game to Ward, of Slack, her porter, and of Herring, who spoke to the directions given him by Palmer as to the disposal of Cook's bets, his Lordship called the particular attention of the jury to the statement in the evidence of Bates, that the prisoner had told him not to let any one see him deliver the letter to Ward.]

The next witness, he continued, is Dr. Curling, and now, gentlemen, you will be called upon to come to some conclusion with regard to the evidence of the scientific men respecting the symptoms of the deceased before death, and the appearance of his body after death. You will have to say how far those symptoms and those appearances are to be accounted for by natural disease, and how far they are the symptoms and appearances produced by strychnine. It will be a question of great importance whether, in your judgment, they correspond with natural, that is with traumatic or idiopathic tetanus, or with any other disease whatever.

[His Lordship read the evidence of Dr. Curling and the examination in chief of Dr. Todd without comment, and directed the Clerk of Arraigns to read the depositions of Dr. Bamford. The depositions were accordingly read, and his Lordship then remarked,—]

When this deposition was first given in evidence, Dr. Bamford was too ill to come into court, but he partially recovered, and on a subsequent day he was examined and gave the *vivâ voce* evidence, which I will now read.

[The learned Lord here read the evidence, observing with regard to the pills made up by Dr. Bamford that the prisoner certainly had an opportunity of changing them, if he pleased; that circumstance deserved their consideration.]

There is not, he continued, the slightest reason to impute any bad faith to Dr. Bamford, but it is allowed on all hands that the old man was mistaken in saying that the death was caused by apoplexy. All the witnesses on both sides say that, whatever the disease may have been, it was not apoplexy; but he filled up a certificate that it was apoplexy, in compliance with a recent Act of Parliament which renders a certificate of the cause of death necessary.

[The cross-examination of Dr. Todd was then read, and his Lordship pointed out that the case of strychnine seen by that witness bore a certain resemblance to Cook's attack on the Monday night.]

The next witness is a gentleman of high reputation and unblemished honour, Sir B. Brodie, one of the most distinguished medical men of the present time.

[His Lordship read Sir B. Brodie's evidence.]

That distinguished man tells you, as his solemn opinion, that he never knew a case in which the symptoms he had heard described, arose from any disease. He is well acquainted with the various diseases which afflict the human frame, and he knows of no disease answering to the description of the symptoms which preceded Cook's death. If you agree with him in opinion, the inference is that Cook died from some other cause than disease.

[The learned Judge then read the evidence of Dr. Daniel, who agreed with Sir B. Brodie, and of Dr. Solly, who also thought that natural disease would not account for death.]

Mr. *Serjeant Shee* wished to have the cross-examination of this witness read.

Lord CAMPBELL. — Certainly. I dare say it is very applicable.

Mr. *Serjeant Shee* read a part of the cross-examination:— "Is not the *risus sardonicus* very common in all forms of violent convulsions? — No, it is not common.

Does it not frequently occur in all violent convulsions which assume, without being tetanus, a tetanic form and appearance? — Yes, it does.

Are they not a very numerous class? — No, they are not numerous.

Is it not very difficult to distinguish between them and idiopathic tetanus? — In the onset, but not in the progress.

I think you say you have only seen one case of idiopathic tetanus? — I have only seen one.

When you answered that question of mine, you spoke from your reading, and not from your experience? — I did not know your question applied to idiopathic tetanus alone.

Does epilepsy sometimes occur in the midst of violent convulsions? — Epilepsy itself is a disease of a convulsive character.

I am aware of that; but you heard the account that was given by Mr. Jones of the few last moments before Mr. Cook died? — Yes, I did.

That he uttered a piercing shriek, fell back and died; did he not? — Yes.

Tell me whether that last shriek and the paroxysm that occurred immediately afterwards — would not that bear a strong resemblance to epilepsy? — In some respects it bears a resemblance to it.

Are all epileptic convulsions — I do not mean epileptic convulsions designated by scientific men as of the epileptic character — are they all attended with an utter want of consciousness? — No, not at all.

Does not death by convulsions frequently occur without leaving any trace in the body behind it? — Death from tetanus, accompanied with convulsions, leaves seldom any trace behind; but death from epilepsy leaves a trace behind it generally.

Lord CAMPBELL. — The jury have heard you read it. It is for them to say whether it is important in their view or not.

Evidence is then given of various cases of tetanus arising from strychnine; it is for you, gentlemen, to consider how far the symptoms in those cases resemble the symptoms in this case, or how far the symptoms in this case resemble those of ordinary tetanus, idiopathic or traumatic.

[The learned Judge read his notes of the evidence given by Dr. Robert Corbett, Dr. Watson, Dr. Patterson, and Mary Kelly, witnesses examined to prove the symptoms in the Glasgow case, and then proceeded to call the attention of the jury to the testimony of Caroline Hickson, Mr. Taylor, surgeon, and Charles Broxholme, all of whom were examined with reference to the case of Mrs. [Sarjantson] Smyth, of Romsey. He then passed on to the Leeds case — that of Mrs. Dove, whose name had transpired so frequently in the course of the trial that it would be vain to affect any reserve on the subject now. After reading the evidence of Jane Witham and George Morley, the learned Judge observed,—]

It is beyond all controversy that strychnia was not discovered in the dead body of Cook, but it is important to bear in mind that the witness Morley declares that in cases where the quantity of strychnine administered had been the minimum dose that will destroy life it is to be expected that the chymist should occasionally fail in detecting traces of the poison after death. That case of Mrs. Dove's is a very important one, because it is a case in which it is beyond all question that death was caused by strychnine, however administered. It is for you to determine how far the symptoms of this unhappy lady correspond with or differed from those of Cook. You will remember that she had repeated attacks of convulsions. She recovered from several, but at last a larger dose than usual was given, and death ensued.

With regard to the possibility of the poison being decomposed in the blood, that appears to be a vexed question among toxicologists, and Mr. Morley differs on the point from other and, I doubt not, most sincere witnesses. The great question for your consideration at this part of the inquiry is whether there may not be cases of death by strychnia in which, nevertheless, the strychnia has not — let the cause be what it may — been discovered in the dead body.

[The learned Judge then read the evidence of Edward Moore in the Clutterbuck case, where an over-dose of strychnia had been administered; and proceeded as follows:-]

I have now to call your attention to the evidence of Dr. Taylor, but before doing so, I think it right to intimate that I fear it will be impossible to conclude this case to-night. It is most desirable, however, to finish the evidence for the prosecution this evening. When that is concluded, I shall be under the necessity of adjourning the Court, and asking you to attend here again to-morrow, when, God willing, this investigation will certainly close.

[The learned Judge then proceeded to read his notes of Dr. Taylor's evidence, and on arriving at that portion of it in which the witness described the results of his own experiments upon animals, observed,—]

There is here a most important question for your consideration. Great reliance is placed by the prisoner's counsel, and very naturally so, upon the fact that no trace of strychnine was detected in the stomach of Cook by Dr. Taylor and Dr. Rees, who alone analysed it and experimented upon it.

But, on the other hand, you must bear in mind that we have their own evidence to show that there may be and have been cases of death by strychnine in which the united skill of these two individuals has failed to detect the presence of the strychnine after death. Both Dr. Taylor and Dr. Rees have stated upon their oaths that in two cases where they knew death to have been occasioned by strychnine — the poison having, in fact, been administered with their own hands — they failed to discover the slightest trace of the poison in the dead bodies of the animals on which they had experimented. It is possible that other chymists might have succeeded in detecting strychnine in those animals and strychnine also in the jar containing the stomach and intestines of Cook; but, however this may be, it is beyond all question that Dr. Taylor and Dr. Rees failed to discover the faintest indications of strychnine in the bodies of two animals which they had themselves poisoned with that deadly drug.

Whatever may be the nature of the different theories propounded for the explanation of this fact, the fact itself is deposed to on oath; and, if we believe the witnesses, does not admit of doubt.

With regard to the letter from Dr. Taylor to Mr. Gardner, stating that neither strychnia, prussic acid, nor opium had been found in the body, his Lordship said this letter was written before Cook's symptoms had been communicated to Dr. Taylor and Dr. Rees; but they had been informed that prussic acid, strychnia, and opium had been bought by Palmer on the Tuesday. They searched for all those poisons, but they found none. The only poison they found in the body was antimony, and therefore they did not, in the absence of symptoms, attribute death to strychnia, as they could not at that time; but they say that it possibly may have been produced by antimony, because the quantity discovered in the body was no test of the quantity which might have been taken into the system.

[As to the letter which was written by Professor Taylor to the *Lancet*, the learned Judge remarked,]—

I must say I think it would have been better if Dr. Taylor,

trusting to the credit which he had before acquired, had taken no notice of what had been said; but it is for you to say whether, he having, as he says, been misrepresented, and having written this letter to set himself right, that materially detracts from the credit which would otherwise be given to his evidence.

[Having concluded his reading of Dr. Taylor's evidence, his Lordship said,—]

This is Dr. Taylor's evidence. I will not comment upon it, because I am sure that you must see its importance with regard to the antimony and the strychnia. For the discovery of strychnia Dr. Taylor experimented upon the bodies of two animals which he had himself killed with that poison, but in them no strychnia could be found.

[The learned Judge next read the evidence of Dr. Rees, in commenting upon which he said,—]

I do not know what interest it could be supposed that Dr. Taylor had to give evidence against the prisoner. He was regularly employed in his profession, and knew nothing about Mr. Palmer until he was called upon by Mr. Stevens and the jar was given to him. He could have no enmity against the prisoner and no interest whatever to misrepresent the facts.

[Mr. Serjeant Shee reminded the learned Judge that the experiments upon the two rabbits were not made until after the inquest.]

That makes no difference. If the witnesses are the witnesses of truth they are equally cases where there has been the death of an animal by strychnia and no strychnia can be found in the animal; if that experiment had been made this morning the fact would have been the same.

Dr. Taylor has been questioned about some indiscreet letter which he wrote, and some indiscreet conversation which he had with the editor of the *Illustrated Times*. Against Dr. Rees there is not even that imputation, and Dr. Rees concurs with Dr. Taylor that in these experiments the rabbits were killed by strychnia; that they did whatever was in their power, according to their skill and knowledge, to discover the strychnia, as they did with the contents of the jar, and no strychnia could be discovered.

As to the antimony, he corroborates the testimony of Dr. Taylor. Antimony is a component of tartar emetic, tartar emetic produces vomiting, and you will judge from the vomiting at Shrewsbury and Rugeley whether antimony may have been administered to Cook at those places. Antimony may not have produced death, but the question of its administration is a part of the case which you must seriously consider.

His Lordship then read the evidence of Professor Brande, of Dr. Christison, a man above suspicion, who said that if the quantity of strychnia administered was small, he should not expect to find it after death, and of Dr. John Jackson, who spoke to the symptoms of idiopathic and traumatic tetanus as he had observed them in India, which concluded the evidence on the part of the Crown.

Having thus gone through all the evidence for the prosecution, his Lordship intimated that he should defer the remainder of his charge until the following day; and the court was therefore (at 8 o'clock) adjourned till 10 o'clock to-morrow (Tuesday) morning.

TWELFTH DAY.—May 27, 1856.

This was the 12th day of the trial, and on no previous morning was there a greater crowd, either within the court or waiting on the outside for admission. Among the persons of distinction upon the bench were the Earl of Denbigh, Lord G. Lennox, Mr. Gaskell and other members of Parliament.

Counsel for the Crown: the Attorney-General, Mr. E. James, Q.C., Mr. Bodkin, Mr. Welsby, and Mr. Huddleston; for the prisoner: Mr. Serjeant Shee, Mr. Grove, Q.C., Mr. Gray, and Mr. Kenealy.

The learned Judges, Lord Campbell, Mr. Baron Alderson, and Mr. Justice Cresswell, came into court about 10 o'clock, accompanied by the Sheriffs, Sir R. W. Carden, and other aldermen.

No sort of change has taken place in the appearance and general bearing of the prisoner. Once, only, while the learned Judge was summing up the case which had been made out by the prosecution, a slight shade passed across his countenance, but it was gone in a moment. He was continually writing notes on small slips of paper and handing them to one or other of his counsel. As soon as he had been placed at the bar,

Lord CAMPBELL proceeded with the charge. He said:— Gentlemen of the jury, — At the adjournment of the Court yesterday evening I had finished the task of laying before you all the evidence on the part of the prosecution, and that evidence, if unanswered, does certainly present for your consideration a very serious case against the prisoner at the bar. It appears that in the middle of November he was involved in pecuniary difficulties of the most formidable nature, that he had engagements to perform which he was unable to perform without some most extraordinary expedients, that he had to make payments for which he was unprepared, that actions had been brought against him and against his mother upon forged bills, and that he had no credit in any quarter from which money could be raised.

It so happened that at that time, on the 13th of November, Cook, the deceased, by winning a race, became master of at least £1,000; and there is evidence from which the inference may be drawn that the prisoner formed the design of appropriating that money to his own use. Whether he did endeavour to accomplish that object or not, it is for you to determine. We find, however, that he did appropriate the money to the payment of debts for which he alone was liable.

There is evidence from which it may be inferred that he drew a cheque in the name of Cook, which was a forgery, and by means of which he endeavoured to obtain payment of part of the money. There is further evidence that he employed Herring to collect the money on the Monday, and to appropriate it to his own use. What effect would have been produced by the survival of Cook under such circumstances you are to infer.

It further appears that on Cook's death the prisoner contemplated the advantage of obtaining possession of the horse Polestar, which had just won the race.

We also have evidence of his having fabricated a document declaring that certain bills of exchange, in which it appears that Cook had no concern, were negotiated for Cook's advantage, and that he derived no benefit from them. That document, gentlemen, was brought forward after Cook's death, and, if Cook had survived, the fraud must have been exposed.

With respect to the joint liability of Cook and the prisoner, it has been represented on behalf of the prisoner that after Cook's death that liability would be thrown entirely upon him, and he would be a severe loser. Now, such liability would be rather a distant object; and, on the other hand, it must be remembered that if the prisoner had obtained possession of all Cook's property by the means to which he resorted he would not have been a severe loser by his death.

Upon the important question of whether Cook died from natural disease or from poison we have the evidence of Sir B. Brodie and of other most honourable and skilful men, who say that in their opinion he did not die from natural disease, as they know of no natural disease which will account for the symptoms attending his death. Many of them further say that they believe the symptoms exhibited by him were the symptoms of strychnine — that they were what might be expected to be produced by strychnine, and that, comparing them with the symptoms of natural tetanus, they do not correspond with those symptoms, but that they do correspond with the symptoms of strychnine.

Then, gentlemen, you are to take into consideration the fact that no strychnine was found in the body, but there is no rule of law according to which poison must be found in the body of a deceased person before a charge of poisoning can be maintained, and all we know respecting strychnine not being in the body is that in that part of the body which was analyzed by Dr. Taylor and Dr. Rees they found none.

Witnesses of great reputation, Dr. Christison among the number, have said where strychnine has been administered under certain circumstances they should not expect that it would be found; and you have the evidence of Dr. Taylor and Dr. Rees that, having experimented upon animals certainly killed by strychnine, having resorted to the same means for its detection which they employed in examining the body of Cook, no strychnine was to be discovered.

Then with regard to the length of time that occurs between the administration of strychnine and its operation the evidence seems to me to lead to this conclusion, that, although when administered to animals with the view of making experiments it generally operates more rapidly than it is said to have operated in this instance, yet there is a difference in its operation upon animals and upon the human frame; and that where it is administered in the shape of pills much may depend upon the manner in which those pills are made up, and likewise, looking to the state of body of the person to whom it is administered, upon whether there was any previous tampering with the health of that person. It is asserted, too, that there are instances in which a greater space of time elapsed than in this case between the administration of the poison, if poison was administered, and the appearance of the symptoms.

Mr. *Serjeant Shee.* — I do not think those instances were proved, my Lord.

Lord CAMPBELL. — There are instances in the books which it has been agreed on both sides should be referred to in the course of the trial — there are instances recorded by medical writers, and spoken of in the evidence I have read, in which a long time has elapsed.

With regard to no blood having been found in the heart, the result of the evidence seems to be, when death is produced by contraction of the respiratory organs, causing asphyxia, blood is found in the heart; but when it is produced by a spasm in the heart itself, the heart contracts, and the blood is expelled, so that after death no blood is found in it.

You must also look at the evidence with regard to the conduct of the prisoner at the bar before the death of the deceased. You must consider the evidence as to his having tampered with the health of the deceased by administering something to him in brandy-and-water and in other things, one of them being the broth, a part of which was taken by Mills, and, according to her evidence and that of Barnes, caused her to be attacked, as the deceased has been, with vomiting.

It seems clear that antimony was found in the body. It is for you to say whether it was administered by the prisoner.

I again say that if you believe the witnesses you cannot doubt that the prisoner procured this very poison of strychnine on the Monday and on the Tuesday — three grains on the Monday, six grains on the Tuesday. For what purpose was that poison obtained? The witness who proved the purchase upon the Monday is impeached, but no impeachment rests on the evidence of the witness who swears that poison was sold by him on the Tuesday to the prisoner at the bar. What was his intention in buying that poison? What was to be its application! No explanation is given!

OF THE TRIAL OF WILLIAM PALMER

Then it is impossible that you should not pay any attention to the conduct of the prisoner after the death. From the instances which have been given in evidence you will say whether his conduct was what might be expected from an innocent or from a guilty man.

With regard to the betting-book, there is certainly reasonable evidence from which you may infer that in order to obtain possession of it he abstracted it from the room of the deceased. You may further take into consideration his attempt to bribe the postboy to overturn the jar containing those parts of the body which were to be sent up to London for analysation, and from which evidence might be obtained against him.

You find him tampering with the post-master to induce him to open a letter from the medical men who were examining the body to Mr. Gardner, solicitor for the prosecution; then, again, tampering with the coroner, and trying to induce him to procure a verdict from the jury that no murder had been committed.

These are serious matters for you to consider. You must say what inferences you draw from them. Certainly they present, if unanswered, a very serious case for your consideration.

If, however, you think either that the case for the prosecution is insufficient, or that the answer to it is satisfactory, the prisoner is entitled to your verdict. The answer consists of two parts — first, the medical evidence, and, secondly, the evidence as to facts.

With regard to the medical witnesses on the part of the prisoner, I must observe that, although there were among them gentlemen of high honour, consummate integrity, and profound scientific knowledge, who came here with a sincere wish to speak the truth, there were also gentlemen whose object was to procure an acquittal for the prisoner.

It is, in my opinion, indispensable to the administration of justice that a witness should not be turned into an advocate, nor an advocate into a witness. You must say, gentlemen, whether some of those who were called for the prisoner belonged to the category I have described, — that of a witness becoming an advocate.

[His Lordship then proceeded to read the evidence for the defence, beginning with that of Dr. Nunneley, who expressed the opinion that the death of Cook was caused not by strychnine, but by some convulsive disease, and who produced reports of the *post-mortem* examination which he had made in two cases of death from strychnine. These reports were also read by the Clerk of Arraigns. Having gone through the examination and cross-examination of the witness without comment, his Lordship observed,—]

This, gentlemen, is the evidence of Dr. Nunneley. You recollect the manner in which he gave it, and you must form your own opinion as to the weight to be attached to it. Certainly he seemed to display an interest not quite becoming a witness in a court of justice, but you will give every attention to the facts to which he refers and to the evidence he gives. He differs very materially in general opinion from several of the witnesses examined on the part of the prosecution, — especially in the statement that there is no extraordinary rigidity of body after death from tetanus, a point which is clearly of considerable importance in coming to a conclusion as to the cause of Cook's death.

[His Lordship next read Mr. Herapath's evidence, and at the close of it remarked,—]

Mr. Herapath is a very distinguished chymist, and, no doubt, says what he sincerely thinks. He is of the opinion that where there has been death by strychnine, strychnine ought to be discovered. But he seems to have intimated an opinion that the deceased in this very case died by strychnine, and Dr. Taylor did not use proper means to discover it. Now, the only evidence we have in this case that there is no strychnine is that it was not discovered by the analysis of Dr. Taylor and Dr. Rees; but, as I before pointed out, in two of the instances in which they certainly had poisoned animals by strychnine the result was the same — no strychnine was discovered.

[The learned Judge then read the evidence of Mr. Rogers, who agreed with Mr. Herapath as to the possibility of detecting the poison.]

There is no reason to doubt, his Lordship continued, that this witness does sincerely entertain the opinion he expresses. According to these witnesses, where strychnine exists, even mixed with impure matter, it should be discovered by skilful experimenters using the proper tests.

[After reading the evidence of Dr. Henry Letheby, who said that the symptoms in this case were not, in his opinion, those of strychnine, his Lordship proceeded,—]

Dr. Letheby speaks sincerely, according to his experience; but I must say that cases of this kind seem to vary very much. There are cases which are, as this witness says, exceptional, and among them he mentions that of the lady, Romsey. The fair result would probably be that enough is not known of cases of this kind for us to be aware of all their varieties, and where there is a strong probability that strychnine has been administered any peculiarity in the symptoms would not be anything like conclusive evidence to rebut that probability.

[The evidence of Dr. Gay was then read.] This witness [said his Lordship] gives you a case of idiopathic tetanus. You are to say whether, from the symptoms he describes, you can infer that the case of Cook was one of idiopathic tetanus. The weight of evidence seems to me to show that it was not idiopathic any more than traumatic tetanus.

[The learned Judge read his notes of the evidence of Mr. J.B. Ross, house surgeon to the London Hospital, who, it will be remembered, described a case of tetanus admitted into that institution on the 23rd of March last. There were on the body of the patient three wounds — two at the back of the right elbow, each about the size of a shilling, and one on the left elbow, about the size of a sixpence. The man had had those wounds for twelve or sixteen years. They were old chronic indurated ulcers, circular in outline, the edges thickened and rounded, and covered with a white coating, without granulation.]

Call that tetanus by what medical name you please, it is admitted upon all hands that it was to be referred to certain wounds plainly discernible upon the body of the patient. On the body of John Parsons Cook no such wounds were discovered. No doubt witnesses have been examined for the defence who have stated that in their opinion Cook's was not a case of tetanus at all, and it is for you to say what amount of credit should be attached to their representations. At all events, it is beyond controversy that the case cited by Mr. Ross is distinguishable from the present in these important respects — that there was no suspicion of poison, and that death was obviously attributable to external wounds.

We now come to the evidence of Dr. Wrightson, who, you will remember, had been a pupil of Liebig at Giessen, and is at present a teacher of chymistry in a medical school at Birmingham.

[The learned Judge, having passed in review the evidence in question, observed,—]

This witness, who, I have no doubt, is a most scientific and honourable man, has stated that, assuming a man to have been poisoned by strychnine, he should expect to find traces of the poison in the stomach within five or six days after death; but he gave his testimony with that caution which is never so proper and becoming as in treating on questions of science; and, taking all the facts of this case together, and contrasting the testimony of the various witnesses, it will be for you to say whether, under particular circumstances, the poison may not be unobservable, or whether the chymiste to whom the duty of analysation was intrusted in the present instance may not have failed to employ the proper means to detect it.

And now we come to the evidence of Mr. Partridge, who has been for many years in extensive practice as a surgeon, and is professor of anatomy in King's College, London.

[The learned Judge read his notes of the evidence of Professor Partridge.]

It is very true that this most respectable witness gave it as his opinion that some of the symptoms in Cook's case were inconsistent with the tetanus of strychnine, but then it is important to bear in mind that he only spoke from his own experience, and that we have abundant evidence to show that the symptoms attending the tetanus of strychnia vary very much in different cases.

[The learned Judge then called the attention of the jury to the evidence of Mr. Gay, Fellow of the Royal College of Surgeons, who had described a case of traumatic tetanus that came under his observation in the Royal Free Hospital in 1843.]

The patient was a boy, the middle toe of whose left foot had been completely smashed by the accidental fall of a large stone upon it. This being a case of tetanus incontestably occasioned by the smashing of the patient's toe, I cannot see that it bears any analogy whatever to the case now under consideration, for there is not the slightest pretext for saying that any such accident ever happened to Cook.

But there is in the evidence of Mr. Gay another matter well deserving of your attentive consideration. The witness told you that in the event of a given set of tetanic symptoms being proposed for the judgment of a medical man it would be extremely difficult, if not quite impossible, without collateral evidence, to ascribe the attack to any particular cause. On you devolves the duty of inquiring and deciding whether that collateral evidence is supplied by the conduct of any particular person, or by the means that he may have had in his possession; and, if so, whether the prisoner is that person.

[The learned Judge then passed on to the evidence of Dr. W. Macdonald, a licentiate of the Royal College of Surgeons of Edinburgh, who had described a case of idiopathic tetanus that came under his own notice in the month of October, 1855. The Clerk of Arraigns read Dr. Macdonald's report of the circumstances attending this case, the subject of which was Catherine Watson, a young woman, twenty-two years of age, who, after going about her ordinary occupation during the day, was attacked with tetanus at ten o'clock at night. By the administration of chloroform the violence of the spasms was gradually diminished and she recovered. After her recovery she slept for thirty-six hours.]

His Lordship continued,— It is very certain that the patient here alluded to did not die. She is still alive, and gave evidence before you; and you will, after a fair review of all the circumstances, decide for yourselves whether there is any similarity between her case and that which resulted in the death of Cook. Dr. Macdonald has gone the length of introducing a new term of disease, "epilepsy with tetanic complications," and not only does he state that this may have been such a case, but he declares his belief that it was so, adding that it might have arisen from mental, moral or sexual excitement. You will have to determine what weight you will attach to this evidence as compared with the medical testimony adduced by the Crown.

[Having read without comment the evidence of Dr. Bainbridge, the medical officer of St. Martin's workhouse, the learned Judge next called the attention of the jury to the testimony of Mr. Steddy, a surgeon in practice at Chatham, who in 1854 had attended a person named Sarah Ann Taylor for trismus and pleuro-tothonos.]

The convulsions in that case came on in paroxysms, and she is still alive, but it is important that you should bear in mind that it was elicited in cross-examination that the woman had received a blow upon her side from her husband. The case was therefore one of traumatic tetanus, and, having heard it described, you will say whether there were manifested in the course of it any symptoms resembling in the slightest degree those that were observed in the case of Cook.

[In commenting on the evidence of the witness next in order, Dr. George Robinson of Newcastle-on-Tyne, the learned Judge remarked,—]

You have here the testimony of a respectable physician, from whose opinions you are called upon to infer that this was a case of epilepsy. Dr. Robinson thought that, putting aside the assumption of death by strychnia, Cook may have died of epilepsy; but, on being asked by the Attorney-General whether all the symptoms spoken to by Mr. Jones were not indicative of death by strychnia, he at once replied, "They certainly are." Nor is it immaterial to remember that the witness failed to mention a single case as having fallen under his own observation where an epileptic patient retained his consciousness during the fit.

Dr. Richardson, who, I am bound to say, appears a very respectable witness, was next examined, and was the first to suggest the theory that Cook may have died of angina pectoris. In 1850 the witness had under his care a girl of 10 years old, whom he believed to be afflicted with that malady, and he has described her symptoms with great minuteness; but you will remember that he candidly admitted that if he had known as much then as he knows now he would have analysed the stomach of the girl after death, with a view to ascertain whether strychnia might not be detected.

And here again arises the important question I have already propounded for your consideration. You will have to determine whether Cook's symptoms were or were not consistent with death by strychnia. If they were not, your conclusion will be in favour of the prisoner; if they were consistent with death by strychnia, I do not say that on that fact alone you should find a verdict against him, but this I say, that it will be your duty to consider the fact in connection with other evidence that has been brought before you, in order that you may come to a clear conclusion as to whether this was a death by strychnia, and, if so, whether the prisoner at the bar was the man who administered it to the deceased.

After Dr. Richardson had given his evidence Dr. Wrightson was recalled, and, in reply to a question put to him by the counsel for the Crown, stated that if a minimum dose to destroy life were given and a long interval elapsed before death the more complete would be the absorption and the less the chance of finding the poison in the stomach.

Mr. *Serjeant Shee.* — He added, my Lord, that he should still expect to find it in the spleen, liver, and blood.

Lord CAMPBELL. — You are quite right; he certainly did say so, and you have done well in calling attention to the statement.

[The learned Judge then read, without comment, his notes of the evidence given by Catherine Watson and Oliver Pemberton, and added,—]

This is the close of the medical testimony adduced on behalf of the prisoner, and I propose that the Court should now adjourn for a brief period.

[The Court then adjourned for about 20 minutes, and it may be mentioned, as an instance of the tenacity with which the human mind will cling to hope under the most desperate circumstances, that just as he was leaving the dock the prisoner threw over the bar to one of the learned gentlemen engaged in his defence a slip of paper, on which were written, in a clear and firm hand, these words,— "I think they'll find a verdict of not guilty."

When the trial was resumed the learned Judge said, that, having concluded the medical evidence, he now came to that of the witnesses who spoke as to facts.]

Having read the evidence of Henry Matthews as to the time at which the express train, by which alone the prisoner could have left London on the Monday night, arrives at Stafford, and that of Joseph Foster, who gave it as his opinion that Cook was of weak constitution, and stated that he founded this opinion upon having during seven years' time seen him suffer from bilious attacks, the noble Lord said,—

Of the evidence of the latter witness I must say that this is very slender evidence to show that Cook was in such a state of health as might produce the result which has been spoken to by several of the witnesses as likely to result from weak health.

[Upon the evidence of Myatt as to the transactions at Shrewsbury, the learned Judge said,—]

The materiality of the evidence of this witness seems to be to show that Palmer could not have left the room to have brought in such an ingredient as it is suggested he used, and that he could not have given anything of the sort to Cook. Upon this point Myatt's evidence is at variance with that of the witnesses for the Crown, and is not consistent with that of Mrs. Brooke. You are to judge between them.

That there was this scene — that Cook drank his brandy-and-water and complained that there was something in it, and that it was tasted by some one who said that there was nothing in it — has been proved by the evidence for the prosecution, and is corroborated by this witness.

[His Lordship next read the evidence of John Serjeant as to the diseased state of Cook's throat, and as to the effect produced upon him by swallowing a gingerbread nut containing cayenne pepper. On this his Lordship observed,—]

You are to say whether this evidence induces you to think, contrary to the evidence which you have heard on the other side, that Cook was at the time he had these attacks in bad health. As to the cayenne pepper nut, it would have happened to any of you who had swallowed such a nut to exhibit the same symptoms.

Next comes a very material witness, a part of whose statement would, if you believe him, be very important — I mean Jeremiah Smith. It is for you to say, looking at the whole of the evidence which he has given, both upon his examination and re-examination, what value you attach to it.

[In the course of reading the evidence of this witness his Lordship said,—]

If Smith's testimony as to what occurred on the Monday evening be true, it would show to you that the very identical pills which Bamford had made were in the state in which he had prepared them taken by Cook before Palmer arrived from London, at all events before he went to the Talbot Arms.[1]

As to the broth, there is no explanation why it was not sent to the Talbot Arms, where Cook was, but was taken to Palmer's house. The dressing of Cook's throat by Thirlby, which is spoken to by this witness, is material, and it is very extraordinary, that Thirlby is not here to give evidence with respect to it.

[After reading [Jeremiah] Smith's evidence the learned Judge said,—]

Gentlemen, it is for you to say whether you think that this witness is to be believed. You saw how he conducted himself, how he at last denied that the signature to a deed which he had attested, and which he received from the prisoner at the bar, was his handwriting. Then, it appears that he did receive £5. The counterfoil of the cheque book of

---

[1] As mentioned above, Fletcher presents evidence in his biography that Palmer wrote several letters to Smith coaching him on his testimony. See pp. 93-95 of the Peschel Press edition.

William Palmer is produced, and shows that he gave to this witness a cheque for £5, which this witness took to the bank and got cashed, and you are to say whether it is not clear that Smith received that for attesting this very deed. Further, you are to say what weight you can attach to the evidence of a witness who has been engaged in transactions such as those in which Smith admits that he was concerned.

We are now upon the question of veracity, and you must say whether you can believe a witness who acknowledges that he was engaged in procuring the insurance upon the life of Walter Palmer, who had been a bankrupt six years ago, and who had no means of living except the allowance from his friends and the allowance made to him by the prisoner. He also acknowledged that he was engaged in the proposal to insure the life of Bates for £10,000, Bates being at that time superintending the stables of the prisoner, and living in lodgings for which he paid only 6s. 6d. a-week. Bates apparently had no property, and nothing depended upon his life, yet it was to be insured for £10,000. Smith gets himself appointed agent to an insurance-office, with a knowledge of these facts, and proposes that this insurance should be accepted by the office which he represents.

Can you believe his evidence when he acknowledges himself to have been engaged in such fraudulent transactions, and, being now examined upon his oath, denies his own attestation to that document? Of his credit you are the judges. His evidence would be material as to what took place on the evening of Monday, because it would show that the pills which Cook took that night were taken as they were prepared by Bamford, and before the prisoner at the bar could have had any opportunity of substituting others for them.

The evidence as to what took place on the Tuesday night remains exactly as it stood at the conclusion of the case for the Crown. The only other evidence is this letter from Cook to Palmer:—

"LUTTERWORTH, JAN. 4, 1855.

"MY DEAR SIR, — I sent up to London on Tuesday to back St. Hubert for £50, and my commission has returned 10 to 1. I have therefore booked 250 to 25 against him, to gain money. There is a small balance of £18 due to you, which I forgot to give you the other day. Tell Will to debit me with it on account of your share of training Pyrrhine. I will also write to him to do so, as there will be a balance due from him to me. Yours faithfully,

"W. PALMER, ESQ.
"J. PARSONS COOK."

Now, gentlemen, this shows, what has never been disputed, that Cook and the prisoner had transactions together in bets; but it does not at all contradict what appears from the other evidence, that the prisoner had large dealings in which Cook had no concern. He (Palmer) had borrowed these large sums from Pratt and from Wright upon bills purporting to be accepted by his mother, but which his mother did not accept, and which were forged.

Now, gentlemen (continued the learned Judge), this is the evidence on the part of the prisoner at the bar. You are to say how far it affects the case for the prosecution. So far as concerns the pecuniary transactions between the parties, with respect to the motive by which the prisoner may have been actuated, you will probably think that the case remains untouched.

Then, gentlemen, comes that most important question whether the symptoms exhibited by the deceased were consistent with death from poisoning by strychnia. It is for you to say whether your opinion upon that subject is altered by the evidence given on the part of the prisoner. Several of the witnesses called on his behalf have said that these symptoms were reconcileable with poisoning by strychnine, but in the absence of evidence of the administration of that poison they will not say that the symptoms arose from it.

With regard to the facts of the case you have the witness Myatt, whose account of what occurred at the Raven Hotel, at Shrewsbury, with respect to the brandy-and-water, differs from that given by the witnesses for the prosecution; and the witness Jeremiah Smith, respecting what took place when the prisoner returned from London on Monday night; it is for you to say whether you can rely upon that evidence, to alter any opinion which you had formed before it was given.

The conduct of the prisoner remains. As to that no answer has been given, either with regard to his anxiety to have the body speedily fastened up, with respect to the betting-book, or with respect to the tampering with the postboy and with the coroner. Above all, no explanation has been given of what became of the strychnia purchased on the Tuesday morning, which has been proved, and which stands entirely uncontradicted. Of the purpose for which that was bought no explanation has been given.

The case is now in your hands. Unless by the evidence for the prosecution a clear conviction has been brought to your minds of the guilt of the prisoner, it is your duty to acquit him. You are not to convict him on suspicion, even on strong suspicion. There must be a strong conviction in your minds that he is guilty of this offence; and if you have any reasonable doubt you will give him the benefit of that doubt. But if you come to the clear conclusion that he is guilty, you will not be deterred from doing your duty by any consideration such as has been suggested to you. You will remember the oath that you have taken, and you will act upon it. Gentlemen, I now dismiss you to consider your verdict, and may God direct you! [At the close of his address the learned Judge was sensibly affected. His voice trembled with emotion, and the concluding sentences were almost inaudible.]

Mr. *Serjeant Shee*. — The question which your Lordship has submitted to the jury is whether Cook's symptoms were consistent with death by strychnia. I submit —

Lord CAMPBELL. — That is not the question which I have submitted to the jury; it is a question. I have told them that unless they consider the symptoms consistent with death by strychnia they ought to acquit the prisoner.

Mr. *Serjeant Shee*. — It is my duty not to be deterred by any expression of displeasure; it is my duty to a much higher tribunal than even your Lordships' to submit what occurs to me to be the proper question. I submit to your Lordships that the question whether Cook's symptoms are consistent with death by strychnia is a wrong question, unless it is followed by this, "and inconsistent with death by other and natural causes," and that the question should be whether the medical evidence establishes beyond all reasonable doubt the death of Cook by strychnia. It is my duty to submit that. It is your Lordships' duty, if I am wrong, to overrule it.

Mr. Baron ALDERSON.— It is done already. You have done it in your speech.

Lord CAMPBELL (addressing the jury),— Gentlemen, I did not submit to you that the question upon which alone your verdict was to turn was whether the symptoms of Cook were those of strychnia, but I said that that was a most material question, and I desired you to consider it. I said that if you thought that he died from natural disease — that he did not die from poisoning by strychnia — you should acquit the prisoner; but then I went on to say that if you were of the opinion that the symptoms were consistent with death from strychnia, you should consider the other evidence given in the case to see whether strychnia had been administered to him, and whether it had been administered by the prisoner at the bar.

These are the questions that I again put to you. If you come to the conclusion that these symptoms were consistent with death from strychnia, do you believe that death actually resulted from the administration of strychnia, and that that strychnia was administered by the prisoner at the bar? Do not find a verdict of guilty unless you believe that the strychnia was administered to the deceased by the prisoner at the bar; but, if you believe that, it is your duty to God and man to find the prisoner guilty.

The Jurors' Retiring Room at the Central Criminal Court.

THE TIMES REPORT

At the conclusion of this address from the Lord Chief Justice the Jury retired from the court, at eighteen minutes after two o'clock.[2]

The Jury re-entered their box at twenty-five minutes to four, after an absence of one hour and seventeen minutes, and the prisoner, who had been removed upon the retirement of the Jury, was placed in the dock at the same moment.

The buzz of excitement which ran round the court on the reappearance of the Jury, was instantly hushed by the formal question of the Clerk of the Arraigns, who asked, "Gentlemen of the Jury, are you all unanimous in your verdict?"

The Foreman. — We are.

The Clerk of the Arraigns. — How say you, gentlemen, do you find the prisoner at the bar guilty, or not guilty?

The Foreman (rising, and in a distinct and firm tone.) — We find the prisoner GUILTY.

The prisoner, who exhibited some slight pallor and the least possible shade of anxiety upon the return of the jury to the box, almost instantly recovered his self-possession and his demeanour of comparative indifference. He maintained his firmness and perfect calmness after the delivery of the verdict; and when the sentence was being passed, he looked an interested, although utterly unmoved spectator. We think we may truly say that during the whole of this protracted trial his nerve and calmness have never for a moment forsaken him.

The Clerk of the Arraigns. — Prisoner at the bar, you stand convicted of murder; what have you to say why the Court should not give you judgment to die according to law?

The question is one of a formal nature, and the prisoner made no answer.

The learned Judges then assumed the black cap;[3] and

The LORD CHIEF JUSTICE pronounced sentence in the following terms:— William Palmer, after a long and impartial trial you have been convicted by a jury of your country of the crime of wilful murder. In that verdict my two learned brothers, who have so anxiously

---

[2] At this point, Palmer tossed a note to his solicitor: "It is the riding that did it!" This is usually taken as a reference to the attorney-general or the chief justice, both of whom marshaled the facts and ordered them to show clearly Palmer's guilt. Tennyson Jesse, however, suggested that it was Palmer who did the riding, allowing his passions and desires to roam unchecked and leading him into disaster.

[3] The black cap — actually a plain square of black fabric worn over the judicial wig with the point over the forehead — was traditionally donned by the judge when passing a sentence of death. Although the death penalty was abolished in England and Wales, the cap is still part of the judge's official regalia.

watched this trial, and myself entirely concur, and we consider the conviction altogether satisfactory. The case is attended with such circumstances of aggravation that I will not dare to touch upon them. Whether this be the first and only offence of this sort which you have committed is certainly known only to God and your own conscience. It is seldom that such a familiarity with the means of death should be shown without long experience; but for this offence, of which you have been found guilty, your life is forfeited. You must prepare to die; and I trust that, as you can expect no mercy in this world, you will, by a repentance of your crimes, seek to obtain mercy from Almighty God.

The act of Parliament on which you have been tried, and under which you have been brought to the bar of this court, at your own request, gives leave to the Court to direct that the sentence under such circumstances shall be executed either within the jurisdiction of the Central Criminal Court or in the county where the offence was committed. We think that for the sake of example the sentence ought to be executed in the county of Stafford. I hope that that terrible example will deter others from committing such atrocious crimes; and that it will be seen, whatever art, or caution, or experience may accomplish, that such an offence will surely be detected and punished. However destructive poison may be, it is so ordained by Providence, for the safety of his creatures, that there are means of detecting and punishing those who administer it. I again implore you to repent, and to prepare for the awful change which awaits you.

I will not seek to harrow up your feelings by any enumeration of the circumstances of this foul murder; but I will content myself now by passing upon you the sentence of the law, which is,— that you be taken from hence to the gaol of Newgate, and be thence removed to the gaol of the county of Stafford, being the county in which the offence for which you stand convicted was committed, and that you be taken thence to the place of execution, and be there hanged by the neck until you be dead, and that your body be afterwards buried within the precincts of the prison in which you shall be last confined after your conviction, and may the Lord of Heaven have mercy on your soul! — Amen.[4]

The prisoner was immediately removed from the dock, and the trial was at an end.

Mr. *James*, Q.C., applied that the bills bearing the acceptance of Mrs. Sarah Palmer, which had been proved to have been forged, should be impounded — an application which the Court without hesitation granted.

---

[4] It's clear Chief Justice Campbell was impatient to sentence Palmer. Not only did he breach etiquette by personally sentencing him, a task usually reserved for the junior judge, but he announced that his fellow justices concurred without the pretence of consulting them.

CELLS BELOW THE CENTRAL CRIMINAL COURT.

Turning then to the jury,

The LORD CHIEF JUSTICE said,— I beg to return to you, Gentlemen, the warm thanks of my learned brothers and myself for the service which you have rendered to your country upon this occasion. Your conduct throughout this protracted trial, which you have attended, no doubt at much serious inconvenience to yourselves, has been such as to merit our utmost commendation. I only hope, and I doubt not, that you will be rewarded for your patient attention and for the sacrifices which you have made by the approbation of your own consciences and the approving voice of your country.

Turning next, to the Sheriffs, his Lordship continued:— We have also to thank the Sheriffs of London for the manner in which the court has been kept during the trial, for their excellent arrangements, and for the facilities which they appear to have afforded to every one who had any business here to trial.

Before quitting the bench, the learned Judges signed the warrants for the removal of the prisoner to the gaol of Stafford, and for the execution to be carried out there by the Sheriffs of that county.

Additional Material

(Editor's note: The following material was added to the trial transcript that was published, without illustrations, as "The Most Extraordinary Trial of William Palmer, for the Rugeley Poisonings" by W.M. Clark. The article below was reprinted from a contemporary newspaper. The account of Palmer's execution that follows was from the Illustrated Times.*)*

Removal of Palmer to Stafford Gaol.

Last night the convict William Palmer was taken from Newgate in a cab to the Euston station in charge of two gaolers, and thence conveyed to Stafford gaol by the eight o'clock train, which would arrive at Stafford about twelve o'clock.

When the cab which contained the prisoner and his keepers drove into the yard of the Euston Station, the prisoner alighted and walked through the large room on to the platform. He was immediately recognized by some persons who had seen him in court, and the news of his being at the station spread rapidly.

In a few moments there was a tremendous rush through the station on to the platform, and in an incredibly short space of time the prisoner was the object of general curiosity, although the fact of his removal had been kept as secret as possible. He walked rapidly to the train, with a gaoler on each side, followed by the crowd which had collected. He wore a cloak and a cap, and was, we understand, fettered to one of his gaolers by the leg and arm. He was placed in the middle compartment of a first-class carriage, a gaoler being on each side of him.

When he was seated in the carriage the crowd surrounded the window, eager to catch a glance of one who had attained such an unenviable notoriety. This was evidently annoying to Palmer, and the blind of the carriage window was drawn down, much to the disappointment of the curious. He looked as cool and collected as during the trial.

THE END.

Printed by G. Lawrence, 29, Farringdon Street, City.

APPENDIX

TO

CLARK'S EDITION

OF THE

LIFE, TRIAL, AND EXECUTION

OF

WILLIAM PALMER.

W. M. CLARK, 16 AND 17, WARWICK-LANE.

THE TIMES REPORT

Execution of William Palmer.

Stafford, June 14.

This morning, a few minutes before eight o'clock, William Palmer was executed in front of the County Gaol in this town for the murder of John Parsons Cook under circumstances with which, it were scarcely too much to say, the whole civilised world is familiar.

This atrocious crime, of which thousands have just witnessed the terrible but appropriate denouement, from the very first moment at which it became the subject of investigation in the coroner's court at Rugeley, excited and sustained an unusual degree of interest throughout the whole country, which went on augmenting as the varied and striking incidents of which it was composed became publicly known from time to time. The friendship subsisting between the murderer and his victim, arising out of a community of tastes and pursuits, — the agent used in his destruction, at once so subtle and potent, which, though resorted to for the purpose of evading detection, eventually became the principal means of conviction, and, by the revelations it elicited in a court of justice may be said to have elevated an interesting department of toxicological science from the region of purely professional knowledge to the rank of a social question of great public importance — the extraordinary motives leading to the commission of the crime, and all its collateral events — its investigation before a criminal tribunal under circumstances of singular solemnity and interest, and the inherent characteristics of the circumstantial evidence upon which the whole trial and conviction turned — all these considerations have combined to invest this case with an importance never before, perhaps, surpassed on any previous occasion of the kind, and, by raising it to the position of a *cause celebre* in the criminal history of the country, to denude its judicial investigation of the vulgar and repulsive associations which cling round the crime itself. They have also lent a kindred interest to the execution of the criminal, who had otherwise nothing to distinguish him from the class of monsters to which he belonged, except, perhaps, in the heartless and unredeemed atrocity with which he at once disgraced and outraged humanity.

After the revulsion of feeling consequent upon his conviction, Palmer seems to have been all along buoyed up with the belief that the Government would not carry his sentence into execution, from the conflict of evidence as to the absorption or otherwise of strychnine by the body before or after death. He grounded this belief also on the circumstance, so much relied on by the counsel for his defence, that the *post-mortem* examination of the body of Cook wholly failed to discover any trace of strychnine.

These considerations, and the knowledge that his friends out of doors were making great exertions to procure a respite, encouraged his hopes that his sentence would be stayed or commuted; and he may be said to have clung to this feeling, in a greater or less degree, to the last, notwithstanding an official visit paid him by Lieutenant-Colonel Dyott, the High-Sheriff of the County, accompanied by Mr. Hand, the Under-Sheriff, on the afternoon of yesterday, by whom he was informed that there was no possibility of the Royal clemency being extended to him, and that he must prepare himself for execution.

He received this terrible intimation, which destroyed all ground for hope, in silence, and without any perceptible emotion, and, though from that moment a great change came over him, it was evident to those about him that he still entertained the notion that mercy would be shown to him. The almost inevitable effect of all overtures, however well meant, to stay the execution of a criminal upon grounds which admit of no chance of such a result, unhappily is to divert the current of his mind from those solemn considerations which ought most to engage the attention of one so awfully circumstanced, and to lead him to fritter away, in alternations of hope and despair, the brief interval still left him for preparation and repentance.

To a great extent this was the result produced in the case of Palmer, though he appears to have allowed religious considerations to occupy his mind to some degree, and even received the ministrations of the chaplain with respect and gratitude.

This was especially so after Tuesday last, from which time he applied himself to religious meditation with some earnestness, though the impressions derived from it were constantly liable to be diminished by the hope that his life would be prolonged, which he cherished to the last.

He was not remarkably communicative to the officers of the prison in attendance upon him, and when he did break silence it was mostly to complain of what he called the partisan spirit with which Lord Campbell summed up the evidence on his trial. His eyes occasionally became suffused with tears, but that was almost the only sign of emotion exhibited by him, and he would wipe them away and immediately regain his composure.

From the time of his condemnation he ate and slept well, and even on the night preceding his execution, though it was a very advanced hour before he retired to rest, he slept two hours and a half.

Since his conviction he has seldom or never availed himself of the privilege permitted by the prison regulations of having additional diet; he has been contented with the ordinary gaol allowance; and all he has asked for besides has been a salad, and of this he ate frequently.

For the first time since his return to Stafford he attended the service in the chapel of the prison twice on Sunday last. He occupied a seat, which was screened from the gaze of the rest of the prisoners, in the immediate vicinity of the communion table, and was accompanied by an officer of the gaol. Upon both occasions the Rev. Mr. Goodacre, the chaplain, delivered an impressive sermon, taking for his text, on one occasion, the appropriate words, "Let no man deceive himself." The culprit listened with marked attention and frequently shed tears. He never afterwards attended the service, however, though he had the opportunity of doing so twice a day.

His subsequent religious meditations, which were chiefly conducted by the chaplain, took place in his cell. Of late he has been in the daily habit of reading the morning and evening service and the Commination service from the Book of Common Prayer.[1]

The Rev. Thomas Palmer, a clergyman of the Church of England, his brother, visited him almost daily after his conviction, as did also his brother George several times, and his sister, Miss Sarah Palmer, twice at least. A Mr. Heywood, who married an elder sister — now dead — of the convict, also saw him on Friday morning. A venerable gentleman, named Wright, who has long made it his chief mission to administer religious consolation and advice to criminals under sentence, had likewise frequent interviews with him; and towards the end of the week the Rev. Henry Sneyd, a clergyman residing in this county, who was not before known to the convict, came to see him from a benevolent impulse, and was on several occasions admitted to his presence.

Yesterday he received a letter from the Rev. Mr. Davis, the ordinary at Newgate,[2] of whom since his return to Stafford he has frequently spoken in terms of gratitude, but the contents of the communication have not transpired. His brothers George and Thomas, accompanied by his sister, visited him for the last time yesterday evening. They arrived at the prison about seven o'clock, and, after remaining in his company for several hours, took a final leave of him. The scene at parting was most distressing, but the

---

[1] Subtitled a "denouncement of God's anger and judgment against sinners," it reminds the congregation that hellfire awaits those who live ungodly lives. It warns that God will "pour down rain upon the sinners, snares, fire and brimstone, storm and tempest" and encourages them to repent. The service is traditionally read on Ash Wednesday.

[2] A clergyman appointed as chaplain to attend condemned criminals. Not much is known about the Rev. John Davis except that at this time he had been ordinary at Newgate for more than 20 years.

convict himself is said to have evinced comparatively little emotion.

Yesterday morning Mr. [John] Smith, his solicitor, was summoned by telegraph from London to Stafford, at Palmer's earnest request, and he arrived here at half-past ten o'clock last night, and had an interview with the convict, in the presence of Major Fulford, the Governor of the gaol. The prisoner had declined to retire to rest until Smith came, and from that circumstance, and the anxiety he had shown to have him sent for it was supposed that he had some important communication to make to him; but it was not so.

On going into the cell, the Governor informed Palmer that if he had anything confidential to say on family affairs to Mr. Smith, he (the Governor) would keep it a secret. The prisoner replied that he had not, and he hoped the Governor would lose no time in publishing all he said. He also added, all he had to say was to thank Mr. Smith for his great exertions — the officers of the prison for their kindness to him — and that Cook did not die from strychnine.

Major Fulford expressed a hope that in his then awful condition he was not quibbling with the question, and urged him to say "Ay" or "No," whether or not he murdered Cook. He answered immediately "Lord Campbell summed up in favour of poisoning by strychnine."

The Governor retorted, it was of no importance how the deed was done, and asked him to say "Yes" or "No" to the question.

Palmer said "he had nothing more to add. He was quite easy in his conscience, and happy in his mind."

This is the Governor's version of the conversation; but upon the material point Mr. Smith stated last night, just after leaving the convict, that what Palmer said to him was, "I am innocent of poisoning Cook by strychnine; and all I ask is, that you will have his body examined and that you will see to my mother and boy."

The county gaol at Stafford, in front of which the culprit was executed, is situated in the western suburb of the town, but occupies so low a position as not to attract attention until you approach it. It is built of red brick, and surrounded by a wall of the same material of considerable height, forming a large square, in the interior of which are the various offices of the prison, and flanked at intervals by a series of large round castellated towers, also of brick, which serve as residences for the warders, and give the building all the character it possesses in an architectural point of view. This formidable rampart completely conceals from the public eye the whole of the interior edifices and economy of the prison.

The entrance to the building is situated directly in the centre of the southern side of the square, which is skirted by a public thoroughfare, and, from this road, and at right angles with it, a short narrow street runs in a straight line from the entrance.

THE TIMES REPORT

It was in this limited space in front of the prison that the vast concourse of people who assembled to witness the execution was densely packed. Strong barriers were erected at intervals across the various approaches to the scaffold, so as to relieve the pressure of the immense multitude in that direction. Nearly 200 of the country constabulary were in attendance under the direction of Mr. Hatton, the chief constable, and these were assisted by 150 special constables sworn in for the occasion.

The scaffold, a huge square, unsightly machine, painted black, fixed upon low metal wheels, and about eight or ten feet high, was drawn in front of the gaol in the dead of the night preceding the execution, and placed in position. The platform was surrounded by a chain about four feet high; and a rope suspended from a beam, which projected across the scaffold, completed the grim apparatus of death which the light of the early morning gradually revealed to the immense crowd below.

Balconies and platforms were erected on several of the housetops and in almost every imaginable place commanding a view of the spectacle, and the windows of the houses in the front and near the scaffold had their full complement of eager spectators. The express train and others from London on Friday night brought down a great number of well-dressed persons; but these bore no comparison in point of force with the crowds which kept constantly arriving during the night by railway and other means of conveyance from the adjacent towns for fifty miles round, including the Pottery districts, Birmingham, Wolverhampton, Walsal, Tipton, and the rest of what is called "the black country."[3] The trampling heard in the streets throughout the whole night indicated the number of pedestrians who were hastening to the scene.

As early as nine o'clock last night, in spite of a brisk rain, a considerable number of people had taken possession of the various places commanding a near view of the scaffold, but the prospect of the long dreary interval before the hour fixed for the execution, added to the still drearier state of the weather, wore out their patience and compelled them to retire. The rain continued to fall heavily at intervals during the night, and that circumstance, no doubt, kept hundreds away.

So early as 4 o'clock this morning, however, almost every available point from which a view of the drop, however remote, could be obtained was occupied, and those who arrived afterwards were obliged to hang on the outskirts of the crowd. The great bulk of the

---

[3] Traditional name for the area north and west of Birmingham, inspired by the cascades of soot from the coal mines, iron foundries and steel mills. The nickname dates from the 1840s, at the start of the Industrial Revolution.

people were young men and lads, labourers and artisans, thousands of whom had left their ordinary occupations and travelled many miles to witness the spectacle; but the great number of umbrellas raised during the rain showed, in addition to other indications, that a large proportion of the crowd belonged to a better class of people.

A clear open space of considerable size was kept all round the scaffold, and it was painful to note the wan looks of those in the front rank of the crowd, who were pinned against the barriers by the pressure from behind. A more orderly and patient concourse was, perhaps, never assembled on any similar occasion. By this it is not meant that their behaviour was exactly in harmony with the terrible spectacle had which collected them together. That could not have been expected in a crowd congregated for such a purpose; but, as a body, they were free from that savage brutality which is said to characterise a mob assembled on similar occasions in front of the Old Bailey, though the indecent laughter to which little incidents among them now and then gave rise must have broken sadly on the ear of the doomed man inside the prison. In this state of things the night wore on with the crowd outside, the physical sufferings of many of whom must have been almost unendurable.

Far different was the scene passing within the precincts of the prison. The wretched man on whom all this intense interest hung was spending the few last hours given him to live.

Towards midnight he had taken a painful leave of his immediate relatives, and was now awaiting his irrevocable doom. He had slept two hours and a-half in the early morning, and, on awakening, the chaplain entered his cell. He said, in reply to a question asked by the rev. gentleman, that he felt comfortable, and was quite prepared. He continued in bed until half past five, when he had some tea, and again at half past seven. To the warder who brought him the tea on the last occasion and who asked how he was, he said he was very comfortable. The chaplain remained in almost constant attendance upon him until the hour of his execution.

Shortly after seven o'clock Lieutenant-Colonel Dyott, the High Sheriff, and Mr. Hand, the Under-Sheriff, arrived at the gaol, and at once proceeded to the prisoner's cell, where they found him in earnest conversation with the chaplain. After a brief interval the High-Sheriff asked him if he was prepared to admit the justice of his sentence.

He replied, with the most energetic gesticulation, "No, Sir, I do not and I go to the scaffold a murdered man." He added that several persons, whose names he would not mention, were guilty of his murder, and that he could not acknowledge the justice of his sentence.

The cell of the prisoner was one of a series situated on the first

THE TIMES REPORT

floor of an oblong building, around which a light iron gallery was thrown. Almost immediately opposite the door of his cell a bridge went across to the gallery on the opposite side, and from the centre of the bridge an ornamental stair of iron descended into a large corridor on the basement story. Here were stationed, shortly before eight o'clock, the High-Sheriff of the county and the Under-Sheriff; Mr. W.H. Chetwynd, a magistrate of the county; Major Fulford, the governor of the gaol; Mr. Hatton, the chief of the county constabulary, and the representatives of the press, awaiting the awful ceremony about to take place.

At that moment a tall, broad-shouldered, elderly man, with short grey hair, and dressed in a white smock-frock,[4] emerged from a room in the corridor, and ascending the light iron stairs, entered the condemned cell. This was the executioner, a labouring man residing at Dudley, named John Smith, and this was his first introduction to the convict, whom he at once proceeded to pinion[5] in the presence of the High-Sheriff and the chaplain.

While this operation was being performed Palmer betrayed no symptoms of emotion, and simply requested that the cord might not be drawn too tightly. The High-Sheriff and the chaplain then left the cell for a short time, and the prisoner remarked to the officers who attended him that they would observe that he had not changed from what he had always said, and he then said, "All I have to ask of you is to pray for my child."

The High-Sheriff and chaplain again visited the cell, and thinking that the prisoner might, perhaps, object to say anything in the presence of the officers, they were requested to withdraw. At this moment all the preparations were complete. The unhappy man was pinioned, the executioner was standing by him, and nothing was required but the signal to move forward to the scaffold.

The chaplain, in the most solemn manner, exhorted him to admit the justice of his sentence. The prisoner firmly replied that it was not a just sentence. "Then," said the chaplain, "your blood be upon your own head." To this observation the prisoner made no answer.

At this moment the prisoner appeared for an instant at the door of his cell, and took a cursory look at the official gentlemen waiting below to conduct him to the scaffold. He entered his cell again, and immediately afterwards the chaplain and the High-Sheriff emerged

---

[4] An outer garment made of heavy linen used to protect one's clothing, traditionally used by shepherds and waggoners.
[5] Fletcher adds in his biography that before his arms were tied behind him, Palmer was given a glass of bubbling wine that was poured out quickly. Palmer blew off the foam, explaining that "They always give me indigestion next morning if I drink in a hurry."

from it, accompanied by the convict, who tripped nimbly down the stairs into the corridor, followed by the executioner.

The remarkable appearance of the prisoner at this time will not easily be forgotten. Contrary to all usage, he wore the prison dress, consisting of a dark grey jacket, trousers, and waistcoat, all of the coarsest description, a blue checked cotton shirt, and a pair of thick list shoes.[6] He carried a handkerchief in one hand of the same coarse material. At his request his light sandy hair had been closely cropped, which brought the whole configuration of his large round head and face into striking prominence, and, with the dress he wore, gave to his whole physique an air of singular repulsiveness which was not at all natural to him.

It ought, however, to be stated that the wearing the prison dress was not intended as an indignity, but simply arose from the circumstance of his having no clothes of his own in the prison.[7]

The melancholy procession was now formed which was to conduct him to his doom. The chaplain went first, reading the burial service, followed by the Under-Sheriff, then by the High-Sheriff, carrying their wands of office,[8] next by Palmer, then by the executioner, and finally by Major Fulford, the governor of the prison, Mr. Hatton, the chief constable, and several of the officers of the gaol; and in this way he was escorted to the scaffold amid the tolling of the prison bell.

His bearing in these last moments of his life elicited the amazement of all who witnessed it. As he passed Major Fulford, who was waiting to fall into the procession, he bowed to him in an easy off-hand manner, and then stopped to shake hands with one of the officials of the prison whom he recognised.

He marched along with a light, jaunty step; but the expression of his mouth and the pallor with which his features were suffused indicated the deep current of natural emotion which he strove in vain to conceal. The distance he had to traverse from his cell to the scaffold was very considerable, and included three short flights of stairs, but his step never for an instant faltered.

As the procession reached the entrance of the prison, Mr. Wright, the philanthropist, who was standing near, stepped back to allow it to

---

[6] Soft-sided cloth slippers made without a hard sole. Especially useful when you need to walk about quietly, either early in the morning so as to not awaken the rest of the house or when committing a burglary. Sailors working with gunpowder aboard ships would wear list slippers instead of shoes, because the nails on their soles could strike sparks.

[7] An unconvincing excuse. Palmer spent the last two weeks of his life in a prison that was nine miles from his Rugeley home.

[8] A length of wood carried on ceremonial occasions.

pass; the convict bowed courteously to him, and then walked lightly up the steps leading to the scaffold, and of his own accord placed himself under the beam.

The executioner at once proceeded to adjust the rope round the culprit's neck, and was about to retire from the scaffold when he seemed to remember that he had not drawn the white cap over Palmer's face. He returned to do so, and then the convict shook hands with him and bade him good-bye.

An instant elapsed before the bolt was withdrawn, and the rapid inflation and collapsing of the part of the cap which covered his mouth evinced the intensity of his feelings at this awful moment. The drop at length fell, and he died almost without a struggle. Once or twice, when the executioner was gently holding down his legs, he raised himself slightly up, and there was a simultaneous convulsive moment of the shoulders for an instant; but he exhibited no other sign of life. He held a handkerchief in one of his hands, where it still remained tightly clenched when the body was cut down.[9]

With some very slight exceptions the deportment of the crowd, among whom were many decently dressed women, was decorous in the extreme. When the prisoner first made his appearance on the scaffold there was a slight shout of disapprobation from one part of the crowd, but it was never repeated, and from this time until the drop fell there was almost a dead silence. So deeply impressed did the people appear to be with the dreadful character of the spectacle that by far the greater part of them left shortly after the drop fell, and comparatively few remained to see the body cut down.[10]

The weather underwent a change just before the hour fixed for execution. The rain ceased, and it took place in an interval of sunshine.

On the removal of the body, Mr. Bridges, a gentleman from

---

[9] Hanging kills in one of two ways, depending upon the weight of the prisoner and the length of the drop. If done correctly, the spinal cord is severed between the second and third cervical vertebrae near the base of the skull, causing instantaneous death similar to Lord Blackwood's at the end of the "Sherlock Holmes" movie. Otherwise, the victim strangles slowly, as Brendan Fraser's character demonstrated in "The Mummy." Pulling down the victim's legs is a merciful act to hasten the process.

Despite the claims of numerous websites and trivia books, Palmer did not say, before stepping on the trap door, "do you think it is safe?" The phrase originated in Barnaby Conrad's 1969 trivia book "Fun While It Lasted."

[10] While the crowd may have been "decorous in the extreme," another witness said he heard cries of "Murderer!" and "Poisoner!" Given the speed of the execution before a large crowd, their spirits dampened by the long, wet wait, it seems most likely that those near the scaffold engaged in catcalling while the rest of the crowd remained silent.

Liverpool, engaged in phrenological pursuits,[11] was permitted to take a cast of the convict's head, and this process over, his remains were buried in a grave behind the chapel, within the precincts of the prison. A barbarous custom prevails in the prison at Stafford in the burial of criminals subjected to capital punishment, and it was adhered to in the case of Palmer. It will, perhaps, scarcely be credited that his body, on being removed from the scaffold, was divested of every article of clothing, and buried in a perfectly nude state, without even a shell. But so it was, and this was his ignominious end.

It will be seen that the convict contented himself with denying that Cook was poisoned by strychnine, and that no direct answer was ever given by him to the question of whether he murdered him by other means. The impression conveyed by all the proceedings of the wretched man down to the very latest moment of his existence was, that when he denied the justice of his sentence in so determined a manner he had some mental reservation, and that he applied the observation to the charge of poisoning Cook by means of strychnine only. Should there be any foundation for the suggestion that the death was caused by other means it would tend still further to complicate this most extraordinary case.

It is but an act of justice to acknowledge the debt of obligation due to Major Fulford, the governor of the gaol, and to Mr. Hatton, the chief constable of the county, from the correspondent of this journal on this occasion, for the facilities they afforded him, in common with other representatives of the press, in the discharge of a painful duty.

The Jury's Deliberation.

The following has been addressed to the *Times* by one of the jury: —

TO THE EDITOR. — SIR,— A paragraph having appeared in the *Times* affecting the jury who tried Palmer's case, and mis-stating facts, I beg to trouble you with a statement of what actually took place on our retirement to consider our verdict.

On reaching the room there was a dead silence for about twenty minutes. A discussion of the facts that had been laid before us was then commenced, and it lasted for about ten minutes, after which each man took pen and paper and wrote his decision and name, it having been agreed that no one should pronounce his opinion lest any other should receive a bias. The papers were then laid on the table;

---

[11] Phrenology is a pseudoscience that contended a person's personality, including his character and thoughts, could be discerned by measuring the shape and bumps on the skull.

the foreman opened them and read them aloud, when "Guilty" was found to be the unanimous verdict.

An earnest conversation then ensued, having no relation to William Palmer. This is a precise account of the proceedings of the jury.

It is very material to the dignity of justice and the jury's credit that it should be known that no portion of our time was spent in sham; that no hollow pretence to appear decorous on such a solemn occasion was resorted to. Our situation was too dreadful and too solemn to admit of humbug. It is quite untrue that we were absent a long time for the mere sake of appearances. The long account you published must have been obtained from one of the jury, though at second-hand. I claim the right of giving you direct a full and true account, and shall be obliged by your publishing it word for word.

The Expenses of the Prosecution.

The circumstances attending the financial proceedings in the case of the Queen v. William Palmer, are without precedent in the annals of criminal trials in this country. Although the prisoner was only tried on one indictment, there were upwards of a hundred witnesses subpoenaed, and the total number of persons connected either immediately or remotely with the proceedings, exceeded two hundred.

The expenses incidental to a prosecution of such a nature, and to a defence in which the Crown were met foot to foot, were necessarily very great. Medical men and scientific witnesses of considerable attainments were summoned from all parts of the kingdom to give evidence, and many of them were kept in town for more than a fortnight.

Several exaggerated statements have been made with reference to the cost of the trial, but so far as it can be ascertained it will not exceed £9,000. Of this sum two-thirds, or about £6,000, will be borne in the first instance by the Crown, and the remaining one-third by the family of the prisoner. This calculation is, however, independent of the earlier expenses incurred for the *post-mortem* examination on the body of Cook, the subsequent chemical analysis by Drs. Taylor and Rees, and the expenses connected with the coroner's inquest, all of which were defrayed by Mr. Stevens, the stepfather and executor of the deceased.

After the coroner's jury had returned their verdict of wilful murder against Palmer, in Cook's case, the Solicitor to the Treasury took up the proceedings, and the Crown has discharged the whole of the subsequent disbursements.

The fees to the Attorney-General, Mr. Edwin James, and the other counsel retained for the prosecution, have not yet been paid, as it is not the practice of the Crown in such cases to mark any specific amount on the briefs when delivered.

The fees payable by the Crown to the counsel engaged in Palmer's case cannot be less than £800, including "refreshers" and additional fees in consultation. The consultations were held not at the chambers of the Attorney-General in the Temple, but at the private residence, of the hon. and learned gentleman in Hertford-street, Mayfair. The consultations for the defence were held at the chambers of Mr. Serjeant Shee; and the fees actually paid to counsel exceeded £500.

The Crown has paid the whole of the expenses incurred by the witnesses during their stay in London, their allowance for loss of time, and the charges incurred for the maintenance of the jury at the London Coffee House. A portion of this sum will be received back from the Central Criminal Court upon the certificate of the presiding Judge and the Recorder of the City; and the county of Stafford will have to recompense the City. The Crown will ultimately allow the county of Stafford half of the expense to which it has been put by the prosecution, that amount becoming a charge upon the consolidated fund.

Though the prisoner complained that he had not had the advantage of a fair trial, it must be admitted that the Crown gave him every possible facility for defending himself. In the case of ordinary criminals, a person charged with the offence of murder by a coroner's inquisition, is allowed copies of the depositions sworn before the coroner, and also a list of the names of the witnesses endorsed on the back of the indictment. It is supposed that with this assistance a prisoner can prepare his defence so as to meet and answer the case of the Crown.

But in Palmer's case, his solicitors not only had copies of the depositions taken before the coroner, and a list of the names of all the witnesses sent before the grand jury, but they were furnished by the Crown with the nature of the evidence which they were subpoenaed to give. A fairer trial, therefore, is absolutely impossible to imagine.

Palmer's Diary.

(Editor's note: Palmer's 1855 diary, more like a ledger and account book than a recounting of events, can be found in The Illustrated Life and Career of William Palmer *(Peschel Press, 2015).)*

After the conviction of Palmer he expressed to the under-sheriff his deep regret that he was unable during his sojourn in Newgate to attend the daily performance of divine worship. He added that the early hour fixed for his trial, and the time that it was necessary for him to bestow in the preparation for his defence each morning, precluded the possibility of his being present.

His diary (for 1855) which appears to have been kept with great care, notes the fact that on the Sunday after his wife's death, and on the Sunday after Walter Palmer's death, he was at church and took the sacrament.[12] The diary is one of Lett's half-crown editions, with a space for every day in the year. Under the head of the 25th of January there is the following entry:— "At church (sacrament), Willie (his son) poorly." The word "poorly" is underlined twice. Then on the 3rd of February there is the following:— "Mr. Pratt came here from London to get receipts endorsed on Sun and Norwich assurances." 5th of February, "15 dozen of wine in from Pratt." 7th Feb. "Jere (Jeremiah Smith) and Ben (Thirlby) packed the wine; gave them a bottle each for their trouble." 16th Feb. "dined with Jere at the 'yard'" (Mrs. Sarah Palmer's). 11th Feb. "Quinquagesima Sunday,[13] at church; Mr. Atkinson preached; dined at the yard."

The first entry in the diary having reference to Cook is under the head of March 6th — "Cook dined here." The Fast Day, the 19th of March, is duly recorded, and also the circumstance of his having gone to London on the 12th "to see Pratt." On the 6th of April (Good Friday) "At church with Willie." On the 10th of May there is an entry, "Paid Sarah Palmer's bill due." The last entry in the diary records the *post-mortem* examination on Cook, and runs thus:— "Attended a p. m. examination on poor Cook, with Dr. Harland, Mr. Bamford, Newton, and a Mr. Devonshire."

The following Gentlemen were sworn on

THE JURY.

THOMAS KNIGHT, of Leytonstone.
RICHD. DUMBRELL, Fore Street.
WM. MAVOR, Park Street.
WM. NEWMAN, Coleshill Street.
GEORGE MILLER, Duke Street, Grosvenor Square.
GEORGE OAKSHOTT, Ham Lane, West Ham.
CHARLES BATES, Borough Road.
WM. ECCLESTONE, Ham Lane.
SAMUEL MULLETT, Great Portland Street.
JOHN OYER, Grosvenor Road, Pimlico.
WM. NASH, Conduit Street.
WM. FLETCHER, Fore Street.

---

[12] The diary for that year, consisting of payments for bills and brief notes of his visits to races and his bets, can be found in "The Illustrated Life and Career of William Palmer" (Peschel Press, 2015).
[13] The Sunday before the season of Lent. It is the Latin word for fiftieth and refers to the 50 days before Easter.

Glossary of Medical Terms, Doctors and Hospitals

While these definitions appear in the footnotes, most of them occur so frequently in the transcript that they are reproduced here for the convenience of readers.

Abdominal viscera: The organs in the abdominal cavity below the diaphragm, including the stomach, liver, intestines, spleen, and pancreas.

Ammonia pills: Pills containing ammonia and carbon dioxide, used as a stimulant to treat problems such as chronic bronchitis, dyspepsia, and heart palpitations.

Angina pectoris: A pain in the chest due to an obstruction or spasm of the coronary arteries.

Anodyne draught: A drug such as laudanum (tincture of liquid opium) used to relieve pain.

Antimony: A naturally occurring chemical element. While it is poisonous — its symptoms make it easy to mistake for arsenic — it was used in low doses to cause vomiting.

Aperient: Any medicine used to relieve constipation.

Apoplexy: The medical term for a stroke or a fit. Nowadays, it is used to describe a stroke, an inability to feel or move a parts of the body due to a loss of blood flow to the brain, or hemorrhage in a body cavity or organ.

Apothecaries' Company: A society, founded in 1617, that until 1999 was responsible for licensing doctors in England. It wasn't until soon after Palmer's time, however, that doctors had to meet any general set of standards to practice medicine.

Aorta: The large artery that moves blood from the heart into the body.

Arachnitis: An inflammation of the membrane protecting the central nervous system, including the spinal cord.

Arachnoid: A membrane that surrounds the brain and the spinal cord. The layer between it and the skull is the dura mater.

Arrowroot: A starch obtained from the root of the tropical plant. Ground into a powder, it was used in biscuits, cakes, puddings, and jellies. Easily digestible and nourishing, it was boiled with flavoring or dissolved in beef tea or milk and fed to children and invalids with dietary problems.

Bilious attack: An ailment caused by the disruption of the digestion system or excessive bile.

Black draught: A mixture used as a purgative to encourage the bowels to empty.

Brucia: An alkaloid derived from the bark of the nux vomica tree whose seeds yield strychnia, used to create strychnine. Brucia is a weaker poison than strychnine, but produces the same symptoms.

Calomel: Mercury chloride, a chemical compound used as a laxative and purgative and to treat syphilis.

Carbonate of potash: Potassium carbonate, a chemical compound used to create the bubbling in effervescence mixtures. It was used to increase urine flow and have a soothing effect on the stomach.

Cardamine: Also called bittercress, the flowering plant was used to treat stomach and heart ailments.

Catarrh: Inflammation of the mucus membrane in which the nose and air passages become filled with mucus.

Caustic: A substance that dissolves organic tissue by chemical action. For example, a stick with lunar caustic (silver nitrate) would be brushed on the tongue to heal ulcers.

Cicatriced over: Healed over.

Copland: James Copland (1791-1870) was a Scottish physician and Fellow of the Royal Society. He wrote a number of medical books, including the three-volume "Dictionary of Practical Medicine," which promoted circumcision and suggested that socialism caused insanity.

Cranium: The part of the skull that encloses the brain.

Cupping: The technique of heating a glass vessel, creating a partial vacuum, to draw blood to the surface of the skin. When the cup is removed, a small incision is made and blood drawn.

Distended: A swelling caused by pressure from inside the organ.

Drachm: A unit of measurement, also called a dram, equal to an eighth of an ounce.

Dura mater: The first of three membranes inside the skull that surrounds the brain and the spinal cord. The others are the arachnoid and pia mater.

Effervescing state: A bubbling or foaming mixture. From the Latin *ex-* plus *fervescere* for "to begin to boil."

Embrocations: Liniments rubbed on the skin to relieve muscle pain.

Emetic: A drug or object, such as a toothbrush, used to induce vomiting.

Epileptic fits: Abnormal brain activity that can cause a range of reactions, from a momentary loss of awareness to violent, uncontrolled jerking movements. These seizures also can occur in people who do not have epilepsy.

Esquirol: Jean-Etienne Esquirol (1772-1840) was a psychiatrist who advocated government-supported treatment of the mentally ill. He also founded an asylum devoted to the study and treatment of insanity.

Excoriation: An abrading or wearing off of the skin.

Extravasation: A forcing of fluid, such as blood, from the body.

Farinaceous: Rich in starch. The patient was being fed by injections of food into his stomach.

Fauces: The narrow passage that is part of the pharynx between the soft palate and the base of the tongue.

Glasgow Infirmary: The Glasgow Royal Infirmary, a large teaching hospital founded in 1794. It was here, in the same year as the Palmer trial, that British surgeon Joseph Lister (1827-1912) began experimenting with carbolic acid to reduce the number of deaths from sepsis.

Good: John Mason Good (1764-1827) was a surgeon and writer on religious and medical subjects.

Grain: A unit of measurement roughly equivalent to the size of a grain seed. Its weight varied from country to country; in England it was equal to 64.8 milligrams.

Gravitation: The effect of gravity on an object.

Guy's Hospital: A teaching hospital founded in 1721 by Thomas Guy (1644-1724), funded with the fortune he made in the South Sea Bubble, a notorious investment scandal.

Hydrocele: An accumulation of fluid around a testicle.

Indurated: A substance that is made harder by the introduction of fibrous elements. In other words, the attorney general is saying that if the pill was made harder to dissolve, it will delay the effects of the poison.

Integument: A tough outer layer. From the Latin *integer* for "to cover."

James's powders: A drug containing phosphate of lime and oxide of antimony created by Dr. Robert James (1705-1776), who claimed it cured fever, gout and rheumatism. James also edited a three-volume "Medical Dictionary" which contained a dedication from longtime friend Samuel Johnson.

King's College Hospital: A teaching hospital in the London borough of Lambeth that opened in 1840.

Liebig: Justus von Liebig (1803-1873), a German chemist and innovative teacher. His discovery that nitrogen was an essential plant nutrient helped create the fertilizer industry. He taught at the University of Giessen, where he established the world's first school of chemistry.

Loaded tongue: Thick with mucus.

Lock Hospital: The world's first clinic to treat venereal diseases, founded in 1747 near Hyde Park Corner. The term "lock hospital" was a common one. As early as medieval times, they were used to confine leprosy patients. The word "lock" could come from the Anglo-Saxon *loc*, or enclosure, referring to the conditions the lepers were kept, or its alternative meaning as a tuft of cotton or wool, a reference to how the patients' lesions were wrapped.

Lockjaw: A condition in which the mouth is clamped shut by the jaw muscle. While it can be caused by tetanus, it can also be brought on by infections, traumatic injuries, the side effect of drugs such as antidepressants, and even tonsillitis.

Materia Medica: Materia Medica: Latin for "medical materials," later renamed pharmacology. A teacher on the therapeutic properties of substances used for healing.

Medulla oblongata: The part of the spinal cord that extends into the skull.

Mercury: A highly toxic metallic element notable for being the only one that remains liquid at room temperature. It has been used as a medicine since ancient times. In Victorian England, it was an ineffectual treatment for syphilis.

Morphia / opium: Morphia is an outdated term for morphine, the main chemical found in the opium poppy plant. Morphine operates on the central nervous system to relieve pain. It is effective, but also has a high potential for addiction. It was isolated in 1804 and reached commercial markets in 1827, but it wasn't until the hypodermic needle was invented in 1857 that its use exploded.

Nux vomica: A substance containing strychnine and brucia, derived from grinding into a powder seeds from the tree of the same name.

Ophisthotonos: A condition in which the body's muscles turn rigid. In extreme cases, the body forms into the shape of an arch. It can be caused by tetanus, severe cerebral palsy, brain injury, lithium intoxication, or strychnine.

Orfila: Mathieu Orfila (1787-1853) was a French toxicologist and chemist who is credited with founding the science of toxicology.

Papilla: A small protuberance from an organ. One example would be the taste buds on the tongue.

Pericardium: A double-walled sac that contains the heart and the roots of the great blood vessels.

Pleura-tothonos: A condition in which the spine flexes involuntarily so that the person is leaning. Also called Pisa syndrome.

Poultices: A soft mass of material held against the body with a bandage to ease soreness and inflammation.

Precipitates: Separates from the solution.

Pulmonary: Something that is related to or affecting the lungs.

Respiratory muscles: Muscles responsible for breathing. In the human body, the intercostal muscles that run between the ribs expand and shrink to help the chest cavity bring in and expel oxygen.

Rhubarb: A plant used as a laxative.

Rigor mortis: The stiffening of the muscles that begins about three hours after death and lasts up to three days.

Risus sardonicus: A facial expression caused by a spasm of the muscles creating a distorted grin. From the Latin for "sardonic smile."

Royal Free Hospital: A teaching hospital in the Hampstead area of London. It was founded in 1828 by surgeon William Marsden to provide free care to the poor.

Royal Institution: A group founded in 1799 devoted to scientific education and research.

St. George's Hospital: One of the country's largest teaching hospitals, founded at Hyde Park Corner in 1733. During the 1970s, a new school was built at Tooting in Wandsworth, South-West London.

St. Thomas's Hospital: Probably London's oldest hospital, in existence since 1215, when it was named for St. Thomas Becket. It was founded in Southwark, but moved across the Thames to Lambeth opposite the Houses of Parliament in 1871.

OF THE TRIAL OF WILLIAM PALMER

Saline medicine: A salt-water solution used to rehydrate cholera patients.

Senna: A flowering plant used as a laxative.

Serum: The thin watery part of the blood.

Seton: A skein of cotton inserted below the skin with the end left protruding to promote drainage and healing.

Simple syrup: Refined sugar dissolved into water.

Syphilis: A sexually transmitted disease caused a spiral-shaped bacterium. It initially appears as ulcers on the skin, particularly in the groin, then forms large, painful abscesses and sores all over the body. The disease would fall dormant for a while, sometimes for years, before returning with more painful and wide-spreading symptoms, until the victim became insane, disfigured, and then dead. Syphilis was treated with mercury, which was ineffective and caused severe mouth ulcers, teeth loss, and at high levels death. It wasn't until 1943 when penicillin was introduced as the first effective treatment against syphilis.

Tartaric acid: A type of acid found in fruits used in the creation of effervescent draughts.

Tetanus: Nowadays, it is recognized as a medical condition, characterized by the contraction of muscle fibres throughout the body, caused by a bacterium. But at the time of Palmer's trial, it was defined simply as a type of convulsion. It was divided into three groups: idiopathic, or spontaneous tetanus, a rare disease with an unknown origin; traumatic tetanus caused by external wounds, open sores or lockjaw; and tetanus caused by strychnine. The trial's medical evidence hinged on whether Cook died from traumatic tetanus or strychnine.

Tartar emetic: Potassium antimony tartrate, a compound used to treat animals, in dyes, and to cause vomiting in patients (which is what an emetic does).

Thorax: A part of the chest that is protected by the ribcage. From the Latin word for "breastplate."

Trismus: Lockjaw.

Tubercles: Small protuberances or lumps.

Ulcerated: An opening in the skin caused by the disintegration of tissue.

Vascularity: Anything relating to blood vessels or ducts in the body.

Watson: Sir Thomas Watson (1792-1882), a physician who was the first to describe the water hammer pulse found in aortic regurgitation. In 1859, he was appointed physician extraordinary to the queen, and was created a baronet in 1866.

OF THE TRIAL OF WILLIAM PALMER

Profiles of the Justices and Counsel

Reprinted from "William Palmer" (Notable British Trials series, 1922).

The Justices

JOHN CAMPBELL, Baron Campbell, Lord Chief Justice of the Queen's Bench. Lord Campbell had been Lord Chief Justice six years when he had presided at the trial. He was seventy-seven years of age. Three years after he resigned the Chief Justiceship, and became Lord Chancellor at eighty, a greater age than any of his predecessors on the Woolsack had reached on being appointed. He held his office for two years longer, and died at eighty-two, an age which none of his successors reached while holding it. On the day of his death, in 1861, he had sat in Court and attended a Cabinet Council. Lord Campbell's life as Chancellor and politician, and as the writer of the celebrated lives of the Lord Chancellors and Chief Justices, forms too considerable a part of general history and literature to be detailed here. As a lawyer and judge his name stands high. His contemporaries never denied his abilities; but they considered his personal character and ambitions were selfish and by no means magnanimous. He is said by Sir John Macdonnell in the Dictionary of National Biography to have shown on the bench somewhat too openly an unworthy love of applause; and a tradition still lingers amongst lawyers of an ostentatious kind of politeness assumed by him when he intended anything deadly. The Usher of the Court at the Palmer trial is credited with saying that he knew the Chief meant to hang Palmer; he was so polite in requesting him to be seated. The tone of the letter we print from Palmer's brother expresses much of a prevalent feeling against Campbell.[14] But, in Sir John Macdonnell's words, whatever difference of opinion there may be as to the spirit in which he served his country, there is none as to the value of the services themselves.

MR. BARON ALDERSON. Sir Edward Hall Alderson was in 1856 a Baron of the Court of Exchequer, where he was transferred in 1834, his original appointment as judge having been in 1830 to the Court of Common Pleas. He was born in 1787, so that he was now sixty-nine

---

[14] Published as "A Letter to the Lord Chief Justice Campbell." Falsely attributed to the Rev. Thomas Palmer, the letter claimed that Campbell used his influence to take the case, believed before hearing the evidence that Palmer was guilty, and was prejudicial in summing up the case against the prisoner.

years of age. He was of Norfolk, and his father was Recorder of Yarmouth, Norwich, and Ipswich. His career at Cambridge was remarkable. In the year 1809, when he took his degree, he was Senior Wrangler and first Smith's prize-man, besides being first Chancellor's medallist, which was the highest honour then for classics.[15] From 1817 to 1822 he was joint editor of the well-known Barnewall and Alderson's Reports of those years in the Court of King's Bench; and whilst so reporting he was, unlike reporters of these days, rapidly acquiring a practice, though he never took silk.[16] He made no particular mark on the bench during his twenty-seven years of occupancy, and he died in 1857, the year after the trial. It is rather curious, in view of the attack made on him for prejudice in the letter to Lord Campbell, that he should have been known as a humane judge, with a desire to restrict capital punishment.

MR. JUSTICE CRESSWELL. Sir Cresswell Cresswell[17] was the junior judge on the bench. His age was sixty-two, and he had been on the bench in the Court of Common Pleas since 1842, where he had established a reputation as a learned and strong judge. At the bar he had a large practice, and his legal name, apart from his judicial career, would have lived as one of the editors of the Barnewall and Cresswell's Reports in the King's Bench from 1822 to 1830. But his most abiding fame rests on his having been the first appointed judge of the new Probate and Divorce Court, which was established in 1858. He became for the new principles and practice of divorce what Mansfield had been for commercial law — their creator and expounder. He sat in this Court, achieving a distinction which falls to the lot of few judges, until 1863. In July of this year he was knocked down in Constitution Hill by runaway horses belonging to Lord

---

[15] A word about the prizes Alderson earned. Wranglers were senior students who scored above a certain mark in the notoriously tough mathematical tripos exams. The Senior Wrangler, therefore, earned the top score. The Smith's Prize was awarded to the two students in physics, mathematics and applied mathematics who earned high marks in examinations. The Chancellor's Gold Medal was given for the best poem submitted to the competition.
[16] Became a King's Counsel, or K.C. (or Q.C. when a queen rules Britain), a title bestowed by the monarch to indicate that they're senior members of the profession. The status allows the lawyer to wear silk gowns, hence "taking silk."
[17] That's not a mistake. Cresswell Easterby (1794-1863) was named for his mother's family, and with good reason. The Cresswells were as wealthy as they were noble; their ancestors had served in the Crusades. In 1807, after his mother inherited their wealth, dad changed the family's last name to keep it alive. Hence: Cresswell Cresswell.

Aveland, which had been frightened by the breakdown of the carriage, and he died from the shock. On being made judge of the Probate and Divorce Court he was offered a peerage, but declined it, probably, as he was a bachelor, being sufficiently content with the ancestral name of Cresswell of Cresswell, near Morpeth. Though as a judge he was considered overbearing, it is noticeable that he did not intervene very much in the trial; the letter to Lord Campbell makes a point of contrasting his opinions on admission of evidence, and in other respects, as being in favour of the prisoner, while those of Lord Campbell and Mr. Baron Alderson were asserted to show bias and even strong and unfair prejudice.

For the Crown

SIR ALEXANDER JAMES EDMUND COCKBURN was appointed Solicitor-General in July, 1850, and early next year, in succession to Sir John Romilly, was made Attorney-General. He had up to the former year been obtaining considerable reputation as an advocate, had been appointed Q.C. in 1841, and especially had attracted attention by his defence of M'Naughten, who shot Mr. Drummond, Robert Peel's secretary. He obtained his acquittal on the ground of insanity; a defence less credible and easy in 1843 than it subsequently became.[18] But he first obtained real public distinction, and proved his qualifications to be of the highest class, in 1850 by speeches in Parliament, which led immediately to his appointment as Solicitor and Attorney-General as above mentioned. In the Don Pacifico debate Lord Palmerston had made the great speech of his life; and the law had been prepared for him by Cockburn. On the fourth night of the debate Mr. Cockburn replied to a long speech made by Mr. Gladstone against Palmerston's policy. At the end of his reply, according to a description by Sir Robert Peel, "one-half of the Treasury benches were left empty, while honourable members ran one after another, tumbling over each other in their haste to shake hands with the honourable and learned member."[19] He remained

---

[18] Daniel M'Naughten (or McNaughtan or McNaughton) (1813-1865) suffered from paranoid delusions when in 1843 he shot Prime Minister Robert Peel's private secretary Edward Drummond, possibly thinking he was assassinating Peel. After he was found not guilty of murder by reason of insanity, Britain created the first legal test of criminal insanity called the M'Naghten Rules.

[19] In 1850, while acting as Portuguese consul in Athens, British national David Pacifico's house was attacked by an anti-Semitic mob. Police did nothing as the crowd, including the sons of a government minister, invaded the home and destroyed its contents. When Pacifico's claim for compensation from the Greek government was denied, Foreign Minister Lord Palmerston

Attorney-General in the Palmerston Government until November, 1856; and thus it fell to him to conduct the Palmer prosecution. It is worth mentioning that Cockburn's reply at the end of the case was made without a single note. Palmer had therefore against him the greatest figure at the bar, and one of the most accomplished orators of his generation. It was in November, 1856, that Cockburn gave up his enormous income, and his Parliamentary position, to become Chief Justice of the Common Pleas; and the rest of his distinguished career, until his death in 1880, was spent in that office, or in that of Lord Chief Justice of England, which under the Judicature Acts superseded the two ancient Chief Justiceships. Sir Alexander Cockburn was of an ancient Scottish family; he was several times offered a peerage, but declined; he was never married, and his baronetcy expired with him.

JOHN EDWIN JAMES was forty-four years of age in 1856. "With the appearance of a prize fighter," he failed when he went on the stage as a young man and played "George Barnwell."[20] His father, being a solicitor and an officer of the city of London, it was natural for him to turn to the bar, and he was called at the Inner Temple in 1836, when he was twenty-four. By 1856 he was a noted advocate, had been made a Queen's Counsel, was Recorder of Brighton, and had a professional income of £7,000 a year. He was member of Parliament for Marylebone in 1859; but in 1861 his retirement was announced. He was overwhelmed with pecuniary difficulties, and owed £100,000. Lord Brampton says of him in his "Reminiscences" — "He was a Queen's Counsel, a brilliant advocate in a certain line of business, and a popular, agreeable, intellectual, and amusing companion. ... In every society paper, amongst its most fashionable intelligence, there was he. ... One Sunday afternoon I was reading in my little chambers when this agreeable member of the élite called upon me. ... At this time he was making at the bar seven or eight thousand a year. [Here Lord Brampton relates James' request for a loan.] I borrowed the

---

ordered a blockade of Piraeus, the main port of Athens, and the seizure of Greek ships. After eight weeks Greece agreed to pay Pacifico. After a long debate on June 17, 1850, the House of Lords voted to condemn Palmerston's actions. Later that month, the House of Commons reversed it. Palmerston defended his foreign affairs policy in a five-hour speech that promised British subjects overseas "that the watchful eye and the strong arm of England will protect him from injustice and wrong."
[20] "The London Merchant (Or the History of George Barnwell)," a 1731 play by George Lillo, traces the decline of a young apprentice, whose lust for a prostitute drives him to steal money from his employer, then rob and murder his uncle. The play's combination of moral instruction and moral turpitude made it a popular favorite.

whole amount (£2,500) at 5 per cent., and placed it to the credit of this brilliant Queen's Counsel. The only terms I made with him was that he should, out of his incoming fees, pay my clerk £500 a quarter until the whole sum was liquidated. This he might easily have done, and this he arranged to do, but the next day he pledged the whole of his prospective income to a Jew . . . and left me without a shadow of a chance ever seeing a penny of my money again, and I need not say every farthing was lost, principal and interest." An inquiry by his Inn in 1861 showed that he had in 1857 and 1860 inveigled a young man, a son of Lord Yarborough, into debts of £35,000; had obtained, three years before the trial, £20,000 from a solicitor by false misrepresentations; and in a case in which he was acting for the plaintiff had borrowed £1,250 from the defendant, promising to let him off easily in cross-examination. He was disbarred; went to America in 1861; was admitted to the bar there and practised; but in 1865 was playing at the Winter Garden Theatre, New York. He returned to England in 1873, and failed in persuading the judges to reconsider his case. He had married in 1861, but his wife divorced him in 1863. After his failure to return to the bar he was articled as a solicitor, but was not admitted; and he even offered himself again as candidate for Marylebone. He practised as an expert in American and English law, but sank into very poor circumstances, and a subscription was being made for him when he died in 1882.

SIR WILLIAM HENRY BODKIN. Three years after the trial Mr. Bodkin was appointed assistant judge of the Middlesex Sessions, and in 1867 was knighted. He held his office until a few weeks of his death, in 1874, at the age of eighty-three. At the time of the trial he was sixty-five, and was the most distinguished of the practitioners in specialised criminal business. In 1832 he had been appointed Recorder of Dover, after being only six years at the bar. He acquired a large practice on the Home Circuit and at the Middlesex, Westminster, and Kentish Sessions; he was counsel to the Treasury at the Central Criminal Court in 1856, and was ex officio of the counsel for the Crown in prosecutions in that Court. He retained this appointment until he was made a judge. As an expert on the practice of the poor law and secretary of the Mendicity Society he took great interest in poor law questions. In 1841 he had been returned to Parliament as a Conservative member for Rochester, but lost his seat at the election in 1847 for having supported Sir Robert Peel's Corn Law Bill. While he sat in Parliament he brought forward and passed an important measure of reform as to the chargeability of irremovable poor, which has become a permanent feature of our poor law system.[21] Sir William held several distinguished and important offices. He was President of the Society of Arts, a Deputy-Lieutenant of Middlesex, and chairman of the Metropolitan Assessment Sessions. By his marriage in 1812 to Sarah Sophia, daughter of Peter Raymond Poland of Winchester Hall, Highgate, he became connected with the family of the distinguished lawyer, Sir Harry Bodkin Poland, whose own professional career has followed so closely that of his uncle. Sir Harry Bodkin Poland succeeded him in his Recordership of Dover and his office at the Central Criminal Court. This family and legal collection alike suggested the dedication of this book to Sir Harry Bodkin Poland. None of those who actually took part in the trial are now living.

WILLIAM NEWLAND WELSBY had been called to the bar in 1826, was made Recorder of Chester in 1841, and eventually became the leader on the North Wales Circuit. When Sir John Jervis, who became Lord Chief Justice of the Common Pleas, was made Attorney-General in 1846, Welsby was appointed by him junior counsel to the Treasury; in other words, junior counsel with the Attorney-General in all his legal duties, thence known in English legal professional slang as the Attorney-General's "devil," a very important and lucrative post, which generally leads to a judgeship. It was probably his experience of criminal law in this office, and his general reputation for knowledge of criminal law, founded on his editing numerous law books, as well as on his practice at the bar, that led to his being associated with the Attorney-General at the trial. He had enormous industry, and besides editing a large number of legal books, was an editor of one of the most celebrated series of Reports, the seventeen volumes of "Meeson and Welsby," the product of their reports for years in the Court of Exchequer in the earlier part of Welsby's career. He died eight years after the trial, at sixty-one, without having reached the bench, broken down, it was believed, by his excessive labours.

SIR JOHN WALTER HUDDLESTON (Mr. Baron Huddleston). A year after the trial Mr. Huddleston was made a Q.C. From 1865 to 1875 he was Judge-Advocate of the Fleet. In the latter year he became a judge of the Common Pleas, and was afterwards transferred to the Court of Exchequer; hence the name of Mr. Baron Huddleston,

---

[21] Beginning in the 16th century, Britain enacted laws regarding the care of the poor and indigent. In 1834, the country was organized into poor law unions that were jointly responsible with parishes for administering poor relief. Bodkin's Act 1847 shifted the cost of relief from the parish to the union.

by which in later years he continued to be known, even after the reconstitution of the Courts by the Judicature Acts, when all the judges took the title of Justices of the High Court. Huddleston was a remarkable man. His father was a captain in the merchant service. He was educated at Trinity College, Dublin, but did not take a degree, and he became usher in an English school. He was called by Gray's Inn in 1839, when he was twenty-four years of age, so that he was forty-one at the time of the trial. He was member of Parliament for Canterbury from 1865 to 1868, and for Norwich in 1874 and until he was made a judge. He was a great advocate, but not so great a judge. His reputation increased rather on the social than the legal side. He had married in 1872 Lady Diana De Vere Beauclerk, daughter of the ninth Duke of St. Albans, and he was accounted to be ambitious most of all of social distinction. He was fitted for this, if not by family connections, by his brilliance as a conversationalist, and his gifts as a man of the world and his associations with the theatre and the turf. His accomplishments included an extensive knowledge of French literature and a facility of speaking in French which few Englishmen have. He thus represented gracefully the English bar at the funeral in 1868 of Berryer, the great French advocate, over whose grave he made a speech in French. He died in 1890, aged seventy-five.

For the Defence

SIR WILLIAM SHEE. The leading counsel for Palmer, Mr. Serjeant Shee, was in his fifty-second year; seven years afterwards he was appointed a judge of the Queen's Bench, the first Roman Catholic judge since the Reformation. He was Irish, but educated at a French school in Somers Town, London, subsequently at St. Cuthbert's College, near Durham, where his cousin, afterwards famous as Cardinal Wiseman, was, and then at Edinburgh University. A student of Lincoln's Inn when nineteen, he had become a serjeant at law by 1840, and was one of the leading counsels in London and on the Home Circuit. In 1852 he became member of Parliament for Kilkenny, and represented it for five years. He had been prominent as an advocate for Catholic Emancipation very early in his career, and in Parliament he was a zealous promoter of measures connected with Irish land tenancy, and dealing with the Church endowments, measures precursory of later land legislation and the Disestablishment of the Irish Church. He lost his seat for Kilkenny in 1857, and he never sat in Parliament afterwards. In 1860, three years before he was made a judge, he refused the Chief Justiceship of Madras. Four years after his appointment, in 1868 he died of apoplexy, at the age of sixty-three. It is noticeable that, though

Serjeant Shee had been in most of the great trials, he had never defended in a murder trial until he defended Palmer. We have referred to his declaration of belief in Palmer's innocence; and this was not the only point on which his speech was criticised at the time. The leading legal journal characterized it in terms which will most likely be agreed with by the present-day reader, even more decisively than by the reader of half a century ago, when the taste was more for florid speaking than it is now.[22] "The defence of Mr. Serjeant Shee was clever, ingenious, and eloquent, but wanting in judgment and taste. The peroration was a striking instance of this defect, for the allusion to the family of the prisoner, and to his supposed affection for his wife, grated sorely, and almost ludicrously, on the sense of propriety in the face of the undisguised fact, known to all his audience, that he was accused of murdering his wife, that he slept with his maidservant on the very night she died, and that he had confessed himself guilty of forgery upon his mother. Equally injudicious was the philippic against the insurance offices. In worse taste still was his solemn assertion to the jury that he was convinced by the evidence of the prisoner's innocence."

SIR WILLIAM EGBERT GROVE. Palmer's second counsel, Mr. Grove, Q.C., was in one respect the most distinguished of all the persons who took part in the trial. At the time he had a European reputation, but this was due to his career as a scientific investigator, and not as a lawyer. Without mentioning more, it is sufficient to say that he had published in 1846 the great book, "The Correlation of Physical Forces," which placed him in the front rank of European science. The book was translated into French in the year of the trial. He had been called to the bar in 1835, and was in 1856 forty-five; but he had ill-health, and he turned to science rather than to practice. He was at his call a member of the Royal Institution, and in 1844 he had become its vice-president. By 1853 his health had improved, and he was then a Q.C., having a practice chiefly in patent and scientific cases; but he had also become a leader on his Circuit. It was probably his scientific eminence that led to his brief in the Palmer case. Grove was appointed a judge in 1871, retired in 1887, and died in 1896 at eighty-five. He did not gain any special distinction as a judge nor add

---

[22] The anonymous correspondent for The Law Times added: "Men's minds were in doubt whether there was sufficient evidence for a conviction; but there was no question on any mind that he was in fact guilty. . . . The effect of Serjeant Shee's assertion of his own belief in the prisoner's innocence could not be to win over any other man to his opinion, but to produce a doubt of the soundness of a judgment which could come to such a conclusion with such facts before it."

OF THE TRIAL OF WILLIAM PALMER

to his scientific reputation after he left the bench, though he published several scientific studies.

EDWARD VAUGHAN HYDE KENEALY was the junior counsel for Palmer, and was thirty-seven years old. He was a graduate of Trinity College, Dublin, in 1840, the year of his call to the Irish bar. In 1847 he was called to the English bar by Gray's Inn, and by 1850 he was a Doctor of Laws of Trinity College, Dublin. He had published poems as translations from many Eastern and European languages, and especially in 1850 a poem which has been described as marked by genius, "Goethe, a New Pantomime." Between the year of the trial and 1868 he had risen rapidly, and in the latter year he was made a Queen's Counsel and a Bencher of his Inn. He was the leading counsel for the prosecution in the great Overend and Gurney case of 1869; and in 1873 came the most extraordinary period of his career, when he became chief counsel for the Tichborne claimant.[23] His conduct of that person's defence on the prosecution for perjury, and his editing of the wild paper called The Englishman, and his scurrilous attacks on the Chief Justice and others, led to his expulsion from the Circuit, the deprival of his legal distinctions, and finally to his disbarring. He was elected in 1875 as member for Stoke, solely as the champion of the Tichborne claimant. He sat until 1880, but was defeated then at the General Election, and in that year he died. He was an accomplished and successful advocate, and a scholar of unusual learning, but his gifts seemed of that order of genius which is allied to madness. In 1860 he published a translation of a Celtic poem, and in 1864 a volume of "Poems"; in 1878, "Prayers and Meditations," "An Introduction to the Apocalypse," and "Fo, the Third Messenger of God."

---

[23] In 1866, the Overend, Gurney & Co., a wholesale discount bank that specialized in making loans to other banks, collapsed with a loss of £11 million. The company's directors were accused of defrauding investors, but were acquitted. *Tichborne claimant:* A notorious case in which an Australian man claimed to be Roger Tichborne, the heir to the family's ancient title and fabulous fortune. In 1854, Tichborne disappeared in a shipwreck off Brazil. There were rumors that survivors were picked up and taken to Australia, so his mother advertised extensively in the newspapers there. Twelve years later, Thomas Castro stepped forward to claim the Tichborne title. The case became even more complicated when evidence appeared that Castro was born Arthur Orton, a Londoner who went to sea as a boy and ended up in Australia. The claimant lost his case in 1871, was tried and convicted of perjury in 1874, and sentenced to 14 years in prison. He continued to insist for the rest of his life that he was Tichborne. When he died in 1898, the family agreed to have a card placed in his coffin bearing the names "Sir Roger Charles Doughty Tichborne."

THE TIMES REPORT

JOHN GRAY. Mr. Gray was born at Aberdeen in 1807, and educated at Gordon's Hospital. First a solicitor in London, he was called to the bar in 1833. After attaining the rank of Queen's Counsel in 1863, several years after the Palmer trial, he was appointed solicitor to the Treasury in 1870. It was while holding this office, in 1873, that he conducted the prosecution of Arthur Orton; so that his career and Dr. Kenealy's touched in two points.[24] He was the author of a number of valuable contemporary legal text-books. He died in 1875, owing, it was said, to his labours in preparing and directing the Orton prosecution.

---

[24] The possible birth name of Thomas Castro, a.k.a. the Tichborne claimant. See the previous footnote.

Bibliography

Anonymous, "New Zealand Items," The Star (Lyttelton, New Zealand), 29 August 1874, http://paperspast.natlib.govt.nz/cgi-bin/paperspast?a=d&d=TS18740829.2.13, accessed July 25, 2014.

Bache, Franklin. *A System of Chemistry for the Use of Students of Medicine.* Philadelphia: William Fry, Printer. 1819

Bates, Stephen. *The Poisoner: The Life and Crimes of Victorian England's Most Notorious Doctor.* New York: Overlook Duckworth, 2014.

Fletcher, George, Bill Peschel (editor). *The Life & Career of Dr. William Palmer of Rugeley.* Hershey, Pa.: Peschel Press, 2014.

Gilbert, James. *Gilbert's Visitor's Guide to London.* London: James Gilbert, 1851.

Goodman, Ruth. *How To Be a Victorian.* New York: Liveright Publishing Corp., 2013.

Kirwan, Daniel Joseph. *Palace and Hovel, Or Phases of London Life.* London: Columbian Book Company, 1878.

Mitchell, Sally (editor). *Victorian Britain: An Encyclopedia.* New York: Garland Publishing, Inc., 1988.

Pool, Daniel. *What Jane Austen Ate and Charles Dickens Knew.* New York: Touchstone, 1993.

Taylor, Alfred Swaine. *Medical Jurisprudence.* London: J. Churchill, 1858.

Victorian London. "Mrs. Beeton's Book of Household Management, by Isabella Beeton, 1861 - Recipes - Chapter 39 - Invalid Cookery." http://www.victorianlondon.org/publications7/beeton-39.htm, accessed Jan. 12, 2015.

William Clift (1775-1849). "19 May – 15 June 1813." http://wmcliftrcseng.wordpress.com/2013/06/, accessed Dec. 5, 2014.

… THE TIMES REPORT

Index to Witnesses.— Medical Evidence and Counsel.

PAGE

Armshaw, John (solicitor at Rugeley)..191
Attorney-General's (The) Opening Address for the Prosecution.........20
Attorney-General's Reply to the Evidence for the Defence 312

Bainbridge, Dr. John Nathan (medical officer to St. Martin's Workhouse)..287
Bamford, Mr. William (surgeon at Rugeley) 182
Barnes, Lavinia (waitress at the Talbot)...72, 84
Bates, George (Palmer's stable-keeper)..121
Bond, Sarah (housekeeper at the Talbot)..76
Boycott, John (clerk to Messrs. Landor and Gardner).......................108
Brande, William Thomas (professor of chymistry at the Royal Institution)..172
Brodie, Sir Benjamin (senior surgeon to St. George's Hospital) 135
Brooks, Mrs. Ann (a lady who attends races).......................................70
Broxholme, Charles (apprentice to Mr. Jones, chemist) 144
Burgen, Daniel Scully (chief superintendent of Stafford Police)115, 178
Butler, Johnson Rogerson (jockey)...196

Cheshire, Samuel (late postmaster at Rugeley)................ 110, 112, 115
Christison, Dr. Robert (professor of Materia Medica to the University of Edinburgh)..173
Corbett, Henry (physician, of Glasgow)...140
Crisp, Ellis (inspector of police at Rugeley)..115
Curling, Thomas Blizard (surgeon)...124

Daniel, Dr. Henry (retired surgeon to the Bristol Hospital) 137
Deane, Henry Augustus (attorney of Gray's Inn) 179
Devonshire, Mr. Charles James (late assistant to Dr. Monckton)....106

Espin, John (solicitor of London)..181

Fisher, Ishmael (wine merchant) 48
Foster, Joseph (farmer at Sibbertoft) 295

Gardner, Mr. James (solicitor of Rugeley)..68
Gay, Mr. John (surgeon to the Royal Free Hospital) 279
Gay, Mr. Robert Edward (member of the Royal College of Surgeons)
....270

Gibson, William Scaife (surgeon's assistant) 52

Harland. Dr. John Thomas (physician at Stafford) 98
Hatton, Captain John Haines (chief constable of Stafford) 114
Hawkes, Juliet Elizabeth (boarding-house keeper) 116
Herapath, Mr. William (professor of toxicology at the Bristol Medical School) 262
Herring, George (independent) 116
Hickson, Caroline (lady's maid) 142
Horley, Charles (gardener to Palmer) 76

Jackson, John (member of the College of Physicians) 177
Jones, Thomas (law stationer) 51
Jones, William Henry (surgeon) 77

Keeling, Mary (widow at Rugeley) 97
Kelly, Mary (patient at Glasgow Infirmary) 141

Lee, Henry (surgeon to King's College and Lock Hospitals) 139
Letheby, Dr. Henry (medical officer of Health to the City of London) 267

Macdonald, Dr. William (licentiate of the Royal College of Surgeons of Edinburgh) 280
Mantell, Mr. Ryners (house-surgeon at the London Hospital) 274
Matthews, Henry (inspector of police at Euston-square Railway Station) 295
Mills, Elizabeth (chambermaid at the Talbot Arms) 54, 84
Monckton, Dr. Henry (physician at Rugeley) 107
Moore, Edward D. (surgeon) 149
Morley, Mr. George (surgeon at Leeds) 145
Myatt, James (postboy at the Talbot Arms) 108
Myatt, George (saddler at Rugeley) 296

Newton, Charles (assistant to Mr. Salt, chemist) 85
Nunneley, Mr. Thomas (professor of Surgery at Leeds) 248

Patterson, Dr. James (Glasgow Infirmary) 141
Partridge, Richard (professor of anatomy in King's College) 277
Pemberton, Oliver (lecturer on anatomy, Queen's College) 294
Pratt, Mr. Thomas (solicitor, Mayfair) 184

Read, Mr. George (sporting housekeeper) 52
Rees, Dr. George Owen (lecturer at Guy's Hospital) 171

Richardson, Benjamin Wall (physician of London) 290
Roberts, Mr. Charles Joseph (apprentice to Mr. Hawkins, chemist) .. 90
Robinson, George (physician to the Newcastle-on-Tyne Fever
Hospital) 289
Rogers, Mr. Julian Edward Disbrowe, (professor of chymistry at St.
George's School of Medicine) 265
Ross, Mr. John Brown, (house-surgeon to the London Hospital) 273
Rowley, Ann (charwoman to Palmer) 75

Savage, Dr. Henry (physician) 84
Serjeant, John (attendant at races) 299
Shee, Serjeant William, opening for the Defence 197
Slack, Frederick (porter to Mrs. Hawkes) 119
Smith, Jeremiah (attorney at Rugeley) 300
Solly, Mr. Samuel (surgeon of St. Thomas's Hospital) 138
Spillbury, Mr. John (farmer, near Stafford) 191
Steddy, Edward Austin (surgeon at Chatham) 288
Stevens, Mr. William (stepfather to the deceased, Cook) 92
Strawbridge, Mr. Thomas Smerdon (of the Bank) 191

Taylor, Dr. Alfred Swaine (fellow of the College of Physicians) 151
Taylor, Mr. Francis (apothecary at Romsey) 143
Todd, Dr. Robert Bentley (physician at King's College Hospital) 129

Wallbank, John (butcher at Rugeley) 191
Watson, Catherine of Garnkirk, Glasgow 292
Watson, Dr. Ebenezer (surgeon at Glasgow Infirmary) 141
Weatherby, Charles (treasurer of the Jockey Club) 194
Witham, Jane (a lady's attendant) 144
Wright, Mr. Herbert (solicitor, Birmingham) 192
Wrightson, Dr. Francis (pupil of Liebig's) 275

About the Editor

Bill Peschel is a former journalist who shares a Pulitzer Prize with the staff of The Patriot-News in Harrisburg, Pa. He also is mystery fan who has run the Wimsey Annotations at Planet peschel.com for nearly two decades. He is the author of the 223B series of Sherlock Holmes parodies and pastiches, *The Complete, Annotated Mysterious Affair at Styles*, *The Complete, Annotated Secret Adversary* and *The Complete, Annotated Whose Body?* as well as *Writers Gone Wild* (Penguin Books). He lives in Hershey, where the air really does smell like chocolate.

For more information about Peschel Press, visit www.PeschelPress.com.

WORKS PUBLISHED BY W. M. CLARK,
16 & 17, WARWICK-LANE.

(Editor's Note: One of the many books on the Palmer trial we consulted contained several pages of ads for other books. We include them here as a curiosity.)

In Six Volumes, Royal Octavo, 420 Pages. Containing 312 Splendid Engravings, Handsomely Bound,
price 6s 6d. each, Cloth,
THE MYSTERIES OF LONDON.
In Volumes One to Four.
First and Second Series, forming four volume, by G. W. M. Reynolds, Esq. Vol. Five, by Thomas Miller, Esq. Vol. Six, by E. L. Blanchard, Esq.
Developing Narratives of Thrilling Interest. Novel Scenes and Sketches of Character. It Discloses those Thrilling Realities of Every-day Life, and imparting features of an extraordinary and attractive kind; it aims Truthfully, Graphically to depict the men and manner of the present day.
Can be had in Penny Numbers, or Monthly Parts.

II.

In One Thick Volume, price 5s, Forty-seven Steel Engravings,
SYLVESTER SOUND, THE SOMNAMBULIST.
By Henry Cockton, Esq., Author of "Valentine Vox," "The Steward," "The Sisters," "The Love Match," &c, This most extraordinary Work has gained unprecedented popularity. It is decidedly the most exquisitely humorous Work ever issued from the Press, and as may be well expected, a Somnabulist's midnight wanderings form one continuation of incident and interest from the first page to the last.

III.

Uniform with the above, Handsomely Bound, price 5s.,
THE LOVE MATCH.
By the same Author. Designed to Illustrate the Ups and Downs, the Joys and Griefs, which sprang from the Marriage of Mr. and Mrs. Tom Todd. Illustrated with Twenty-three Steel Engravings. The author of the inimitable "Sylvester Sound," and "Valentine Vox," has given the aid of his powerful pen to the ever popular subject of Love! This tale abounds with life-like sketches, and the most exciting incidents.

IV.

Cloth, Gilt. price 5s.
THE STEWARD.
A ROMANCE OF REAL LIFE.
By Henry Cockton Esq. This Work is a complete denouncer of Hypocrisy, and exhibits it, stripped of its cloak, in all its hideous vice and deformity; it pictures, in well-drawn scenes, its baneful influence upon human nature, and shows how oft, — in lieu of aggrandizement, — it has paved the way to Sin, Disgrace, and Death.

V.

In Cloth, Gilt, uniform with "Sylvester Sound," and "The Love Match," &e.,
price 5s., Cockton's

Celebrated Novel.
THE SISTERS; OR, THE FATAL MARRIAGE.
This Work, considered by the majority of Readers the masterpiece of the inimitable Author of "Valentine Vox," abounds throughout with magnificent Scenes from Life, and splendid delineations of Character. It embraces the period of the wars of France and England; disclosing some secrets of the "Grand Emperor Napoleon," hitherto unknown and unpublished. It also portrays, in brilliant and powerful language, the evils of ill-assorted marriages. "The Sisters" is splendidly illustrated on Wood, by Kenny Meadows and Alfred Crowquill, and on Steel by Onwhyn.

VI.
In One Volume, Quarto, 960 Pages, Elegantly Bound, 153 engravings, by Landells and others — Gilt Edges, price 7s 6d.
TALES OF SHIPWRECKS, AND ADVENTURES AT SEA.
Containing talented sketches of Sea and Seamen, and truthful Narratives of Shipwrecks, Fires, Mutinies, Famines, and every danger of this life of peril, rendering it the handsomest, cheapest, and best Publication ever offered to the Public.

VII.
In One Handsome Volume, Quarto, price 6s. 6d.
TALES OF HEROISM.
AND RECORD OF STRANGE AND WONDERFUL ADVENTURES.
Being a Chronicle of the Lives of those Men whose gallant deeds, bravery, and intrepidity, have been the glory and the wonder of the world. This, with many amusing Tales and Anecdotes, coupled with the numerous Engravings from the first Artists of the day, which adorn its Pages, render it a fit companion to the last much admired and highly popular Work.

VIII.
Just Published, price Half-a-Crown, Handsomely Bound.
THE ORPHEAN WARBLER.
Containing upwards of Two Thousand of the Choicest and most Favourite Songs, Glees, Duets, &c., with a complete
Alphabetical Index. All lovers of harmony will find this Book an invaluable companion. It has sold immensely, and has deserved its sale from the excellency of its arrangement, as well as its general correctness.

IX.
Price Sixpence,
CLARK'S CICERONEAN RECITER,
AND COMPANION TO THE ORPHEAN WARBLER.
Being a selection of the choicest specimens of Elocution, Dramatic Scenes, and Pathetic and Humorous Recitations, now so popular at the various London Entertainments, &c.

X.
CLARK'S TALES OF THE WARS,
AND NAVAL AND MILITARY CHRONICLE.
Each engraving represents some memorable Naval or Military exploit, and the whole comprises a complete history of every celebrated battle by Sea and Land, together with innumerable anecdotes of individual heroics forming a Naval and Military History of Britain to the year 1845.

Works Published by W.M. Clark, 16 and 17, Warwick-Lane.

XIII.
PEOPLE'S EDITION OF COOPER'S NOVELS
Comprising the following:—

The Pilot. The Pioneer.
The Spy. The Prairie.
The Last of the Mohicans. The Red Rover.
Lionel Lincoln. The Water Witch.

In one handsome Volume, price 7s. 6d., consisting of nearly 1,000 Octavo pages, and 200 Engravings. Beautifully printed in Nonpareil Type. Originally published to 24 Vols., at Twelve Guineas.

XIV.
Price Sixpence.
CLARK'S CRICKETER'S GUIDE.
Containing the History and Origin of that manly Game, an account of the Celebrated Players, and Remarkable Matches, Instructions to Cricketers, and the New Laws of Cricket. By a Member of the Marylebone Cricket Club.

XV.
CLARK'S LAW OF LANDLORD, TENANT, AND LODGER, AND SMALL TENEMENT ACT.
Arranged in a plain, easy, and simple manner; embodying the new Law of Ejectment, and the New Building Act, House Duties Act, the New Agricultural Tenant Act, and other recent enactments which relate to Landlords and Tenants, with all necessary forms and modes of proceedings in every possible case. Corrected to the present time. Price Sixpence.

XVI.
In one handsome Volume, Octavo, bound, Five Shillings.
WILL WATCH, THE BOLD SMUGGLER.
A TALE OF THE COAST.

XVII.
In One handsome Volume, Octavo, bound, price Five Shillings.
THE LIFE AND TIMES OF DICK TURPIN, THE HIGHWAYMAN.
With nearly Seventy Engravings. A New Historical Romance of the 17th Century. By H. D. Miles.

XVIII.
In One Volume, price Threepence.
DIBDEN'S SEA SONGS.
This work contains the whole of the Songs of the immortal Charles Dibden, and many others of celebrity, of anonymous authorship.

XIX.
THE WANDERING JEW; A TALE OF THE JESUITS.
By M. Eugene Sue. Price 3s. 6d. With Twenty-four Portraits, after Gavaroi, and others.

XX.
THE MYSTERIES OF PARIS.
By M. Eugene Sue: Price 2s. 6d. Being the only perfect Translation exact, from the Paris Edition: Revised by the Author, with explanatory Notes by the Translator.

XXI.
In One Volume, Quarto, price Four Shillings, with Numerous Engravings,
THE NEWGATE CALENDAR.
Giving a truthful account of the Lives, Trials, and Daring Deeds, of the greatest Villains that ever lived.

XXII.
Price Twopence, Gilt Edges.
CLARK'S BALL-ROOM GUIDE AND DANCER'S COMPANION.
Containing many of the Popular Dances of the day, being a complete Guide to Etiquette.

XXIII.
Price Threepence, Gilt Edges.
CLARK'S BOOK OF THE BALLROOM,
Containing plain instructions for the execution of every Fashionable Dance recognised in Polite Society,

XXIV.
Price Twopence.
THE GAMES OF CHESS AND DRAUGHTS.
Together with the Revised Laws of the London Chess Club, as sanctioned by the celebrated player Mr. Staunton.

XXV.
In One Volume, price Seven Shillings and Sixpence.
THE RUINED COTTAGE, or the Farmer's Maid.
By HANNAH MARIA JONES.

XXVI.
In One Volume, price Five Shillings.
ALICE LEIGHTON, or the Murder at the Druids' Stones.

XXVII.
In One Volume, price Five Shillings.
DE LISLE, or the Shipwrecked Stranger. A Tale of Love and War.

XXVIII.
In One Volume, price Five Shillings.
EMMA MAYFIELD, or the Rector's Daughter.

XXIX.
In Two Volumes, 600 Coloured Engravings, price One Guinea.
BROOK'S CYCLOPÆDIA OF BOTANY.

XXX.
In One Volume, With Coloured Engravings, price Four Shillings.
BROOK'S CULPEPPER'S HERBAL.

The whole of the above Works are constantly kept in print, and will be forwarded POST FREE on receipt of published price in Postage Stamps.

www.ingramcontent.com/pod-product-compliance
Lightning Source LLC
Chambersburg PA
CBHW030144100526
44592CB00009B/119